D1566869

JESUS AND THE TEMPLE

Most Jesus specialists agree that the Temple incident led directly to Jesus' arrest, but the precise relationship between Jesus and the Temple's administration remains unclear. *Jesus and the Temple* examines this relationship, exploring the reinterpretation of Torah observance and traditional Temple practices that are widely considered central components of the early Jesus movement. Challenging a growing tendency in contemporary scholarship to assume that the earliest Christians had an almost uniformly positive view of the Temple's sacrificial system, Simon J. Joseph addresses the ambiguous, inconsistent, and contradictory views on sacrifice and the Temple in the New Testament. This volume fills a significant gap in the literature on sacrifice in Jewish Christianity. It introduces a new hypothesis positing Jesus' enactment of a program of radically nonviolent eschatological restoration, an orientation that produced Jesus' conflicts with his contemporaries and inspired the first attributions of sacrificial language to his death.

SIMON J. JOSEPH is Adjunct Professor of Religion at California Lutheran University. He is the author of *Jesus, Q, and the Dead Sea Scrolls* and *The Nonviolent Messiah*.

SOCIETY FOR NEW TESTAMENT STUDIES

MONOGRAPH SERIES

General Editor: Paul Trebilco

165

JESUS AND THE TEMPLE

SOCIETY FOR NEW TESTAMENT STUDIES

MONOGRAPH SERIES

Recent titles in the series:

Jesus and the Temple

The Crucifixion in its Jewish Context

SIMON J. JOSEPH
California Lutheran University

CAMBRIDGE
UNIVERSITY PRESS

CAMBRIDGE
UNIVERSITY PRESS

University Printing House, Cambridge CB2 8BS, United Kingdom

Cambridge University Press is part of the University of Cambridge.

It furthers the University's mission by disseminating knowledge in the pursuit of education, learning and research at the highest international levels of excellence.

www.cambridge.org
Information on this title: www.cambridge.org/9781107125353

© Simon J. Joseph 2016

First published 2016

Printed in the United States of America by Sheridan Books, Inc.

A catalogue record for this publication is available from the British Library

Library of Congress Cataloguing in Publication data
Joseph, Simon J., 1966–
Jesus and the temple : the crucifixion in its Jewish context / Simon J. Joseph.
    pages   cm. – (Society for New Testament studies monograph series; volume 165)
Includes bibliographical references and index.
ISBN 978-1-107-12535-3 (hardback)
1. Jesus Christ – Jewishness.   2. Jesus Christ – Jewish interpretations.
3. Jesus Christ – Passion – Role of Jews.   4. Jesus Christ – Crucifixion.
I. Title.
BM620.J67   2015
232.96–dc23   2015028166

ISBN 978-1-107-12535-3 Hardback

For Jennifer

CONTENTS

ix

PREFACE

The present study builds on a number of earlier studies that investigated various aspects of Early Judaism and the Jesus tradition. My first book, *Jesus, Q, and the Dead Sea Scrolls: A Judaic Approach to Q* (2012), critically compared a number of Q and Dead Sea Scrolls passages and drew attention to the literary, historical, and theological similarities between the early Jesus tradition and the Qumran corpus. My second book, *The Nonviolent Messiah: Jesus, Q, and the Enochic Tradition* (2014), explored the relationship(s) between Jesus Research, Jewish messianism, and Q.

The present study had its genesis in my article " 'For Heaven and Earth to Pass Away'? Reexamining Q 16,16–18, Eschatology, and the Law," published in 2014, where I investigated the relationship between Q and the Torah, arguing that some of its sayings emerge from a highly realized restorative eschatology focused on the inauguration of a new era and a newly (re)interpreted law. More recently, in an article to be published in the *Journal for the Study of the Historical Jesus* entitled, "Jesus and the Temple Incident: A New Proposal," I have argued that Jesus' critical stance toward the Temple's administration represents a symbolic enactment of eschatological Temple restoration.

Here I would like to thank Matthias Konradt, editor of *Zeitschrift für die neutestamentliche Wissenschaft*, and Robert L. Webb, editor of the *Journal for the Study of the Historical Jesus*, and these journals' anonymous reviewers, for their constructive criticism. Special thanks to F. Stanley Jones for reading a draft of this book and providing constructive comments and recommendations, and to Matti Myllykoski, for reading through a full draft of the study and for making a number of constructive comments. I would also like to thank Petri Luomanen for accepting two papers in the Jewish Christianity Section of the SBL, for his engagement with my paper on "Q and the Ebionites: Testing a Conjecture," and for a pre-publication copy of his book, *Recovering Jewish Christian Sects and Gospels*. Daniel Ullucci graciously responded to my SBL paper on sacrifice and vegetarianism in the Pseudo-Clementines, helpfully clarifying its argument. Markus Tiwald kindly provided me with a copy of his book on Q and the law, *Kein Jota wird vergehen*. Brian Pounds provided access to his Cambridge University Ph.D. dissertation on the "crucifiability" of Jesus. Steve Wiggins provided encouragement and support at an early stage of the project.

I have been very fortunate to teach in the Department of Religion at California Lutheran University over the last three years and would like to thank the Interlibrary Loan staff at Pearson library, in particular Kathy Horneck and Nick Millar, for tracking down numerous publications.

A very special thank you to Professor Paul Trebilco, Laura Morris, and the two Cambridge reviewers for their favorable comments and acceptance of this work for publication in the Society for New Testament Studies Monograph Series.

It is to my wife, Jennifer – who has patiently listened, engaged, strengthened, fortified, supported, and celebrated all these years – that this book is dedicated.

1

THE DEATH OF JESUS AS A HISTORICAL AND THEOLOGICAL PROBLEM

Why Did Jesus Die?

Of all the questions regularly asked about Jesus, the question "Why did Jesus die?" must be among the most frequent.
– N. T. Wright, *Jesus and the Victory of God*[1]

Why did Jesus die? The traditional *theological* answer to this question, of course, is "for our sins," but that is not exactly a *historical* explanation of Jesus' death. Every semester I ask incoming students this seemingly simple, straightforward question. Invariably, most respond, as if on cue, with the same answer, yet I am always struck by how easily a theological answer is assumed to be *the* answer to the question, illustrating how theological interpretations of Jesus' death often overshadow the causal historical factors. I spend much of the semester problematizing this presupposition by encouraging students to differentiate between historical and theological responses to the data. Typically, students are not sure precisely *why* they think the way they do. Some of them are familiar with the idea that Jesus fulfilled certain "messianic prophecies" or replaced the Temple sacrifices with his own voluntary sacrifice; however, while the idea that it was God's will for Jesus to die so that He could give us eternal life may be a theologically and emotionally edifying doctrine and belief,[2] and is certainly part of the historical *tradition*, it is not a historical *explanation* of Jesus' death.

The present work is a critical investigation into the cultural, political, economic, and religious contexts of the historical Jesus and the politico-religious conflicts that led to his arrest, trial, and

---

[1] N. T. Wright, *Jesus and the Victory of God, Vol 2: Christian Origins and the Question of God* (Minneapolis: Fortress, 1996), 540.

[2] Mark 8:31; 10:32–34; 10:38; 10:43–45; 14:22–25; John 10:17–18.

execution.[3] Most Jesus specialists agree that the Temple incident led directly to Jesus' execution, but what few scholars seem to agree on is precisely what Jesus *did* during this incident or why he was so upset with the Temple in the first place.[4] Reexamining the historical sequence of Jesus' Temple incident, arrest, and trial – events which all point to high priestly initiation and participation in Jesus' Roman execution, *Jesus and the Temple* provides a new historical explanation of *why* Jesus died. It is the contention of this study that the traditional theological explanation of Jesus' death does not adequately represent the social, economic, political, and religious contexts within which Jesus lived and died. The historical Jesus was engaged in disagreements over the interpretation of the law, or Torah, the administration of the Temple, and the role of violence in the redemption of Israel, and his death was the end result of his ministry and critique of the Temple's administration.

Since the Enlightenment, traditional views about Jesus' identity, miracles, atoning death, and resurrection have come under constant and increasing scrutiny. The historical Jesus is now routinely constructed within the context of Second Temple Judaism, a sectarian world of diverse Jewish groups and individuals with divergent views of the proper role and interpretation of the Torah and Temple. Yet the greatest challenge still facing critical scholarship on Jesus is identifying what *kind* of Jew Jesus was; simply being "Jewish" does not tell us enough about Jesus' distinctive and particular identity. The dominant paradigm for the historical Jesus – that he was an apocalyptic prophet who predicted and/or threatened the destruction of the Temple – is plausibly based on a surface-level reading of the Gospel narratives, but identifies Jesus as a preacher of doom and judgment, a failed messiah who died an unnecessarily tragic death. Moreover, when it comes to reconstructing what Jesus objected to in the Temple, why Jesus offended the Temple leadership, and why

---

[3] N.A. Dahl, "The Problem of the Historical Jesus," in C.E. Braaten and R.A. Harrisville (eds.) *Kerygma and History: A Symposium on the Theology of Rudolf Bultmann* (Nashville: Abingdon, 1962), 158: "Historical research must begin with the death of Jesus if it will inquire not only into the preaching but also into the life of Jesus."

[4] Adele Reinhartz, "The Temple Cleansing and the Death of Jesus," in C. S. Ehrlich, A. Runesson, and E. Schuller (eds.), *Purity, Holiness, and Identity in Judaism and Christianity: Essays in Memory of Susan Haber* (WUNT 305; Tübingen: Mohr Siebeck, 2013), 110, notes that the Gospels "seem uninterested, uninformed, or both, on ... the event which sparked the process by which Jesus meet (sic) his death."

they in turn orchestrated his execution, most exegetes appeal to the Temple incident but focus on Jesus' critique of its commerce, corruption, or illegitimacy, common enough complaints in this period, but arguably insufficient to warrant crucifixion by political conspiracy. If Jesus was simply a loyal, observant Jew who practiced "common Judaism," then why was he engaged in so many religious controversies? Why did he seem to generate such intense hostility? If Jesus revered the Temple and participated in the Temple cult, then why did he predict, if not threaten, its destruction? What gave Jesus the authority to interpret, let alone correct, the Torah? If Jesus' execution is best explained by positing a conspiratorial alliance initiated by *religious* leaders and authorities, it seems safe to assume that the thrust of Jesus' offense was directed squarely at *them*.

Jesus was executed for sedition but he led no armies and mounted no rebellion.[5] Nonetheless, if it is reasonable to presume that Jesus was executed for a reason – whatever that reason may be – then we must be willing to reexamine the Gospel narratives for clues, especially as their authors either did not know why Jesus offended the Temple's authorities or they wished to obscure their knowledge by emphasizing other explanations for their Master's death. The reverence in which Jesus was held by his disciples and the horror of his brutal death created an immediate need for an explanation that could reconcile the historical and theological elements of the event and make meaning out of them.[6] Jesus' followers "remembered" Jesus' conflict with the Temple, his arrest, trial, suffering, and death in Jerusalem during the Passover festival – events ritually commemorated in the sacred meal they "remembered" Jesus instituting – but they did so in different contexts.[7] Moreover, those

---

[5] Dale B. Martin, "Jesus in Jerusalem: Armed and Not Dangerous," *JSNT*, 37.1 (2014), 3–24, suggests that Jesus attempted to occupy the Temple and take up arms against the Romans, "advocating" for the Temple's destruction (14, 16–17). For critique, see Paula Fredriksen, "Arms and the Man: A Response to Dale Martin's 'Jesus in Jerusalem: Armed and Not Dangerous,'" *JSNT*, 37.3 (2015), 312–25. On the violent revolutionary hypothesis, see Simon J. Joseph, *The Nonviolent Messiah: Jesus, Q, and the Enochic Tradition* (Minneapolis: Fortress, 2014), 23–50.

[6] On early Christian cultic-performative remembrances of Jesus' death, see Ellen Bradshaw Aitken, *Jesus' Death in Early Christian Memory: The Poetics of the Passion* (NTOA/SUNT 53; Göttingen: Vandenhoeck and Ruprecht, 2004), esp. 27–54.

[7] Alan Kirk, "The Memory of Violence and the Death of Jesus in Q," in A. Kirk and T. Thatcher (eds.), *Memory, Tradition, and Text: Uses of the Past in Early Christianity* (SS 52; Atlanta: Society of Biblical Literature, 2005), 203, links Jesus'

"memories" were rapidly transformed into community *traditions* and then came to influence the composition of the Gospels, producing a controlling effect on how the story of Jesus was told and re-told.

The New Testament contains four *different* accounts of the Temple incident and Jesus' Temple-related sayings. It is not always clear, however, whether the events of Jesus' last week in Jerusalem were "remembered" by "eyewitnesses," and, even if they were, whether those "memories" were reliable.[8] "Memories" can be "manufactured."[9] In the case of the Temple incident, each Gospel represents a different literary-theological *interpretation* of a sequence of events infused with scriptural allusions *and* historical reminiscence.[10] In other words, we must still sift through the different "memories" and traditions inscribed and re-inscribed in the Gospels in order to construct persuasive historical accounts of *"wie es eigentlich gewesen war."* At the same time, we must also attempt to explain the emergence of *different* interpretations of "what happened."[11] Our sources must be critically scrutinized and sorted according to their relative chronological, redactional, and theological fingerprints and

---

death in Q 11:47-51 to the commemorative and "moral exhortation" of martyrdom, arguing that Q's view of Jesus cannot be "collapsed into the images emerging in other streams of early Christian tradition."

[8] Judith C. S. Redman, "How Accurate are Eyewitnesses? Bauckham and the Eyewitnesses in the Light of Psychological Research," *JBL*, 129 (2010), 177-97. On the unreliability of memory, see also Dale C. Allison, *Constructing Jesus: Memory, Imagination, and History* (Grand Rapids: Baker, 2010), 1-30. Allison concludes that "our Synoptic writers thought that they were reconfiguring memories of Jesus" (459). See also J. Fried, *Der Schleier der Erinnerung: Grundzüge einer historischen Memorik* (Munich: C.H. Beck, 2004).

[9] Zeba A. Crook, "Collective Memory Distortion and the Quest for the Historical Jesus," *JSHJ*, 11 (2013), esp. 64-76.

[10] On the role of *interpretation* in "eyewitness" testimony, see Samuel Byrskog, *Story as History—History as Story: The Gospel Tradition in the Context of Ancient Oral History* (WUNT 123; Tübingen: Mohr Siebeck, 2000). See also Jens Schröter, *From Jesus to the New Testament: Early Christian Theology and the Origin of the New Testament Canon* (trans. W. Coppins; Waco: Baylor University Press, 2013), 25. On memory as "distortion" or "*refraction*," see Anthony Le Donne, *The Historiographical Jesus: Memory, Typology, and the Son of David* (Waco: Baylor, 2009), 13. On the Markan passion narrative as (liturgical) "scripturalization," see Mark Goodacre, "Scripturalization in Mark's Crucifixion Narrative," in G. van Oyen and T. Shepherd (eds.), *The Trial and Death of Jesus: Essays on the Passion Narrative in Mark* (CBET 45; Leuven: Peeters, 2006), 33-47.

[11] Le Donne, *The Historiographical Jesus*, 74.

tested against the known historical context.[12] In this case, it is the Palestinian Jewish cultural context of the early Jesus movement that can serve as a control to our interpretive and reconstructive efforts related to Jesus' teaching, his relationship to the Temple, conflict with Jewish religious authorities, and political execution.

The present study seeks to shed new light on the historical circumstances which led to Jesus' death by problematizing Jesus' relationship to the Temple and the identification of Jesus and his death as a "sacrifice" in the New Testament. Chapter one reviews the Gospels' accounts of Jesus' death as a politico-religious conspiracy and assassination orchestrated by the high priesthood in collaboration with the Roman prefect. Chapter two explores the role of the Torah in Second Temple Judaism, with special attention given to the theme of eschatological restoration and the different ways that the New Testament authors portrayed the Mosaic Law in relationship to Jesus' teachings, life, and death. Chapter three focuses on contemporary critical discussions on the origins, function, and significance of sacrifice in antiquity, with particular emphasis on how sacrifice is represented in the Torah, the prophetic literature, and the Qumran corpus. Chapter four surveys the New Testament sources on the Temple incident. Chapter five re-examines the hypotheses that the Temple incident represented either a prophetic demonstration of the symbolic destruction of the Temple or an eschatological "cleansing" of its administration and proposes a new hypothesis that attempts to more adequately account for the full range of data. Chapter six further explores and supports this hypothesis by tracing its role and function in "Jewish Christianity." Finally, chapter seven re-examines the identification of Jesus as a sacrifice in the New Testament as interpreted within multiple discourses on sacrifice in Paul's letters, Isaiah's Servant Songs, and the Last Supper narratives.

The early association of Jesus' death with the language and vocabulary of *sacrifice* made meaning out of a tragic event, but it also obscured the original circumstances that led to Jesus' death. The original participants in these events were recast as characters in a divine drama brought to life in the Gospels' passion narratives, which

---

[12] Richard Bauckham, *Jesus and the Eyewitnesses: The Gospels as Eyewitness Testimony* (Grand Rapids: Eerdmans, 2006), 506: "The question is whether it is trustworthy, and this is open to tests of internal consistency and coherence, and consistency and coherence with what other relevant historical evidence we have and whatever else we know about the historical context."

downplayed the original tensions, conflicts, and cultural dynamics that led to the cross. Pilate became the reluctant governor and Jesus the willing victim of a divine sacrifice orchestrated by God. The Gospel of Jesus became the Gospel about Jesus. The idea that Jesus died because he offended the religious authorities who conspired against him was supplemented by the idea that it was God who had purposefully orchestrated his death all along. Jesus' death was viewed through the lens of a theological conviction that God intended Jesus to die as a divine sacrifice for sin.[13] Christianity was soon envisioned as the covenantal replacement of Judaism, with Jesus' sacrifice being the effective replacement of the Temple system. These theological perspectives have overshadowed the historical circumstances of the Temple incident. It is not surprising that some scholars consider the incident itself a fictional account, with the evangelists framing Jesus' last week as a kind of showdown between him and the religious leaders.[14] Such severe scepticism, however, seems unwarranted. The authors of the Gospels certainly *highlight* the conflict between Jesus and the Temple's administration for dramatic tension, but that does not mean that they *invented* the tale.

Today most scholars recognize that it was Jesus' criticism of the Temple's administration, his offense to traditional forms of piety, his contested authority,[15] and his growing popularity that led to his death. Jesus' death was clearly influenced by sociopolitical, economic, and religious conflicts with his contemporaries, particularly the Temple administration.[16] Craig Evans, for example, suggests that this can

---

[13] On Jesus' death as remembered "around Passover," see Helen K. Bond, "Dating the Death of Jesus: Memory and the Religious Imagination," *NTS*, 59.4 (2013), 471: "both the Markan and the Johannine chronologies with which we are familiar are based on theological reflections derived from the memory that Jesus died *at around the time of the Passover*."

[14] David Seeley, "Jesus' Temple Act," *CBQ*, 55 (1993), 263–83, here 274. For criticism, see James G. Crossley, *The Date of Mark's Gospel: Insights from the Law in Earliest Christianity* (London: T & T Clark, 2004), 62–71.

[15] Chris Keith, *Jesus Against the Scribal Elite: The Origins of the Conflict* (Grand Rapids: Baker Academic, 2014).

[16] James H. Charlesworth (ed.), *Jesus and Temple: Textual and Archaeological Explorations* (Minneapolis: Fortress, 2014). On the Temple, see Martin Goodman, "The Temple in First-Century CE Judaism," in John Day (ed.), *Temple and Worship in Biblical Israel* (New York: T & T Clark, 2007), 459–68; Moshe David Herr, "Jerusalem, the Temple, and Its Cult – Reality and Concepts in Second Temple Times," in A. Oppenheimer et al. (eds.), *Jerusalem in the Second Temple Period: Abraham Schalit Memorial Volume* (Jerusalem: Yad Ben-Zvi, 1980), 166–77.

be understood as a politico-ideological battle between the family of Jesus and the family of the high priest.[17] Alternatively, Bruce Chilton proposes that Jesus' death was the end result of his sacrificial "program" to reform the Temple cult.[18] Our interpretive problem is that the historical and theological aspects of Jesus' death were quickly confused and conflated.[19] The historical realities of first-century Judea were relegated to the status of theological stage-props so that Jesus, Caiaphas, and Pilate became unwitting actors in a literary drama of divine salvation. This historical and theological confusion has resulted in major difficulties of interpretation.

The idea that Jesus died as an atoning blood sacrifice is a theological dogma. It cannot be affirmed or confirmed by historiographical analysis. It is a matter of faith. It has been an enduring source of spiritual comfort for millions of Christians for two thousand years, dramatically illustrating the love, mercy, and forgiveness of God.[20] The primary way this concept of atonement has been viewed is that Jesus' suffering, death, and resurrection were divine mysteries that reconciled humanity and God. It is an idea embedded in the very earliest recorded Christian commemorative reflections on Jesus' death.[21] It is a central component of ancient and contemporary Christian faith. It is also a serious historical problem.

Scot McKnight's recent study, *Jesus and His Death*, is illustrative.[22] McKnight surveys a spectrum of views on Jesus' death and concludes that Jesus saw himself as "the Passover victim whose blood would protect his followers from the imminent judgment of God."[23] Jesus

---

[17] Craig A. Evans, *From Jesus to the Church: The First Christian Generation* (Grand Rapids: Westminster John Knox, 2014); Eyal Regev, "Temple Concerns and High-Priestly Prosecutions from Peter to James: Between Narrative and History," *NTS*, 56 (2010), 64–89.

[18] Bruce Chilton, *The Temple of Jesus: His Sacrificial Program within a Cultural History of Sacrifice* (University Park: Pennsylvania State University Press, 1992), 138.

[19] Frances M. Young, "Temple Cult and Law in Early Christianity: A Study in the Relationship between Jews and Christians in the Early Centuries," *NTS*, 19 (1972), 335, argues that Jesus was "condemned for criticism of the Jewish Law and the Temple-cult." In *Sacrifice and the Death of Christ* (Cambridge University Press, 1975), 96, Young affirms that Jesus died *as* a sacrifice.

[20] Martin Hengel, *The Atonement: The Origins of the Doctrine in the New Testament* (trans. John Bowden; Philadelphia: Fortress, 1981).

[21] 1 Cor. 15:3.

[22] Scot McKnight, *Jesus and His Death: Historiography, the Historical Jesus, and Atonement Theory* (Waco: Baylor University Press, 2005). See also James D. G. Dunn, *Jesus Remembered* (Grand Rapids: Eerdmans, 2003), 824.

[23] McKnight, *Jesus and His Death*, 339, also 280–1.

took God's wrath upon himself.[24] The New Testament witness, there-fore, "goes right back to Jesus."[25] It is true, evidently, that the Gospels contain multiple passages in which Jesus foresees his death, predicts his suffering, and proclaims its salvific, atoning power to his disciples, but that is precisely the point: *the Gospels were written to proclaim the Good News of Jesus' saving death and resurrection.* It is not difficult, therefore, to find passages affirming this proclamation. But this "Jesus" both cel-ebrates the Passover by bringing a lamb to the Temple for sacrifice and predicts, even inaugurates, its destruction.[26] This Jesus, in other words, affirmed the Temple cult, participated in its sacrificial rites, criticized its administration, *and* predicted its destruction while instituting an alter-native cultic meal *as* a blood sacrifice that would be "the sacrifice of all sacrifices."[27]

The idea that Jesus' death was a sacrifice may conform to traditional *Christian theology*, but this conceptual language originated in and was derived from Second Temple *Jewish* ideology, theology, and ritual prac-tice. The Temple was a powerful center of cultic ritual, meaning, and identity for ancient Jews. There is no doubt that most Jews (at most times) thought highly of the Temple and experienced their participa-tion in it with reverence and piety. On the other hand, the Temple could also be perceived as a political symbol of collaboration, corruption, inequality, oppression, and religious illegitimacy. There were a variety of positions taken on sacrifice, ranging from pro-sacrifice critique of the Temple and its administration to explicitly antisacrificial stances. We will need to respect this ancient Jewish cultural diversity as we attempt to reconstruct how early Christianity – in and through its adoption of Jewish sacrificial logic, efficacy, vocabulary, imagery, ritual, and soteri-ology – became a "sacrificial" religion.[28]

The contemporary study of Jesus and the early Jesus movement's relationship to the Temple cult is complicated, however, by religious and cultural biases that continue to inform our understanding of what ancient Jews and early Christians believed about sacrifice.[29]

[24] McKnight, *Jesus and His Death*, 142–3.

[25] McKnight, *Jesus and His Death*, 372.

[26] McKnight, *Jesus and His Death*, 254–5.

[27] McKnight, *Jesus and His Death*, 325, 87.

[28] Guy G. Stroumsa, *The End of Sacrifice: Religious Transformations in Late Antiquity* (trans. Susan Emanuel; University of Chicago Press, 2009), 72.

[29] Jonathan Klawans, *Purity, Sacrifice, and the Temple: Symbolism and Supersessionism in the Study of Ancient Judaism* (New York: Oxford University Press, 2005), 75–100. See also Maria Zoe Petropoulo, *Animal Sacrifice in Ancient Greek*

Christianity has a long and disturbing legacy of theological supersessionism.[30] Whether it is a Christian bias that sacrifice was superseded by the death of Jesus, a Jewish bias that prayer and Torah study effectively replaced the Temple, a Reform-Jewish bias that ancient sacrifice was inferior, barbaric, or obsolete, or a scholarly prejudice toward seeing animal sacrifice as a "primitive" rite to be located on an evolutionary spectrum of progress,[31] these biases are "methodologically unsound," "inadequate and inaccurate" understandings of the evidence.[32] Jonathan Klawans suggests that modern readers misrepresent animal sacrifice because of modern concerns regarding the environment, animal abuse, capitalism, and consumerism, and seeks to go beyond the "current antisacrificial bias" by providing a sympathetic view of the ancient system.[33] Klawans denies that the anti-Temple traditions in the New Testament go back to the earliest Christians. According to Klawans, the fact that Acts 2 reports the earliest (Jewish) Christians as living in Jerusalem and visiting the Temple regularly suggests that they did *not* object to the Temple cult.[34] The earliest Christians "*chose* to be headquartered in Jerusalem" and this is virtually inexplicable if "a radically antitemple program was part of the picture from the earliest stage."[35] Moreover, there are a number of Jesus traditions which "assume his followers worship in the temple, and will continue to do so."[36] After all, Jesus' disciples visit the Temple to prepare for the Passover immediately after the Temple incident.[37] For Klawans, neither Jesus nor his followers nor Paul ever

Religion, Judaism, and Christianity, 100 BC to AD 200 (Oxford: Oxford University Press, 2008); Christian A. Eberhart (ed.), *Ritual and Metaphor: Sacrifice in the Bible* (RBS 68; Atlanta: Society of Biblical Literature, 2011).

[30] Jon D. Levenson, *The Death and Resurrection of the Beloved Son: The Transformation of Child Sacrifice in Judaism and Christianity* (New Haven: Yale University Press, 1993), x.

[31] See especially William Robertson Smith, *Lectures on the Religion of the Semites* (London: Adam and Charles, 1894); Réne Girard, *Violence and the Sacred* (trans. P. Gregory; Baltimore: John Hopkins University Press, 1977); Walter Burkert, *Homo Necans: The Anthropology of Ancient Greek Sacrificial Ritual and Myth* (trans. P. Bing; Berkeley: University of California Press, 1983).

[32] Klawans, *Purity, Sacrifice, and the Temple*, 3.

[33] Klawans, *Purity, Sacrifice, and the Temple*, 10.

[34] Klawans, *Purity, Sacrifice, and the Temple*, 217.

[35] Klawans, *Purity, Sacrifice, and the Temple*, 218, citing Paula Fredriksen, *Jesus of Nazareth, King of the Jews* (New York: Alfred A. Knopf, 1999), 94–6, 106, 147.

[36] Matt 8:4, Mark 1:44, and Luke 5:14, Matt 23:21.

[37] Klawans, *Purity, Sacrifice, and the Temple*, 218.

rejected the Temple. Paul simply "borrowed" concepts from the sacrificial lexicon of Judaism and regarded the Temple cult as "proper and effective."[38]

Similarly, Daniel Ullucci argues that early Christian "nonparticipation" in sacrifice was "part of a larger argument over what sacrifice ought to be" made by people committed to the practice.[39] Early Christians were cultural "producers" and their "positions on sacrifice cannot and should not be construed as critiques ... Their texts are evidence of their participation."[40] In short, "there is nothing antisacrificial in the earliest Christian sources,"[41] Paul "fully supports animal sacrifice in the temple of Jerusalem," and "Rejections of sacrifice in second- and third-century Christian sources are post-facto rationales for a non-participation that came decades before." Ullucci proposes that Christians only rejected sacrifice because the destruction of the Temple put an end to their participation; the *earliest* Christians had a *positive* view of the Temple cult.[42] Nonetheless, the Christian rejection of blood sacrifice was a challenge not only to the social and political structures of Roman society but to a widely shared view of the cosmos as well.[43] Klawans and Ullucci seem to represent "a growing scholarly recognition of the early Christian appreciation of the Temple and the sacrificial cult."[44]

In a recent study comparing the early Jerusalem community to alternative "temples" in Samaria, Leontopolis, and Qumran, Timothy Wardle shows that a number of Jewish communities were willing to create an "alternative" temple. He also notes that both the historical Jesus and the early Jesus movement engaged in polemical

[38] Klawans, *Purity, Sacrifice, and the Temple*, 221.

[39] Daniel C. Ullucci, *The Christian Rejection of Animal Sacrifice* (New York: Oxford University Press, 2011), 3; "Before Animal Sacrifice: A Myth of Innocence," *R & T*, 15 (2008), 357–74.

[40] Ullucci, *The Christian Rejection of Animal Sacrifice*, 8.

[41] Ullucci, *The Christian Rejection of Animal Sacrifice*, 12.

[42] Oskar Skarsaune, *In the Shadow of the Temple: Jewish Influences on Early Christianity* (Downer's Grove: InterVarsity, 2002), 157, argues that "the early believers purposefully ignored the sacrificial cult going on in the temple." Contra Johannes Zachhuber, "Modern Discourse on Sacrifice and Its Theological Background," in J. Zachhuber and J. T. Meszaros (eds.), *Sacrifice and Modern Thought* (Oxford University Press, 2013), 12–28, here 15, 17: "At no point, then, in the New Testament or throughout late antiquity were Christians opposed to sacrifice as such."

[43] See George Heyman, *The Power of Sacrifice: Roman and Christian Discourses in Conflict* (Washington, DC: Catholic University of America Press, 2007).

[44] Regev, "Temple Concerns," 89.

conflict with the priestly leaders of the Jerusalem Temple, and that Jesus' criticism and demonstration against its administration led to his death. It is less clear, however, that all early Jewish Christians continued to participate in the Jerusalem Temple cult.[45] Here we are on less secure ground. Wardle proposes that Jesus began his ministry with a "positive" view of the cult,[46] which is "what one would expect to find in a first-century C.E. Jew."[47] He appeals to passages in which Jesus appears to display such a positive attitude, including Jesus' multiple visits to the Temple in the Gospel of John,[48] Jesus' lament over the Temple,[49] Jesus' apparent deference to priestly authority in the Gospel of Mark,[50] Matthew's sayings about reconciling with a brother before offering a gift and swearing by the sanctuary,[51] and Jesus' presumed participation in Passover rites. The problem is that Wardle does not engage counter-indications within these very passages that might yield a less "positive" view of the Temple cult. He also over-interprets, as when he states that Jesus is "portrayed as celebrating the Passover meal with a lamb ritually slain according to the temple's regulations."[52] This sacrificial act is not *explicit* anywhere in the Gospels. There is no such detail in the texts.[53] Moreover, the symbolic association of Jesus with the Passover lamb is implicit in the Markan narrative,[54] rendering the identification of the Last Supper as a *Passover* meal suspect. The idea that Jesus had an essentially positive attitude toward the Temple cult also renders problematic the idea that Jesus' attitude toward the Temple cult suddenly *shifted* during his last week.

Wardle appeals to E. P. Sanders's argument that Jesus' demonstration in the Temple was a prophetic act of symbolic destruction *and*

---

[45] Timothy Wardle, *The Jerusalem Temple and Early Christian Identity* (WUNT II.291; Tübingen: Mohr Siebeck, 2010), 10.

[46] Wardle, *The Jerusalem Temple*, 170.

[47] Wardle, *The Jerusalem Temple*, 170.

[48] John 2:13; 5:1; 7:10; 11:55.

[49] Q 13:34–35.

[50] Mark 1:40–44

[51] Matt 5:23–24; 23:21.

[52] Wardle, *The Jerusalem Temple*, 170.

[53] Similarly, P. Maurice Casey, *Aramaic Sources of Mark's Gospel* (SNTSMS 102; Cambridge University Press, 1998), 222, locates Jesus sacrificing in the Temple ("Jesus slit the throat of a one-year old lamb") by retroverting the Greek of Mark 14:12 ("when the Passover lamb was being sacrificed" (ὅτε τὸ πάσχα ἔθυον) into the Aramaic כדי פסחא דבחין ("when *they* were sacrificing the Passover").

[54] Cf. 1 Cor 5:7.

a critique of the Second Temple's economic corruption.[55] Similarly, Wardle proposes that Jesus expected that "a new temple would replace the current one upon its destruction,"[56] although there is precious little evidence that Jesus anticipated the building of a new *physical* Temple.[57] Wardle discusses Mark's Parable of the Wicked Tenants and affirms that its setting in Mark "has an air of authenticity to it,"[58] but this assertion re-inscribes Mark's narrative agenda, which is to *transfer* the covenantal relationship of the vineyard ("Israel") to a new temple-community ("Christians"). While it is highly likely that economics played a role in Jesus' critique of the Temple's administration, this was already a common enough critique throughout the Second Temple period. Yet if such is the case, it becomes less clear how Jesus could have held a "positive" view of the Temple, participated in its cultic rites, and encouraged his followers to do so. Moreover, despite the fact that the identification of Jesus as a sacrifice is a pervasive theme in the New Testament,[59] Wardle does not discuss or address the topic of sacrifice – as his primary interest is reconstructing early Christian self-identification as an alternative "temple" – but in doing so he tends to overlook the complex diversity of early Christian attitudes toward the Temple.

More recently, James H. Charlesworth has challenged the "supposition, or claim, that Jesus led a movement that was, in principle, opposed to the Temple or its worship ... and sought, symbolically at least, to destroy the Temple."[60] Charlesworth illustrates this supposition by surveying the work of four scholars who focus on the relationship between Jesus and the Temple: Walter Bauer, John Dominic Crossan, E. P. Sanders, and Nicholas Perrin. Bauer, infamous for seeking to distance Jesus from Judaism altogether, "influenced generations of Europeans to adopt the hypothesis that Jesus was not only against any form of sacrifice but was against the Temple."[61] Crossan "explicitly portrays Jesus as setting himself against the Temple."[62]

---

[55] Wardle, *The Jerusalem Temple*, 174.
[56] Wardle, *The Jerusalem Temple*, 184.
[57] Wardle cites *1 En.* 90.28–29, 11Q19 29.7–10, *4 Ezra* 10.25–54, and *2 Bar.* 4.2–7; 6.7–9, but the latter two texts represent *post*-70 CE traditions.
[58] Wardle, *The Jerusalem Temple*, 189.
[59] Rom 12:1; 15:16; Phil 2:17; 4:18; 2 Tim 4:6; Heb 13:15–16; Rev 8:3–4.
[60] Charlesworth, "Jesus and the Temple," in *Jesus and Temple*, 150.
[61] Charlesworth, "Jesus and the Temple," 151.
[62] Charlesworth, "Jesus and the Temple," 151, citing John D. Crossan, *The Historical Jesus: The Life of a Mediterranean Jewish Peasant* (San Francisco: HarperSanFrancisco, 1991), 355.

Sanders "gives the impression that Jesus directs his words and actions against the Temple as an institution."[63] And finally, Perrin's claim – that "Jesus claimed to embody the Temple" – is found to be methodologically unsound as it removes Jesus from Judaism "by attributing to him a Christology that in fact appeared only after Jesus."[64]

Charlesworth's contribution is a major step forward in Jesus Research. According to Charlesworth, Jesus felt "at home" in the Temple, taught in its precincts, and defended its sanctity.[65] Jesus, in other words, was a faithful, "observant Jew" who traveled to Jerusalem during his last week not in order to complete his ministry, but rather "to obey the *halakah* that faithful Jews must be in Jerusalem to celebrate Passover and to worship in the Temple."[66] Charlesworth rejects the idea that Jesus and his *earliest* followers saw themselves as *replacing* the Temple and argues that they "hallowed the Temple and worshipped in it."[67] In doing so, however, he tends to take the author of Luke-Acts' tendentious accounts of early Christian participation in the Temple at face value.[68] At the same time, he dismisses the historical value of "Jewish Christian" traditions.[69] Charlesworth rightly urges *discrimination* in assessing the evidence, noting that Jesus may have "loved the Temple" but disliked its administration, objecting to certain "operational" aspects of the Temple system.[70] Nonetheless, it is still not clear precisely what Jesus objected to in the Temple.[71] Charlesworth suggests that Jesus *may* have

[63] Charlesworth, "Jesus and the Temple," 152, citing E. P. Sanders, *Jesus and Judaism* (Philadelphia: Fortress, 1985), esp. 66, 70, 70–1, 75, 76.

[64] Charlesworth, "Jesus and the Temple," 153–4, citing Nicholas Perrin, *Jesus the Temple* (Grand Rapids: Baker Academic, 2010), 12.

[65] Charlesworth, "Jesus and the Temple," 160, 162.

[66] Charlesworth, "Jesus and the Temple," 179.

[67] Charlesworth, "Jesus and the Temple," 154.

[68] See esp. Acts 2:46; Luke 24:53; Acts 21:26–36; 22:17. On the (un)reliability of Acts (and its traditions) as history, see Richard I. Pervo, *Profit With Delight: The Literary Genre of the Acts of the Apostles* (Philadelphia: Fortress, 1987), 8. See also Gerd Lüdemann, *Early Christianity According to the Traditions in Acts: A Commentary* (Minneapolis: Fortress, 1989), 1–17.

[69] Charlesworth, "The Temple," 200, refers to the *Gospel of the Ebionites* (209) as "rhetoric" that "informs us of attitudes to the Temple by Christians who lived after the first century CE ... These 'gospels' inform us neither of Jesus' attitude nor of his disciples' attitude."

[70] Charlesworth, "Jesus and the Temple," 154–5, 212, n. 101.

[71] Charlesworth, "Jesus and the Temple," 161, suggests that Jesus either "became angry at abuse and cheating within the Temple," was "offended" and driven to "a righteous outrage" by the iconography on the coins, or "hated" the money changers, and the "unjust" measures (155).

rejected the sacrificial system, either because the priests were corrupt and illegitimate, or because he suddenly changed his mind during his last days.[72] He thus leaves open the pressing question of whether Jesus actually offered animal sacrifices in the Temple, although he admits that "The Gospels do not depict Jesus in this action."[73]

Modern scholarly attempts to portray early Jewish and Gentile Christians as affirming the validity and sanctity of the Temple *cult* may be more politically correct and ecumenically palatable than historically accurate.[74] Identifying Jesus as "a devout Jew faithful to Torah" may be a laudable attempt to undermine anti-Judaic readings of the Jesus tradition,[75] but the more Jesus is characterized as an "observant Jew," the more difficult it becomes to explain the subsequent departure of his Jewish followers from Jewish practices. If the Gospels are any indication, Jesus seems to have offended, scandalized, challenged, criticized, and reinterpreted Jewish traditions.[76] Any re-construction of the relationship between Jesus and the Temple must account for *all* the evidence, including the ambiguities within the tradition, early Christian criticism of the Temple cult, Luke's apologetic portrait of early Christian activity in the Temple, and the radically innovative redeployment of sacrificial ideology and supersessionistic theology in early Christian representations of Jesus' death.

While many scholars today correctly affirm Jesus' Jewish identity, the portrayal of Jesus as an essentially observant Jew seems to fly in the face of significant currents of religious conflict running through the early Jesus tradition. Similarly, the assumption that the earliest Christians *participated* in the Temple cult is problematic for several reasons. First, the available evidence is ambiguous: the New

---

[72] Charlesworth, "Jesus and the Temple," 176–7, considers the idea that Jesus "might have turned against the Temple sacrifices in his last days" as "possible" and "conceivable," appealing to Christopher Rowland, "The Temple in the New Testament," in John Day (ed.), *Temple Worship in Biblical Israel* (London: T&T Clark, 2007), 472.

[73] Charlesworth, "Jesus and the Temple," 178.

[74] On the fallacy that "all Jews in the postexilic period held the temple in high regard," see George W. E. Nickelsburg, *Ancient Judaism and Christian Origins: Diversity, Continuity, and Transformation* (Minneapolis: Fortress, 2003), 153.

[75] Charlesworth, "Introduction," 16–17.

[76] Martin Hengel, *Die Zeloten: Untersuchungen zur Jüdischen Freiheitsbewegung in der Zeit von Herodes 1.bis 70 n. Chr.* (AGJU 1; Leiden: Brill, 1961), 346, n. 3, notes that Jesus' critique was directed "nicht gegen die römische Oberherrschaft sondern gegen die religiös und politisch herrschende Schicht im Judentum selbst."

Testament contains both positive *and* negative views of the Temple; we cannot simply privilege one set of the data.[77] Second, early Christians refused to participate in animal sacrifice. Why? Third, how did the conception of Jesus' death as a sacrifice and his body as a temple arise? And fourth, why did some "Jewish Christians" emphatically claim that Jesus *rejected* animal sacrifice? If *Jesus* was regarded as an efficacious atoning sacrifice, why would Jesus' Jewish followers continue worshipping, that is, *sacrificing*, in the Temple? Did Jesus and his first followers participate in the Temple cult – or not? These are the questions this book will investigate. Although this study challenges certain historical assumptions about Jesus – for example, the assumption that the historical Jesus and his followers participated in the Temple cult – I am not particularly interested in courting controversy. What I am interested in is understanding how the early Jesus movement emerged, developed, and transformed from a Palestinian Jewish renewal movement into a Gentile-inclusive empire-wide network of faith-communities which ultimately came to identify themselves as non-Jewish. The reinterpretation of Torah observance and traditional Temple practices were central components of this new faith. Yet the precise relationship between Jesus and Second Temple Judaism remains unclear. It is our task to reconstruct this transformation.

Who Killed Jesus? The Politico-Religious Conflict

Who killed Jesus? In today's post-Holocaust sensitivity toward Christian anti-Judaism, it is tempting to remove the blame for Jesus' brutal death from the Jewish religious leadership – where it has traditionally rested – and place it squarely on the shoulders of Rome. Historically speaking, however, our focus should be as much on identifying *who* or *what* killed Jesus as on *why* Jesus died. It is not possible to answer these questions, however, without first establishing the political context of Roman Judea.[78] Since the days of Alexander

---

[77] Hengel, *The Atonement*, 47.

[78] E. Mary Smallwood, *The Jews Under Roman Rule: From Pompey to Diocletian: A Study in Political Relations*, second edn.; (Leiden: Brill, 1981). See also Jean Juster, *Les Juifs dans l'Empire Romain: Leur Condition Juridique, Économique, Sociale* (Paris: Paul Geuthner, 1914), and Emil Schürer, *The History of the Jewish People in the Age of Jesus Christ (175 B. C. – A. D. 135)*, revised and edited by Geza Vermes, Fergus Millar, and Matthew Black with Pamela Vermes (Edinburgh: Clark, 1973–1979). More recently, see Richard Horsley, *Scribes, Visionaries, and the Politics of Second Temple Judea* (Louisville: Westminster John Knox, 2007).

the Great, the political relationship between various occupying imperial forces and the Judean Temple priesthood had resulted in a long history of political compromise and collaboration. By the time Rome annexed Judea in 63 BCE, the high priesthood had survived Antiochus' attempt to Hellenize the Temple and the rise and fall of the Hasmonean/Maccabean dynasty. Following the deposition of Herod's son Archelaus in 6 CE, the three districts of Judea, Samaria, and Idumaea – once governed under the temporary policy of electing client-kings – finally came under direct Roman rule as the province of "Judea."

The Romans had adopted a policy of toleration toward Judaism as a *religio licita* ("permitted religion") and Jews were exempt from participating in the imperial cult. Instead, they offered a daily sacrifice for the emperor's "well-being." Nonetheless, the high priest was appointed directly by the prefect. Josephus tells us that the Romans "entrusted" the aristocracy and the high priesthood with the "leadership of the nation,"[79] yet the fact that the high priest's ceremonial vestments were kept under lock and key in the Antonia Fortress symbolized Rome's control over both the political and religious landscape.[80] The presidency of the Sanhedrin and the role of the high priest were both supervised and controlled by the Roman governor, illustrating the complex intersection of politics and religion in first-century Judea, a province ever on the brink of nationalistic fervor, resentment toward Roman taxes, and a willingness to resist, rebel, and revolt. It is within this turbulent context that we must locate the high priest and evaluate his efforts to maintain control and order.

It is virtually certain that the high priest who co-orchestrated Jesus' arrest, trial, and crucifixion was a man named Joseph Caiaphas.[81] Appointed by Valerius Gratus in 18 CE (and deposed in 37 CE), Caiaphas was the son-in-law of Annas (Ananus), a former high priest appointed by Quirinius in 6 CE. Luke 3:2 refers to the "high-priesthood of Annas *and* Caiaphas" as if they worked together.

---

[79] *A.J.* 20.251.

[80] Smallwood, *The Jews Under Roman Rule*, 149.

[81] Smallwood, *The Jews Under Roman Rule*, 168. For a sympathetic biographical portrait, see Helen K. Bond, *Caiaphas: Friend of Rome and Judge of Jesus* (Louisville: Westminster John Knox Press, 2004); *Pontius Pilate in History and Interpretation* (Cambridge University Press, 1998). See also J.-P. Lémonon, *Pilate et le gouvernement de la Judée* (Paris: Gabalda, 1981); Rainer Metzner, *Kaiphas. Der Hohepriester jenes Jahres. Geschichte und Deutung* (AJEC 75; Leiden: Brill, 2010).

Annas may have been the real power behind the scenes, since Annas had served as high priest from 6 CE to 15 CE. Eventually, five of his sons were to become high priests themselves.[82] This was a family dynasty. John the Baptist, Jesus, Stephen, and James were all put to death during the offices of priests of the house of Annas.[83]

The quest for the "historical Caiaphas" is difficult. After all, Caiaphas has been judged rather harshly by history and no less so by biblical scholars. Helen Bond and others have recently tried to rehabilitate Caiaphas' reputation by challenging the tendency to view the high priesthood as a group of self-serving hypocrites and cynical collaborators. She suggests that rather than being seen as a corrupt and/or greedy politician, Caiaphas should be recognized as dutiful and pious, and our portrait of him should sympathetically reflect the difficult position he was in, perhaps even absolving him of any complicity in Jesus' death. According to Bond, Caiaphas may have been far more concerned about Jesus' ability to gather crowds and incite a riot during Passover than on anything Jesus taught or thought about himself. Caiaphas, in other words, may not have cared about Jesus or his teachings. Bond's sympathetic portrait is a necessary corrective to stereotypical representations of Caiaphas as the quintessential villain. Yet there is something to be said for the fact that Caiaphas – unlike his predecessors or successors – retained the high priesthood for almost twenty years. Surely this suggests that he was not simply pious, but also politically savvy in his ability to maintain a strategic working relationship with Pilate. We may not agree with Solomon Zeitlin who identified the high priests as "Jewish Quislings" who proved to be "traitors to their own people" by doing "the bidding of Roman masters,"[84] but Caiaphas *was* a "collaborator." For Zeitlin, the high priest "delivered" Jesus to Rome, but he was either "compelled to do so to save himself" or to "sell out Judea to the Romans for personal gain."[85] In either case, Zeitlin finds neither the Pharisees

---

[82] Annas was appointed high priest in 6 CE by Sulpicius Quirinius, legate in Syria, and deposed by Valerius Gratus, prefect in Judea, in 15 CE. In the subsequent fifty years, five of his sons became high priests (*A.J.* 20.9.1 § 198). Caiaphas, Annas' son-in-law, was appointed in 18 CE. (*A.J.* 18.2.3 § 34–35). Pontius Pilate was Valerius' successor in 26 CE. Caiaphas remained high priest throughout the eleven years of the rule of Pilate (26–36 CE).

[83] Brawley, *Luke-Acts*, 117.

[84] Solomon Zeitlin, *Who Crucified Jesus?* (New York: Harper & Brothers, 1942), 209.

[85] Zeitlin, *Who Crucified Jesus?*, 172.

nor the Sadducees, nor the Jewish people to be responsible for the death of Jesus: Jesus was crucified by Rome, the victim of "a universal evil, imperialism."[86]

Similarly, Ellis Rivkin dissociates the high priest from his traditional allegiance to the Temple and Jewish people by highlighting his political collaboration with Rome, thus absolving Jews and Judaism in the death of Jesus, and shifting the blame entirely onto the Roman "system."[87] Whereas Zeitlin asked *who* crucified Jesus, Rivkin asks *what* crucified Jesus. According to Rivkin, Caesar, Pilate, the high priest, and his "privy council" were "tied together by two interests: the preservation of imperial power ... and the smooth collection of tribute."[88] The Jewish high priest was essentially "an arch sinner" appointed directly by a foreign power, and not, as legislated in the Torah, a descendent of Aaron, Eleazar, Phineas, and Zadok. The post-Herodian high priesthood was thus *halakhically* illegitimate, the result of political compromise under Roman occupation. A charismatic preacher like Jesus did not stand a chance: there was no way to predict when such a figure's teachings "*would have unintended political consequences.*"[89] For the Romans, charismatics were "politically dangerous" because they attracted crowds, and crowds were unpredictable. Caiaphas would have lost no time in "silencing so ominous a threat to law and order."[90] Pilate "made short shrift of a case like this."[91] Jesus was simply another victim of "Rome's determination to eradicate anyone who challenged its rule."[92]

More recently, John Dominic Crossan has echoed these sentiments by indicting the imperial Roman system, arguing that Jesus – a "peasant nobody" – was executed in Jerusalem through a *conjunction* of the highest Jewish and Roman authorities. Jesus was simply "a dangerous peasant nuisance" and was eliminated without any official trials or "consultations." It was just "handled under general procedures for maintaining crowd control during Passover."[93] Crossan lays

---

[86] Zeitlin, *Who Crucified Jesus?*, 211.

[87] Ellis Rivkin, *What Crucified Jesus? The Political Execution of a Charismatic* (Nashville: Abingdon, 1984).

[88] Rivkin, *What Crucified Jesus?*, 38.

[89] Rivkin, *What Crucified Jesus?*, 63.

[90] Rivkin, *What Crucified Jesus?*, 82.

[91] Rivkin, *What Crucified Jesus?*, 87.

[92] Rivkin, *What Crucified Jesus?*, 105.

[93] John Dominic Crossan, *Who Killed Jesus? Exposing the Roots of Anti-Semitism in the Gospel Story of the Death of Jesus* (San Francisco: HarperSanFrancisco, 1995), 212.

the blame squarely at this conjunction of Jewish and Roman authority. Yet while it seems reasonable to hold Pilate responsible for signing Jesus' death-warrant, Jesus does not seem to have been arrested by the Romans, but rather by a Jewish squad of armed Temple guards (representing the "high priests, the scribes and the elders").[94] Jesus was brought before Pilate because Jewish priests had arrested him. Therefore, a more precise solution to why Jesus was arrested may have less to do with how he may have offended or brought Roman attention to himself and far more to do with why the high priest wanted Jesus out of the way.[95]

Jesus was brought to Pilate by the Jewish authorities and it was the high priest(s) that made the accusation against Jesus and provoked the "crowd,"[96] presumably constituted by priestly supporters, to demand his execution.[97] Does *Caiaphas* then bear "the ultimate official responsibility?"[98] A few scholars have suggested that Caiaphas was actually trying to *save* Jesus by attempting to give him an opportunity to deny being a messianic figure.[99] According to this theory, Caiaphas was tragically compromised by Jesus' disrespect for the Temple, his potentially political following, and the possibility that the Romans could slaughter thousands of Jews along with Jesus for treason. Here Caiaphas' ripping of his garments – a scene typically interpreted as his indignation at Jesus' blasphemous claim to be messiah – is understood as an act of *mourning* for Jesus. Should Caiaphas be celebrated as a hero for trying to rescue Jesus from the Romans? This does not seem very likely. It is fairly certain that Caiaphas was "the moving agent on the Jewish side in the final proceedings against Jesus."[100] Jesus may not have been

---

[94] Mark 14:43; 14:33; cf. John 18:3.

[95] On Jesus' crucifixion as a Roman misunderstanding of a (false) charge by Jewish authorities, see Bornkamm, *Jesus of Nazareth*,151; H.-W. Kuhn, "Die Kreuzesstrafe während der frühen Kaiserzeit. Ihre Wirklichkeit und Wertung in der Umwelt des Christentums," *ANRW* 25.1 (Berlin and New York: Walter de Gruyter, 1982), 735; Rudolf Bultmann, "Das Verhältnis der urchristlichen Christusbotschaft zum historischen Jesus," in D. Dinkler (ed.), *Exegetica. Aufsätze zur Erforschung des Neuen Testaments* (Tübingen: Mohr Siebeck, 1967), 453.

[96] Mark 15:3.

[97] Mark 15:11.

[98] Simon Légasse, *The Trial of Jesus* (trans. J. Bowden; London: SCM, 1997), 33.

[99] Haim Hermann Cohn, *The Trial and Death of Jesus* (New York: Ktav Publishing, 1977).

[100] Raymond E. Brown, *The Death of the Messiah: From Gethsemane to the Grave – A Commentary on the Passion Narratives in the Four Gospels*, 2 vols., (New York: Doubleday, 1994), 392, 458.

mounting a rebellion against Rome, and his ministry could not have been mistaken as a military uprising, but his popular following and talk about a new "kingdom" could easily be mistaken as a royal claim. The Synoptics tell us that Jesus' ministry had grown more popular than John the Baptist's, whose ministry was also familiar to the priests. Jesus' activities in Judea, Galilee, and Samaria had earned him a reputation as a charismatic healer, exorcist, prophet, and potential king. His arrival in Jerusalem could have been seen as a direct challenge to priestly religious and political authority. Jesus was arrested by a group of Temple guards representing the "high priests, the scribes, and the elders."[101] While it is possible that the Jewish authorities had already consulted with Pilate before Jesus' arrest, the time and setting suggests a more clandestine effort on their part. According to Mark, the Sanhedrin met at night and condemned him to death.[102] What is more likely, however, is a hasty informal meeting.[103] It is unlikely that this examination was intended to be a formal capital trial. This was rather an expedient way to have Jesus executed directly by Pilate. The high priest did not need to call an official assembly.[104]

The Gospels repeatedly refer to a "Sanhedrin" (Συνέδριον/סנהדרין) in the trial of Jesus.[105] Josephus refers to a senate of elders or *Gerousia* as well as a Sanhedrin when he claims that Jewish law "forbids us to slay someone, even an evildoer, unless this person has first been condemned by the Sanhedrin to suffer this fate."[106] Josephus tells us that "the chief priests were entrusted with the leadership of the nation" following Herod the Great's death,[107] a body largely comprised of Sadducees in Jerusalem including the high priest, noblemen, elders, and Pharisees.[108] The New Testament *seems* to support this general Josephan description.[109] The Jewish trial of Jesus *seems*

---

[101] Mark 14:43; John 18:3; Mark 14:33.

[102] Mark 14:53–72.

[103] Mark 14:53–65, Matt. 26:57–68, and Luke 22:54–71.

[104] Simon Légasse, *The Trial of Jesus* (trans. John Bowden, London: SCM, 1997), 25.

[105] Mark 15:1; Matt 26:59; Luke 22:66; John 11:47.

[106] For *Gerousia*, see *A.J.* 12.3.3 §138. For Sanhedrin, see *A.J.* 14.9.3 §167. Josephus uses both *Sanhedrin* and *Boulē*. See also *A.J.* 20.9.1 §200–3; *A.J.* 20.9.6 § 216–217; *Life* 12 §62; *A.J.* 20.1.2 §11; *B.J.* 2.15.6 §331; *B.J.* 2.16.2 §336; *B.J.* 5.13.1 §532; *B.J.* 5.4.2 §142–144).

[107] *A.J.* 20.10.5 § 251; *A.J.* 20.10.4 §244.

[108] *B.J.* 1.8.5 §170; *A.J.* 14.4.4 §91.

[109] Cf. John 11:47–53; Acts 4:5–6, 15.

to have involved a Sanhedrin of the high priest, chief priests, scribes, and elders which had the authority, under Roman jurisdiction, to sentence legal transgressions. The Sanhedrin was essentially under the authority and control of the high priest.[110] In a much disputed passage, Josephus' Testimonium refers directly to Jesus' death at the instigation of Jewish authorities:

> At this time there appeared Jesus (Ἰησοῦς), a wise man (σόφος ἀνήρ) ... for he was a doer of wonderful works (παραδόξων ἔργων), a teacher of people who receive the truth with pleasure. He won over many Jews and many of the Greeks ... And when Pilate, because of an accusation/indictment (ἐνδείξει) made by the leading men among us (πρώτων ἀνδρῶν), condemned him to the cross, those who had loved him previously did not cease to do so.[111]

Josephus' Testimonium implicates the Jewish religious leadership's participation in Jesus' death.[112] According to the Babylonian Talmud (*Sanh.* 43a), Yeshu is described as "one who leads the people astray":[113]

> On the eve of Passsover Yeshu (ישוע) (the Nazarene) was hanged. For forty days before the execution took place, a herald went forth and cried, 'He is going forth to be stoned because he has practiced sorcery and enticed Israel to apostasy. Anyone who can say anything in his favor, let him come

---

> forward and plead on his behalf.' But since nothing was brought forward in his favor, he was hanged on the eve of Passover.

Although this passage suggests that Jesus was executed on the evening of the Passover (which contradicts the Synoptics, but corresponds to the Gospel of John), the passage also implies that both the accusers and executioners were Jewish authorities, with no reference to Pilate or the Roman cross. In the late 100s, the pagan critic Celsus quotes a Jewish position stating that

> We punished this fellow (Jesus) who was a cheater ...
>   We had convicted him, condemned him, and decided that he should be punished.[114]

Justin also states to his dialogue partner, Trypho, that "You crucified him."[115] Similarly, the book of Acts attributes a significant role in Jesus' death to Jews and/or Jewish authorities,[116] while our earliest Christian text (1 Thess 2:14–15, c. 49 CE) explicitly implicates "the Jews/Judeans" in Jesus' death:

> For you, brothers and sisters, became imitators of the churches of God which are in Judea in Christ Jesus because you too suffered the same things from your own countrymen as they did from the Jews/Judeans (Ἰουδαίων) who killed both the Lord Jesus and the prophets, and drove us out; they displease God and oppose everyone by hindering us from speaking to the Gentiles so that they may be saved.[117]

The authenticity of this passage has been disputed, yet the allegedly anti-Judaic tone and content of 1 Thess 2:14–15 is fairly consonant with Pauline theology. In Romans, Paul writes that the Jews have been "broken off" or "cut off" from the tree of Abraham ("because

---

[114] Origen, *Contra Celsum* 2.4, 2.9, 2.5.

[115] Justin, *Dial.* 17.1.

[116] Acts 3:14–15; 4:10; 5:30; 7:52; 13:27–28.

[117] On the authenticity of the passage, see Frank D. Gilliard, "The Problem of the Antisemitic Comma Between 1 Thessalonians 2.14 and 15," *NTS*, 35 (1989), 481–502; Markus Bockmuehl, "1 Thessalonians 2:14–16 and the Church in Jerusalem," *TB*, 52.1 (2001), 1–31; Todd D. Still, *Conflict at Thessalonica: A Pauline Church and its Neighbours* (JSNTSup 183; Sheffield Academic Press, 1999), 24–45; Karl Paul Donfried, *Paul, Thessalonica, and Early Christianity* (Grand Rapids: Eerdmans, 2002), 195–208.

of their unbelief"; Rom 11:20) and will not be grafted back until the future, when God's "wrath" against them comes to an end (cf. Rom 11:11–29). Paul repeatedly appeals to the theme of God's "wrath" in Romans (2:5, 8; 3:5; 4:15; 5:9; 9:22; 12:19). It seems safe to conclude that not only were *some* Jews involved in the death of Jesus, but we can be even more specific by identifying the high priest (and chief priests) as disliking him enough to form conspiratorial attempts to stop him, a dislike that ultimately led to a judicial action by the "Sanhedrin" and to Jesus being "handed over" to Pilate, who sentenced him to death.[118]

The idea that at least *some* Jews had *no* role in Jesus' death is a modern fiction.[119] Jesus was involved in an inner Jewish conflict at a time when Jews committed acts of great violence against each other over religious issues.[120] Jesus claimed to be able to speak for God. He called for religious renewal and reform.[121] But what was it about Jesus that offended the high priest? It must have been "something that could be interpreted as presenting a danger to the Temple."[122] The Gospel of John intimates as much, quoting Caiaphas as saying that "if we permit him thus, all will believe in him. And the Romans will come and take from us both the place and the nation."[123] We can be confident that the high priest and other religious authorities were involved even if it is difficult to determine their precise motives. At least some of those involved may have thought it their religious duty to interrogate Jesus. Others may have been motivated by political or economic factors. The high priest was appointed directly by the Roman prefect and could be deposed at will. There is certainly reason to believe that political considerations were involved.

What we can be quite sure about, however, is that Jesus' trial was *not* an official meeting of the Sanhedrin according to Mishnaic and rabbinical law. There are significant differences between the Gospel

---

[118] Brown, *The Death of the Messiah*, 1:377: [there is] "no ancient indication of any Jewish tradition that calls into doubt the involvement of Jewish authorities in the death of Jesus."

[119] David R. Catchpole, "The Problem of the Historicity of the Sanhedrin Trial," in E. Bammel (ed.), *The Trial of Jesus – Cambridge Studies in Honour of C. F. D. Moule* (SBT 2.13; London: SCM, 1970), 47–65; *The Trial of Jesus* (SPB 18; Leiden: Brill, 1971).

[120] Brown, *The Death of the Messiah*, 394.

[121] Brown, *The Death of the Messiah*, 392–3.

[122] Brown, *The Death of the Messiah*, 458.

[123] John 11:47–53.

trial scenes and the Mishnah's description of the Sanhedrin.[124] The Mishnah reflects a much later (third-century) rabbinical idealization of the Sanhedrin and so cannot be affirmed as evidence of any first-century Sanhedrin or priestly council. Yet the fact that the trial of Jesus was not conducted according to Mishnaic rules does not mean that Jesus' trial was "illegal." It simply suggests that the first-century Sanhedrin was not bound by Mishnaic rules. The Sanhedrin operated by procedures more in keeping with its actual religious and political configuration(s) at the time.

In the Gospels, Jesus is accused of blasphemy. Mark tells us that the high priest asked Jesus if he is the messiah, the "Son of God/ Son of the Blessed."[125] According to Mark, Jesus simply says "I am" (Mark 14:62). In Matthew 26:64 and Luke 22:70, Jesus' reply invokes the son of man sitting at the right hand of God, a quotation from Psalm 110:1:

> "Are you the Messiah, the Son of the Blessed One?"
> "I am, and you will see the son of man seated at the right hand of the Power/Almighty and coming with the clouds of heaven."

According to Mark and Matthew, Caiaphas regarded this reply as blasphemous, but it was not blasphemous to declare oneself to be the messiah. Jesus may have claimed to speak for God or even identified himself as an eschatological judge, but such claims, while perhaps misguided and dangerous in the eyes of his opponents, were not blasphemous.[126] Mishnaic blasphemy requires the use of the divine name.[127] Jesus does not do so, although it is likely that "blasphemy"

---

[124] A *Mishnaic* Sanhedrin would have required a meeting of seventy elders in a special room in the Temple complex during the day (*Sanhedrin* 4.1; *b. Megillah* 14a). Verdicts of condemnation cannot be reached on the same day as the trial (*Sanh.* 4.1). The trial also cannot be held in the high priest's house (*m. Sanh.* 11.2). The Mishnah rules against judging alone (*'Abot* 4.8). Capital cases cannot be tried on the evening of the Sabbath or the evening of a festival day (*Sanh.* 4.1) and must begin with reasons for acquittal and that witnesses for the defense have been brought in (*Sanh.* 5.4). In addition, contradictory testimony is not only nullified, but false witnesses are to be punished with the same penalty reserved for the accused (*Sanh.* 5.2; 11.6).

[125] Mark 14:61–64.

[126] Geza Vermes, *Jesus the Jew: A Historian's Reading of the Gospels* (Philadelphia: Fortress, 1981 [1973]), 35, states that Mark 14:62 is not blasphemous "by virtue of any known Jewish law, biblical or post-biblical." See also Sanders, *Jesus and Judaism*, 55, 298.

[127] *m. Sanh.* 7.5.

included insulting God. In Acts, Stephen is tried for his "blasphe-mous" words against Moses, God, and the Temple, implying that Jesus wanted to change the Mosaic customs of the Jews.[128] What seems clear from these accounts is that the *Jewish* charges against Jesus may have included *blasphemy*. The charge of blasphemy is consistent with the idea that Jesus said and did something against the Temple and/or the authority of the Mosaic Torah.[129] Rabbinical Jewish tradition accuses Jesus of deception, practicing "sorcery," and leading Israel to "apostasy,"[130] crimes punishable by death,[131] but Jews did not have full authority to carry out capital punishment under Roman rule, which in this case would have involved stoning.[132] The Roman gover-nor had the power of life and death over the Jews in cases of political offenses, although religious offenses were left to the discretion of the Sanhedrin.[133] It is not clear whether the Sanhedrin could sentence capital cases.[134] The Gospels suggest that the Sanhedrin decided on the death penalty, but needed their decision to be authorized by Rome. John 18:31 has "The Jews" remind Pilate that "it is not per-mitted to us to put anyone to death." Josephus tells us of Greek and Latin inscriptions warning foreigners not to cross from the Court of the Gentiles to the inner court of the Temple under penalty of death.[135] Josephus describes James' death at the hands of Annas II (Ananus) as unethical because he convened a "Sanhedrin of judges" and delivered James to stoning. Many people apparently knew that Annas II (Ananus) had conducted an illegal Sanhedrin without the procurator's consent,[136] which suggests that Rome held the *imperium* to try, convict, and punish capital crimes. There is no doubt that Jesus challenged the position and authority of the high priest. He was claiming an exalted authority of his own, which he claimed came directly from God. Caiaphas may have been insulted and offended by Jesus' lack of response and deference to his authority, but since Pilate

[128] Acts 6:11–14.
[129] Brown, *The Death of the Messiah*, 1:525.
[130] *b. Sanh.* 43a.
[131] *m. Sanh.* 7.4.
[132] *B.J.* 2.117; *A.J.* 18.2; John 18:31; 19:10.
[133] *A.J.* 18.2; *B. J.* 6.334, respectively.
[134] Smallwood, *The Jews under Roman Rule*, 150, suggests that they could.
[135] *B.J.* 5.5.2 §193; *A.J.* 15.11.5 §417; Philo, *Ad Gaium* 31 §212. This seems to have been one instance in which Rome gave the Temple authorities permission to execute (*B.J.* 6.2.4 § 124–126).
[136] *A.J.* 20.9.1 §200–203.

would not be interested in a Jewish religious dispute over blasphemy, the leaders needed a political charge.

Jesus disturbed commerce in the Temple. He was said to have threatened the destruction of the Temple, but there were no reliable witnesses. Jesus was said to have advised followers not to pay taxes, but the charge didn't stick.[137] The Gospels recount how Jesus avoided being cornered into making a dangerous political decision when he said "render unto Caesar what belongs to Caesar."[138] The only certain offense was sedition, revolt, rebellion. It is reasonable to conclude that Caiaphas told Pilate that Jesus was a prospective *king*. He was either calling himself king or was being hailed as a king. Caiaphas knew that declaring oneself a king was a political crime against Rome. It is unlikely that he told Pilate that they had "handed him over" (παραδεδώκεισαν) out of "jealousy" (φθόνον), as Mark suggests.[139] Caiaphas may have accused Jesus of *blasphemy*,[140] but the official charge became "perverting the nation," "forbidding to pay taxes to Caesar," and claiming that Jesus declared himself to be "Christ or King."[141]

Jesus was executed as a political figure.[142] The historical origins of crucifixion are difficult to determine, although the Romans seem to have reserved it for such enemies of the state.[143] Josephus describes a number of mass executions in Judea,[144] and skeletal remains of a

---

[137] Mark 12:12.

[138] Matt. 22:15–22; Luke 23:1–4.

[139] Mark 15:10; cf. Matt 27:18.

[140] Mark 14:61.

[141] Luke 23:2.

[142] On crucifixion, see Martin Hengel, *Crucifixion in the Ancient World and the Folly of the Message of the Cross* (trans. John Bowden; Philadelphia: Fortress, 1977); David W. Chapman, *Ancient Jewish and Christian Perceptions of Crucifixion* (WUNT II.244; Tübingen: Mohr Siebeck, 2008); Kuhn, "Die Kreuzesstrafe während der frühen Kaiserzeit.," 648–793. On the language of crucifixion (i.e., ἀνασταυροῦν, ἀνασκολοπίζειν, σταυρός), with crucifixion described as "an executionary suspension," see Gunnar Samuelsson, *Crucifixion in Antiquity: An Inquiry into the Background and Significance of the New Testament Terminology of Crucifixion* (WUNT II.310; Tübingen: Mohr Siebeck, 2011), 306.

[143] See Plato, *Gorgias* 473c. Herodotus describes the Persians using it. Demosthenes knew about being "nailed up" as the worst form of execution (*Oration* 21; *Against Meidias* 105). See also Cicero (*Against Verres* 2.5.64), Seneca (*To Marcia on Consolation* 20.3); Philo, *On Dreams* 2.213; Plutarch, *Morals* 499d; Seneca, *On the Happy Life* 19.3.

[144] *B.J.* 5.451; 2.75; 2.241; 2.305–8; Seneca *Dial.* 6.20.3; Philo, *Spec. Laws* 3.160; *Flaccus* 84–85; Cicero, *Verr.* 2.5.64,6 § 165, 169; Quintilian, *Decl.* 274.13; Cassius Dio, *Hist. Rom.* 49.22.6; Tacitus, *Hist.* 2.72.

crucified man with a Roman nail still in his heel-bone were found in Jerusalem in 1968.[145] Pilate executed Jesus as a political response to a punishable, political crime. The Gospels portray Pilate as suspicious of the Jewish authorities and not altogether trusting their motivations.[146] But Passover was a popular religious festival and this was a potentially explosive political problem. Pilate could be callous in his disregard for the religious beliefs and practices of Jews. There is little reason to think that he was motivated by any desire to appease a high priest. There is no compelling historical reason to think that there was a Roman custom of letting a rebel prisoner free at Passover. There is even less reason to think that Pilate was reluctant to order an execution.[147]

The Gospels describe Pilate as sympathetic to Jesus' situation, even trying to find a reason, excuse, or justification to release him. Is this likely? This portrayal seems to be part of the early Christian tradition's attempt to transfer the blame from Rome to the Jews. Sympathetic portrayals of Pilate almost certainly reflect the anti-Jewish post-70 CE atmosphere in which the Gospels were written. Jews had just revolted against Rome, and anti-Jewish sentiment was rife in the later decades of the first century.[148] Nonetheless, the ancient evidence does not entirely support the idea that Pilate was nothing but a ruthless, brutal, insensitive thug. In 26 CE, when Pilate took office, he is reported to have sent troops into Jerusalem with medallions or busts of Tiberius attached to their standards.[149] The Jews revolted against this pagan iconography and protested before Pilate in Caesarea. Pilate, although reluctant to remove the standards, realized that the Jews were willing to die, and acquiesced, removing the standards. On another occasion, Pilate appropriated

---

[145] N. Haas, "Anthropological Observations on the Skeletal Remains from Giv'at ha-Mivtar," *IEJ*, 20 (1970), 38–59; J. Zias and E. Sekeles, "The Crucified Man from Giv'at ha-Mivtar: A Reappraisal," *IEJ*, 35 (1985), 22–7.

[146] See, for example, John 18:30–31.

[147] The Synoptics use the term "governor" (Matt. 27:2; Luke 20:20), while Tacitus and Josephus use "procurator" (*Annals* 15.44). Josephus uses the Greek *epitropos* ("procurator"; *B.J.* 2.169). A Latin inscription found in Caesarea in 1961 properly identifies Pontius Pilate, in particular, as the "*prefect*" of Judea ([PON]TIUS PILATUS [PRAEF]ECTUS IUDA[EA]E).

[148] According to Tertullian, Pilate was a kind of secret "Christian" (*Apologeticum* 21.18,24). The *Didascalia Apostolorum* claims that Pilate did *not* go along with the Jews (5.19.4). Hippolytus (*On Daniel* 1.27) regarded Pilate as innocent.

[149] *B.J.* 2.9.2–3 §169–174; *A.J.* 18.3.1 §55–59.

Temple treasure to build an aqueduct into Jerusalem.[150] Although thousands of Jews seem to have protested, this time Pilate did not back down, but sent soldiers in disguise out into the crowd to attack the protestors and many Jews seem to have died in the ensuing chaos. It is difficult, however, to see this admittedly bold move as justification for characterizing Pilate as greedy or rapacious: he was, after all, making a significant improvement to the health and welfare of the city. On yet another occasion, Philo reports that Pilate dedicated golden shields in the Herodian palace in Jerusalem c. 31 CE.[151] Philo tells us that the shields did not have pagan iconography or imagery on them, but may have named the (divine) emperor. This time, a contingent of four Herodian princes and a larger group of Jews protested, and Pilate was ordered by Tiberius to take the shields from Jerusalem to Caesarea. Finally, Josephus tells us about a Samaritan prophet who announced that he would reveal Moses' sacred vessels on Mount Gerizim.[152] Pilate opposed this eschatological enthusiasm, and a number of Samaritans were killed and the leaders executed. It was after this last episode that Pilate was ordered to leave Judea and report back to Rome. In most of these accounts, however, Pilate is not portrayed as especially violent or brutal, but rather a religiously insensitive yet politically shrewd and calculating governor.

The Jewish high priest had charged Jesus with sedition. Jesus was brought before Pilate. The high priest delivered the accusations,[153] provoked a crowd of supporters, and pressed for execution.[154] According to Luke, Pilate sent Jesus to Herod Antipas because Jesus, as a Galilean, was under his jurisdiction. Herod was in Jerusalem for the Passover, but Jesus refused to speak. Herod and his soldiers put a royal robe on him and mocked him as a king. He was then taken back to Pilate, who took Jesus inside for questioning. Jesus may have refused to answer.[155] After the charges were pronounced,[156] Pilate ordered Jesus to be delivered to the guards, and they flogged him in the courtyard. A severe beating with whips was standard practice for condemned criminals. The soldiers then apparently put a twisted cap

[150]   *B.J.* 2.9.4 §175–177; *A.J.* 18.3.2 § 60–62.
[151]   Philo, *Ad Gaium* 38 §299–305.
[152]   *A.J.* 18.4.1–2 §85–89.
[153]   Mark 15:3.
[154]   Mark 15:11.
[155]   At least according to Mark 15:5.
[156]   Luke 23:2.

of thorns on his head, a reed in his hand, and bowed, hailing him as "King of the Jews." Pilate ordered the charge to be written in Latin, Greek, and Hebrew (Aramaic): "This is Jesus, the King of the Jews."

The death of Jesus may be easy enough to reconstruct in terms of *who* and *what* led to his Roman crucifixion – a religious conflict translated into political language and a capital crime in the hands of political collaborators – but we still do not have a firm grasp on *why*. Why was Jesus such a threat to the high priest? If Jesus' death was not simply incidental to his ministry – a tragic accident neither foreseen nor expected – but rather the climax of his ministry, then we need to re-evaluate why Jesus offended his contemporaries. Some scholars have traced the origins of Jesus' offense to scribal authority conflicts. Others have sought it in his subversive interpretations of religious traditions and/or his criticisms of Pharisaic or Sadducean practices. The accusation of blasphemy seems to follow Jesus around like the crowds of curious Galileans who affirmed his charisma and authority. While the general consensus among specialists is that Jesus' demonstration in the Temple got him killed, what led up to this climactic moment might also have played a role in his demise. The question we need to ask, therefore, is: What *led* Jesus to challenge the Temple's administration? To answer this, we need to re-examine Jesus' relationship to the Torah. That is, in order to understand *what* Jesus objected to in the *Temple*, we must first understand Jesus' attitude to the *Torah* in the context of first-century Judaism.

2

THE ESCHATOLOGICAL TORAH

If one takes the Gospels at face value ... there emerges a
Jesus capable of generating intense dislike. Indeed, that is
the usual result of asking self-consciously religious people
to change their minds.[1]

Raymond E. Brown, *The Death of the Messiah*

The Torah in Second Temple Judaism

The Torah was the constitution of Israel, a body of ritual, civil, crim-
inal, and international law that guided the people of Israel in their
relationships, not only toward their neighbors and the nations, or
Gentiles, but also to each other.[2] Yet the Torah was interpreted dif-
ferently by different Jews, causing divisions, disagreements, and conflicts throughout the Second Temple era. Since the Persian period,
the Mosaic Torah had come to represent the ancestral laws and customs of the Jewish *ethnos*, a tradition which drew from Hellenistic
concepts of associating people with their ancestral laws. That is why
challenging the Jewish law or customs could be viewed as breaking
with the tradition of a people, its constitutional and nationalistic

---

[1] Brown, *The Death of the Messiah*, 392.

[2] On the law, see Philip S. Alexander, "Jewish Law in the Time of Jesus: Towards
a Clarification of the Problem," in B. Lindars (ed.), *Law and Religion: Essays on
the Place of the Law in Israel and Early Christianity* (Cambridge: James Clarke and
Co., 1988), 44–58; K. Müller, "Gesetz und Gesetzeserfüllung im Frühjudentum," in
K. Kertelge (ed.), *Das Gesetz im Neuen Testament* (Freiburg: Herder, 1986), 11–27;
P. Richardson and S. Westerholm, *Law in Religious Communities in the Roman
Period: The Debate over Torah and Nomos in Post-Biblical Judaism and Early
Christianity* (SCJ 4; Waterloo: Wilfred Laurier University Press, 1991). For the *liter-
ary* development of the Torah, see Bernard M. Levinson, *Legal Revision and Religious
Renewal in Ancient Israel* (Cambridge University Press, 2008), 23–7; Aharon Shemesh,
Halakhah in the Making: The Development of Jewish Law from Qumran to the Rabbis
(TLJS 6; Berkeley/Los Angeles: University of California Press, 2009).

legislation. The post-Maccabean period led to new emphases on the Torah's identity-markers, an increase in *halakhic* interpretations, and the rise of sectarianism based on those interpretations.[3]

The Torah was not just an ancestral law-code. It was also the symbolic cultural currency in and through which *new* claims of divine revelation could be made and authorized. This tension between the Torah's ancestral laws and the idea that the Torah could incorporate new interpretations, hidden laws, *pre*-Mosaic Law, "heavenly tablets," and the divinely designed natural order of creation, complicated Torah-interpretation in this period. The Torah could also be *prioritized*, with some laws trumping other laws – the way the Markan Jesus cites Genesis 1 in order to challenge Deuteronomy 24 in the Markan saying on divorce – and so the role of the Torah was a subject of ongoing conflict and debate. It will be useful to illustrate this in some detail here with several examples from Second Temple Jewish literature, with a particular focus on the Enochic literature and its influence on the book of *Jubilees* and the Qumran corpus.

The idea that the history of Israel began at creation was a popular idea in the Second Temple period (Ben Sira, the book of *Jubilees*, the *Animal Apocalypse*) and supported the idea that the covenant was eternal.[4] The Wisdom of Ben Sira (c. 200–175 BCE), for example, identified Wisdom with the Torah:

> From eternity, in the beginning, he created me, and for eternity I will not cease to exist (Sirach 24:9; cf. 24:23).

Ben Sira "grounded a conception of history as timeless by viewing creation as the beginning of Israel's history."[5] Sirach refers to the "law of life" (νόμον ζωῆς), an "eternal covenant" (διαθήκην αἰῶνος), and "decrees" (τὰ κρίματα) ordained by God,[6] echoing the "eternal

---

[3] The word *halakhah* is commonly associated with rabbinical Judaism and is not used in the Dead Sea Scrolls. Nonetheless, as L. H. Schiffman, "Halakhah and Sectarianism in the Dead Sea Scrolls," in T. H. Lim, L. W. Hurtado, A. G. Auld and A. Jack, (eds.), *The Dead Sea Scrolls in their Historical Context* (Edinburgh: T & T Clark, 2001), 123–4, points out, "no English term can possibly describe this system of law and practice as well as the term halakhah." See also Philip R. Davies, "Halakhah at Qumran," in P. R. Davies and R. T. White (eds.), *A Tribute to Geza Vermes: Essays on Jewish and Christian Literature and History* (Sheffield: JSOT, 1990), 37–50.

[4] See Ari Mermelstein, *Creation, Covenant, and the Beginnings of Judaism: Reconceiving Historical Time in the Second Temple Period* (JSJ Sup 168; Leiden: Brill, 2014).

[5] Mermelstein, *Creation*, 16.

[6] Sir 17:11–12. See Mermelstein, *Creation*, 25.

order" (ἐκόσμησεν εἰς αἰῶνα) in which God arranged the heavenly bodies.[7] Like Ben Sira, Philo also refers to the eternal Torah:

> The provisions of this law alone, stable, unmoved, unshaken, as it were stamped with the seal of nature itself, remain in fixity from the day they were written until now, and for the future we expect them to abide through all time as immortal.[8]

In the *Epistle of Enoch* (*1 En.* 91–108), Enoch refers to "the eternal law" (*1 En.* 99.2) as well as "the words of the Holy and Great Ones" (104.9). What is this mysterious "eternal law" that Enoch refers to? It cannot be the *Mosaic* Torah, at least not historically speaking, since it had not yet been revealed to Moses. It is, rather, an explicit appeal to a *pre-Mosaic* Torah. That is, there were revelations from the heavenly tablets *prior* to Moses.[9] In the *Astronomical Book* (*1 En.* 81.1–10), there is a tradition of heavenly "tablets" upon which "all the deeds of humanity and all the children of the flesh upon the earth for all the generations of the world" were written (81.2).[10] Enoch sees these "heavenly tablets" on his heavenly journey. The book of *Jubilees* – so obviously influenced by and indebted to the Enochic literature – can be seen as a kind of non-Mosaic Torah.

The book of *Jubilees* is later than the Enochic books. The author of *Jubilees* uses the Enochic tradition of "heavenly tablets" to imply that Enoch wrote down what he saw on these tablets – and that other revealers after Enoch also "saw" these heavenly tablets. Enoch is

---

[7] Sirach 16:27.

[8] Philo, *De vita Mosis* 2.14–16.

[9] George W. E. Nickelsburg, "The Nature and Function of Revelation in 1 Enoch, Jubilees, and Some Qumranic Documents," in E. G. Chazon and M. Stone (eds.), *Pseudepigraphic Perspectives: The Apocrypha and Pseudeipgrapha in Light of the Dead Sea Scrolls* (STDJ 31; Leiden: Brill, 1999), 92–120, here 101.

[10] Gabriele Boccaccini, "From a Movement of Dissent to a Distinct Form of Judaism: The Heavenly Tablets in Jubilees as the Foundation of a Competing Halakah," in G. Boccaccini and G. Ibba (eds.), *Enoch and the Mosaic Torah: The Evidence of Jubilees* (Grand Rapids: Eerdmans, 2009), 193–210; F. García Martínez, "The Heavenly Tablets in the Book of Jubilees," in M. Albani, et al. (ed.), *Studies in the Book of Jubilees* (TSAJ 65; Tübingen: Mohr Siebeck, 1997), 243–59; Martha Himmelfarb, "Torah, Testimony, and Heavenly Tablets: The Claim of Authority of the Book of Jubilees," in B. G. Wright (ed.), *A Multiform Heritage: Festschrift: Robert A. Kraft* (Atlanta: Scholars, 1999), 19–29; Hindy Najman, "Interpretation as Primordial Writing: Jubilees and Its Authority Conferring Strategies," *JSJ*, 30 (1999), 379–410.

revered as "the first who learned writing and knowledge and wisdom … He saw and knew everything and wrote his testimony and deposited the testimony upon the earth" (4.17–19). An angel gave seven tablets to Jacob, who wrote them down (32.21–26). Levi and his sons are entrusted with a library of books containing these heavenly secrets (45.16). Moses, too, is part of this tradition. An angel shows Moses "the tablets of the division of years from the time of the creation of the law and testimony" (1.29). *Jubilees*, in other words, claims to be a pre-Mosaic heavenly revelation.[11]

The book of *Jubilees* affirms that the covenant between God and Israel began at creation.[12] The author downplays the Mosaic covenant in order to accentuate and prioritize the pre-Mosaic covenants based on creation. This appeal to creation and the heavenly tablets is not intended to prioritize or privilege the authority of the Mosaic Torah, but rather to re-describe the Mosaic Torah as *part* of the pre-Mosaic divine revelation.[13] The motif of the heavenly tablets became the center of a complex history of revelation that included the patriarchs Enoch, Noah, Abraham, Jacob, and Moses. The Mosaic Torah was only *part* of the heavenly tablets revealed to Enoch.[14] The implication is that God's will is found in these heavenly tablets, not in the incomplete revelation received by Moses.[15] The heavenly tablets are *not* to be *equated* with the Mosaic Torah nor are they intended to *replace* the Mosaic Torah. Rather, they serve as a narrative device to identify the original divine *source* of the Mosaic Torah, that is, the Torah's heavenly prototype or template. The book of *Jubilees* refers to the Sabbath as an "eternal law" (2.30–33). The eternal law is written in heaven and manifest in the divine order of creation. This association of heavenly tablets = eternal law = divine creation suggests that the

---

[11] Hindy Najman, "Reconsidering Jubilees: Prophecy and Exemplarity," in *Enoch and the Mosaic Torah*, 229–43, here 231: "a second Torah that is already prior to the first Torah from Sinai." David R. Jackson, *Enochic Judaism: Three Defining Paradigm Exemplars* (LSTS 49; London: T & T Clark, 2004), 104, notes that "the Pentateuchal law is but a manifestation at one point of time of the eternal law of God as recorded more fully in the heavenly tablets."

[12] Mermelstein, *Creation*, 91.

[13] Mermelstein, *Creation*, 129. On the idea of an eternal covenant, see James C. VanderKam, "Genesis 1 in Jubilees 2," *DSD*, 1 (1994), 300–21.

[14] Boccaccini, *Enoch and the Mosaic Torah*, 89.

[15] Shemesh, *Halakhah in the Making*, 109, notes that "the Damascus Document's principle of the 'foundation of the Creation' is very similar to or even identical with the book of Jubilee's idea of 'laws written on the heavenly tablets.'"

Mosaic Torah could be conceived as a partial revelation of the fuller eternal law of the heavenly tablets or Torah of creation.[16]

The *concept* of the Torah could not be contested, but the *content* of Torah – in and through various appeals to pre-Mosaic authority and revelation – could be modified, corrected, challenged, and subverted.[17] This theme of heavenly tablets is echoed throughout the Qumran library,[18] where the language of mysteries, secrets, and revelations are a central theme of the community's preoccupations. This enacted or realized eschatology is related to the "fulfillment hermeneutics" characteristic of the Qumranic *pesharim*, where writers "construed sacred traditions as repositories of divine promises coming to fruition in their community's recent past and more contemporary circumstances."[19]

A number of Second Temple Jewish authors understood contemporary events in light of creation.[20] The authors of Ben Sira, the book of *Jubilees*, and the *Animal Apocalypse* each envisioned the story of Israel – albeit in their own distinctive ways – as beginning at creation and being fulfilled by restoring God's plan from creation.[21] This restoration of creation is made explicit in the *Animal Apocalypse*,[22]

[16] The idea of a preexistent Torah was also developed by the rabbis. M. S. Jaffee, *Torah in the Mouth: Writing and Oral Tradition in Palestinian Judaism, 200 BCE-400 CE* (New York: Oxford University Press, 2001); Gabriele Boccaccini, "The Preexistence of the Torah: A Commonplace in Second Temple Judaism, or a Later Rabbinic Development?" *Hen*, 17 (1995), 329–50.

[17] Alex P. Jassen, *Scripture and Law in the Dead Sea Scrolls* (New York: Cambridge University Press, 2014), 29, describes the period as "a shared world of scriptural exegesis that sought to make ancient Israelite law portable to new sociological, theological, and geographic contexts."

[18] 1QM 12.1–3; 4Q177; 4Q180 1 (*Ages of Creation*); 4Q537 1; 1QHᵃ 9.23–24; 4Q417 2 i15.

[19] Loren T. Stuckenbruck, "The Dead Sea Scrolls and the New Testament," in Nóra Dávid and Armin Lange (eds.), *Qumran and the Bible: Studying the Jewish and Christian Scriptures in Light of the Dead Sea Scrolls* (Leuven: Peeters, 2010), 131–70, here 141.

[20] Mermelstein, *Creation*, 181, notes that each author re-imagines historical events as "indicators" that God would "eventually realize the plan that he had formulated at creation."

[21] These appeals to creation are not to be confused with the idea of an alleged "Zion Torah" for all nations developed by Hartmut Gese, *Essays in Biblical Theology* (Minneapolis: Augsburg, 1981) and Peter Stuhlmacher, *Reconciliation, Law and Righteousness: Essays in Biblical Theology* (Philadelphia: Fortress, 1986), 110–33. For criticism, see Heikki Räisänen, *Jesus, Paul and Torah: Collected Essays* (JSNT Sup 43; Sheffield: JSOT, 1992), 241.

[22] Mermelstein, *Creation*, 146–7.

an Enochic text which envisions the end of violence and the birth of a new eschatological Adamic messiah who transforms both Israel and humanity. Loren Stuckenbruck notes how such language "about the *Urzeit* also functioned to provide *a basis for being confident about such an outcome.*"[23] It is now possible to speak of an ancient *theology of creation* associated with both the Torah and Temple.[24] The Torah was contested sacred *text*. The Temple was contested sacred *space*, the central axis and navel of creation. It is within this spectrum of interpretation – that is, within the heightened eschatological communities of Second Temple Judaism – that we can locate the historical Jesus.

Jesus and the Law

The law was "the single most divisive issue in the first Christian century."[25] The New Testament contains diverse interpretations and representations of Mosaic Law. For the author of Mark, as perhaps for Paul, Jesus abolished the Jewish dietary restrictions of the law,[26] or "declared all foods clean."[27] Certainly for Paul, Christ was "the *end* (or fulfillment) (τέλος) of the law."[28] But what about *Jesus*' understanding of Torah? Jesus' distinctive understanding of the law is embedded within the Gospels' narrative accounts of his sayings and deeds and can only be accessed after the evangelists' individual interests are isolated and identified.[29]

[23] Loren T. Stuckenbruck, *The Myth of Rebellious Angels: Studies in Second Temple Judaism and New Testament Texts* (WUNT 335; Tübingen: Mohr Siebeck, 2014), 252–3.

[24] Bernard Och, "Creation and Redemption: Toward a Theology of Creation," in L. M. Morales (ed.), *Cult and Cosmos: Tilting toward a Temple-Centered Theology* (BTS 18; Leuven: Peeters, 2014), 331–50; B. W. Anderson (ed.), *Creation in the Old Testament* (Philadelphia: Fortress, 1984). Gerhard von Rad, "The Theological Problem of the Old Testament Doctrines of Creation," in *The Problem of the Hexateuch and Other Essays* (Edinburgh: Oliver and Boyd, 1966), 131–43, notes that the concept of creation has been neglected in modern biblical theology.

[25] David Sim, "Matthew's Use of Mark: Did Matthew Intend to Supplement or to Replace His Primary Source?" *NTS*, 57 (2011), 185.

[26] See H. Sariola, *Markus und das Gesetz: Eine redaktionskritische Untersuchung* (AASF dhl 56; Helsinki: Suomalainen Tiedeakatemia, 1990).

[27] Mark 7:19b.

[28] Rom 10:4. E. Lohse, "Christus, des Gesetzes Ende? Die Theologie des Apostels Paulus in kritischer Perspektive," *ZNW*, 99 (2008), 18–32, argues that the law belonged to a former age.

[29] On the law in the Synoptic Gospels, see K. Berger, *Die Gesetzesauslegung Jesu. Ihr historischer Hintergrund im Judentum und im Alten Testament. Teil I: Markus und*

Here we encounter the vexing problem of identifying Jesus' distinctiveness *within* Judaism. James Crossley has recently suggested that a significant amount of "supersessionist rhetoric concerning Jews and Judaism continues in contemporary scholarship."[30] While Jesus researchers regularly appeal to Jesus' Jewishness, many also (re)construct a "Jewish-but-not-that-Jewish" Jesus who "overrides, makes redundant, transcends, intensifies, subverts, or ignores ... *Jewish identity as constructed by contemporary scholarship.*"[31] According to Crossley, "This pattern of finding ways for Jesus to 'transcend' or intensify Judaism, or at least find a get-out clause or do something new and unparalleled" is a holdover from the history of "the perceived cultural superiority of Christianity over Judaism."[32]

There is much to be commended in this ideological critique of contemporary Jesus Research. There is no doubt that Jesus' "Jewishness" *can* (and sometimes does) function as a cipher for the Christian Christ's "difference" from and superiority to Judaism. On the other hand, contemporary Jesus Research's emphasis on the Jewishness of Jesus remains a necessary corrective, a constant reminder that Jesus' "Jewishness" *was* "Christianized" by an increasingly Gentile Jesus movement. Furthermore, Jesus-scholars continue to disagree on the particular details of Jesus' attitude to the Torah and Temple cult. In other words, it is not Jesus' Jewishness that is in question; it is his *halakhah*. At the same time, recent scholarship on the diversity within Second Temple Judaism warns us against presuming that all Jews shared the same degree of Torah observance or participation in the Temple cult. In short, the solution to the problem of supersessionistic readings of Jesus' "Jewishness" (in which Jesus rejects Judaism,

Parallelen (WMANT 40; Neukirchener-Vluyn: Neukirchener, 1972); H. Hübner, *Das Gesetz in der synoptischen Tradition* (Witten: Luther, 1973); R. Banks, *Jesus and the Law in the Synoptic Tradition* (SNTSMS 28; Cambridge University Press, 1975); F. Vouga, *Jésus et la Loi selon la Tradition synoptique* (Geneve: Labor et Fides, 1988). On Jesus' *halakhah*, see Markus Bockmuehl, *Jewish Law in Gentile Churches: Halakhah and the Beginning of Christian Public Ethics* (Edinburgh: T & T Clark, 2000), esp. 3–48; Peter J. Tomson, "Halakhah in the New Testament: A Research Overview," in R. Bieringer, et al. (eds.), *The New Testament and Rabbinic Literature* (JSJ Sup 136; Leiden: Brill, 2010), 135–206.

[30] James G. Crossley, "A 'Very Jewish' Jesus: Perpetuating the Myth of Superiority," *JSHJ*, 11 (2013), 109–29, here 110. See also William E. Arnal, *The Symbolic Jesus: Historical Scholarship, Judaism, and the Construction of Contemporary Identity* (London: Equinox, 2005).

[31] Crossley, "A 'Very Jewish' Jesus," 116.

[32] Crossley, "A 'Very Jewish' Jesus," 117.

condemns the Temple, criticizes the Law, and somehow replaces all of this with "Christianity") is not to assume that Jesus participated in the Temple cult and fully observed the Law, but rather to identify each and every recoverable aspect of his particular *halakhah*.[33] Our discussion should focus less on *identity* and more on *praxis*.

The question of whether or not the historical Jesus opposed or affirmed the law is a contested and divisive issue in New Testament scholarship. In his influential monograph *Jesus and Judaism*, E. P. Sanders admitted that the theory of Jesus' opposition to the "validity" of the law "would account for his meeting opposition during his ministry," could have led to his death, and could account for "a new sect which broke with Judaism."[34] The problem with this theory, according to Sanders, is that "the apostles in Jerusalem apparently did not know that the Torah had been abrogated."[35] Sanders concludes that Jesus never opposed the law,[36] even while he concedes that the Mosaic Law was neither "final" nor adequate for the eschatological era.[37] It is highly unlikely, as Sanders notes, that Jesus opposed the *entire* Mosaic Law in practice or principle. But this does not mean that Jesus never criticized, corrected, or reinterpreted the law.[38] Second, Jesus' movement was not "a new sect which broke with Judaism," but a multi-regional movement *within* Judaism that ultimately came to adopt a radical view of the Torah, including the abolition of the Temple's sacrificial system. Moreover, the "apostles in Jerusalem" are *not* portrayed as consistently upholding the Torah or sacrificing in the Temple. The historical Jesus' relationship to the Torah is more complex than simple dichotomous constructions of opposition or affirmation.

Tom Holmén has explored whether Jesus sought to "remain faithful" to the "covenant."[39] The Gospels, of course, do not portray

[33] Bockmuehl, *Jewish Law in Gentile Churches*, 33: "The implausibility of occasional Jewish and other programmes to assert a wholly observant and uncontroversial Jesus should not prevent us from adopting a pragmatic posture that will assess each case on its own merits."

[34] Sanders, *Jesus and Judaism*, 56.

[35] Sanders, *Jesus and Judaism*, 246: the evidence of early Church participation in the Temple is "fatal to the view that Jesus openly and blatantly opposed the law."

[36] Sanders, *Jesus and Judaism*, 269, 272, 275.

[37] Sanders, *Jesus and Judaism*, notes that the Mosaic law was "not final" (252, 269) and thus not adequate for the eschatological era (255, 260; cf. 250, 267–9).

[38] Keith, *Jesus Against the Scribal Elite*, 145–6.

[39] Tom Holmén, *Jesus and Jewish Covenant Thinking* (BI 55; Leiden: Brill, 2001), 23.

Jesus as referring to the "covenant" (ברית/διαθήκη) outside the Last
Supper traditions (Mark 14:24; cf. 1 Cor 11:25), so Holmén must
look for "clues and connotations" of the covenant in Jesus' teaching.[40] Holmén coins the phrase "path searching"[41] to describe how
many Second Temple Jews remained loyal to the covenant as an
"enacted reality" manifesting in individual choices of Torah observance.[42] He concludes that Jesus did *not* participate in "covenant
path searching" and was indifferent to these path-markers because
he found this pursuit to be ineffective and unnecessary.[43] Jesus was
focused on the kingdom of God as that which "set aside covenant
path searching."[44] For Holmén, as for Sanders, Jewish opposition
toward Jesus did not arise from any "particular violation of the
law," but rather from the general suspicion that Jesus rejected "covenant path searching."[45] Holmén assumes Jesus maintained a certain level of Torah-observance, holding that there is "no reason to
doubt that he usually kept the Sabbath according to the common
demands ... he surely participated in the religious feasts in the
Temple and even otherwise in general lived as a law-abiding Jew."[46]
Nonetheless, Holmén recognizes that Jesus defied the Sabbath
commandment, devalued tithing, implied that the Torah was inadequate, and proclaimed that the Temple cult was "futile." In other
words, Holmén identifies the ambiguity inherent in the Jesus tradition, but does not resolve it.[47] So while Holmén has indeed made a
major contribution to Jesus Research, isolating Jesus' scandalous
indifference to covenantal "path markers" as indicative of his allegiance to the kingdom, he does not here establish the hermeneutic
that informed Jesus' distinctive approach to the Torah, that is, the
guiding principle(s) that allowed Jesus to intensify the demands of
marital law but relax the *halakhic* restrictions of Sabbath law. We

---

[40] Holmén, *Jesus and Jewish Covenant Thinking*, 17.
[41] Holmén, *Jesus and Jewish Covenant Thinking*, 48.
[42] See G. E. Mendenhall and G. A. Herion, "Covenant," *ABD*, 1 (1992), 1201.
[43] Holmén, *Jesus and Jewish Covenant Thinking*, 332–3.
[44] Holmén, *Jesus and Jewish Covenant Thinking*, 334. On Jesus' "new covenant," see
Dale C. Allison, Jr., "Jesus and the Covenant: A Response to E.P. Sanders," *JSNT*, 29
(1987), 57–78. On the "new covenant," see esp. Ezek 37:21–22; Jer 3:17; 24:7; 31:31;
31:33–4; 32:40; Ezek 11:19–20; 36:27; 37:24.
[45] Holmén, *Jesus and Jewish Covenant Thinking*, 339; Sanders, *Jesus and Judaism*,
270–81.
[46] Holmén, *Jesus and Jewish Covenant Thinking*, 342.
[47] Holmén, *Jesus and Jewish Covenant Thinking*, 337.

have yet to properly identify Jesus' *particular* hermeneutic of Torah interpretation within Judaism.

If the fundamental question in Jesus Research is what *kind* of Jew was Jesus, then the best way to answer that question is by identifying Jesus' *halakhah*. Jesus' conflict with his contemporaries was primarily a conflict over Torah-interpretation. And while we need not deny that Jesus was probably capable of spontaneous responses to *halakhic* challenges, it is nonetheless reasonable to suppose that Jesus was guided by some coherent internal sense, unifying principle, or hermeneutic, that he had some idea of how to interpret the tradition and a distinctive way that he positioned himself in relationship to it. To think otherwise is to assume that his *halakhah* was haphazard. If we conclude, moreover, that Jesus was part of the apocalyptic-eschatological world of Early Judaism, and that his kingdom-vision represented a realization of that expectation – reminiscent of similar expectations in the Enochic literature and the Qumran corpus – then Jesus' enactment of eschatological restoration would have been perceived as a politically subversive movement interpreting the Torah and the tradition in such a way as to further threaten the stability of an already divided sectarian society.[48] It may be when we ask what such an enacted eschatological program might have *looked like* that we will begin to see Jesus' ministry emerge in a clearer light.

In a recent study, Thomas Kazen locates the historical Jesus' "motives and principles" within recent discussions of "halakic reasoning" in Second Temple Judaism.[49] Kazen analyzes three areas of *halakhic* debate – Sabbath observance, purity law, and divorce practices – in rabbinical *halakhah*, the Qumran texts, and the Gospel conflict narratives. He concludes that in all three cases the Jesus tradition "seems to appeal to divine intent, viewing revelation as based on plain reading and a realist understanding of Scripture, rather than on individual or halakic authority."[50] Kazen suggests that Jesus' *halakhah* appealed, in part, to the "order of creation."[51] The divorce

---

[48] On Jesus' "realized" restorative eschatology, see Steven M. Bryan, *Jesus and Israel's Traditions of Judgement and Restoration* (SNTSMS 117; Cambridge University Press, 2002). See also Sanders, *Jesus and Judaism*, 72.

[49] Thomas Kazen, *Scripture, Interpretation, or Authority? Motives and Arguments in Jesus' Halakic Conflicts* (WUNT 320; Tübingen: Mohr Siebeck, 2013), 30–1.

[50] Kazen, *Scripture*, 290.

[51] Kazen, *Scripture*, 6.

saying, in particular, "suggests underlying motives based on a realist interpretation of the Genesis creation narratives as reflecting the divine will."[52] Kazen affirms Jesus' "eschatological motive" as a prophet,[53] but Jesus neither "abrogated" the Torah nor expected a literal end of the world. Rather, Jesus' *halakhah* is best understood in light of "an *Urzeit-Endzeit* schema."[54] Jesus seems to have been capable of responding to different situations with a certain kind of interpretive spontaneity and should not be reduced to an overly rigid and dogmatic *halakhic* approach,[55] but it is apparent that a certain coherent vision has begun to emerge of Jesus as a prophet of eschatological restoration.[56] The question is whether we can further refine and focus this discussion by re-examining Jesus' *halakhah* in the Jesus tradition. Let us begin, then, with a chronological inventory of our sources.

Jesus, Q, and the Law

The Synoptic Sayings Source or "Gospel" Q is widely regarded as the most important source for reconstructing the teachings of the historical Jesus.[57] The historical Jesus, however, cannot be conflated with the Jesus of Q. The Jesus of Q is "a literary character, constructed from a network of sayings, stories, and editorial comments."[58] Nonetheless, the study of Q does have significant implications for the study of the historical Jesus and the law.[59] The relationship between Q and the law

[52] Kazen, *Scripture*, 288.

[53] Kazen, *Scripture*, 298, 300.

[54] Kazen, *Scripture*, 300. See also Lutz Doering, "*Urzeit-Endzeit* Correlation in the Dead Sea Scrolls and Pseudepigrapha," in J. Eckstein, C. Landmesser, and H. Lichtenberger (eds.), *Eschatologie: Eschatology* (WUNT 272; Tübingen: Mohr Siebeck, 2011), 19–58.

[55] Kazen, *Scripture*, 298.

[56] Thomas Kazen, "The Christology of Early Christian Practice," *JBL*, 127.3 (2008), 591–614.

[57] See James M. Robinson, "*The Jesus of the Sayings Gospel Q*" (OPIAC, 28; Claremont: Claremont Graduate School, 1993); "The Critical Edition of Q and the Study of Jesus," in A. Lindemann (ed.), *The Sayings Source Q and the Historical Jesus* (Leuven: Peeters, 2001), 27–52; Daniel Kosch, "Q und Jesus," *BZ NF*, 36 (1992), 30–58; John S. Kloppenborg, "The Sayings Gospel Q and the Quest of the Historical Jesus," *HTR*, 89 (1996), 307–44; Richard Horsley, "Q and Jesus: Assumptions, Approaches, and Analyses," *Semeia*, 55 (1991), 175–209.

[58] Kloppenborg Verbin, 'Discursive Practices,' 161–2.

[59] Kloppenborg, "The Sayings Gospel Q and the Quest for the Historical Jesus," 315–19.

is still a subject of considerable debate.[60] John Kloppenborg suggests that there is now a consensus that Q is not "preoccupied" with Torah.[61] The Q group sought salvation not in the Temple or Torah, but on "the model of paideia."[62] The "redemptive significance of the Temple has been already abandoned."[63] Q is "indifferent" to the law.[64] Daniel Kosch argues that the Q group regarded the teachings of Jesus as an *eschatologische Tora* which did not oppose the Torah, but effectively replaced it.[65] Karl H. Schelkle sees the work of Jesus as a replacement for the salvific significance of the law as the law and the prophets were only authoritative until the arrival of the kingdom: Q is a community in which the Holy Spirit and Wisdom now work.[66] Paul Meyer argues that the Q community saw itself as the manifestation of the kingdom inaugurated by the ministry of Jesus.[67] The community maintained an allegiance to the authority of the law, but a significantly greater allegiance to the authority of Jesus.

On the other hand, David Catchpole proposes that the Q community was "Torah-centered."[68] The status of the Torah may even be normative in Q, given that "le cadre de pensée de la source Q

---

[60] See, e.g., Daniel Kosch, *Die eschatologische Tora des Menschensohnes: Untersuchungen zur Rezeption der Stellung Jesu zur Tora in Q* (NTOA 12), Freiburg/ Göttingen: Vandenhoeck and Ruprecht, 1989; David R. Catchpole, "The Law and the Prophets in Q," in G. F. Hawthorne and O. Betz (eds.), *Tradition and Interpretation in the New Testament: Essays in Honor of E. Earle Ellis for his 60th Birthday* (Grand Rapids: Eerdmans, 1987), 95–109; C. M. Tuckett, "Q, the Law and Judaism," in B. Lindars (ed.), *Law and Religion: Essays on the Place of the Law in Israel and early Christianity* (Cambridge University Press, 1988), 90–101; John S. Kloppenborg, "Nomos and Ethos in Q," in J. E. Goehring, et al. (ed.), *Gospel Origins and Christian Beginnings: In Honor of James M. Robinson* (Sonoma: Polebridge, 1990), 35–48.

[61] John S. Kloppenborg, "Preface," in Kyu Sam Han, *Jerusalem and the Early Jesus Movement: The Q Community's Attitude Toward the Temple* (JSNT Sup 207; Sheffield Academic Press, 2002), 7–8; "City and Wasteland: Narrative World and the Beginning of the Sayings Gospel (Q)," *Semeia*, 52 (1991), 157.

[62] Kloppenborg, "Nomos," 35–6, 47.

[63] Kloppenborg, "City and Wasteland," 157.

[64] Kloppenborg, "Nomos," 35–6, 47.

[65] Kosch, *Die eschatologische Tora des Menschensohnes*, 453: "Q sieht zwischen den Forderungen Jesu und der Tora keinen Gegensatz, sondern Uebereinstimmung."

[66] See K. H. Schelkle, "Israel und Kirche im Anfang," *TQ*, 163 (1983), 86–95, here 89.

[67] P. D. Meyer, "The Community of Q," Ph.D. dissertation, University of Iowa, 1967, 14–15.

[68] David R. Catchpole, *The Quest for Q* (Edinburgh: T & T Clark, 1993), 279, 273–4; Allison, *The Jesus Tradition in Q*.

est profondément judéo-chrétien."[69] Christopher Tuckett sees Q as representing "a strongly conservative Jewish Christian group within primitive Christianity"[70] that upholds "the abiding validity of the Law."[71] Siegfried Schulz also sees Q as representative of an early Jewish Christian, Torah observant community.[72] Was the Q group Torah observant? Are Q's Torah passages late redactional additions? What role did Torah observance play? Our models range from the proposition that the Q group was not interested in the law (i.e., until the text's latest compositional stages) to the proposal that we can unproblematically assume full Torah observance in Q. Let us proceed by reviewing the Jewish ethnic and religious content of Q.

Q is an ethnically Judean "text."[73] Q presupposes the God of Israel (Q 6:36; 11:2.13; 12:30), contains Aramaic loan-words, refers to synagogues, purity issues (Q 11:39–41), and tithing (Q 11:42). Q contains a high number of biblical references.[74] Jesus quotes directly from the book of Deuteronomy (Q 4:4; 4:10; 4:8). Q is hostile to those who presume to call themselves "children of Abraham" (Q 3:8), including the Pharisees (Q 11:42.39b.43–44), the "exegetes of the law" (11:46b.52), the religious leaders of Jerusalem (Q 13:34–35), and "this generation" (Q 7:31; 11:29–30, 32; 11:49–51). These are *inter*-Jewish tensions in the context of first-century Judaism. A dominant compositional theme of Q is the pronouncement of judgment on "this generation."[75] This

[69] Andreas Dettwiler, "La source Q et la Torah," in A. Dettwiler and D. Marguerat (eds.), *La source des paroles de Jésus (Q): Aux origines du christianisme* (MoBi 62; Geneva, 2008), 221–54, here 253–4.

[70] Tuckett, "Q, the Law and Judaism," 100.

[71] Christopher M. Tuckett, *Q and the History of Early Christianity: Studies on Q* (Peabody: Hendrickson,1996), 406. Tuckett sees Q 16:17 as affirming the law ("Q, the law and Judaism," 91). Similarly, Q 16:18 is not an attack on the law (93).

[72] Siegfried Schulz, *Q: Spruchquelle der Evangelisten* (Zurich: Theologischer, 1972), 104.

[73] For Q's Judean/Jewish ethnicity, see Markus Cromhout, *Jesus and Identity: Reconstructing Judean Ethnicity in Q* (Eugene: Cascade, 2007); Catchpole, *Quest*, 279; Paul Hoffmann, *Studien zur Theologie der Logienquelle* (NTA 8; Münster: Aschendorff, 1972), 332–3; James M. Robinson, *The Sayings Gospel Q: Collected Essays*, C. Heil and J. Verheyden (eds.), (BETL 189; Leuven: Peeters, 2005), 195; John S. Kloppenborg Verbin, *Excavating Q: The History and Setting of the Sayings Gospel* (Edinburgh: T & T Clark, 2000), 256; Tuckett, *Q*, 435, n. 37.

[74] Cf. Dale C. Allison, *The Intertextual Jesus: Scripture in Q* (Harrisburg: InterVarsity, 2000), 182–4.

[75] Cf. Dieter Lührmann, *Die Redaktion der Logienquelle* (WMANT 33; Neukirchener-Vluyn: Neukirchener, 1969), 93; A. D. Jacobson, *The First Gospel: An Introduction to Q* (Sonoma: Polebridge, 1992), 39, 152–3,167–9; John S. Kloppenborg,

theme is characteristic of the final redaction of Q. It is found in sayings framing the entire document and complements the theme of the rejected prophets (Q 6:23c; Q 11:47–51; Q 13:34–35). These two major themes create a distinctive thematic unity to Q. Q is a Jewish text representing inner- and intra-Jewish conflicts.[76]

While the social history of the early Jesus movement and its relationship to the existence, composition, and social history of the Q tradition continues to be debated, the traditions preserved in Q indicate that loyalty to the Jesus movement seems to have been at odds with some traditional norms of Jewish cultural identity and community belonging. We find hints of this in Q 3:8, where John warns the crowds that Jewish ethnic identity in and of itself was not deemed sufficient to avoid the coming judgment. Consequently, the author(s) of Q seem to have *distanced* themselves from those norms, to *differentiate* themselves from Pharisaic customs,[77] normative family values, and ethnic identity. This differentiation may have led to social conflict and "hearings before synagogues." Q's evidently strained accounts of its author's relationship(s) with fellow Jews provides us with an ideal text-historical case-study of nascent sectarian formation in social identity theory. A social identity approach to Q suggests a process of self-definition emerging from disagreements over ethnic and traditional practices.[78] Social identity theory is a socio-psychological research method that explains how identity is constructed in and through the exclusion of others by discrimination, prejudice, stereotyping, and intergroup conflict, attitudes and orientations that often lead to violence. New religious movements emerge through constructing difference, that is, new religions create a new world, give new meanings to old symbols, and create new symbols and rituals to define themselves in reaction, response, or *opposition* to earlier traditions. Since ancient Jews, Jewish Christians, Gentile Christians, and Samaritans all claimed an identity as "true Israel," it was inevitable that competition, rivalry, and

The Formation of Q: Trajectories in Ancient Christian Wisdom Collections (Philadelphia: Fortress, 1987), 102–69.

[76] Kloppenborg, *Formation*, 246–8.

[77] Q 11:42, 39b, 41, 43–4.

[78] On social identity theory, see Henri Tajfel and John C. Turner, "The Social Identity Theory of Intergroup Behavior," in Stephen Worchel and William G. Austin (eds.), 2nd edn., *Psychology of Intergroup Relations* (Chicago: Nelson-Hall, 1986), 7–24, esp. 13; Michael A. Hogg and Dominic Abrams, "Intergroup Behavior and Social Identity," in Michael A. Hogg and Joel Cooper (eds.), *The Sage Handbook of Social Psychology* (Los Angeles: Sage, 2007), 335–60.

conflict would be the result of this contestation. It is not difficult to detect the process of sectarian identity formation in Q, whether in its willingness to redefine who belongs to Israel (Q 3:8, 13:29, 28, 13:30, 14:11, 14:16–23), its polarized self-definition (Q 11:23), its criticism of other Jews (Q 11:42, 39b, 43–44, 46b, 52, 47–48), its rejection of those villages that have rejected Jesus' message (Q 10:10–12, 13–15), its self-awareness as a marginalized group (Q 10:2–3, 12:11–12), its stance toward "this generation," (Q 7:31, 11:16, 29–30, 11:49–51), its pronouncement of judgment on Israel (Q 13:34–35), its subversive intensification of normative, Mosaic Torah (Q 16:18), its cautious admiration of Gentiles (Q 7:9), its radical, eschatological reversal of the "blessed" (Q 6:20–23), its apocalyptic knowledge of salvation (Q 10:21) or its promotion of Jesus as the "Coming One" through appeals to scripture (Q 7:22–23). Q is a classic example of nascent sectarian identity formation.

Q contains numerous traces and echoes of the social conflict dynamics delineated in social identity theory. It employs stereotypes, like "this generation," to criticize its opponents. It combats stereotypes directed at its leaders, John and Jesus. Q labels Pharisees as "empty tombs" and the "wicked" Jews of "this generation" who fail to respond to Jesus (Q 11:44). Q draws "symbolic boundaries" between its in-group and those who rejected its message and are consigned to judgment. It emphasizes faithfulness to Jesus and his teachings. It draws "social closure" around the Jesus people by claiming that the "last will be first and the first last." Some will enter the kingdom and others will be excluded. The faithful servant will be given charge over his master's estate. Q differentiates Jesus and the Jesus people of Q from Pharisees, the Temple establishment, and scribes; it challenges traditional Jewish norms and assumptions of familial piety and ethnic identity: Q 3:8 criticizes those who "presume" that having Abraham as forefather is enough whereas Q 16:18 suggests that the Mosaic Law is not strict enough. A new social and group identity is being formed and Q witnesses the birth of this distinctive voice within Judaism in tension and competition with other groups. The Jesus people of Q seem to have differentiated themselves from other Jews as a result of social conflict, ideological differences and contestations over law, Jesus' identity, worship, prayer, ethics, and the Temple.[79] Q's worldview is polarized: its symbolic boundaries have

---

[79] Han, *Jerusalem and the Early Jesus Movement*, 181, refers to Q's "lost allegiance" to the Temple.

been clearly drawn. There was the Q community and then there was everybody else.

While Q's rhetoric clearly reflects inner-Jewish conflicts and tensions, it still maintains its right and claim to represent authentic Jewish tradition. The Temptation narrative affirms that Jesus is faithful and obedient to the Torah.[80] Jesus rebukes the devil by citing passages from Deut 6–8. The Temptation narrative is followed by the Inaugural Sermon (Q 6:20–49), an instructional collection where Jesus speaks *as* the obedient Son of God, and (re)interprets the Torah.[81] A distinctive feature of both the Temptation narrative and Q's Inaugural Sermon is how Jesus' approach to the Torah stands in tension with politico-military expectations associated with the Conquest narrative and Davidic messianism. Jesus' "interpretation of God's will ... is primarily oriented towards loving attitudes and behavior."[82] At the same time, the Jesus of Q also engages in heated religious polemic with his contemporaries. Q 11:42 sharply criticizes Pharisees for tithing "mint and dill and cumin," but neglecting "justice and mercy and faithfulness." While it is not clear that Pharisees actually tithed these things,[83] the Jesus of Q admonishes that tithing should be done "without neglecting the others," by which he means, weightier matters.[84] It would seem, therefore, that Q's value system is able to differentiate and prioritize between different levels of Torah observance.[85] Similarly, Q 11:39b seems to criticize Pharisees for focusing on the external purification of vessels, but uses this *halakhic* observance as an opportunity to insinuate that they neglect their own internal purification. A distinction between the outside and the inside of cups may underlie this passage,[86] but the point is that "attitude

---

[80] Tuckett, "Temptation," 487–8, argues that the temptation narrative emphasizes Jesus' obedience to Torah. William R. G. Loader, *Jesus' Attitude towards the Law: A Study of the Gospels* (Grand Rapids: Eerdmans, 2002), 403.

[81] See Catchpole, *Quest*, 107–16, citing Q 6:31, 32–3, 35c as exegetical developments of Lev 19:18b. See also Q 6:36–45 (cf. Lev 19:17). See also Horsley, "Q and Jesus: Assumptions, Approaches, and Analysis," 175–209, here 184–5.

[82] Loader, *Jesus' Attitude*, 430.

[83] The Mishnah suggests that tithing was an issue in the Second Temple period (*m. Sheb* 9.1)

[84] Kloppenborg, "Nomos and Ethos," 41–3.

[85] Loader, *Jesus' Attitude*, 415.

[86] See Jacob Neusner, "'First Cleanse the Inside," *NTS*, 22.4 (1976), 486–95, on the dispute between Hillel and Shammai. Kloppenborg, "Nomos," 39, sees Q as ridiculing these concerns.

and morality in contrast to concern with ritual cleansing of externals" is what is truly important.[87] This is not an attack on the ritual purification of vessels.[88] In this same series of woes, Q 11:43 criticizes Pharisees for seeking honor and public recognition, the "front seat in the synagogues, and accolades in the markets." Q 11:44 condemns them as unclean tombs. Q 11:46b criticizes them for loading people "with burdens hard to bear," that is, difficult interpretations of Torah observance, while they refuse to lift their fingers to help others observe them.[89] Finally, Q 11:52 criticizes them for hiding the kingdom of God and neither going in nor allowing others to enter it.

While Q's woes against Pharisees represent some of its most scathing indictments of "this generation," it is in Q 11:49–51 and Q 13:34–35 that we see how Q envisions Judaism's highest religious institutions. Here the theme of judgment comes to a climax with Jerusalem's rejection of Jesus. In response, Jesus declares the "house" (οἶκος), that is, the Temple, to be "forsaken."[90] Jerusalem must repent before it ever sees Jesus again:

> O Jerusalem, Jerusalem, who kills the prophets and stones those sent to her!
> How often I wanted to gather your children together, as a hen gathers her nestlings under her wings, and you were not willing!
> Look, your House (οἶκος) is forsaken! I tell you: You will not see me until you say: Blessed is the one who comes in the name of the Lord!

While there is no explicit evidence of a cultic critique here,[91] a "forsaken" Temple is not one in which sacrifices are either efficacious or capable of reconciling Israel and God. The Temple is a place where prophets are killed.[92]

---

[87] Loader, *Jesus' Attitude*, 416.

[88] Tuckett, "Q, the law and Judaism," 96.

[89] Catchpole, *Quest*, 264; Loader, *Jesus' Attitude*, 417.

[90] Schulz, *Spruchquelle*, 356. Hoffmann, *Studien*, 174, thinks it refers to the city. Horsley, "Q and Jesus," 195–6, thinks it refers to Jerusalem's ruling house. For the theme of God's departure from the Temple, see Jer 12:7; 22:5; Ezek 7:22; 8:6; 10:18–19. See also *2 Bar* 8:2; 44:7; Josephus *B.J.* 2.539; 4.323; *A.J.* 20.166.

[91] So Loader, *Jesus' Attitude*, 422.

[92] John S. Kloppenborg, "The Sayings Gospel Q: Recent Opinion on the People behind the Document," *CR BS*, 1 (1993), 9–34, here 25.

While certain aspects of Torah observance in Q have now been surveyed, the *only* passage which specifically refers to the law is Q 16:16–18.[93] A clear concern for the law unites three sayings. We will proceed by re-examining each individual saying and then re-assessing their coherence as a unit, beginning with Q 16:16. According to Q 16:16, the "law and the prophets" were "*until* John." But is John in or out of the kingdom? On one hand, John dies a violent death, and Q 16:16b focuses on *violence* to the kingdom. John and Jesus are also portrayed as parallel figures,[94] even colleagues, in the Jesus tradition. Q also begins with John's announcement of Jesus as the "One Who Is To Come," and Q 7:31–35 identifies their ministries as complementary, climaxing with both John and Jesus being called "Wisdom's children."[95] Q 16:16a can thus be understood to mean that John is associated with and regarded as the last in a series of prophets.

On the other hand, Q also seems to *separate* John from the kingdom (Q 7:18–23; Q 7:28) and there are clear *temporal* distinctions between Jesus and John's ministries in Q. John looks toward the future for the "One Who Is To Come" whereas Jesus announces the kingdom as present and implicitly accepts the title (Q 7:22–23). The interpretive key here is ἕως: John is relegated to a past era.[96] He belongs to the old order.[97] The final redaction of Q, at least, *excludes* John from the kingdom.[98] The kingdom, not the law and the prophets, is now the center of religious attention.[99] The kingdom "impinges upon the law."[100] Q 16:16 contrasts the law and the prophets with

---

[93] See *The Critical Edition of Q*, James M. Robinson, Paul Hoffmann, and John S. Kloppenborg (eds.), (Minneapolis: Fortress, 2000), 468; Tuckett, "Q, the Law, and Judaism," 90–102; Kloppenborg, "Nomos," 35–48; Kosch, *Tora*, 435–43. As a unit, see also D. Kosch, *Die Gottesherrschaft im Zeichen des Widerspruchs. Traditions- und redaktionsgeschichtliche Untersuchung von Lk 16,16/Mt 11,12 bei Jesus, Q und Lukas* (EHS 23/257; Bern/New York: Peter Lang, 1985), 63. Paul Foster, "Matthew's Use of 'Jewish' Traditions from Q," in M. Tiwald (ed.), *Kein Jota wird vergehen. Das Gesetzesverständnis der Logienquelle vor dem Hintergrund frühjüdischer Theologie* (BWANT 200; Stuttgart: W. Kohlhammer, 2013), 179–201, here 184.

[94] Kloppenborg, *Formation*, 114.

[95] Catchpole, *Quest*, 234.237.

[96] See H. Conzelmann, *The Theology of Saint Luke* (London: Faber and Faber, 1960), 16–17, 21.

[97] Fleddermann, *Q*, 790.

[98] Fleddermann, *Q*, 790. Cf. Schulz, *Q*, 265. Hoffmann, *Studien*, 50–79, esp. 63–75.

[99] Dale C. Allison Jr., *Resurrecting Jesus: The Earliest Christian Tradition and Its Interpreters* (New York: T & T Clark, 2005), 173.

[100] Allison, *Resurrecting Jesus*, 189.

the kingdom. The kingdom is "a new beginning: it supercedes the old revelation."[101] Like Q 7:18–35 – the major Baptist-unit in Q – Q 16:16 explicitly contrasts John with the kingdom.[102]

A third view might see John as part of the fulfillment of scripture (Q 7:27),[103] and his activity inaugurating the end time,[104] so he is both part of the new era and yet still part of the old era. Q 7:28a places John above Abraham, Moses, and David; yet Q 7:28b states that "even the smallest in the kingdom is greater than he." This secondary addition represents a later attempt to clarify Jesus' superiority to John.[105] John represents a *former* age and the kingdom represents a *new* age. The law's obligations were only valid "*until* John."[106]

Q seems to reflect a relatively radical vision of the law re-interpreted and secondarily domesticated.[107] Q 16:17, like Matthew 5:17–20, seems to have been composed to mitigate an antinomian reading of Q 16:16,[108] a redactional afterthought intended to correct the idea that the Torah has been abrogated. Q may have been composed before the Jewish/Gentile controversies over the law.[109] Daniel Kosch even sees the emergence of Q as a response to law-free Pauline Christianity: the theology of the Inaugural Sermon was based on Q 16:17 in order to reject the idea that Jesus had abolished the law. Kosch also argues that the addition of 16:17 reflects an *early* compositional stage in Q.[110] In so far as Q 16:16–17 rejects antinomianism,[111] Q 16:17, like Matt 5:17,

---

[101] Fleddermann, *Q*, 789.

[102] Cf. H. Koester, *Ancient Christian Gospels: Their History and Development* (Philadelphia: Fortress, 1990), 161.

[103] Cf. Catchpole, *Quest*, 241.

[104] Kloppenborg, *Formation*, 114.

[105] Cf. Rudolf Bultmann, *The History of the Synoptic Tradition* (trans. J. Marsh; New York: Harper, 1963), 177; Hoffmann, *Studien*, 218, 220; Lührmann, *Redaktion*, 27; Schulz, *Q*, 229, 230.

[106] Allison, *Resurrecting Jesus*, 172. On the historicity of Q 16:16, see Kosch, *Gottesherrschaft*, 20–1, 46–7; John P. Meier, *A Marginal Jew*, Vol. 2: *Mentor, Message, and Miracles* (New York: Doubleday, 1994), 157–63.

[107] Cf. S. Schulz, "Die Bedeutung des Markus fur die Theologiegeschichte des Urchristentums," *SE*, 2.1 (1964), 135–45, here 138–9, argued that the Q community intensified its Torah-observance. See also Schulz, *Q*, 114–16.

[108] Cf. R. Bultmann, "Was läßt die Spruchquelle über die Urgemeinde erkennen," *Oldenburgisches Kirchenblatt*, 19 (1913), 35–7, 41–4, here 42. See also H. Merklein, *Die Gottesherrschaft als Handlungsprinzip. Untersuchung zur Ethik Jesu* (FzB 34; Würzburg: Echter, 1978), 94; Kosch, *Tora*, 473–80.

[109] Koester, *Gospels*, 162.

[110] Kosch, *Tora*, 166, 458, 462.

[111] Kosch, *Tora*, 474–5, also 163–4. Kloppenborg suggests that the "intrusive" redactional fingerprint of Q 16:17 (with Q 11:42c and Q 4:1–13) provides evidence of

is a "redactional modification(s) of an earlier tradition."[112] Matt 5:17
seems to be another example of a developed response to Q 16:16 since
Matt 5:17–20 endorses the Torah, responding to Q 16:16, which was
perceived as critical of the law.[113]

"From the Beginning of Creation": Jesus and Divorce

The divorce saying is widely regarded as authentic Jesus tradition.[114]
In an apparent contrast to the legally recognized norms of the day
(cf. Deut 24:1–4), Q 16:18 proscribes divorce.[115] The ruling on divorce
is so contrary to popular sentiment and Mosaic Law that this "hard
saying" should be regarded as belonging to early Q tradition. Q's version is arguably earlier than Paul's (1 Cor 7:10–11), which Paul cites
as from "the Lord" (ὁ κύριος). As in Matt 5:17, here also Matt 5:32's
exception clause παρεκτὸς λόγου πορνείας maintains the validity of the
Mosaic Law's allowance for divorce and corrects possibly antinomian
interpretations suggested by Q, where the prohibition is given without
further qualification. The Jesus of Q seems to forbid divorce within an
eschatological context: he neither contradicts the law nor is entirely satisfied with it.[116] In contrast to the book of Deuteronomy, which presupposes the validity of both divorce and polygamy, Q forbids what is
sanctioned in the Torah. Q's hard line approach can be contrasted both
with Matthew's version and later rabbinical traditions, which allowed
for divorce.[117] Q 16:18 is not rejecting or implying an abolition of the

---

a *late* stage in the development of Q ("Nomos," esp. 45–6). See also Christoph Heil,
"Nachfolge und Tora in Q 9 57–60," in *Kein Jota*, 111–40, here 130.

[112] Tuckett, *Q*, 422.

[113] Allison, *Resurrecting Jesus*, 173.

[114] Kosch, *Tora*, 443: "16,16 und 16,18 sind authentische Jesusworte." Cf. also
E. P. Sanders, *The Historical Figure of Jesus* (London: Penguin, 1993), 198–204; John
P. Meier, "The Historical Jesus and the Historical Law: Some Problems within the
Problem," *CBQ*, 65 (2003), 69, n. 38.

[115] For the divorce sayings, see Joseph A. Fitzmyer, "The Matthean Divorce Texts
and Some New Palestinian Evidence," *TS*, 37 (1976), 197–226; Amy-Jill Levine, "Jesus,
Divorce, and Sexuality: A Jewish Critique," in B. F. le Beau (ed.), *The Historical Jesus
through Catholic and Jewish Eyes* (Harrisburg: T & T Clark, 2000), 113–29. See also
John S. Kloppenborg, "Alms, Debt and Divorce: Jesus' Ethics in their Mediterranean
Context," *TJT*, 6 (1990), 182–200.

[116] Sanders, *Jesus and Judaism*, 256–60. See also David R. Catchpole, "The
Synoptic Divorce Material as a Traditio-Historical Problem," *BJRL*, 57 (1975),
92–127, here 125.

[117] Deut 24:1 does not clarify the grounds for divorce. Targum Onqelos and the
Palestinian Targum interpreted it to mean any sinful matter. The Hillelite R.'Akiba
allowed for divorce for any reason (*m. Git.* 9,10). Shammai limited divorce to cases of

law. If anything, this Q saying appears to be more rigorous, not more lenient, than the Torah.[118] Here Q shares with the Qumran community a tendency to re-write scripture. Their similar use of scriptural references as well as their high regard for their founding teachers, suggest a shared cultural tradition.[119]

The central importance of the law at Qumran has been recognized in recent years.[120] Since the publication of 4QMMT, with its concerns regarding Temple law, the calendar, and ritual purity, there has been a growing awareness that legal disagreements played a major role in the Qumran group's separation from the Temple.[121] Some have concluded that the community was "legalistic," but that is an overstatement.[122] The Qumran community believed that they were receiving a renewed revelation of the law. They simply did not live by the same understanding or interpretation of law as other Jews. They accepted neither the Pharisaic oral law nor the Sadducean assumption that the law was fixed. God's revelations were ongoing and the law could be renewed through prophetic revelation. The law was both eternal and subject to change, both hidden and revealed. The law needed to be continually reinterpreted and clarified. The law at Qumran consisted of both "revealed things" (נגלות) and "hidden things" (נסתרות) (CD 3.14). The revealed law was known to all of Israel while the hidden law was the Qumran community's esoteric interpretation received through divine inspiration.[123]

---

sexual immorality (*y. Git.* 50d; *y. Sot.* 16b). The Mishnah recognizes the validity of polygamy (*m. Yeb.* 1,1; *m. Ket.* 10,1).

[118] Kloppenborg, "Nomos," 45.

[119] Cf. George J. Brooke, "Shared Intertextual Interpretations in the Dead Sea Scrolls and the New Testament," in M. E. Stone and E. G. Chazon (eds.), *Biblical Perspectives: Early Use and Interpretation of the Bible in Light of the Dead Sea Scrolls* (STDJ 28; Leiden: Brill, 1998), 35–57.

[120] Cf. Schiffman, "Halakhah and Sectarianism in the Dead Sea Scrolls," 124.

[121] *Qumran Cave 4,* V, *Miqsat Ma'aśe Ha-Torah,* J. Strugnell and E. Qimron (eds.), (DJD 10; Oxford: Clarendon, 1994); L. H. Schiffman, "The Place of 4QMMT in the Corpus of Qumran Manuscripts," in J. Kampen and M. J. Bernstein (eds.), *Reading 4QMMT, New Perspectives on Qumran Law and History* (SBLSS 2; Atlanta: Scholars, 1996), 81–98.

[122] Cf. J. J. Collins, *Apocalypticism in the Dead Sea Scrolls* (London/New York: Routledge, 1997), 29.

[123] Cf. L. H. Schiffman, *The Halakhah at Qumran* (SJLA 16; Leiden: Brill, 1975), 48. Cf. M. Tiwald, "Jewish-Christian Trajectories in Torah and Temple Theology," in Tom Holmén (ed.), *Jesus in Continuum* (WUNT 289; Tübingen: Mohr Siebeck, 2012), 385–409, here 386, 392: "'Torah' for the Qumran community is nothing other than the fulfilment of God's cosmological law … the manifestation in words of God's creation order."

According to 1QS 9.11, the community was to live by the laws in which it was first instructed "*until* the coming of the prophet and the messiahs of Aaron and Israel" (עד בוא נביא ומשיחו אהרון וישראל). Qumran law was a *temporary* legal code expected to change when the messiah(s) arrived. The laws described in CD only apply to observing the Sabbath during the *current* age of wickedness.[124]

The messianic age would alter how the community interpreted the law, presumably now instructed by their messiah(s). We see traces of this expected transformation in various Qumran texts. In 4Q521, for example, there seems to be an implicit relationship between the *Urzeit* of creation, when God created "the heaven(s) and the earth" (השמים ואת הארץ) (Gen. 1:1), and the *Endzeit*, when "the heavens and the earth will *listen* to his messiah" (ישמעו למשיחו השמים והארץ). The Qumran community seems to have anticipated the eschatological restoration of the "glory of Adam" (כבוד אדם).[125] In 4Q171 3.1–2, the "inheritance of Adam" (נחלת אדם) will be made available to the community. This "inheritance" is "a crown of glory with majestic raiment in eternal light" (1QS 4.7–8). 1QS envisions "some kind of metamorphosis"[126] to be inaugurated at the renewal (1QS 4.25), a profound transformation of the community. 4Q174 1.6 identifies the community as an eschatological temple, a "Temple of Adam" (מקדש אדם),[127] an "eschatological sanctuary" as well as an "Adamic sanctuary of Eden restored."[128] The Thanksgiving Hymns also refer to an "Eden of glory" and a hidden fountain supplying "living water."[129] The eschatological orientation of the Qumran community clearly affected their understanding and interpretation of the law.

CD and 11QT contain sectarian rules regarding marriage as well as prohibitions of polygamy and remarriage after divorce. According

[124] Schiffman, *Halakhah*, 78.

[125] 1QS 4.22–23, CD 3.20, and 1QH 4.15. Cf. Oscar Cullmann, *The Christology of the New Testament* (London: SCM, 1963), 141; Geza Vermes, *Discovery in the Judean Desert* (New York: Desclee Co., 1956).

[126] Geza Vermes, *The Complete Dead Sea Scrolls in English* (New York: Penguin, 1997), 87.

[127] Cf. Gärtner, *The Temple and the Community*, 30–42; Michael A. Knibb, *The Qumran Community* (New York: Cambridge University Press, 1987), 258–62; Michael O. Wise, "4QFlorilegium and the Temple of Adam," *RdQ*, 15 (1991), 103–32.

[128] George J. Brooke, *The Dead Sea Scrolls and the New Testament* (Minneapolis: Fortress, 2005), 245.

[129] 16.21.

to 11QT 57.17–18, the king is forbidden from taking a second wife.[130] 11QT refers to the king in its prohibition of polygamy.[131] It is still debated whether CD refers explicitly to divorce or simply prohibits polygamy.[132] CD 4.19–21 – 5.1–2 *certainly* proscribes polygamy.[133] Yet the exact meaning of the CD passage, and whether it refers to anti-polygamy, divorce, and/or remarriage after divorce, remains unclear.[134] Interpretations range from a total prohibition of divorce,[135] to divorce being regarded as legitimate, but remarriage following divorce being prohibited.[136] It is perhaps best to view CD as referring to polygamy,[137] but not necessarily to divorce. Divorce is

[130] Cf. J. R. Mueller, "The Temple Scroll and the Gospel Divorce Texts," *RQ*, 10 (1980), 247–56, here 253–4; M. Klinghardt, *Gesetz und Volk Gottes: Das lukanische Verständnis des Gesetzes nach Herkunft, Funktion und seinem Ort in der Geschichte des Urchristentums* (WUNT II.32; Tübingen: Mohr Siebeck, 1988), 83–96.

[131] Cf. Fitzmyer, "Divorce Texts," 216.

[132] See G. Brin, "Divorce at Qumran," in M. Bernstein, et al. (eds.), *Legal Texts and Legal Issues: Proceedings of the Second Meeting of the International Organization for Qumran Studies Cambridge 1995* (Leiden: Brill, 1997), 231–49.

[133] Cf. Brooke, *Dead Sea Scrolls*, 71. Allison, *Jesus*, 64–5.

[134] Cf. F. García Martínez, "Man and Woman: Halakhah Based upon Eden in the Dead Sea Scrolls," in G. P. Luttikuizen (ed.), *Paradise Interpreted: Representations of Biblical Paradise in Judaism and Christianity* (TBN 2; Leiden: Brill, 1999), 95–115, here 104; J. Murphy O'Connor, "An Essene Missionary Document? CD II, 4-VI, 1," *RB*, 77 (1970), 201–29, here 220; P. R. Davies, *Behind the Essenes: History and Ideology in the Dead Sea Scrolls* (Atlanta: Scholars, 1987), 73–85; L. H. Schiffman, "Laws Pertaining to Women in The Temple Scroll," in D. Dimant and U. Rappaport (eds.), *The Dead Sea Scrolls: Forty Years of Research* (STDJ 10; Leiden: Brill, 1992), 210–28, here 217; Fitzmyer, "Divorce Texts," 79–111, here 96; J. Baumgarten, "The Qumran-Essene Restraints on Marriage," in L. H. Schiffman (ed.), *Archaeology and History in the Dead Sea Scrolls: The New York University Conference in Memory of Yigael Yadin* (Sheffield Academic Press, 1990), 13–24, here 15; Geza Vermes, "Sectarian Matrimonial Halakhah in the Damascus Rule," *JJS*, 25 (1974), 197–202; D. Instone-Brewer, "Nomological Exegesis in Qumran 'Divorce' Texts," *RdQ*, 18 (1998), 561–79.

[135] See Mueller, "Temple Scroll," 253–4.

[136] Schiffman, "Laws Pertaining to Women," 217–18; A. Shemesh, "4Q271.3: A Key to Sectarian Matrimonial Law," *JJS*, 49 (1998), 244–63, here 245–6; Baumgarten, "Restraints," 15.

[137] M. Kister, "Divorce, Reproof, and Other Sayings in the Synoptic Gospels: Jesus Traditions in the Context of 'Qumranic' and Other Texts," in R. A. Clements and D. R. Schwartz (eds.), *Text, Thought, and Practice in Qumran and Early Christianity: Proceedings of the Ninth International Symposium of the Orion Center for the Study of the Dead Sea Scrolls and Associated Literature, Jointly Sponsored by the Hebrew University Center for the Study of Christianity, 11–12 January, 2004* (Leiden: Brill, 2009), 195–229, here 201.

allowed in Deuteronomy and is explicitly mentioned in CD 13.17, 4Q266 9 iii 1–5, and 11QT 54.4. It seems reasonable to conclude that CD refers to polygamy.[138] Divorce seems to have been recognized as a legitimate practice at Qumran.[139] The community may have objected to divorce under certain conditions.[140] The Torah allows for both polygamy and divorce, yet the authors of CD and 11QT seem to have assumed the scribal and exegetical freedom to *revise* Torah. We find a similar exegetical freedom, based on similar exegetical principles, in the Gospel of Mark.[141]

In Mark 10:2, Jesus states that "Moses allowed a man to write a certificate of dismissal and to divorce her," but this was because of Israel's "hardness of heart." Jesus justifies his position by arguing that the allowance for divorce was due to an inability to uphold the original intention of creation. Mark's Jesus corrects a Mosaic concession and restores the original design of creation.[142] He appeals to Gen 1:27 (ἀπὸ δὲ ἀρχῆς κτίσεως ἄρσεν καὶ θῆλυ ἐποίησεν αὐτούς, Mark 10:6) and Gen 2:24. As William Loader puts it, "Jesus' appeal to the Genesis creation narrative ... is more than citing one scripture against another. It is an appeal to origins and reflects a theology and ideology: God's original purpose has priority."[143] The use of Genesis here is instructive: first, because it suggests that Q's saying on divorce should also be understood in an eschatological context; and second, because the Qumran community used this passage to justify their view on remarriage.[144] Both Mark 10 and CD 4–5 appeal to Gen 1:27: Mark to denounce divorce; CD to ban polygamy.[145] This common appeal to Genesis "shows most clearly a common interpretative

---

[138] Fitzmyer, "Divorce Texts," 220.

[139] Brin, "Divorce," 231. See CD 13.16–17; 11QT 54.5.

[140] Brin, "Divorce," 237.

[141] Cf. M. Fander, *Die Stellung der Frau im Markusevangelium. Unter besonderer Berücksichtigung kultur- und religionsgeschichtlicher Hintergründe* (MThA 8; Altenberge: Telos, 1990), 200–57.

[142] Cf. Levine, "Jesus," 121; Lutz Doering, "Marriage and Creation in Mark 10 and CD 4–5," in F. García Martínez (ed.), *Echoes from the Caves: Qumran and the New Testament* (STDJ 85; Leiden: Brill, 2009), 133–63, here 160–3; H. Stegemann, "Der lehrende Jesus: Der sogenannte biblische Christus und die geschichtliche Botschaft Jesu von der Gottesherrschaft," *NZSTh*, 24 (1982), 3–20.

[143] Loader, *Jesus' Attitude*, 89.

[144] See J. De Waard, *A Comparative Study of the Old Testament Text in the Dead Sea Scrolls and in the New Testament* (STDJ 4; Leiden: Brill, 1965), 31.

[145] Cf. Doering, "Marriage," 133–163. Sanders, *Jesus and Judaism*, 257; Geza Vermes, *The Authentic Gospel of Jesus* (London: Allen Lane, 2003), 56; E. B. Powery,

horizon, in which issues pertaining to marriage law are addressed by reference to texts from Gen 1–2 … and by appeal to creation."[146] In Mark, Jesus explains that Moses allowed for divorce as a concession to human weakness.[147] Lifelong marriage was God's intention in creation ("from the beginning") and cannot be terminated. The Mosaic Law was a temporary concession,[148] and eschatologically inadequate.[149] Mark's text is a "model of restoration of paradisiacal conditions."[150] The Mosaic Torah is being replaced by a *Schöpfungstora*, the Mosaic concession with God's original intention for marriage. Jesus is in accord with Mal 2:14–16, where the prophet declares that God "hates divorce," and refers back to the original creation (2:10).

Mark 10:6–8 combines two passages from the creation account, Gen 1:27 and Gen 2:24.[151] Mark's argument is that God created the first humans ἄρσεν καὶ θῆλυ, "male and female." The force of the preposition ἀπό (*"from* the beginning of creation") indicates that the hermeneutical principle of creation is still valid.[152] Mark 10:9 shows that this is by divine command: "what God has joined together, let man not separate." Jesus thus restores God's original intention at creation.[153] Q 16:18 represents a tension between Jesus and Torah. The law requires a new interpretation.[154] Q, like 11QT, alters Mosaic Law and creates *new* Torah.[155] Q 6:27–45 modifies and adds to Mosaic

---

Jesus Reads Scripture: The Function of Jesus' Use of Scripture in the Synoptic Gospels (Leiden: Brill, 2003), 52.

[146] Doering, "Marriage," 163.

[147] Cf. M. Hooker, *The Gospel According to St. Mark* (BNTC 2; Peabody: Hendrickson, 1991), 236.

[148] Doering, "Marriage," 145.

[149] Sanders, *Jesus and Judaism*, 260.

[150] Doering, "Marriage," 158. See also Sanders, *Jesus and Judaism*, 116, 230. D. Dungan, *The Sayings of Jesus in the Churches of Paul: The Use of the Synoptic Tradition in the Regulation of Early Church Life* (Philadelphia: Fortress, 1971), 117.

[151] See William Loader, *The Septuagint, Sexuality, and the New Testament: Case Studies on the Impact of the LXX in Philo and the New Testament* (Grand Rapids: Eerdmans, 2004), 80.

[152] Doering, "Marriage," 142. Tiwald, "Hat Gott sein Haus verlassen (vgl. Q 13,35)? Das Verhältnis der Logienquelle zum Frühjüdentum," in *Kein Jota*, 63–89, here 82, concludes that "Zumeist sollten diese Endzeitpropheten den *protologisch* von Gott festgelegten Sinngehalt der Tora nun *eschatologisch* aktualisieren."

[153] J. Jeremias, *New Testament Theology* (New York: SCM, 1971), 225. Cf. R. Le Déaut, "Le Targumic Literature and New Testament Interpretation," *BTB*, 4 (1974), 243–289, here 251.

[154] Allison, *Resurrecting Jesus*, 166.

[155] Allison, *Jesus*, 212.

Law.[156] Q 14:26 inverts the commandment to "honor your father and mother."[157] Like Mark, Q 16:18 also seems to affirm an Edenic eschatology, a "prelapsarian standard that revokes a temporary concession in the Torah."[158] Jesus' sayings revise Mosaic Law.[159] Matthew enhances this Mosaic motif by locating his Sermon on a "Mount" as a series of antitheses intended to correct, intensify, and "fulfill" Mosaic Law.[160]

Q 16:16–18 is a major interpretive key to understanding the relationship(s) between Jesus, the law, and eschatology in Q.[161] If Q 16:16 suggests that in some way the era of the law has ended,[162] Q 16:17 seems to modify this saying, probably in response. That is, Q 16:17 *qualifies* Q 16:16. On one hand, a new era has begun and it is contrasted with the law. On the other hand, the law is still in effect. In this light, Matt 5:17 represents Matthew's reworking of the (Q) saying in Luke 16:16. Q 16:18 is not an attack on the law.[163] Since Q 16:16 could be interpreted as signifying the end of the law, and Q 16:18 could be interpreted as undermining Deut 24:1–4, the author of Q placed Q 16:17 in between the two sayings, presumably

[156] Cf. Allison, *Jesus*, 33.

[157] Allison, *Jesus*, 62–4. Levine, "Jesus," 121. Cf. Heil, "Nachfolge und Tora," 111–40.

[158] Allison, *Resurrecting Jesus*, 186. Cf. Nickelsburg, *Ancient Judaism and Christian Origins*, 194.

[159] Cf. Dale C. Allison Jr., "Q's New Exodus and the Historical Jesus," in *The Sayings Source Q and the Historical Jesus*, 395–428, here 423; Catchpole, *Quest*, 101–34; C. M. Tuckett, "Scripture in Q," in C. M. Tuckett (ed.), *The Scriptures in the Gospels* (BETL 131; Leuven: Peeters, 1997), 3–26, here 25.

[160] Contra the idea of "abrogation" of Deut 24 in Bultmann, *History*, 135–6; Jeremias, *New Testament Theology*, 251; M. J. Suggs, *Wisdom, Christology and Law in Matthew's Gospel*, (Cambridge: Harvard University Press, 1970), 110–115; R. A. Guelich, "The Antitheses of Matt 5:21–48: Traditional and/or Redactional?" *NTS*, 22 (1976), 444–57, here 445. Michael Tait, "The End of the Law: The Messianic Torah in the Pseudepigrapha," in Michael Tait and Peter Oakes (eds.), *The Torah in the New Testament: Papers Delivered at the Manchester-Lausanne Seminar of June 2008* (LNTS 401; London: T & T Clark, 2009), 196–207, 198, affirms various Second Temple works as "interpretation" and "expansion of the *existing* Torah" (200). Tait affirms the divorce saying as an "eschatological provision" based on "an appeal to the Creation," but points out that the Creation is itself "part of the Torah" (206). On the "Messianic Torah," see Peter Schäfer, "Die Torah der Messianischen Zeit," *ZNW*, 65 (1974), 27–42.

[161] Meier, "Historical Jesus."

[162] Tuckett, *Q*, 407.

[163] Tuckett, *Q*, 408.

to emphasize the permanent validity of the law.[164] Q 16:17 seems to represent a development that emerged in response to Pauline thought.[165] Q 16:17 entered the Q tradition to counter antinomian tendencies when Pauline interpretations were causing controversy (c. 50 CE). Nonetheless, it is Q 16:18 that best represents the climax of this sayings-cluster, and illustrates the intended meaning of the collection.[166] If Q 16:16 and Q 16:18 represent a radical *re-interpretation* of the law, and Q 16:17 and Matt 5:17 a conservative *reaction* against antinomianism, then it certainly seems that the seeds of an eschatological *re-definition* of the law – which would ultimately result in various forms of Jewish-Christian sectarianism – were originally planted by the historical Jesus.

Jesus' teachings and the kingdom inaugurated a new era: the law is now newly interpreted. Q is neither indifferent to the law nor does it "abrogate" the law. Q 16:18 – one of the best attested of Jesus' sayings – *adjusts* Mosaic Law. Q 16:16–18 represents a pivotal moment in early Jewish Christian reflection on the law. Q 16:18 takes the final or concluding position in the unit, warranting its function as an interpretive key to the collection. If Q 16:16 implies that a new era is underway, Q 16:18 confirms that the law has been modified in light of the kingdom, which restores the original law between humanity and God. Q's reaction to antinomian tendencies in the Jesus movement led to the addition of Q 16:17, Matt 5:17, and James 2. This analysis suggests that at least some Q-sayings emerge from a highly realized restorative eschatology, that is, the inauguration of a new era (Q 16:16), a new creation (symbolized by the presence of the kingdom), and a newly interpreted law (Q 16:18). The law is being reinterpreted in the teachings of Jesus.[167] In other words, Jesus' teachings represent a new "law."[168] Salvation lies in Jesus' teachings.[169] Jesus' proscription

---

[164] Catchpole, *Quest*, 237.

[165] Cf. Jens Schröter, "Erwägungen zum Gesetzverständnis in Q anhand von Q 16, 17–18," in C. M. Tuckett (ed.), *The Scriptures in the Gospels* (BETL 131; Leuven: Peeters, 1997), 457.

[166] Cf. Alan Kirk, *The Composition of the Sayings Source: Genre, Synchrony, and Wisdom Redaction in Q* (NovT Sup 91; Leiden: Brill, 1998), 301, n. 89; Fleddermann, *Q*, 781–92.

[167] Tuckett, *Q*, 34.

[168] Q 6:46/Matt 7:24–27. Graham Stanton, *A Gospel for a New People: Studies in Matthew* (Louisville: Westminster John Knox, 1992), 130.

[169] Kloppenborg, "Nomos," 35–6, 47. Kloppenborg, "Preface," in *Jerusalem and the Early Jesus Movement*, 7–8; "City and Wasteland," 157. See also Ra'anan S. Boustan and Annette Yoshiko Reed, "Blood and Atonement in the Pseudo-Clementines and

of divorce is thus a *Jewish* restoration of creation, not Christian supersessionism. Jesus did not abolish the law. Jesus affirmed the original law or Torah of creation. Jesus appealed to an argument from creation: the Mosaic Law was simply not strict enough because it did not uphold God's original intention.

The Torah in the Gospels

The author of the Gospel of Mark inherited a "body of material with a strong coherence in thought and form," material that represents Jesus' most distinguishing features of prioritizing "compassion for human need, of following God's original intention, of ethical behavior and attitude above ritual and cultic."[170] This pre-Markan tradition has much in common with similar emphases in Q.[171] Yet the Gospel of Mark represents a more complex convergence of early Jesus traditions, Pauline theology,[172] and the author's distinctive Christology set within a narrative account of Jesus' ministry.[173] The Markan Jesus "declares all foods clean," replaces the Temple with the community of faith,[174] and asserts that what really matters are not the external, ritual aspects of the law,[175] but the ethics and internal morality of the heart. Mark's Jesus does not "abrogate" the law; the law is often simply irrelevant.[176] Jesus, as the Son of God, is

---

The Story of the Ten Martyrs: The Problem of Selectivity in the Study of 'Judaism' and 'Christianity,'" *Henoch*, 30 (2008), 344.

[170] Loader, *Jesus' Attitude*, 519.

[171] Loader, *Jesus' Attitude*, 519.

[172] On Paul and the law, see James D. G. Dunn, *The New Perspective on Paul*, rev. edn., (Grand Rapids: Eerdmans, 2008), 441; Heikki Räisänen, *Paul and the Law*, 2nd edn., (WUNT; Tübingen: Mohr Siebeck, 1987), xii; M. Wolter, *Paulus: ein Grundriss seiner Theologie* (Neukirchen-Vluyn: Neukirchener Verlagsgesellschaft, 2011), 351–8; Mark D. Nanos, *The Mystery of Romans* (Minneapolis: Fortress, 1996); *The Irony of Galatians: Paul's Letter in First-Century Context* (Minneapolis: Fortress, 2002); Stanley K. Stowers, *A Rereading of Romans: Justice, Jews and Gentiles* (New Haven: Yale University Press, 1994); Peter J. Tomson, *Paul and the Jewish Law: Halakha in the Letters of the Apostle to the Gentiles* (Assen: van Gorcum, 1990); Brian S. Rosner, *Paul and the Law: Keeping the Commandments of God* (NSBT 31; Downers Grove: InterVarsity, 2013); N. T. Wright, *Paul and the Faithfulness of God*, Vol. 4 of *Christian Origins and the Question of God*, 2 vols., (Minneapolis: Fortress, 2013).

[173] On Mark and the law, see Sariola, *Markus und das Gesetz*.

[174] D. Juel, *Messiah and Temple: The Trial of Jesus in the Gospel of Mark* (SBL DS 31; Missoula: Scholars, 1977), 135–6.

[175] Loader, *Jesus' Attitude*, 134.

[176] Loader, *Jesus' Attitude*, 135, 515.

the supreme, authoritative interpreter of the law. Nonetheless, Jesus affirms the Ten Commandments as the key to eternal life (10:17–27), and emphasizes loving God and loving one's neighbor as the two greatest commandments.[177] Similarly, the Sabbath may be observed, but only as God originally intended and as interpreted by Jesus (2:23–28; 3:1–6).[178] For Mark, "Human beings were not made for the Sabbath, but the Sabbath was made for human beings" (2:27). As we have seen, Jesus' position "has the force of an argument about inter-pretation of Torah on the basis of what God intended in creation,"[179] restoring the Sabbath's original purpose (cf. Mark 10:1–12). At the same time, the Markan Jesus repeatedly crosses Jewish purity bound-aries.[180] Paul's letter to the Galatians illustrates that disagreements over the Jewish food laws were a major site of conflict in the early movement; the Markan Jesus removes this impediment to Gentile inclusion as irrelevant compared to the true commandments. Purity is redefined as morality.[181] Jesus' authority sets aside or relaxes Torah commandments so as to open the way to the Gentiles. This is a *par-tial* abrogation of Torah, especially the ritual and cultic apparatus of the Torah,[182] and, simultaneously, an affirmation of the Torah's ethics, its commandments to love God and neighbor, and principles derived from creation.

James Crossley has argued that the Gospel of Mark can be dated c. 35–45 CE based on Synoptic accounts of legal controversies.[183] For Crossley, the Synoptic Jesus is a Torah-observant Jew involved in religious disputes with Pharisees over *their* expansions of Torah.[184] Consequently, the Markan community reflects the Jesus movement *before* early Christians began to question Torah observance, Sabbath observance, and the food laws.[185] In other words, Christianity was "largely law observant for at least the first 10 to 15 years after the

---

[177] 12:28–34; cf. Deut 6:4–5; Lev 19:18.

[178] Loader, *Jesus' Attitude*, 135.

[179] Loader, *Jesus' Attitude*, 33.

[180] Mark 1:41; 5:41; 5:24–28; 2:13–14, 15; 4:35–42; 7:31; 7:24–30; 7:19c; 7:2; 2:23–28; 3:1–6; 11:15–17; 12:33;14:58; 15:29.

[181] Loader, *Jesus' Attitude*, 79.

[182] Loader, *Jesus' Attitude*, 123.

[183] Crossley, *The Date of Mark's Gospel*. See also Casey, *Aramaic Sources of Mark's Gospel*.

[184] Crossley, *The Date*, 123 (emphasis added).

[185] As is found in the Pauline letters and Acts (Acts 6–7; 10:1–11, 18; 15; Gal 2:1–10; 2:11–14).

death of Jesus."[186] Crossley argues that the Markan Jesus never violates biblical law and downplays the pervasive theme of the Temple's destruction,[187] suggesting that he is not declaring *all* foods clean but only those foods allowed in the Torah.[188]

Is the Markan Jesus fully Torah observant? There are a number of reasons we might question this proposal. First, it seems unlikely that *Mark*'s readers knew that Jesus' declaration of "*all* foods clean" was referring *only* to foods permitted in the Torah. Second, it is methodologically problematic to interpret Jesus' controversy with Pharisees in Mark through the lens of *later* rabbinical purity laws (which cannot be properly dated). Third, it is difficult to use an allegedly early *halakhic* controversy as a criterion for dating the composition of Mark. Fourth, there are a number of indicators that Mark's interests are *post*-Pauline, including Mark's preoccupation with the destruction of the Temple, Paul's apparent ignorance of Mark, Mark's Pauline ideas, and the author's interest in Gentiles. Fifth, Mark 7:19's editorial aside (that Jesus declared "all foods clean") is most plausibly read in light of Paul (cf. Rom 14:14). Sixth, Mark's atonement theology (Mark 10:45; 14:24) may also be best read in light of Pauline soteriology. Crossley's model, while provocative and corrective of supersessionist readings, requires that Jesus both endorsed and participated in the Temple's sacrificial system *while* predicting, threatening, and perhaps even inaugurating its imminent destruction.

While Crossley is surely correct in claiming that the early Jewish Jesus movement was *more* Torah-oriented than Paul's Gentile communities, we must be cautious when assessing *Jesus*' own personal Torah observance. Passages like Mark 10:1–12, where Jesus forbids divorce and challenges a Mosaic concession, require more nuance. Crossley argues that Mark "assumed" an exception existed in cases of "sexual immorality."[189] Consequently, the Markan Jesus "in no way opposes biblical law … Divorce is still permissible just as it is in Deut. 24.1ff."[190] Yet this reading does not quite do justice to the full

---

[186] Crossley, *The Date of Mark's Gospel*, 157.

[187] Crossley interprets Mark 11:15–17 as criticism of abuse, not a call for the Temple's abolition. So, too, the rending of the veil is symbolic of God's "mourning" (not judgment), and the cursed fig tree represents the Jewish leaders but not the Temple.

[188] Crossley, *The Date of Mark's Gospel*, 192.

[189] Crossley. *The Date*, 172, 207. Crossley claims that this *assumption* implicit in Mark was then "accurately interpreted" by Matthew.

[190] Crossley, *The Date*, 174.

complexity of the problem. Mark 10:2–9 issues an *absolute* prohibition of divorce based on an appeal to the divine order of creation. It is
Matthew, not Mark, who introduces an exception for πορνεία. It is true
that Mark 10:10–12 does seem to nuance this prohibition with Jesus
elaborating in private about the adulterous consequences of *remarriage*,
but this does not necessarily blunt the force of the earlier prohibition.
Mark 10:10–12 *could* be interpreted as implicitly assuming the *existence*
of divorce, but that does not mean the Markan Jesus approves of it
or endorses its validity.[191] Jesus did not approve of divorce *or* remarriage.[192] He insists that it was not God's original intention at creation.
But the Mosaic Torah permitted it. The inevitable conclusion is that
the Mosaic Torah was a (temporary?) concession. So any attempt to
disallow divorce was an implicit critique of the Mosaic Torah, which
is precisely why the Markan account is framed as a *controversy* story.
The Markan Jesus addresses both concerns: contra the Torah, divorce
is prohibited and remarriage is adultery.

The Gospel of Matthew is widely regarded as the most "Jewish"
of the Gospels,[193] but there is still considerable debate on precisely
how "Jewish" this Gospel is.[194] The general consensus is that Matthew
represents a Jewish-Christian community.[195] But did Matthew agree
with Mark about the law? That is doubtful.[196] Despite substantial

---

[191] Contra, e.g., D. E. Nineham, *Saint Mark* (London: Penguin, 1963), 261–2; D.
Instone-Brewer, "Jesus' Old Testament Basis for Monogamy," in S. Moyise (ed.), *The
Old Testament in the New Testament: Essays in Honour of J. L. North* (Sheffield: Sheffield
Academic Press, 2000), 75–105, here 90; M. Bockmuehl, "Matthew 5:32; 19:9 in the
Light of Pre-Rabbinic Halakah," *NTS*, 35 (1989), 291–5; *Jewish Law in the Gentile
Churches*, 17–21.

[192] Cf. Mal. 2:13–16; *m. Git.* 9.10; *b. Git.* 90b.

[193] J. A. Overman, *Matthew's Gospel and Formative Judaism: The Social World of
the Matthean Community* (Minneapolis: Fortress, 1990); A. J. Saldarini, *Matthew's
Christian-Jewish Community* (Chicago: University of Chicago Press, 1994).

[194] Cf. D. R. A. Hare, "How Jewish is the Gospel of Matthew?" *CBQ*, 62 (2000),
264–77. On Matthew as representing a "new people," see Stanton, *A Gospel for a
New People*; D. A. Hagner, "Matthew: Apostate, Reformer, Revolutionary?," *NTS*,
49 (2003), 193–209; R. Deines, *Die Gerechtigkeit der Tora im Reich des Messias: Mt
5,13–20 als Schlüsseltext der matthäischen Theologie* (WUNT 177; Tübingen: Mohr
Siebeck, 2004); Paul Foster, *Community, Law and Mission in Matthew's Gospel*
(WUNT II.177; Tübingen: Mohr Siebeck, 2004).

[195] Overman, *Matthew's Gospel and Formative Judaism*; Saldarini, *Matthew's
Christian-Jewish Community*; D. C. Sim, *The Gospel of Matthew and Christian
Judaism: The History and Social Setting of the Matthean Community* (Edinburgh: T
& T Clark, 1998).

[196] See William R. G. Loader, "Attitudes to Judaism and the Law and Synoptic
Relations," in P. Foster, et al. (eds.), *New Studies in the Synoptic Problem Oxford*

agreements in theology and Christology, Matthew viewed Mark's account as seriously flawed and sought to replace it with his own,[197] correcting Mark's language, extending its length, and eliminating its most offensive features. In particular, Matthew found Mark to be theologically inadequate because Mark was written from a Pauline perspective.[198] Matthew does not necessarily know the letters of Paul,[199] but wherever Mark is in agreement with Pauline views and traditions, Matthew omits or corrects them.[200] For example, Paul and Mark both share an interest in a law-free mission to Gentiles; Matthew, on the other hand, claims that Jesus' ministry was to the Jews alone.[201] But while the Matthean Jesus declares his exclusive focus on Israel,[202] these passages are better understood as arising "from a Jewish Christian wing of a church pressing its interest

Conference, April 2008 (BETL 239; Leuven: Peeters, 2011), 347–69, here 354; J. Nolland, *The Gospel of Matthew* (NICTC; Grand Rapids, 2005), 218. See K. Müller, "Forschungsgeschichtliche Anmerkungen zum Thema 'Jesus von Nazareth und das Gesetz': Versuch einer Zwischenbilanz," in *Kirche und Volk Gottes. FS. Jürgen Roloff* (Neukirchen-Vluyn, 2000), 58–77.

[197] Sim, "Matthew's Use of Mark," 176–92.

[198] Sim, *Matthew*, 198. Cf. J. Painter, *Mark's Gospel: Worlds in Conflict* (NTR; London: Routledge, 1997), 4–6; W. R. Telford, *The Theology of the Gospel of Mark* (NTT; Cambridge University Press, 1999), 164–9; Joel Marcus, *Mark 1–8: A New Translation with Introduction and Commentary* (AB 27; New York: Doubleday, 2000), 73–5; "Mark – Interpreter of Paul," *NTS*, 46 (2000), 473–87; J. Svartvik, *Mark and Mission: Mk 7:1–23 in its Narrative and Historical Contexts* (CBNTS 32; Stockholm: Almqvist & Wiksell International, 2000), 344–7; "Matthew and Mark," in *Matthew and His Christian Contemporaries* (LNTS 333; London: T & T Clark, 2008), 27–49, here 33.

[199] Paul Foster, "Paul and Matthew: Two Strands in the Early Jesus Movement with Little Sign of Connection," in M. F. Bird and J. Willitts (eds.), *Paul and the Gospels: Christologies, Conflicts and Convergences* (LNTS 411; London: T & T Clark, 2011), 86–114.

[200] D. Sim, "Paul and Matthew on the Torah: Theory and Practice," in P. Middleton, et al. (eds.), *Paul, Grace and Freedom: Essays in Honour of John K. Riches* (London: T & T Clark, 2009), 50–64; D. J. Harrington, "Matthew and Paul," in D. Sim and B. Repschinski (eds.), *Matthew and His Christian Contemporaries* (London: T & T Clark, 2008), 11–26; D. Sim, "Matthew, Paul and the Origin and Nature of the Gentile Mission: The Great Commission in Matthew 28:16–20 as an Anti-Pauline Tradition," *HTS*, 64 (2008), 377–92; "Matthew's Anti-Paulinism: A Neglected Feature of Matthean Studies," *HTS*, 58 (2002), 767–83; "Matthew 7.21–23: Further Evidence of Its Anti-Pauline Perspective," *NTS*, 53 (2007), 325–43.

[201] Matt 15:24; 10:5–6. Amy-Jill Levine, *The Social and Ethnic Dimensions of Matthean Salvation History: "Go nowhere among the Gentiles …" (Matt. 10:5b)* (SBEC 14; Lewiston: Edwin Mellen, 1988).

[202] Matt 10:5–6; 15:24.

against some rival Gentile Christian element."[203] Like Matt 5:17, where Matthew counters Mark's (Pauline) emphasis on Jesus as breaking with Mosaic Law, these Matthean sayings protest too much and presuppose a Gentile *mission* which did not arise until well after Jesus' death. Narratively, these apparently "pro-Jewish" passages also function as "anti-Jewish" polemic,[204] blaming the Jews retrospectively for not having recognized their salvation. These sayings do not likely represent the historical Jesus. This is kin to the Matthean Jesus' apparent endorsement of the Temple system in Matt 5:23–24 as a literary-narratival way of affirming Jesus' regard for the sacrificial system *in spite of which he was rejected and betrayed by his own people.* Matthew 28:19's endorsement of the Gentile mission after Jesus' death and resurrection is thus consonant with Markan and Pauline Christology: Jesus came to the Jews first, but he was rejected, inaugurating salvation for Gentiles.

Whereas Mark criticized Jesus' family and the twelve,[205] Matthew rehabilitates their reputation.[206] Whereas Mark shows a relative disinterest in Jesus' teachings and the ritual demands of the Torah,[207] Matthew takes pains to emphasize Jesus' role as an interpreter of Torah. The Matthean Jesus, accordingly, upholds the law. Matthew omits Mark 7:19c's parenthetical comment that Jesus "declared all foods clean."[208] Matthew essentially re-judaizes Mark for his Jewish Christian community,[209] preserves conservative elements from Q, and embraces a mission to "all nations" (τὰ ἔθνη) (Matt 28:19). Matthew's understanding is that the law – the renewed, restored, or reinterpreted will of God – is fulfilled in Jesus' life and teachings.[210]

---

[203] Michael J. Cook, "How Credible Is Jewish Scholarship on Jesus?" in Zev Garber (ed.), *The Jewish Jesus: Revelation, Reflection, Reclamation* (West Lafayette: Purdue University Press, 2011), 251–70, here 262. Contra Vermes, *The Authentic Gospel of Jesus*, 380.

[204] Cook, "How Credible," 263.

[205] T. J. Weeden, *Mark – Traditions in Conflict* (Philadelphia: Fortress, 1971), 50.

[206] See Svartvik, "Matthew and Mark," 44.

[207] Sim, "Matthew's Use of Mark, "180; B. Repschinski, *Nicht aufzulösen, sondern zu erfüllen: Das jüdische Gesetz in den synoptischen Jesuserzählungen* (FzB 120; Würzburg: Echter, 2009), 143–216.

[208] Svartvik, "Matthew and Mark," 41.

[209] Sim, "Matthew's Use of Mark," 181. See also A. M. O'Leary, *Matthew's Judaization of Mark: Examined in the Context of the Use of Sources in Graeco-Roman Antiquity* (JSNTSup 323; London: T & T Clark, 2006). Svartvik, "Matthew and Mark," 36–7, 49, suggests that Matthew is the first attempt to perform a "*Heimholung Jesu ins Judentum.*"

[210] Saldarini, *Matthew's Jewish-Christian Community*, 161.

Matthew represents a counter-tendency insisting on the ongoing validity of the law (Matt 5:17), increases Q's polemic against the Pharisees, introduces additional parables of eschatological violence, and re-judaizes the tradition to counter-antinomian tendencies in the early movement.[211] Matt 5:17 epitomizes this approach, rejecting the view – presumably present among some early (Pauline?) Christians – that Jesus came to abolish the law.[212] The Matthean antitheses "lay[s] down a stricter law ... (and) do not come into conflict with Torah; they go beyond it ... They run in the direction of asking more of people, rather than less."[213] This is why divorce, once permitted, is only now allowed under certain conditions; the Matthean Jesus can forbid what the law allows. As in Mark, the hermeneutical principle of Jesus' authoritative interpretation is that "Jesus' words interpret and apply *the true intention* of the commandments."[214] Even more distinctive is how the Matthean Jesus interprets the Torah using the criterion of compassion. Matthew downplays the antinomian tendencies in Mark (and Paul) and defends Jesus' stance toward the Temple and Torah.[215]

The author of Luke, like Matthew, portrays Jesus, his family, and his first followers as faithful to the Temple and the Torah.[216] While Luke's representation of Jesus' circumcision (2:21), ceremony in the Temple (2:22, 27), the Holy Family's journey to Jerusalem for Passover, and Jesus' teaching in the Temple both as a child (2:41–51) and as an

---

[211] See also Matt 10, 6; 15, 24.

[212] See G. Barth, "Das Gesetzesverständnis des Evangelisten Mätthaus," in G. Bornkamm, G. Barth, and H. J. Held (eds.), *Überlieferung und Auslegung im Matthäusevangelium* (WMANT 1; Neukirchern: Wageningen, 1961), 62; Reinhardt Hummel, *Die Auseinandersetzung zwischen Kirche und Judentum im Matthäusevangelium* (München: Kaiser, 1966), 68; I. Broer, *Freiheit vom Gesetz und Radikalisierung des Gesetzes* (SBS 98; Stuttgart: KBW, 1980), 24–5.

[213] Loader, *Jesus' Attitude*, 177.

[214] Loader, *Jesus' Attitude*, 180.

[215] Loader, *Jesus' Attitude*, 262–3.

[216] On Luke and the law, see S. G. Wilson, *Luke and the Law* (SNTSMS 50; Cambridge University Press, 1983); Klinghardt, *Gesetz und Volk Gottes*; K. Salo, *Luke's Treatment of the Law: A Redactional-Critical Investigation* (Helsinki: Suomalainen Tiedeakatemia, 1991). On "Luke" as a "Jewish" author and text, see Isaac W. Oliver, *Torah Praxis after 70 CE: Reading Matthew and Luke-Acts as Jewish Texts* (WUNT II.355; Tübingen: Mohr Siebeck, 2013). See also Jacob Jervell, *Luke and the People of God: A New Look at Luke-Acts* (Minneapolis: Fortress, 1972), 133–52. For criticism, see Amy-Jill Levine, review of Oliver, *Torah Praxis after 70 CE*, *Reviews of the Enoch Seminar*, www.enochseminar.org [accessed May 30, 2015].

adult (19:47; 20:1; 21:37) might lead us to conclude that the historical Jesus was fully Torah-observant, these Lukan literary-theological
motifs are not necessarily "historical" reports or "memories" of
Jesus.[217] It is this perspective, ironically, that betrays Luke's apologetic agenda, for he is at pains to defend Paul against the charge that
he both personally transgressed the law and taught others to do so as
well.[218] Luke's larger project, Luke-Acts, is a two-volume work which
sought to represent Christian salvation history.[219] Luke's representation of the authority of the law has often been seen as *temporal* and
belonging to a past, nostalgically recalled era, as in Acts' representation of Jesus' followers continuing to worship in the Temple (2:46;
3:1; 5:12–12, 20–21, 42). This model recognizes that Luke's agenda
was to reconcile the law-free Gentile mission with the origins of the
church within Judaism.[220] Luke consistently portrays Jesus as faithful
and obedient to the Torah because he wants to avoid suggesting that
Jesus had anything to do with "abrogating" Jewish law.[221] The problem is that Acts 10 strongly suggests that ritual purity laws, especially
the food laws, *were* abolished, although not during Jesus' ministry.
Luke tries to show how this came about without antagonizing his
Jewish Christian colleagues. This tension runs throughout Luke-Acts,
whether it is Luke's adoption of the Q tradition on divorce, with its
affirmation of the law's validity and partial "abrogation" in the new
era of the kingdom,[222] or, as in Q, Mark, and Matthew, where Luke's
Jesus fulfills the law yet surpasses it in Christological authority.[223] Is
it possible that Luke (i.e., Stephen) could reject the Temple and the

[217] Cook, "How Credible," 264.

[218] Loader, *Jesus' Attitude*, 379.

[219] Conzelmann, *Saint Luke*; Vouga, *Loi*, 67, 152, 186–7; Salo, *Luke's Treatment of the Law*.

[220] E. Haenchen, *Die Apostelgeschichte* (KEKNT 111; Göttingen: Vandenhoeck & Ruprecht, 1968).

[221] Hübner, *Gesetz*, 208.

[222] C. L. Blomberg, "The Law in Luke-Acts," *JSNT*, 22 (1986), 53–80, here 61–2. P. Esler, *Community and Gospel in Luke-Acts: The Social and Political Motivations of Lucan Theology* (SNTS MS 57; Cambridge University Press, 1987), 120–1. Klinghardt, *Gesetz und Volk Gottes*, 29–36; Fitzmyer, "The Jewish People and the Mosaic Law in Luke-Acts," 197–8, n. 11, argues that Jesus' prohibition of divorce is "not directly contrary" to the Torah.

[223] M. M. B. Turner, "The Sabbath, Sunday, and the Law in Luke/Acts," in D. Carson (ed.), *From Sabbath to Lord's Day: A Biblical, Historical and Theological Investigation* (Grand Rapids: Zondervan, 1982), 99–157, esp. 111. See also Blomberg, "The Law in Luke-Acts," 58.

cultic law without rejecting the Torah, that is, by re-interpreting the Torah?[224]

Luke's goal was to construct a narrative in which Gentiles were welcomed into the new movement without causing offense to their Jewish colleagues.[225] In an effort to harmonize what was in reality a truly contentious time, Luke suppresses evidence to the contrary. For example, in Acts, it is Peter (not Jesus, as in Mark) who receives a divine vision where *God* declares all foods clean and edible so as to ambiguously, yet pre-emptively, permit shared table fellowship with Gentiles without appealing to the Markan tradition that Jesus did so.[226] Luke also has Peter declare the law to be too difficult in Acts 15:10–11. Luke's portrait of a law-observant Paul is particularly suspect (Acts 21:20; 24:17; 25:8), as Paul was known to have regularly eaten with Gentiles.[227] Luke's apologetic agenda "runs up against the hard facts of the case."[228] Like Matthew, Luke's agenda is apologetic. Both evangelists – writing in the 80s and 90s CE, that is, decades after the deaths of Jesus, Peter, Paul, and James – are striving to affirm continuity with Judaism and authority from Jesus. We cannot uncritically take the Matthean or Lukan Jesus' position on the law as faithfully preserving or representing the historical Jesus.'

The Gospel of John represents an even later stage in this process; its author no longer regards the law as authoritative.[229] For example, Jesus commands a man to carry his mat on the Sabbath (5:8). Jesus himself breaks the Sabbath again by making clay (9:4–6). Jesus seems to be "above" the law even while the law witnesses and points to Christ. One may go even further: Jesus effectively *replaces* the law. His body replaces the Temple (2:19–22; 4:20–24). He replaces the old festivals (6:4–14; 2:13; 7:2; 10:22). He is the true manna of the true Passover. He is the true Word (1:1), the true Light (8:12),

[224] So Klinghardt, *Gesetz und Volk Gottes*, 284–303, 306.

[225] J. T. Sanders, *The Jews in Luke-Acts* (London: SCM, 1987), 121.

[226] So Blomberg, "The Law in Luke-Acts," 64. On Luke purposefully intending the reader to see the connection between Peter's vision and the abolition of clean/unclean animals and food, see also Hübner, *Gesetz*, 190–1; Pesch, *Apostelgeschichte I*, 339; Turner, "Sabbath," 116.

[227] Esler, *Community and Gospel*, 127–8.

[228] Esler, *Community and Gospel*, 129.

[229] S. Pancaro, *The Law in the Fourth Gospel: The Torah and the Gospel, Moses and Jesus, Judaism and Christianity according to John* (NovT Sup 42; Leiden: Brill, 1975); M. Kotila, *Umstrittene Zeuge. Studien zur Stellung des Gesetzes in der johanneischen Theologiegeschichte* (Helsinki: Suomalainen Tiedeakatemia, 1988).

Water (7:37–39), and Life (5:39). He is the true means of purification
(2:6, 10). He is greater than Jacob (4:12), Abraham (8:53, 56–58),
and Moses (1:17; 3:13–15; 5:36, 46; 6:31–32). For the author of John,
the Torah is a temporary provision from God now surpassed and
replaced by the Son. The Gospel of John represents a late stage in the
progressive supersessionism of the tradition, an increased hostility
toward "the Jews" and a significantly higher and more other-worldly
Christology which cumulatively suggests a trajectory moving further
and further away from traditional Judaism, with its two dominant
institutions of Torah and Temple.

Conclusion

This chapter surveyed the relationship(s) between Jesus and the
Torah in the New Testament Gospels. Beginning with Q, we found
that the best attested Jesus tradition – the divorce saying – already
represents a relatively radical stance in comparison with the general
Mosaic legal norms of Jesus' day which allowed for divorce. We also
found that the juxtaposition of several legal sayings in Q 16:16–18
represent an early attempt to qualify and limit the possibility of antinomian interpretations of the tradition. The hermeneutical principle
at work in Q's saying on divorce seems to be similar to Mark's – Jesus
affirms and seeks to restore God's original will and intention at creation – *despite* what the Mosaic tradition holds. While Mark (following Paul's radical break with Torah) emphasizes Jesus' discontinuity
with the Torah and prophetic destruction of the Temple, Matthew
and Luke, as later evangelists, attempt to mitigate these radical portraits by defending Jesus' loyalty to the Torah and Temple while John
explicitly replaces the Torah and Temple with Christ and his (new)
Temple-body of followers. Since our literary, historical, and theological survey of the New Testament Gospels has revealed a trajectory moving further and further away from ethnic and ideological
continuities with Judaism, with ever-increasing hostility, separation,
"parting(s)," and mutual condemnations, it is apparent that if we
want to understand the historical Jesus in his original Jewish context,
we are going to have to re-locate Jesus within the *inter*-Jewish sectarian conflict(s) characteristic of Second *Temple* Judaism.

3

THE ESCHATOLOGICAL TEMPLE

A Jesus whose words and deeds did not threaten or alien-
ate people, especially powerful people, is not the historical
Jesus.[1]

John P. Meier, *A Marginal Jew*

Revisiting the Temple Incident

Most historical Jesus specialists agree that the Temple incident played
a pivotal role in Jesus' arrest and death. The historicity of the incident rests on firm ground, well supported by the criteria of multiple
attestation,[2] dissimilarity, and embarrassment.[3] Jesus seems to have
criticized the Temple's administration and predicted its destruction,[4]
but it is not clear precisely what Jesus objected to. What is it *specifically* about Jesus' attitude to the Temple that was the problem? It
seems certain that Jesus must have threatened the Temple in some
way. Threats to the Temple were taken seriously for they "reached
beyond theological concerns to the socioeconomic and political
realms."[5] Threats to the Temple affected the priests' livelihood and
authority as well as the public order. Serious threats to the Temple
were sufficient to result in the punishment of death, but the Gospels
are not in agreement as to the nature of the offense or the *meaning*

[1] John P. Meier, *A Marginal Jew: Rethinking the Historical Jesus, The Roots of the
Problem of the Person* (New York: Doubleday, 1991), 177.
[2] Mark 11.15–18; Matt 21:12–16; Luke 19.45–48; John 2:13–22; *Thomas* L. 64; 71.
[3] Klyne R. Snodgrass, "The Temple Incident," in R. L. Webb and D. L. Bock (eds.),
Key Events in the Life of the Historical Jesus (Tübingen: Mohr Siebeck, 2009), 430–2.
[4] Sanders, *Jesus and Judaism*, 306; *The Historical Figure of Jesus* (London: Penguin,
1993), 254. See also Paula Fredriksen, *From Jesus to Christ: The Origins of the New
Testament Images of Jesus* (New Haven: Yale University Press, 1988); "Did Jesus
Oppose the Purity Laws?" *BR*, 11.3 (1999), 20–25, 42–47.
[5] Brown, *The Death of the Messiah*, 458.

of the incident. While there is a general consensus that Jesus initiated some form of protest, the Temple incident seems to represent a lost historical tradition that only partially surfaces in the Gospels.[6] Our goal here, however, is not to determine precisely what Jesus said or did in the Temple courtyards as much as it is to discern, perhaps even decipher, the implied meaning of his Temple-related sayings and deeds. While there is good reason to suppose that Jesus objected to some aspect of the Temple's current administration and issued a critique not entirely unlike those made by the prophets, we still have to identify the social, economic, and moral questions involved in order to locate the incident within Second Temple Judaism.

The Temple was revered by most Jews as the house of God, the place where God "resided." Serving as a visible symbol of the presence of God and the physical center of Jewish identity, the Temple was not just a place where animal sacrifice was conducted. Other kinds of sacrifices (wine, flour, oil, and grains) were also offered. It was a house of prayer,[7] a place for public gatherings and teaching. Traditional Jewish reverence for the Temple is consistent, therefore, with pro-Temple Christian traditions, especially in Luke-Acts, where the earliest Christians are described as going to the Temple to pray and teach (but not sacrifice).[8] This would also make sense of Jesus advising his followers to pay the Temple tax and forbidding people to carry "vessels" through the Temple.[9] After all, Jesus identifies the Temple as "my Father's house." The Temple incident reflects Jesus' concern for its holiness as the house of God.

At the same time, reverence for the Temple could also lead to criticism of and contestation over the Temple's correct administration.

---

[6] Alexander J. M. Wedderburn, "Jesus' Action in the Temple: A Key or a Puzzle?" *ZNW*, 97 (2006), 1–22. See also J. Roloff, *Das Kerygma und der irdische Jesus. Historische Motive in den Jesus-Erzählungen der Evangelien* (Göttingen: Vandenhoeck and Ruprecht, 1970); M. Trautmann, *Zeichenhafte Handlungen Jesu. Ein Beitrag zur Frage nach dem geschichtlichen Jesu* (FB 37; Würzburg: Echter, 1980); Kurt Paesler, *Das Tempelwort Jesu. Die Traditionen von Tempelzerstörung und Tempelerneuerung im Neuen Testament* (FRLANT 184; Göttingen: Vandenhoeck & Ruprecht, 1999).

[7] See 1 Macc. 7.37; Josephus, *A.J.* 8.108; Philo, *Moses* 2.133.

[8] Acts 2.46; 3.1–26; 5.42; 22.17; 20.16; 21.26–27. L. Gaston, *No Stone on Another: Studies in the Significance of the Fall of Jerusalem in the Synoptic Gospels* (NovT Sup 23: Leiden: Brill, 1970), 98, argues that early Christians only used the Temple to teach and preach. See also Martin Hengel, *The Atonement: The Origins of the Doctrine in the New Testament* (London: SCM, 1981), 57: "the Temple no longer served as a place of sacrifice and atonement."'

[9] Matt 17.24–27, Mark 11.16, respectively.

Despite some dissenting doubt,[10] there is considerable evidence pointing to long-term systemic corruption within the Temple priesthood and administration.[11] The presumption of priestly guilt is a common assumption,[12] and despite some dissenting scholars who argue that commerce in the Temple was a practical necessity,[13] many hold that the Temple was perceived as a flawed institution.[14] There is a great deal of evidence supporting this conclusion. The prophets repeatedly accuse the priests of bribery, theft, murder, and idolatry.[15] The Qumran texts, in particular, criticize the Jerusalem priesthood for betraying the law, stealing from the poor, and seizing public monies.[16] Other Second Temple texts echo the theme.[17] The rabbis also note that the Temple was prone to corruption.[18] We can be confident, therefore, that at least *some* priests abused their positions even while *most* priests may have performed their duties with pious integrity. The office of the high priest in particular was notorious for its illegitimacy, bribery, political machinations, and collaboration with Israel's

[10] Sanders, *Jesus and Judaism*, 62–7; Ådna, *Jesu Stellung zum Tempel*, 339–40; Adela Yarbro Collins, "Jesus' Action in Herod's Temple," in A. Y. Collins and M. M. Mitchell (eds.), *Antiquity and Humanity: Essays on Ancient Religion and Philosophy* (Tübingen: Mohr Siebeck, 2001), 53.

[11] Craig A. Evans, "Jesus' Action in the Temple: Cleansing or Portent of Destruction?" *CBQ*, 51 (1989), 237–70; "Jesus and the "Cave of Robbers": Toward a Jewish Context for the Temple Action," *BBR*, 2 (1993), 92–110; "Predictions of the Destruction of the Herodian Temple in the Pseudepigrapha, Qumran Scrolls, and Related Texts," *JSP*, 10 (1992), 89–146; "Opposition to the Temple: Jesus and the Dead Sea Scrolls," in J. H. Charlesworth (ed.), *Jesus and the Dead Sea Scrolls* (New York: Doubleday, 1992), 235–53.

[12] Sanders, *Jesus and Judaism*, 61–3.

[13] Israel Abrahams, *Studies in Pharisaism and the Gospels* (Cambridge University Press, 1917), 82–9; Sanders, *Jesus and Judaism*, 61–76.

[14] Evans, "Jesus' Action," 395–439; Richard Horsley, *Jesus and the Spiral of Violence: Popular Jewish Resistance in Roman Palestine* (San Francisco: Harper & Row, 1987), 285–317; Marcus J. Borg, *Conflict, Holiness, and Politics in the Teaching of Jesus* (New York: Edwin Mellen, 1984), 174–212; Wright, *Jesus and the Victory of God*, 413–28.

[15] Isa. 28.7; 66.3; Jer. 6.13; 7.9–15; 23.11–12; Lam. 4.13; Hos. 4.4–9; 6.9; Mic. 3.9–12; Zeph. 3.1–4; Mal. 1.6–14; 2.7–8; 3.1–5.

[16] 1QpHab 8.7–13; 4QpNah f3 and 4 1.10; 4QMMT 82–83; CD A 6.14–17; 4QPs 37 2.14, 3.6, 12.

[17] *1 En.* 89.72–73; *Test. Levi* 14.1–15.1; 17.8–11; *Test. Judah* 23.1–3; *Test. Moses* 5.3–6.1.

[18] Evans, "Jesus' Action," 421–4; Casey, "Culture and Historicity," 313–16. See, for example, *m. Keritot* 1.7; *b. Pesahim* 57a; *Lev. Rabbah* 21.9; *b. Yoma* 8b; *t. Yoma* 1.12; *t. Menahot* 13.22.

enemies during the post-Maccabean era. Such sentiments led to the conclusion that there was something wrong with how the Temple was being administrated and that this, in turn, compromised the religious integrity of the people of Israel and could lead to the Temple's destruction.

The Gospels present us with a Jesus who claims to have authority *over* the Temple, a Jesus who predicts, or threatens, the *destruction* of the Temple, a Jesus who forgives sins and mediates forgiveness during his ministry – a Jesus who even thinks of himself as dying an atoning sacrifice and becoming a new temple for his followers. Historically, most scholars think that Jesus criticized the Temple's administration but never questioned the institution itself.[19] The problem with this interpretation is that the Temple incident plays a central role in Jesus' death. It was an immediate causal factor leading to Jesus' arrest, trial, and execution and should be interpreted in its original context. The Temple incident should carry the weight of Jesus' offense. We need a hypothesis that can explain *what* Jesus objected to in the Temple, that is, a hypothesis that has the explanatory power to clarify *what* Jesus risked his life for and *why* he died.

Most scholars today are rightly reluctant to reinscribe supersessionist readings of the early evidence and approach these motifs with due caution (either as redactional or as misguided). But in attempting to eliminate the secondary redaction of the evangelists, Jesus is often remade in the image of the normative Jew who wore "fringes," observed the festivals, debated (but observed) Torah, and couldn't possibly have criticized anything truly fundamental about the Temple. According to this view, if Jesus criticized the Jewish leaders, it was only an administrative disagreement or a relatively common prophetic condemnation of excessive commercialism, greed, or corruption.

Different scholars also have different thoughts about why Jesus died. Some believe that no matter what kind of trouble Jesus got into with the Jewish leaders or the Roman authorities, what *really* happened was that God was replacing the Temple's sacrificial system with Jesus' sacrificial death. We can read it clearly in the gospel-texts – both plainly and as highly sophisticated theological biographies – but

[19] Darrell L. Bock, "What Did Jesus Do That Got Him into Trouble? Jesus in the Continuum of Early Judaism-Early Christianity," in Tom Holmén (ed.), *Jesus in Continuum* (WUNT 289; Tübingen: Mohr Siebeck, 2012), 171–210, here 195 (emphases added).

if we interpret Jesus strictly or even primarily through a predetermined theological lens, we just might miss the radical thrust of Jesus' original critique. It is necessary, therefore, to discuss Jesus' relationship to the Temple *and* the sacrificial system, a relationship which is itself part of, and inseparable from, wider discussions on religion, sacrifice, and violence in contemporary scholarship.

Contemporary Critical Reflections on Sacrifice and Violence

The contemporary study of ancient *sacrifice* (from the Latin *sacrificium*, literally "something made sacred") remains a site of vigorous discussion and debate.[20] Whether we view sacrificial offerings in terms of "feeding" the gods, reciprocal gift-giving,[21] a divine meal or cuisine,[22] part of a broader cross-cultural practice of ascetic renunciation,[23] a communal sharing of a sacred victim,[24] or as complex ritual *processes* involving killing, consumption, and sacralization,[25] the language and vocabulary of sacrifice is polyvalent.[26] No single

[20] On the Latin term "sacrifice" as "various rites which arose from the common meal ... for the purpose of entering into [divine] union," see R. K. Yerkes, *Sacrifice in Greek and Roman Religions and Early Judaism* (London: Adam & Charles Black, 1953), 25–6. For contemporary discussions, see J. Zachhuber and J. T. Meszaros (eds.), *Sacrifice and Modern Thought* (Oxford University Press, 2013); Anne Porter and Glenn M. Schwartz (eds.), *Sacred Killing: The Archaeology of Sacrifice in the Ancient Near East* (Winona Lake: Eisenbrauns, 2012).

[21] Ullucci, *The Christian Rejection of Animal Sacrifice*, 30; Stanley K. Stowers, "Greeks Who Sacrifice and Those Who Do Not: Toward and Anthropology of Greek Religion," in L. Michael White and O. L. Yarbrough (eds.), *The Social World of the First Christians: Essays in Honor of Wayne A. Meeks* (Minneapolis: Fortress, 1995), 293–333; "The Religion of Plant and Animal Offerings Versus the Religion of Meanings, Essences, and Textual Mysteries," in Jennifer W. Knust and Zsuzsanna Várhelyi (eds.), *Ancient Mediterranean Sacrifice* (Oxford University Press, 2011), 35–56; Richard E. DeMaris, "Sacrifice, an Ancient Mediterranean Ritual," *BTB* 43 (2013), 60–73; Edward Burnett Tylor, *Primitive Culture: Researches into the Development of Mythology, Philosophy, Religion, Language, Art, and Custom*, 2 vols., (London: John Murray, 1871), 2:328.

[22] Marcel Detienne and Jean-Pierre Vernant, *The Cuisine of Sacrifice among the Greeks* (trans. Paula Wissing; University of Chicago Press, 1989).

[23] See Gavin Flood, "Sacrifice as Refusal," in *Sacrifice and Modern Thought*, 115–31.

[24] Robertson Smith, *Lectures on the Religion of the Semites*, 226–7.

[25] Henri Hubert and Marcel Mauss, *Sacrifice: Its Nature and Functions*, trans. W. D. Halls (University of Chicago Press, 1964), originally published as "Essai sur la nature et la fonction du sacrifice," *L'Année sociologique* 2 (1898): 29–138.

[26] C. Carter, *Understanding Religious Sacrifice: A Reader* (London: Continuum, 2003).

theory can *explain* the origins or the phenomenon of sacrifice.[27] Yet a particularly problematic point of contention is the assumption that the origins of sacrifice can be explained as vestiges of primitive rites of violent animal or human sacrifice. Walter Burkert, for example, argued that the origins of sacrifice were to be found in Paleolithic hunting rituals that absolved the feelings of guilt induced by the act of killing, produced a sense of community, and survived in ritualized forms.[28]

Fred S. Naiden, however, objects to the idea that ancient Greek sacrifice was primarily about killing animals and argues that sacrifice included animal as well as vegetal and incense offerings that did not require killing or death.[29] Naiden sees such traces of Christian belief in contemporary theories of sacrifice, namely "the universality of sacrifice, of redemptive bloodshed, and of the victim's consent."[30] Yet ancient Greek sacrifice is better understood as a complex system of prayers, requests, and offerings to a god which may or may not have been accepted or rewarded. This is most apparent in the etymological root of the Greek term for sacrifice, θυσία, which refers to the burning, smoke, and "offering" of the sacrificial item. Similarly, Jonathan Z. Smith argues that "The putative 'evidence' for the primitivity of animal sacrifice is far from compelling" and that "*Animal sacrifice appears to be, universally, the ritual killing of a domesticated animal by agrarian or pastoralist societies.*"[31] Smith suggests that

---

[27] Jacob Milgrom, *Leviticus 1–16: A New Translation with Introduction and Commentary* (AB 3; New York: Doubleday, 1992), 442–3.

[28] Burkert, *Homo Necans*.

[29] On θύσειν as nonanimal sacrifice, see Jean Casabona, *Recherches sur le vocabulaire des sacrifices en grec, des origines à la fin de l'époque classique* (Paris: Editions Ophrys, 1966), 72–8. On "bloodless sacrifice," see Benedikt Eckhardt, "'Bloodless Sacrifice': A Note on Greek Cultic Language in the Imperial Era," *Greek, Roman, and Byzantine Studies* 54 (2014), 255–73.

[30] F. S. Naiden, *Smoke Signals for the Gods: Ancient Greek Sacrifice from the Archaic through Roman Periods* (Oxford University Press, 2013), 276. See also C. Faraone and F. S. Naiden (eds.), *Greek and Roman Animal Sacrifice: Ancient Victims, Modern Observers* (Cambridge University Press, 2012); Sarah Hitch and Ian Rutherford (eds.), *Animal Sacrifice in the Ancient World* (Cambridge University Press, 2015). On sacrifice in the Roman world, see Francesca Prescendi, *Decrire et comprendre le sacrifice. Les réflexions des Romains sur leur propre religion à partir de la littérature antiquaire* (Stuttgart: Franz Steiner, 2007).

[31] Jonathan Z. Smith, "The Domestication of Sacrifice," in J. Carter (ed.), *Understanding Religious Sacrifice: A Reader* (London: Continuum, 2003), 325–41, here 332.

animal sacrifice is "a meditation on domestication," a "product of 'civilization.'" It is not to be equated with violence, but rather understood as a *gift* to the gods.

The relationship between sacrifice and violence has long been an active site in the study of religion.[32] *Violence*, of course, tends to be an "outsider" term used to criticize acts committed by *other* people while insiders tend to adopt the language of "justice, a righteous war, martyrdom, heroics, ritual."[33] In the study of religion, this way of speaking about violence is known as "rationalization,"[34] justification, re-description, legitimation, and mythologization.[35] René Girard, a prominent literary critic, cultural anthropologist, and theorist of sacrifice, locates the origins of human violence in "mimetic desire."[36] According to Girard, human beings transfer their desires to surrogates, giving birth to systems of sacrifice, ritual, and religion. Vengeance, or "reciprocal violence,"[37] becomes an act of "unanimous violence,"[38] the murder that lies behind sacrificial practice.[39] The innocent victim's murder establishes peace and sanctifies the victim: human culture is founded on an act of violence. Religion and culture derive from and yet conceal mimetic conflict and violence, the symbolic bloodletting of a community transferring its violence onto an innocent victim or scapegoat. The function of sacrifice is

[32] Chilton, *The Temple of Jesus*; Kathryn McClymond, *Beyond Sacred Violence: A Comparative Study of Sacrifice* (Baltimore: John Hopkins University Press, 2008); Burkert, *Homo Necans*; Girard, *Violence and the Sacred.*

[33] Karel R. Van Kooij, "Iconography of the Battlefield: The Case of Chinnamastā," in Jan E. M. Houben and Karel R. Van Kooij (eds.), *Violence Denied: Violence, Non-Violence and the Rationalization of Violence in South Asian Cultural History* (Leiden: Brill, 1999), 250.

[34] Jonathan Z. Smith, *Imagining Religion: From Babylon to Jonestown* (Chicago University Press, 1982), 62.

[35] Burton L. Mack, "Introduction: Religion and Ritual," in *Violent Origins*, 32–51.

[36] Girard, *Violence and the Sacred*; idem, *Things Hidden since the Foundation of the World* (Stanford University Press, 1987). For an overview of Girard's theory, see Leo D. Lefebure, *Revelation, the Religious, and Violence* (Maryknoll: Orbis, 2000), 20–3, 29–31. For an application of Girard's theory to the Bible, see James G. Williams, *The Bible, Violence, and the Sacred: Liberation from the Myth of Sanctioned Violence* (San Francisco: HarperSanFrancisco, 1991). See also Raymund Schwager, *Must There Be Scapegoats? Violence and Redemption in the Bible* (San Francisco: Harper and Row, 1987); Bradley McLean, "The Absence of an Atoning Sacrifice in Paul's Soteriology," *NTS*, 38 (1992), 531–53.

[37] Girard, *Violence and the Sacred*, 27, 55.

[38] Girard, *Violence and the Sacred*, 85, 93.

[39] Girard, *Violence and the Sacred*, 19, 93.

to transmute violence, but in so far as it selects arbitrary and innocent victims, it is immoral and unjust. Girard identifies Jesus' death
as a classic mythic account of an innocent victim murdered and
commemorated in perpetual ritual reenactment, although in this
particular case Jesus' innocence is said to symbolize the *destruction*
of the sacrificial system altogether because it reveals the foundation of the social order on murder,[40] exposing the powers that uti-
lize violence. According to Girard, therefore, "the sacrificial reading
of Christianity" – and Jesus' death – is a misrepresentation of the
Gospels.[41]

Girard's theory of mimetic desire has been variously applied to
the biblical tradition.[42] Robert G. Hamerton-Kelly applies Girard's
"Generative Mimetic Scapegoating Mechanism" to the Gospel of
Mark.[43] Hamerton-Kelly begins his study with the Temple incident
interpreted as a symbolic attack on the Temple that enacts the end
of sacrifice and rejects the Temple's "sacrificial exclusiveness" and
violence.[44] Jesus becomes the scapegoat who breaks the cycle of violence by subverting the Temple cult-system and inaugurating the
Eucharist,[45] unmasking the violent scapegoat system. Similarly, James
Williams welcomes Girard's work as "the basis for a new Christian
humanism" and attempts to "unveil" the scapegoating mechanism in
the biblical texts which portray God siding with the innocent victim,
thereby revealing "God's will for nonviolent human community."[46]

[40] Girard, *Things Hidden*, 180. Robert Hamerton-Kelly, *Sacred Violence: Paul's Hermeneutic of the Cross* (Minneapolis: Fortress, 1992).

[41] Girard, *The Scapegoat* (trans. Yvonne Frecerro; Baltimore: John Hopkins University Press, 1986), 109. Girard notes a substantial difference between "archaic sacrifices" and the "sacrifice of Christ." See René Girard, *Celui par qui le scandale arrive* (Paris: Desclée de Brouwer, 2001), 76.

[42] See Ann W. Astell and Sandor Goodhart (eds.), "Substitutive Reading: An Introduction to Girardian Thinking, Its Reception in Biblical Studies, and This Volume," in *Sacrifice, Scripture, and Substitution: Readings in Ancient Judaism and Christianity* (CJAS 18; Notre Dame University Press, 2011), 1–36, here 19. For examples of avoidance, see Roger Beckwith and Martin Selman, *Sacrifice in the Bible* (Grand Rapids: Baker Book House, 1995); Gil Bailie, *Violence Unveiled: Humanity at the Crossroads* (New York: Crossroad, 1995), 7. See also Schwager, *Must There Be Scapegoats?*; Andrew J. McKenna, *Violence and Difference: Girard, Derrida, and Deconstruction* (Urbana: University of Illionis Press, 1991).

[43] Robert G. Hamerton-Kelly, *The Gospel and the Sacred: Poetics of Violence in Mark* (Minneapolis: Fortress, 1994).

[44] Hamerton-Kelly, *Gospel and the Sacred*, 17–9.

[45] Hamerton-Kelly, *Gospel and the Sacred*, 44.

[46] Williams, *The Bible, Violence, and the Sacred*, 6, 30.

According to Williams, "The absence of violence in Genesis 1 has endured as a revelatory model of nonviolent creation of the world,"[47] and Israel was "created *through a process of becoming exceptional vis-à-vis the violent structures in the midst of which it came to be*," yet never quite "extricated itself completely from the mythical camouflage of the victimization mechanism."[48] Like Girard, Williams proposes that the Gospels are "the culmination of the Israelite-Jewish tradition of revelation" although here "sacrificial language is used, necessarily, in order to break out of a sacrificial view of the world."[49] Like Hamerton-Kelly, Williams also sees Jesus' Temple incident as "*an attack on the entire sacrificial system.*"[50]

There is no question that mimesis, violence, and scapegoating "mechanisms" are operative in human culture. The origins of sacrifice, however, cannot be explained by grand narratives. Girard's approach has been criticized for its methodological reductionism, oversimplification of human culture, and its facilitation of Christian evolutionary, progressive, and supersessionist readings of the early Jesus tradition.[51] Despite the attraction of a "positive mimesis" based on Jesus' renunciation of violence and the "imitation of Christ,"[52]

[47] Williams, *The Bible, Violence, and the Sacred*, 29.
[48] Williams, *The Bible, Violence, and the Sacred*, 30, 120.
[49] Williams, *The Bible, Violence, and the Sacred*, 224.
[50] Williams, *The Bible, Violence, and the Sacred*, 193.
[51] For criticism, see Richard D. Hecht, "Studies on Sacrifice," *RelSRev*, 8.3 (1982), 253–9, esp. 257–8; Luc de Heusch, *Sacrifice in Africa: A Structuralist Approach*, trans. L. O'Brian and A. Morton (Bloomington: Indiana University Press, 1985), 15–7; Ninian Smart, Review of *Violence and the Sacred*, *RelSRev*, 6.3 (1980), 173–7; Ivan Strenski, *Religion in Relation: Method, Application, and Moral Location* (Columbia: University of South Carolina Press, 1993), 202–16; Chilton, *The Temple of Jesus*, 3–42, 163–80; "René Girard, James Williams, and the Genesis of Violence," *BBR*, 3 (1993), 17–29, esp. 24–5. See also P. Dumouchel (ed.), *Violence and Truth: On the Work of René Girard*, (Stanford University Press, 1988); Hayden White, "Ethnological 'Lie' and Mystical 'Truth,'" *Diacritics*, 8 (1978), 2–9; Luc de Heusch, "L'Evangile selon Saint-Girard," *Le Monde* (25 June 1982): 19; Jean Greisch, "Une anthropologie fondamentale du rite: René Girard," in *Le rite* (Paris: Beauchesne, 1981).
[52] Rebecca Adams proposed a corrective model of "creative mimesis." See "Loving Mimesis and Girard's "Scapegoat of the Text": A Creative Reassessment of Mimetic Desire," in Willard M. Swartley (ed.), *Violence Renounced: René Girard, Biblical Studies, and Peacemaking*, (SPS 4; Telford: Pandora, 2000), 277–307. See also Petra Steinmair-Pösel, "Original Sin, Grace, and Positive Mimesis," *Contagion: Journal of Violence, Mimesis, and Culture*, 14 (2007), 1–12; Pablo Bandera, "Love vs. Resentment: The Absence of Positive Mimesis in Generative Anthropology," *Contagion: Journal of Violence, Mimesis, and Culture*, 14 (2007), 13–26. On positive mimesis, see James G. Williams (ed.), Girard, *The Girard Reader* (trans. Yvonne

and its utility in constructing "peace-oriented" theologies, Girard's readings reinscribe a covert Christian supersessionism in which the revelation of Christ is more read *into* the tradition than deduced *from* historical analysis. Jesus may represent a subversive "revelation" of nonviolent thought and action, but not because he is a scapegoat who somehow exposes and subverts the sacrificial system.

Jonathan Klawans dismisses Girard's mimetic theory as "nothing short of an indictment of sacrificial rituals," a theoretical distortion that posits a crime at the heart of religion, "a collective murder by a frenzied mob of an arbitrarily chosen hapless victim."[53] Klawans calls this "a hybrid Western myth." Moreover, the theory is "thoroughly reductionist," "antiritualist and evolutionist," "distinctively Christian," and "notably supersessionist."[54] Klawans is troubled by the fact that Girard "squarely places much of the blame on Jewish authorities and on the (Jewish) crowd, without entertaining the possibility that post-crucifixion conflicts between Jesus' followers and other Jews may have had an impact on how the passion narratives were constructed."[55] While Klawans's critique may be excessive,[56] he has clearly struck a nerve. It is indeed difficult to imagine how the sacrificial mechanism "was played out in each and every society that has ever existed."[57] Klawans's methodological intervention rejects the quest for the origins of sacrifice as "biased and flawed" because it always requires some form of "evolutionist analysis."[58] He argues that we should rather focus on what the symbolic system of biblical sacrifice "meant" to those who practiced it without looking into either the origins of the cult or its later reinterpretation. Yet in seeking to correct evolutionary and supersessionist interpretations of ancient sacrifice with a "hermeneutic of sympathy," Klawans ultimately undermines "the ideological heterogeneity of the biblical text" itself and disregards its "potential value for re-constructing processes of historical change and social conflict."[59] This has the

Freccero; New York: Crossroad, 1996), 63–4, 269; Vern Neufeld Redekop and Thomas Ryba (eds.), *René Girard and Creative Mimesis* (Lanham: Lexington Books, 2014).

[53] Klawans, *Purity, Sacrifice, and the Temple*, 22, 23.

[54] Klawans, *Purity, Sacrifice, and the Temple*, 24, 24, 25, respectively.

[55] Klawans, *Purity, Sacrifice, and the Temple*, 25.

[56] Goodhart and Astell, "Substitutive Reading," 19, call it "ill-spirited."

[57] Bruce D. Chilton, *Abraham's Curse: The Roots of Violence in Judaism, Christianity, and Islam* (New York: Random House, 2008), 35.

[58] Klawans, *Purity, Sacrifice, and the Temple*, 47.

[59] Ra'anan Boustan, "Review of Jonathan Klawans's *Purity, Sacrifice, and the Temple*," *AJS Review*, 32:1 (2008), 169–219, here 170.

perhaps unintended effect of reinscribing "the highly particular but authoritative perspective articulated in the canonized end product of what were, in fact, messy compositional and historical processes." While the study of ancient Israelite sacrifice is indeed fraught with problematic assumptions and presuppositions, it seems rather odd to privilege the canonical construction of sacrifice. Are we to ignore the historical origins of sacrifice and deny any evidence of development in various sacrificial systems? Is there any way to trace the transformation(s) of sacrifice in Judaism and Christianity over time without succumbing to evolutionary models or supersessionistic theologies?

In *Beyond Sacred Violence*, Kathryn McClymond suggests a comparative approach, arguing that sacrifice, a powerful, "authoritative concept," is "nearly universal in human culture" and "nearly impossible to define."[60] Taking a "polythetic" approach to sacrifice as "a complex matrix of varied and interrelated procedures,"[61] McClymond identifies the "basic activities that characterize sacrificial events," drawing data from the Vedic,[62] brahmanical Hindu, biblical, and Mishnaic Jewish traditions, emphasizing sacrifice as a *process* that includes the *selection, association, identification, killing, apportionment, heating,* and *consumption* of offerings (whether vegetable, incense, liquid, or animal) by ritual participants and/or divine beings. This multi-faceted picture of sacrificial acts illustrates that nonanimal offerings are not simply substitutes for animals and that sacrifice *cannot* be equated with violence or ritual killing.[63] On the contrary, sacrifice is a complex, cross-cultural ritual symbolic language system including violent *and* nonviolent, animal *and* vegetable,

---

[60] McClymond, *Beyond Sacred Violence*, 1. See also Barbara A. Holdrege, *Veda and Torah: Transcending the Textuality of Scripture* (Albany: State University of New York, 1996); Albert I. Baumgarten (ed.), *Sacrifice in Religious Experience* (SHR 93; Leiden: Brill, 2002).

[61] McClymond, *Beyond Sacred Violence*, 2.

[62] On Vedic ritual, see also Brian K. Smith, *Reflections on Resemblance, Ritual and Religion* (Oxford University Press, 1989). On sacrifice (*yajna*), see also Ramesh Chandra Majumdar (ed.), *The History and Culture of the Indian People*, vol. 1: *The Vedic Age* (Mumbai: Bharatiya Vidya Bhavan, 1951); S. Gyanshruti and S. Srividyananda, *Yajna: A Comprehensive Survey* (Munger: Yoga Publications Trust, 2006); F. M. Smith, "Indra Goes West: Report on a Vedic Soma Sacrifice in London," *HR*, 36/3 (2000), 247–67.

[63] Contra Girard, "Mimesis, Sacrifice, and the Bible: A Conversation with Sandor Goodhart," in *Sacrifice, Scripture, & Substitution*, 39–69, here 47: "Violence is essential in sacrifice."

and cultic *and* metaphoric offerings. McClymond's study is a helpful corrective to a pervasive theoretical equation of sacrifice with violence and killing in the literature, but her efforts to rehabilitate the scholarly discussion of sacrifice sometimes downplay the violence inherent in *animal* sacrifice, especially when she denies that "the sacrifice of an animal victim should be interpreted as a violent or even dramatic moment."[64] It is difficult to see how this could possibly ever be true for the animal in question.

The prevailing assumption is that *blood* sacrifice (whether human and/or animal or, as some suspect, of animals as substitutes for humans) is the earliest form of Greek, Egyptian, Vedic, Near Eastern, Israelite, and Native American sacrificial practice, secondarily replaced by liquid or vegetable offerings, with the most recent stage of sacrificial practice being internalized so that one "sacrifices" one's self. This model presupposes that ancient peoples offered various food and gift items to the gods (with the most precious and valuable offering being the gift of a *life*) and secondarily developed polemical, antiritualistic, and antisacrificial readings and interpretations of these traditions. The Eastern ideal of *ahimsā* or "nonviolence," for example, is thought to have developed within the ascetic and renunciation traditions of *post*-Vedic Brahmanism (esp. the Dharma-Sūtras and the Chāndogya-Upanishad), Buddhism, and Jainism.[65]

The earliest historical origins of blood sacrifice may be irrecoverable, but biblical scholars are well aware that ancient Mesopotamian and Near Eastern sacrificial practices influenced the development and concept of ancient Israelite sacrifice.[66] William W. Hallo

---

[64] McClymond, *Beyond Sacred Violence*, 60–1, proposes that since "slaughter was performed publicly," "presumably it was not tremendously traumatic to onlookers."

[65] Henk W. Bodewitz, "Hindu *Ahimsā* and its Roots," in Jan E. M. Houben and Karel R. Van Kooij (eds.), *Violence Denied: Violence, Non-Violence and the Rationalization of Violence in South Asian Cultural History* (BIL 16; Leiden: Brill, 1999), 17–44.

[66] See Gary A. Anderson, *Sacrifices and Offerings in Ancient Israel: Studies in their Social and Political Importance* (HSM 41; Atlanta: Scholars, 1987); David P. Wright, *The Disposal of Impurity: Elimination Rites in the Bible and in Hittite and Mesopotamian Literature* (SBLDS 101; Atlanta: Scholars, 1987); Baruch A. Levine, *In the Presence of the LORD: A Study of the Cult and Some Cultic Terms in Ancient Israel* (SJLA; Leiden: Brill, 1974); Jacob Milgrom, *Cult and Conscience: The Asham and the Priestly Doctrine of Repentance* (Leiden: Brill, 1976); *Studies in Cultic Theology and Terminology* (Leiden: Brill, 1983); Alfred Marx, *Les systèmes sacrificiels de l'Ancien Testament: Formes et fonctions du culte sacrificiel à Yhwh* (VTSup 105; Leiden: Brill, 2005). On a common "temple ideology" in the ancient Near East, see

proposes that Israelite sacrifice originated in imitation of the rituals performed in ancient Mesopotamia, where animal sacrifices served as a means of justifying meat-consumption.[67] Hallo points out that since the spilling of blood was "in some sense an offense against nature," the practice of animal sacrifice was invested with "divine sanction" in order to justify the act.[68] Consequently, biblical attitudes toward meat-consumption underwent "three distinct transformations." In the beginning, "men and beast alike were vegetarians by divine command."[69] After the Flood, this original dispensation was "superseded" by the complete reversal of the original state: now humankind was allowed to eat "every creature that lives" except for "flesh with its life-blood in it."[70] Third, the Holiness code introduced a very different legislation in which blood is now to be used for "making expiation for your lives on the altar" for it is "the blood, as life, that effects expiation."[71] The Levitical code suggests that animal slaughter "*except at the authorized altar* is murder."[72] It is only in the book of Deuteronomy (c. 620 BCE) – with the centralization of the Temple cult under Josiah – that animal slaughter outside of Jerusalem was permitted.[73] For Hallo, the Mesopotamian evidence (especially a mythic epic about Uruk, the biblical Erech [Gen 10:10]),[74] clearly illustrates that in Sumerian and Akkadian myth, human beings were created to "relieve the gods of the need to provide for their own food."[75] Hallo concludes that the Sumerian

---

John M. Lundquist, "The Common Temple Ideology of the Ancient Near East," in T. G. Madsen (ed.), *The Temple in Antiquity: Ancient Records and Modern Perspectives* (Provo: Religious Studies Center, Brigham Young University, 1984), 53–76.

[67] William W. Hallo, "The Origins of the Sacrificial Cult: New Evidence from Mesopotamia and Israel," in Patrick D. Miller Jr., Paul D. Hanson, and S. Dean McBridge (eds.), *Ancient Israelite Religion: Essays in Honor of Frank Moore Cross* (Philadelphia: Fortress, 1987). See also "The Origin of Israelite Sacrifice," *BAR*, 37/6 (Dec. 2011), 59–60, 71.

[68] W. W. Hallo, *The Torah: A Modern Commentary* (New York: Union of American Hebrew Congregations, 1981), 743.

[69] Hallo, "The Origins of the Sacrificial Cult," 5.

[70] Gen 9:3, 4.

[71] Lev 17:11.

[72] Hallo, "The Origins of the Sacrificial Cult," 5, citing Jacob Milgrom, "A Prolegomenon to Leviticus 17:11," *JBL* 90 (1971): 149–56.

[73] Jacob Milgrom, "Profane Slaughter and the Composition of Deuteronomy," *HUCA*, 47 (1976), 1–17; A. R. Hulst, "Opmerkingen over de Ka'aser-Zinnen in Deuteronomium," *NTT*, 18 (1963), 337–61.

[74] See W. W. Hallo, "Lugalbanda Excavated," *JAOS*, 103 (1093), 165–80.

[75] Hallo, "The Origins of the Sacrificial Cult," 7.

deities "physically partake of the best of the meat at a sacred meal con-
voked in their honor" and "sanction the slaughter of the animals that
has made this consumption of their meat possible."[76] Furthermore, the
slaughter is "carried out according to divinely inspired prescriptions,
by a divinely chosen individual." This template functions as "an aetiol-
ogy of meat-eating that explains its origins" as divine and "replacing a
prior, vegetarian order of things."[77] In Genesis, God's original intention
for creation is vegetarian and does *not* include animal sacrifice (Gen 1).
In both the ancient Mesopotamian and biblical traditions, there is an
original vegetarian creation and humanity's role is "domesticating and
cultivating the vegetation."[78] The domestication of animals (for wool,
milk, and sacrifice) may have occurred in the *second* generation with
Abel, but there is no meat-*consumption* until after the Flood. It is not
until the time of Noah that humanity is allowed to eat meat. In the
Sumerian Flood story, Ziusudra emerged from the ark and "slaughtered a large number of bulls and sheep."[79] In the Babylonian epic of
Atra-hasis, the sacrifice is described as an offering (*nīqu*) which the gods
smell. In the *Epic of Gilgamesh*, the sacrifice is burned over cane, cedar-
wood, and myrtle:

> So all set I free to the four winds of heaven, and I poured a
> libation, and scattered a food-offering, on the height of the
> mountain. Seven and seven did I lay the vessels, heaped into
> ther incense-basins sweet-cane, cedarwood and myrtle. And
> the gods smelled the savour, the gods smelled the sweet savour,
> the gods gathered like flies about the priest of the offering.[80]

It is not clear whether the Mesopotamian traditions "linked the inauguration of meat-eating with the immediate aftermath of the flood
as did the Bible."[81] It would seem that Lugalbanda, a member of the
third post-diluvian generation of Uruk represented this new "innova-
tion."[82] While the biblical creation stories and Noah's sacrifice after

[76] Hallo, "The Origins of the Sacrificial Cult," 9.
[77] Hallo, "The Origins of the Sacrificial Cult," 10.
[78] Hallo, "The Origins of the Sacrificial Cult," 10.
[79] Hallo, "The Origins of the Sacrificial Cult," 10, citing *Atra-hasis*, 145 line 211.
[80] Tablet 11, lines 155–61. See J. V. Kinnier Wilson, "The Story of the Flood," in D. Winton Thomas (ed.), *Documents from Old Testament Times* (New York: Harper and Row, 1961), 17–6.
[81] Hallo, "The Origins of the Sacrificial Cult," 10.
[82] W. W. Hallo and W. K. Simpson, *The Ancient Near East: A History* (New York: Harcourt Brace Jovanovich, 1971), 47.

the Flood are clearly modeled on ancient Mesopotamian traditions, they did not develop along similar lines. The Mesopotamian sacrificial cult was understood "as a means of feeding the gods" whereas the Israelite cult ultimately served to "atone for other human transgressions."[83] In both cases, however, blood sacrifice is not envisioned as the original design of creation.

Despite the near-ubiquity of animal sacrifice in antiquity, various voices of dissent were variously registered regarding the efficacy, ethics, and philosophical propriety of blood sacrifice. Today blood sacrifice and Temple rituals seem alien to modern religious sensibilities. Yet animal sacrifice is not solely a primitive vestige of the ancient past, but continues to be practiced in Nepal and Samaria and continues to inform historical and theological interpretations of Jesus' death.[84] Is it even possible to speak of Jesus' death as a sacrifice without presupposing that it served as a blood sacrifice of atonement?

Stephen Finlan has identified six ways in which the language of sacrifice has been (re)interpreted, internalized, and "spiritualized" in different religious systems.[85] The first reinterpretation of sacrificial practice is the (often hypothesized) *replacement* of human sacrifice with animal sacrifice.[86] The second involves investing sacrificial practice with new "*moralizing*" meanings. The third asserts the importance of *inner* preparation in addition to or opposed to the *external* ritual act, emphasizing the internal attitude of prayer and worship using the metaphors, language, and vocabulary of sacrifice to convey inner dispositions.[87] The result of these new emphases can undermine the significance attached to the literal act in favor of its spiritual meaning. Similarly, *metaphorical* interpretations represent a form of rhetorical expertise, employing the vocabulary of sacrifice for nonsacrificial acts and attitudes.[88] These forms of spiritualization

---

[83] Hallo, "The Origins of the Sacrificial Cult," 11.

[84] Stephen Finlan, *Options on Atonement in Christian Thought* (Wilmington: Michael Glazier, 2007), 6.

[85] Stephen Finlan, *Problems with Atonement: The Origins of, and Controversy about, the Atonement Doctrine* (Collegeville: Liturgical Press, 2005), 20–9. On "spiritualization," see Hans Wenschkewitz, *Die Spiritualisierung der Kultusbegriffe: Tempel, Priester und Opfer im Neuen Testament* (AB 4; Leipzig: E. Pfeiffer, 1932).

[86] 1 Kgs. 16:34 relates a story of a man who sacrificed his sons. See also Ps. 50:14; 106:37–40; Jer. 7:30–32; 19:5; 32:35). Levenson, *The Death and Resurrection of the Beloved Son*, 220, 218.

[87] Ps. 141:2; Rom. 2:29; Deut. 10:16.

[88] 1 Cor. 6:19; Phil. 3:3; 2 Cor. 6:16.

can also lead to the redescription of sacrifice as spiritual transformation or renunciation.[89] In addition to the *reinterpretation* and *re-description* of sacrifice, the criticism or *rejection* of sacrifice may also develop from internalizing or metaphorical interpretations.

The rejection of sacrifice can be attributed to a number of factors, including ethics and the rejection of "authority structures," although rejection is often associated with "social change and reform."[90] The rejection of *animal* sacrifice and meat-eating was common among ancient Greek philosophers, including Heraclitus, Empedocles,[91] Theophrastus,[92] Plutarch,[93] Plato,[94] Plotinus, Porphyry,[95] Pythagoras,[96] Apollonius of Tyana,[97] and Orphic initiates.[98] Empedocles rejects

---

[89] Finlan, *Problems*, 27–8, appeals to Rom. 12:1 and the idea of *theosis*, citing 2 Pet. 1:4, Matt. 5:48. Jonathan Klawans suggests "sacrificialization" as an all-encompassing ideology in Second Temple Judaism that inspired Jews to adopt sacrificial language in describing the meaning and purpose of nonsacrificial activities (*Purity*, 171). See also Steven Fine's work on the "templization" of synagogues as a process of *imitatio templi*. Steven Fine, *This Holy Place: On the Sanctity of the Synagogue During the Greco-Roman Period* (University of Notre Dame Press, 1997), 32, 55, 41–55, 79–94, 132–4.

[90] Finlan, *Problems*, 23, citing Mary Douglas, *Natural Symbols: Explorations in Cosmology* (New York: Pantheon, 1982), 52.

[91] Fr. 11 and 124 Inwood = DK 115 and 139.

[92] *On Piety*.

[93] *Precepts for Preserving Health* 131F-132A; *On the Eating of Flesh* 993C-994B; 995D-996A; 996E-997A.

[94] *Republic* 372a-d; *Laws* 781e-783b. Plato criticizes attempts to manipulate the gods by "offerings and prayers" as forms of false flattery or attempts to "persuade" them (*Laws* 10.94C; *Laws* 10.909B). The gods are not hungry, angry, jealous, or interested in animal sacrifice.

[95] *On Abstinence from Killing Animals* (Περὶ ἀποχῆς ἐμψύχων) (c. 270 CE); *On Abstinence from Killing Animals* (trans. G. Clark; Ithaca: Cornell University Press, 2000).

[96] Diogenes Laertius, *Lives of the Philosophers* 8.13; Ovid, *Metamorphoses* 15.75-142. Although see *Vit. Pyth.* 45; Diog. Laert., 8.20.

[97] See Robert J. Penella (ed.), *The Letters of Apollonius of Tyana: A Critical Text with Prolegomena, Translation and Commentary* (Leiden: Brill, 1979), 46–7. See also Philostratus' *Life of Apollonius of Tyana* 1.31.2–1.32.2; 3.41.1; 4.11.1; 5.25.1; 6.4.3; 6.11.3. Apollonius' treatise *On Sacrifices* (Περὶ Θυσίων) is cited by Eusebius (*Praep. Evang.* 4.13.1).

[98] See James W. Thompson, "Hebrews 9 and Hellenistic Concepts of Sacrifice," *JBL*, 98 (1979), 574. See W. K. C. Guthrie, *Orpheus and Greek Religion: A Study of the Orphic Movement* (New York: Norton, 1966), 196. On ancient philosophical vegetarianism, see Johannes Haussleiter, *Der Vegetarismus in der Antike* (RVV 24; Berlin: Alfred Töpelmann, 1935); Daniel A. Dombrowski, *The Philosophy of Vegetarianism* (Amherst: University of Massachusetts Press, 1984).

animal sacrifice based on metempsychosis.[99] According to Porphyry of Tyre, the first sacrifices were plants, wine, and honey: animal sacrifice originated as a result of famine and warfare, a human justification of meat-consumption (2.11.3). Porphyry advocated the pursuit of pure thoughts and "our own uplifting as a holy sacrifice to God" (τὴν αὑτῶν ἀναγωγὴν θυσίαν ἱερὰν προσάγειν τῷ θεῷ) (2.34). Animal sacrifices were "inappropriate to the transcendent philosophical life."[100] Porphyry articulates a critique of animal sacrifice as directed toward intermediary *daimones* (δαίμονες),[101] a tradition paralleled in Paul's criticism of Greco-Roman sacrifice as the "table of demons," and further developed in the Pseudo-Clementine literature.[102] Philostratus refers to Pythagoras as one who "abstained from all food or sacrifices of things that contain a soul" (1.1.1). Pythagoras is reported to have appealed to a "golden age" when human beings ate only plants.[103] In *Fasti*, Ovid suggests that human beings originally sacrificed spelt, salt, and plants. Apollonius tells the priests of Olympia that "The gods do not need sacrifices (θυσιῶν οὐ δέονται)." Apollonius is portrayed as avoiding animal sacrifice, but making other kinds of offerings "of a bloodless and pure kind" (4.11.1, ἀναίμων τε καὶ καθαρῶν).

A common feature of these philosophical critiques is not the rejection of the principle or practice of sacrifice, but a *preference* for nonanimal sacrificial offerings.[104] That is, the practice of sacrifice is affirmed but transformed, a transformation paralleled in certain schools in Hinduism, Buddhism, and Jainism. A second feature is that the impurity of animal sacrifice is *contrasted* with a primordial era *before* animal sacrifice.[105] This is a striking similarity between the Greek philosophical tradition and the biblical tradition of Genesis 1.

---

[99] Diog. Laert. 8.54.

[100] Aaron P. Johnson, *Religion and Identity in Porphyry of Tyre: The Limits of Hellenism in Late Antiquity* (Cambridge University Press, 2013), 123. On Porphyry's theology of sacrifice, see James Rives, "The Theology of Animal Sacrifice in the Ancient Greek World: Origins and Developments," in *Ancient Mediterranean Sacrifice*, 188–197. Cf. Rom 12:1.

[101] Porphyry, *On Abstinence* 2.36–37, 42–43, 49.

[102] On the association of sacrifice with the "table of demons," see 1 Cor. 8:1–13; 10:28–29; Acts 15:29; 21:25; cf. *Hom.* 8.13–19; *Rec.* 1.29; 4.29.

[103] *Metamorphoses* 15.103–106. See also Hesiod, *Theogony*; *Works and Days*.

[104] Rives, "The Theology of Animal Sacrifice," 192, notes the implicit relationship between the refusal to eat meat and the rejection of animal sacrifice in Greek culture, but points out that the rejection of meat need not signify the rejection of the principle or practice of sacrifice.

[105] Ullucci, "Before Animal Sacrifice."

The rejection of sacrifice can now be sub-divided into the follow-ing categories: (1) the rejection of the *idea* of sacrifice; (2) the rejec-tion of *improper* sacrifice (i.e., sacrifices performed with impurity or insincerity); (3) the rejection of impure or corrupt institutions or priesthoods; and (4) the rejection of certain *forms* of sacrificial offer-ings (while retaining the spiritual value of *other* forms of sacrifice). In each case, the "repudiation of tradition" would be "threatening" and potentially alarming to ritual specialists,[106] especially considering the socio-economic, political, and religious factors at play in rejecting the sacrificial system.

The Christian theological tradition remembers Jesus as one who "sac-rificed" himself, renouncing attachment to possessions, family, sex, home, wealth, and even his own life in pursuit of the kingdom of God. The historical Jesus was a first-century Jewish ascetic.[107] The question, however, is how do Jesus' ascetic practices relate to the traditional sac-rificial ideology of the Temple? In a broad sense, *anything* dedicated to the divine can be said to be "sacrificed" in so far as it has been set aside, sanctified, or "made sacred" in divine service. That is why *yogic* tradi-tions could adopt the language of sacrifice, why the (post-70 CE) rab-binical tradition could affirm prayer and Torah study as sacrifice, and why common vernacular appeals to the language of sacrifice exalt those who have dedicated their lives to a higher purpose or calling. Jesus' con-frontation with the Temple was surely a signification of his own "sacri-fice" in the sense that he had dedicated his life to God,[108] but this does *not* mean that he envisioned his life-purpose as a *blood* sacrifice, thought that God needed his blood to forgive Israel, or that his bloody death was somehow a Passover lamb that would protect his followers from God's imminent wrath. It may not be necessary to reject the vocabulary of sacrifice in relationship to Jesus' death altogether, but it will surely not do to collapse and conflate multiple "sacrificial" concepts either.[109]

---

[106] Finlan, *Problems*, 24.

[107] See Simon J. Joseph, "The Ascetic Jesus," *JSHJ*, 8 (2010), 146–81.

[108] Donald Senior, "The Death of Jesus and the Meaning of Discipleship," in J. T. Caroll and J. B. Green (eds.), *The Death of Jesus in Early Christianity* (Peabody: Hendrickson, 1995), 242–5, refers to the "heroic witness" as a central motif in the Gospels. See also David Seeley, *The Noble Death: Graeco-Roman Martyrology and Paul's Concept of Salvation* (JSNTSup 28, Sheffield: JSOT, 1990).

[109] Raymund Schwager, "Christ's Death and the Prophetic Critique of Sacrifice," *Semeia*, 33 (1985), 109–123, maintains that Jesus' death is determined theologically as a "self-offering" in *obedience*, his *identification* with his enemies, and his *intercession* to God (121).

Rather than constructing a kind of normative Judaism in which the legitimacy and necessity of blood sacrifice are taken for granted, we might well imagine a spectrum of attitudes toward blood sacrifice *within* Judaism. Just as modern Judaism contains different denominations, with different attitudes toward blood sacrifice (and the desirability of its future restoration), so too could ancient Jews have registered different attitudes toward the practice, ranging from regarding it as necessary to optional to objectionable, depending on the context.

Given the complexity of the data – the polyvalent language and vocabulary of sacrifice, its obscure origins in prehistoric culture, and its diverse manifestations and expressions even within a single religious tradition – it is imperative that we first pay close attention to what those who actually practiced, criticized, rejected, and transformed sacrificial rites thought and believed about what they were doing before we attempt to re-construct Jesus' own attitude toward the Temple cult.

"An Aroma Pleasing to the LORD" (Num 29:2): Ancient Israelite Sacrifice in the Law and the Prophets

The Israelite sacrificial system was complex and multi-faceted, legislating an entire symbolic system of reparation and re-conciliation between the people and God. The Temple was variously understood either as a symbolic representation of the cosmos,[110] or the earthly counter-part to a heavenly Temple,[111] although here, too, we must be cautious not to assume that the idea of a heavenly or future Temple suggests that the present-day physical Temple was somehow rejected. Moreover, understanding ancient Israelite sacrifice also involves understanding that sacrificial practice involved a number of material items like grains, wine, bread, oil, and incense, as well as first-born, unblemished animals. Critiques of the current Temple's

---

[110] Josephus, *B.J.* 5.212–213, 218; *A.J.* 3.180. Josephus also tells us that God left the sanctuary (*B.J.* 5.412; 6.300; *A.J.* 20.166) as a result of Israel's unethical behavior (*B.J.* 2.539; 5.19; 7.328). See also Philo, *Special Laws* 1.6–67; Raphael Patai, *Man and Temple in Ancient Jewish Myth and Ritual* (London: Thomas Nelson, 1947), 105–17.

[111] For angelic Temple worship, see *1 En.*; *Testament of Levi*; *Songs of the Sabbath Sacrifice*. For heavenly models of a future ideal Temple seen in heavenly journeys or divine revelations, see Philo, *Life of Moses* 2.74–76; Ezek 40–4. For the eschatological new Temple to appear on earth, see *1 En.* 90.28–37; *2 Bar.* 4:1–6; *2 Ezra* 10:25–28; 11QT 29:9–10. See also C. T. R. Hayward, *The Jewish Temple: A Non-Biblical Sourcebook* (London: Routledge, 1996).

administration, legitimacy, corruption, and commercialism need not signify a critique of "sacrifice" *per se*, let alone a critique of the Temple as an institution or site of religious ritual and communion. Sacrifice is not "inherently violent."[112] The sacrificial system involved complex processes of ritual purification and preparation designed to attract and maintain "the presence of God within the community" as well as avoid and correct ritual and moral impurity.[113] Sacrifices attract God; sin repels God.[114] Sacrifice is not just corrective, but *creates* relationship, and was practiced as a way of attracting and maintaining the divine presence in Israel.[115] This concern for maintaining boundaries and ritual purity lies behind the Temple Warning inscriptions forbidding Gentiles to enter the holy areas on penalty of death:

> No foreigner may enter *within the balustrade around the sanctuary and the enclosure* (ἐντὸς τοῦ περὶ τὸ ἱερὸν τρυφάκτου καὶ περιβόλου). Whoever is caught doing so will have himself to blame for his death which will follow.[116]

The problem with Israel's acts of moral impurity was that God may not continue to abide in the Temple as a result of this ethical defilement.[117] Ritual impurity could be contracted via various natural processes including childbirth, skin disease, fungus, genital discharges, and corpses.[118] Moral impurity could arise from unethical acts like sexual sin, idolatry, and murder.[119] Acts of moral impurity defile

---

[112] Klawans, *Purity, Sacrifice, and the Temple* 9; McClymond, *Beyond Sacred Violence*.

[113] Klawans, *Purity, Sacrifice, and the Temple*, 53. See also Smith, "The Domestication of Sacrifice," 191–205.

[114] On the daily sacrifices, see Exod. 29:38–45; Num 28:3–8.

[115] Klawans, *Purity, Sacrifice, and the Temple*, 68. See Exod. 25:8; 40:35; 29:41, 42–46. On attraction, see Levine, *In the Presence of the Lord*, 22–27; "On the Presence of God in Biblical Religion," in J. Neusner (ed.), *Religions in Antiquity: Essays in Memory of Erwin Ramsdell Goodenough*, (Leiden: Brill, 1968), 71–87, here 79–80.

[116] Peretz Segal, "The Penalty of the Warning Inscription from the Temple in Jerusalem," *IEJ*, 39.1/2 (1989), 79–84; Elias J. Bickerman, "The Warning Inscriptions of Herod's Temple," *JQR*, 37.4 (1947), 387–405. The Mishnah reports the Aramaic inscriptions on the shekel trumpets (תקלין עתיקין and תקלין חדתין) (*m. Sheq* 6.5).

[117] Num 35:30–34; Ezek 8–11.

[118] On *ritual* impurity, see Lev 11–15; Num 19. On contracting ritual impurity from childbirth, see Lev 12:1–8; from skin diseases, see Lev 13:1–46; 14:1–32; from fungus, see Lev 13:47–59; 14:33–53; from genital discharges, see Lev 15:1–33; from dead animals, see Lev 11:1–47; from dead human beings, see Num 19:10–22.

[119] Lev 18:24–30; 19:31; 20:1–3; and Num 35:33–34, respectively.

the one who commits them,[120] the land,[121] and the Temple.[122] The sacrifices offered by the morally impure are "abominations,"[123] not only because they defile the sanctuary, but also because the fate of Israel depended on the moral behavior of those performing sacrifices and officiating at the Temple. If the priesthood was corrupt, then the sacrifices offered in the Temple were invalid, and there could be no genuine atonement or re-conciliation between Israel and God. Moral impurity may not be contagious, but its effects could not be removed by purification rites, only by punishment or atonement. It follows that although *ritual* purification is a pre-requisite to entering the Temple, one may be in a state of *moral* impurity and still engage in Temple worship. Contrary to popular assumptions, therefore, ancient Israelite sacrifice was not exclusively focused on atonement, but served a variety of purposes including atonement, thanksgiving, prayer, and purification. It would be helpful, therefore, to review the complex range of sacrifices prescribed in the Torah, especially as sacrifices fulfilled a number of different functions and only *some* sacrifices had atoning value.[124]

The "burnt offering" (עלה) removes guilt generated by the neglect of the law. An animal is burnt entirely on the altar as a gift to God. The "burnt offering" or offerings (קרבנות עולה) (literally, "that which goes up") involved the death of an animal and its shed blood substituting for the one offering the sacrifice.[125] Here the laying-on of hands on the victim implies a substitution, signifying the identity and ownership of the one making the offering and wiping the sin of the sinner away by transference. The contraction of sin required purification and the use of an unblemished animal was needed. The animal was identified with the sinner by the laying on of hands and its blood was poured out on the altar, "covering" or making "atonement" for the sin. It was the life-power of the blood, not the suffering or death of the animal, that provided atonement and purification.

[120] Lev 18:24.

[121] Lev 18:25; Ezek 36:17.

[122] Lev 20:3; Ezek 5:11.

[123] Prov 15:8; 21:27.

[124] For the variety of sacrificial rituals, see Ronald S. Hendel, "Sacrifice as a Cultural System: The Ritual Symbolism of Exodus 24, 3–8," *ZAW*, 101 (1989), 366–90. See esp. B. H. McLean, *The Cursed Christ: Mediterranean Expulsion Rituals and Pauline Soteriology* (JSNTSup 126; Sheffield Academic Press, 1996), 27–42. But see Noam Zohar, "Repentance and Purification: The Significance and Semantics of חטאת in the Pentateuch," *JBL*, 107 (1988), 609–18.

[125] Num 28:3; Lev 1:11; 17:11.

The purification (or transgression) offering (חטאת) was designed to atone for sins and purify the Temple of ceremonial uncleanness (Lev 4:2–23) and from unintentional sins committed through carelessness (Lev 4:1–5:13; 6:1–7, 17–23; Num 15:22–29).[126] This offering cannot atone for *intentional* violations of the law. This offering can be offered on behalf of the community as a whole or for individuals. The most important community offering on the Day of Atonement (*Yom Kippur*) provided a means of atonement for the entire nation.[127] Leviticus 16:5 legislates how two goats were required for this ritual purification of sin and explicitly associates the animals with atonement (Num 29:11). One goat was slaughtered and its blood was sprinkled in the center of the ark of the covenant; the other was driven out of the camp (Num 5:1–3). Both the blood ritual and the scapegoat had atoning value (Lev 16:9–10, 16, 21).[128] The goat (not a lamb) became the bearer of sins and was led out of the city into the wilderness; the peoples' sins were transferred to the scapegoat.

The guilt or reparation offering (אשם) also provided atonement (Lev 5:16, 18; Num 5:8) in that the person sought forgiveness of wrongdoing, but this type of offering was used for financial compensation, restitution, or payments in cases of theft, debt, and fraud, although it could also be associated with unintended sin.[129]

This offering involves an animal (Lev 5:1–19; 7:1–7). Whereas the חטאת is offered in response to an unintentional sin, the אשם is performed when a person feels guilt over a past sin. It is also strictly for individuals, not for the community.

The peace (or "well-being") offering (שלם), or peace offerings (זבח שלמים), were not explicitly atoning.[130] These include the thanksgiving or freewill offering (Lev 7:11–21), the wave offering, and the

---

[126] Jacob Milgrom, "Sin Offering or Purification Offering?" *VT*, 21 (1971), 237–9; Gordon J. Wenham, *The Book of Leviticus* (NICOT; Grand Rapids: Eerdmans, 1979), 88–9; J. W. Rogerson, "Sacrifice in the Old Testament: Problems of Method and Approach," in M. F. C. Bourdillon and Meyer Fortes (eds.), *Sacrifice* (London: Academic Press, 1980), 53.

[127] Lev 16:30, 34.

[128] N. Kiuchi, *The Purification Offering in the Priestly Literature: Its Meaning and Function* (Sheffield Academic Press, 1987), 143–59.

[129] Lev 5:15, 17. On sin and guilt offerings, see Levine, *In the Presence*, 91–92, 98–99, 109–10.

[130] Milgrom, "A Prolegomenon to Leviticus 17:11," 149–56. Although see Wenham, "Theology," 82; Rogerson, "Sacrifice," 53.

offering made in fulfillment of a vow. These also involved an animal offering. In this offering, the animal flesh is eaten by those who sacrifice. It is more a gift or expression of thanks to God.

The grain offering, or the food and drink offering (מנחה), devoted human labor to God (Lev 2, 6:14–18), and included cereals and grains – either as substitutes for an animal offering or as integral components of the מנחה rites.

In addition to these sacrificial rites, the festival of Passover was also associated with sacrificial imagery and ideology.[131] A year-old male lamb was slain and its meat was roasted over a fire and consumed.[132] The blood was smeared on the door-frames of the house to ward off the spirit of death.[133] The sacrifice of the lamb served as a sign of protection from the wrath of God as well as a sign of God's liberating power – the spirit of death would "pass over" that particular house – but the Passover sacrifice did not have atoning value.[134] The Passover lamb is slain, but not as a sacrifice in atonement for the peoples' sins.

Blood sacrifice was not always associated with the forgiveness of sins nor was blood sacrifice the *only* means for obtaining atonement available to Israelites.[135] Repentance, suffering, good deeds, and death also had atoning value.[136] This complexity of the Temple cult and its detailed priestly legislation and administration created and required a sophisticated and elaborate socio-economic infrastructure susceptible to corruption and frequently subject to criticism.

Despite the central role of sacrificial legislation in the Torah, the prophetic corpus contains numerous critiques of improper participation in the cultic system. These critiques have sometimes been interpreted to suggest that sacrifice itself is rejected.[137] According

[131] Exod 12:27.
[132] Exod 12:5; 29:1; Lev 1:3, 10; 3:1, 6–7; 9:3; 12:8–10.
[133] Exod 12:7, 13, 22–23.
[134] McLean, *Cursed Christ*, 34–5.
[135] Contra Heb 9:22. The blood atonement passage in Lev 17:11 is not specifically about "atonement," but rather the dietary laws: Israelites are not allowed to eat blood (17:10).
[136] On the need for repentance *and* sacrifice, see Ben Sira 7:8–9; 34:18–20. On repentance alone as atoning, see 5:5–7a; 17:24–26, 29; 18:20. On suffering as atoning, see Pss. Sol. 3:8–10; 10:1; 13:9; 1QS 8.3–4; 1QpHab 5.3–6. On the atoning value of death, see *m. Yoma* 8.8, *Sipre Num.* 5; *m. Sanh.* 6.2; *t. Sanh.* 9.5; *Sipre Num.* 112;
[137] Finlan, *Problems*, 24, differentiates between *critical* and *radical* sayings; the former simply prioritize the value of ethics over ritual, the latter openly attack the

to James G. Williams, for example, the prophetic corpus contains "a polemic against sacrifice and violence," implying that violence is "not the ultimate means by which God desires that Israel renew its common life." Rather, "God's will is that Israel eventually become disengaged from sacrifice." For Williams, "a nonsacrificial reading unmasks the structures of cultic violence in Israel's history and discloses the witness to the God who desires love and justice rather than sacrifice."[138] This reading challenges normative interpretations that affirm divine "regeneration through violence and sacrifice" and contends that "there was a nonsacrificial element of faith and vision" articulated by the prophets who "subverted the primitive, universal foundations of religion and culture that continued to determine Israelite institutions."[139] Can this (Girardian) view of prophetic critique be sustained?[140] It is true that some passages do criticize corruption, impurity, and hypocrisy, but each passage must be examined independently in its original literary, socio-historical, and theological context(s) before passing judgment on any alleged "prophetic criticism of sacrifice."

In 1 Samuel, for example, the author criticizes Saul by contrasting sacrifice and obedience, but this is by no means a *rejection* of sacrifice:

> Has the Lord as great delight in burnt offerings and sacrifices as in obeying the voice of the Lord? Surely to obey is better than sacrifice, and to heed than the fat of rams.[141]

Similarly, Amos compares and contrasts burnt offerings, festivals, and assemblies with the higher ethical requirements of "justice" and "righteousness":

> I hate, I despise your festivals, and I take no delight in your solemn assemblies. Even though you offer me your burnt

practice of sacrifice, citing Ps. 50:12–13; Ps. 40:6; Amos 5:21; Hos. 6:6; and Mic. 6:6–7; Isa 66:3.

138 James G. Williams, "Steadfast Love and Not Sacrifice," in Mark I. Wallace and Theophilus H. Smith (eds.), *Curing Violence* (FF 3; Sonoma: Polebridge, 1994), 71–99, here 71.

139 Williams, "Steadfast Love and Not Sacrifice," 72, 82, 85.

140 See Göran Eidevall, "The Role of Sacrificial Language in Prophetic Rhetoric," in C. Eberhart (ed.), *Ritual and Metaphor: Sacrifice in the Bible* (RBS 68; Atlanta: Society of Biblical Literature, 2011), 49–61.

141 1 Sam 15:22–23.

offerings and grain offerings, I will not accept them … but let justice roll down like waters, and righteousness like an everflowing stream.[142]

Amos 5:25 also seems to deny that Israel performed animal sacrifice before the conquest, suggesting that Israel had misunderstood its divine calling and that God did not command the performance of sacrifices in the wilderness. Israel's call was to perform "justice" and "righteousness" (5:24):

> Did you bring to me sacrifices and offerings the forty years in the wilderness?

Here Amos does seem to undermine the validity of the sacrificial cult.[143] The eighth-century prophet Hosea also appears to negate the value of sacrifice in favor of mercy and the knowledge of God, but this may be prophetic hyperbole:[144]

> For I will have mercy rather than sacrifice, and the knowledge of God *rather than* whole-burnt offerings. (Διότι ἔλεος θέλω ἢ θυσιαν, καὶ ἐπίγνωσιν Θεοῦ ἢ ὁλοκαυτώματα).[145]

Like Amos, Hosea also implies that God did not command or legislate a sacrificial cult; moreover, God did not *want* sacrifice, but rather "steadfast love" and "knowledge" (6:6). Isaiah also seems to criticize sacrifice as an inadequate substitute for ethical righteousness and social justice:

> What to me is the multitude of your sacrifices?
>
> Says the Lord: I have had enough of burnt offerings of rams and the fat of fed beasts; I do not delight in the blood of bulls, or of lambs, or of goats.[146]
>   What is the house that you would build for me, and what is my resting place? … But this is the one to whom I will look, to the humble and contrite in spirit, who trembles at

[142] Amos 5:21–24.
[143] Finlan, *Problems*, 26.
[144] Klawans, *Purity, Sacrifice, and the Temple*, 80.
[145] Hos 6:7.
[146] Isa 1:11.

my word. Whoever slaughters an ox is like one who kills a
human being.[147]

Isaiah criticizes "vain offerings," denies that God enjoys "the blood of
bulls," and criticizes those who have hands "full of blood" (1:16–17).
Moreover, Isaiah envisions the messianic age as one of peace and
Edenic vegetarianism (2:4). It seems unlikely that animal/blood sacrifice is part of this messianic vision.

The seventh-century prophet Jeremiah contrasts the uselessness of
burnt offerings in light of Israel's disobedience:

> because they have not given heed to my words ... Your burnt
> offerings are not acceptable, nor are your sacrifices pleasing
> to me.[148]

Like Amos and Hosea, Jeremiah also suggests that Israel was never
commanded to offer sacrifices:

> in the day that I brought your ancestors out of the land of
> Egypt, *I did not speak to them or command them concerning
> burnt offerings and sacrifices.*[149]

Jeremiah clearly implies that God did *not* require sacrifices when
he led her out of Egypt and into the wilderness. At the same time,
Jeremiah also suggests that there will be neither Temple nor the Ark
of the Covenant in the future because God will create a "new covenant" different from the previous one.[150] Jeremiah lived prior to the
Babylonian destruction of the Temple and is known for delivering
a "Temple sermon" (7:1–15; 26:1–24) in which he proclaims divine
judgment, condemning the Temple as a "den of robbers" (7:11). His
call to repentance criticized the view that the Temple was itself an
insurance policy against foreign destruction (as in Ps 46; 48) and predicted that Zion would be destroyed for the peoples' sins (7:14; 26:6).
Jeremiah's criticism, therefore, should not be read so as to imply that
God rejects sacrifices *per se*, but rather that Israel cannot take the
Temple for granted as Israel's special relationship with God is being

---

[147] Isa 66:1–4.
[148] Jer 6:19–20.
[149] Jer 7:21–22. Cf. Amos 5:22–25.
[150] Jer 31:33b-34. Williams, *The Bible, Violence, and the Sacred,* 161: "Jeremiah
envisioned a new covenant and a new Torah that would be present and real in Israel
apart from the sacrificial cult."

compromised and jeopardized by sin (7:9). It is in this context that Jeremiah predicts God making "a new covenant with the house of Israel, and with the house of Judah," one that would be "written on their hearts" (Jer 31:31–33).

Like Jeremiah, the prophet Ezekiel also foresaw the destruction of Jerusalem:

> because they had not executed my ordinances, but had rejected my statutes and profaned my sabbaths, and their eyes were set on their ancestors' idols. Moreover, I gave them statutes that were not good and ordinances by which they could not live. I defiled them through their very gifts, in their offering up all their firstborn in order that I might horrify them, so that they might know that I am the Lord.[151]

While Ezekiel catalogs Israel's "abominable" sins of idolatry (8:9–18), bloodshed (11:6–7), and sexual transgression (22:10) – acts that defiled the Temple (5:11) and the land (36:17), leading to the departure of God's "glory" (8:6, 11:22–23) and the exile of the people from the land (11:9–10) – Ezekiel also envisioned a new, rebuilt Temple and restored sacrificial worship (40–48). Ezekiel's new Temple requires stricter regulations than those found in the Torah (44:25–27; cf. Num 19:10–13), including the size of the gates surrounding the Temple (40:20–23), access to the altar (44:15–16; cf. Exod 40:29), and the ban on foreigners entering or bringing offerings to the sanctuary in a highly idealized vision of Temple administration.[152] Like Amos, Hosea, and Jeremiah, Ezekiel also comments on the wilderness period of Israel:

> I gave them statutes that were not good and ordinances by which they could not live (20:25).

According to Ezekiel, the sacrificial cult's statutes were "not good." Ezekiel *seems* to envision the sacrificial cult as a temporary concession to Israel's sin:

> that I might horrify them, so that they might know that I am the LORD (20:26).

---

[151] Ezek 20:24–26.
[152] Ezek. 44:6–9; cf. Lev 17:8; Num 15:14–16, 27–29.

While the prophetic witnesses often affirm that prayer, justice, righteousness, humility, faithfulness, mercy, and love please God *more*
than sacrifice, it is also the case that certain prophets emphasize
the *pre*-sacrificial wilderness period and the *post*-sacrificial eschatological era as idealized states in which God's will was (and will
be) more properly followed. Isaiah and Micah envision a future in
which people will turn their swords into plowshares and come to
worship the Lord at the Temple in Jerusalem,[153] but it is not clear
whether these prophets envision the continuation of the Temple
cult. Despite the fact that the prophets do not provide any coherent
let alone systematic rejection of blood sacrifice, it is striking that
some passages do *appear* to reject priestly rituals and that some
prophets articulated *occasional* oppositions to sacrificial practices,
especially when they sought to emphasize the priority of social justice over sacrificial ritual.[154]

The earliest Jewish apocalyptic tradition – the Enochic *Book of
the Watchers* – is also sometimes thought to represent "a dim view
of the Jerusalem temple and its cult."[155] It is not entirely clear that
this is the case, however, as there is no explicit evidence of a critique
of the Jerusalem Temple. Moreover, the *Book of Enoch*, despite its
composition between the early third century and late second century
BCE, is set in the antediluvian age, that is, before the construction of
the Temple. Nonetheless, the *Animal Apocalypse*, written c. 165 BCE,
clearly envisions a "New Jerusalem" and the eschatological restoration of its "house" in conjunction with the conversion of the Gentiles
(90.30), the end of war (90.34), and the birth or appearance of a new
Adam in the form of a "white bull":

> Then I stood up to watch as he folded up that old house.
> And all the columns were removed, and every beam and
> ornament of that house was folded up along with it. It was
> then taken out and deposited in a certain place in the south-
> ern part of the land. I watched until the Lord of the flock
> brought out a new house, greater and loftier than that first
> one, and he set it up on the site of the former one which had
> been rolled up. All its columns were new, its beams new, and
> its ornaments new and larger than those of the first – the

---

[153] Isa 2:1–4; Mic 4:1–5.
[154] Amos 5:23 and 5:10–11; Isa 1:11–15, and 1:17; Jer 6:20 and 6:13.
[155] Nickelsburg, *1 Enoch 1*, 54–5; Himmelfarb, *Ascent to Heaven*, 20–3, here 22.

old one which had been removed. And all of the flock was within it.[156]

Daniel Olson argues that *An. Apoc.* portrays "the ruin of this system" as "absolute. The Second Temple is declared invalid from the beginning (89:73), and the allegory offers no indication that it will ever be reformed or restored, even in the Eschaton … the allegory does not seem to anticipate any cult or temple *at all* in the age to come," although there continues to be debate about whether the allegory's use of the word בית refers solely to the city or includes the Temple.[157] Despite the ambiguity of the *An. Apoc.*, written in the heat of the Maccabean revolt, its author certainly sees a glorious future for Israel and Jerusalem.

The Community as Temple: Qumran, the Essenes, and the Dead Sea Scrolls

The Qumran corpus contains many texts illustrating the community's alienation from the Temple.[158] Whether the origins of the community are to be found in a rival high priest, a group of disaffected Zadokite priests, or a larger multi-regional Essenic movement of both lay and priestly members, the evidence suggests that relationship(s) between the Qumran community, the Essenes, and the Jerusalem Temple establishment and administration were never resolved.

---

[156] *An. Apoc.* 90.28–29. Translation from Daniel C. Olson, *A New Reading of the Animal Apocalypse of 1 Enoch: "All Nations Shall Be Blessed": With A New Translation and Commentary* (SVTP 24; Leiden: Brill, 2013), 225.

[157] Olson, *A New Reading*, 59.

[158] See Lawrence H. Schiffman, "Community without Temple: The Qumran Community's Withdrawal from the Jerusalem Temple," in B. Ego, et al. (eds.), *Gemeinde ohne Tempel-Community without Temple: Zur Substituierung und Transformation des Jerusalemer Tempels und seines Kultes im Alten Testament, antiken Judentum und frühen Christentum* (WUNT 118; Tübingen: Mohr Siebeck, 1999), 267–84; Joseph M. Baumgarten, "Sacrifice and Worship among the Jewish Sectarians of the Dead (Qumran) Scrolls," *HTR*, 46.3 (1953), 141–159; "The Essenes and the Temple: A Reappraisal," in *Studies in Qumran Law* (Leiden: Brill, 1977), 59–62. For secondary texts, see 4QApocryphon of Jeremiah C(e) (or 4Qpseudo-Moses(e)), 4Q390 fr. 2, 1.9; CD 6.11–17; CD B 20.22–23. On priesthood at Qumran, see also Joseph L. Angel, *Otherworldly and Eschatological Priesthood in the Dead Sea Scrolls* (STDJ 86; Leiden: Brill, 2010).

According to the *Temple Scroll*, bribery seems to have been a major concern:

> For the bribe twists judgement, overturns the works of justice, blinds the eyes of the wise, produces great guilt, and profanes the house by the iniquity of sin.[159]

In the *Damascus Document*, priestly sexual impropriety was also a problem:

> they profane the Temple because they do not observe the distinction (between clean and unclean) in accordance with the Law.[160]

The *Pesher Habakkuk* reflects on the many moral failures of the Wicked Priest:

> when he ruled over Israel his heart became proud, and he forsook God and betrayed the precepts for the sake of riches. He robbed and amassed the riches of the men of violence who rebelled against God, and he took the wealth of the peoples, heaping sinful iniquity upon himself. And he lived in the ways of abominations admist every unclean defilement.
> *the city* is Jerusalem where the Wicked Priest committed abominable acts and defiled the Temple of God.[161]

The Wicked Priest became arrogant, stole the wealth of the poor, and defiled the Temple through wicked deeds, sin, theft, and greed. Other texts paint a similar picture of the Temple. The book of *Jubilees* describes how

> A future generation will lift themselves up for deceit and wealth so that one shall take everything of his neighbor; and they will pronounce the great name, but not in truth or righteousness. And they will pollute the holy of holies with their pollution.[162]

---

[159] 11QT 51.11–15. Vermes, *The Complete Dead Sea Scrolls*, 209.

[160] CD 5.6–9. Vermes, *The Complete Dead Sea Scrolls*, 131.

[161] 1QpHab 8.10; 1QpHab 12.8–10. Vermes, *The Complete Dead Sea Scrolls*, 482, 484.

[162] *Jub* 23.21. For the Qumran fragments of *Jubilees*, see J. C. VanderKam and J. T. Milik (eds.), *DJD XIII* (Oxford: Clarendon), 1–185.

The Qumran community withdrew from the Temple because it was ethically corrupt and ritually deficient.[163] 11QT provides detailed instructions for how the new Temple is to be operated (45.7–51.10), implying that the ritually impure were currently allowed to enter its precincts and legislates purity laws even stricter than the Torah (cf. 45.7–10; Lev 15:16; Deut 23:10–11). The current Temple administration was not following proper ritual protocol and procedure.[164] The high priest was illegitimate and the correct calendar was not being used. Purification procedures were inadequate, especially the red heifer rite (Num 19) and ritual impurity was being contracted due to too close proximity to the Temple.[165] The Qumran community abandoned the ethically and ritually impure Temple and regarded their community as a substitute, transforming the idea of Temple worship so that the community itself *substituted* for the sacrificial cult.[166] The law could be fulfilled not simply in ritual but in one's purified heart and mind.[167] It would be their prayers, their righteous deeds,

---

[163] On its ritual inadequacy, see the prohibition of leaving cereal offerings overnight (4QMMT B 9–13; 11QT 20.12–13); and the requirement that fourth-year produce and tithes be given to the priests (4QMMT B 62–64). Other issues involve the "solar" calendar followed by 4QMMT, 11QT, and the Songs of the Sabbath Sacrifice. On its structural inadequacy, the *New Jerusalem* texts anticipate a new Temple (1Q32, 2Q24, 4Q554–555, 5Q15, 11Q18) – a city with a golden wall (11Q18, fr. 10), jeweled buildings (4Q554, fr. 2, II.15), streets paved in white stone, alabaster, and onyx (5Q15 fr. 1, I.6–7), and a radiant Temple (2Q24 fr. 3; fr. 8). The Temple Scroll also envisions a new expanded Temple that will last until God constructs his own sanctuary (29.9–10).

[164] Menahem Kister, "Studies in 4Miqsat Ma'aseh ha-Torah and Related Texts: Law, Theology, Language and Calendar," *Tarbiz*, 68.3 (1999), 317–72; Eyal Regev, "Abominated Temple and a Holy Community: The Formation of the Notions of Purity and Impurity in Qumran," *DSD*, 10/2 (2003), 245–9. Regarding the Red Heifer, 4QMMT B13–17, and 4Q277 1 emphasize that those involved with its preparation are ritually impure until evening (cf. *m. Parah* 3.7).

[165] 11QT XLV.11–12 bans men defiled by semen from the *city*, not just the Temple; in CD 12.1–2, sexual relations must not take place in the city.

[166] 1QS 5.6, 8.3, 9.4. On the community as complementary and analogous to, but not necessarily a *permanent* replacement of the Jerusalem Temple, see D. Dimant, "4QFlorilegium and the Idea of the Community as Temple," in A. Caquot (ed.) *Hellenica et Judaica. Festschrift V. Nikiprowetzky* (Leuven: Peeters, 1986), 165-89, here 187. Similarly, as equivalent and competitive to the Temple, see A. Steudel, "The Houses of Prostration: CD XI 21-XII 1 – Duplicates of the Temple," *RevQ*, 16 (1993), 49-68, here 56-7, 62-5.

[167] See L. H. Schiffman, *Reclaiming the Dead Sea Scrolls: The History of Judaism, the Background of Christianity, the Lost Library of Qumran* (Philadelphia: Jewish Publication Society, 1994), 299.

and inspired exegesis that would now suffice as the true "sacred offerings" that would atone for Israel:

> "the Council of the Community shall be established in truth. It shall be an Everlasting Plantation, a House of Holiness for Israel (בית קודש לישראל), an Assembly of Supreme Holiness for Aaron ... who shall atone for the Land ... It shall be a Most Holy Dwelling for Aaron, with everlasting knowledge of the Covenant of justice, and shall offer up sweet fragrance. It shall be a House of Perfection and Truth ... And they shall be an agreeable offering, atoning for the Land."[168]

The *Community Rule* explicitly states that there will be *no* animal sacrifices:

> "they shall establish the spirit of holiness (רוח קודש) according to everlasting truth. They shall atone for guilty rebellion and for sins of unfaithfullness, that they may obtain loving-kindness for the Land *without the flesh of holocausts and the fat of sacrifice*. And prayer rightly offered shall be as an acceptable fragrance of righteousness, and perfection of way as an acceptable free-will offering."[169]

1QS 9.3–6 states that "offerings of the lips" (תרומת שפתים) and the "perfection of way" (תמים דרך) are kin to a "fragrance of righteousness" (ניחוח צדק) and "an acceptable freewill offering" (מנחת רצון) in place of the flesh of burnt-offerings and the fat of sacrifice.[170] Similarly, 4QFlorilegium 1–2 I, 6–7 envisions a "Temple of Adam" in which the "smoke of incense" (מקטירים) and the "works of thanksgiving" (מעשי תודה) may be sent up instead of sacrifices.[171]

Whether or not the Qumran community saw its alternative means of atonement as a temporary or permanent replacement for an ethically and ritually corrupt Temple,[172] they do seem to have replaced

---

[168] 1QS 8.5–12. Vermes, *The Complete Dead Sea Scrolls*, 109.

[169] 1QS 9.1–5. Vermes, *The Complete Dead Sea Scrolls*, 110.

[170] Knibb, *The Qumran Community*, 138–9.

[171] The reading of מעשי תורה ("acts of Torah") has been suggested by J. Milgrom, *Pesharim, Other Commentaries, and Related Documents* (PTSDSSP 6B; Louisville: Westminster John Knox, 2002), 248.

[172] Klawans, *Purity, Sacrifice, and the Temple*, 163, favors the former.

animal sacrifice with prayer and "perfection of way." There is an ongoing debate whether the Qumran community stopped performing animal sacrifices altogether or whether they built their own altar and performed animal sacrifice within their community.[173] While animal bones were found at the Qumran site, and several Qumran texts do seem to presuppose sacrifice,[174] there is no compelling evidence that the Qumran community ever practiced animal sacrifice.[175] The incense altar discovered there is too small for communal worship and the bone burials are not evidence of any known form of sacrificial practice. The Qumran corpus undoubtedly represents different stages in the community's development, but their nonparticipation in Temple worship seems to have begun in the mid-second century BCE and included "rewriting" the Torah to suit their sectarian interests, redefining Temple practice through their own ethical and ritual practices, and re-imagining themselves as the place where atonement was being offered "for Israel."

The Temple was ritually and morally impure and the sacrifices being offered there were invalid. This would result in destruction, exile, and the departure of the divine presence. *Jubilees* 23.22 asserts that the generation that defiles the Temple will be oppressed, exiled, and destroyed. *T. Levi* 14.5–15.1 asserts that the wages of sin will be the desolation of the Temple. The Qumran community seems to have *abandoned* the Temple (CD 20.22) in expectation of its divine judgment, yet continued to worship God through prayer, common meals, and purification, rather than focusing on the ritual laws of the Temple. The community transformed the ideal of Temple worship through creating alternative Temple services in which the community itself was the Temple. 4Q174 explicitly identifies the community as a "Temple of Adam" (מקדש אדם).[176] There is

---

[173] Cross, *Ancient Library*, 85–6; Humbert, "L'espace Sacre a Qumran," 184–91, 199–201. But see Magness, *Archaeology of Qumran*, 105–32.

[174] 11QTemple and 1/4QM describe burnt offerings; CD 4.2 presupposes sacrifice. It is possible that the Qumran community envisioned a future Temple with burnt offerings. See 1QM 2.4–6; 4Q171 3.10–11; 11QT 29.10; 11Q18, frag. 13, 4; 16–17 II/1:1–5). The *War Scroll* imagines future priests administering burnt offerings and other sacrifices in the Temple (1QM 2.4–6; 7.10–11). The Temple Scroll speaks of a future Temple (29.10) and the New Jerusalem texts imagine a future rebuilt Temple (11Q18, fr. 13, 4; fr. 16–17 II/I.1–5).

[175] Klawans, *Purity, Sacrifice, and the Temple*, 162.

[176] Bertil Gärtner, *The Temple and the Community in: Qumran and the New Testament: A Comparative Study in the Temple Symbolism of the Qumran Texts and*

an ongoing debate whether מקדש אדם refers to a sanctuary "among the people" or a kind of "Adamic sanctuary of Eden restored,"[177] a new "holy place that will signify the fulfillment of God's original creation,"[178] but there is no doubt that the community saw itself as inheriting the eschatological "glory of Adam" (אדם כבוד).[179] The community's ethical and ritual acts were envisioned as an effective alternative to the illegitimate atonement offered in Jerusalem.

The Essenes also seem to have withdrawn from participating in the sacrificial system. Josephus' account of the Essenes' worship is ambiguous,[180] and has been interpreted both to mean that the Essenes declined to take part in Temple sacrifices *and* that they offered their own sacrifices apart from other Jews.[181]

---

the New Testament (Cambridge University Press, 1965), 30–42; Knibb, *The Qumran Community*, 258–62. See also Wise, "4QFlorilegium and the Temple of Adam," 103–32. 4Q500 & *Jub* 3.9–12 associates Eden w/the Holy of Holies (see Wise, *Thunder*, 179, n.78). See also Brooke, *The Dead Sea Scrolls and the New Testament*, 242–3; *Exegesis at Qumran*, 184–93; *Exegesis at Qumran: 4QFlorilegium in its Jewish Context* (JSOT Sup 29; Sheffield: JSOT, 1985).

[177] Brooke, *The Dead Sea Scrolls and the New Testament*, 245; "Miqdash Adam, Eden and the Qumran Community," in B. Ego, et al. (eds.), *Gemeinde ohne Tempel-Community without Temple: Zur Substituierung und Transformation des Jerusalemer Tempels und seines Kultes im Alten Testament, antiken Judentum und frühen Christentum* (WUNT 118 ; Tübingen: Mohr Siebeck, 1999), 285–301. On the cult and Eden, see *Jub.* 3:26–27, 8:19; Martha Himmelfarb, "The Temple and the Garden of Eden in Ezekiel, the Book of Watchers, and the Wisdom of Ben Sira," in Jamie S. Scott and Paul Simpson-Housely (eds.), *Sacred Places and Profane Spaces: Essays in the Geographies of Judaism, Christianity and Islam* (Westport: Greenwood, 1991), 63–78; *Ascent to Heaven in Jewish and Christian Apocalypses* (Oxford University Press, 1993); Sandra R. Shimoff, "Gardens: From Eden to Jerusalem," *JSJ*, 26 (1995), 145–55; Lawrence E. Stager, "Jerusalem and the Garden of Eden," *Eretz-Israel*, 26 (1999), 183–94.

[178] Klawans, *Purity, Sacrifice, and the Temple*, 163, notes that the community uses the term "house" (בית) to refer to itself, instead of "sanctuary/Temple" (מקדש) which typically referred to the Jerusalem Temple. 1QS uses "house" (8.5–6, 9.6). CD uses "a sure house in Israel" (CD 3.19), but also uses "sanctuary" (CD 1.3, 4.1, 18, 5.6, 6.12, 16, 12.1, 2, 20.23); 4Q171 *does* use מקדש.

[179] 1QS 4.22–23, CD 3.20, and 1QH 4.15.

[180] *A.J.* 18.1.5; *Quod omnis probus liber* 75.

[181] L. H. Schiffman, *Texts and Traditions* (Hoboken: Ktav, 1998), 275–6. See Albert I. Baumgarten, "Josephus on Essene Sacrifice," *JJS*, 45 (1994), 169–83. Joan E. Taylor, *The Essenes, the Scrolls, and the Dead Sea* (New York: Oxford University Press, 2012), 98–9, suggests that the Essenes held to a higher standard of purity than other Jews and avoided the nonpriestly areas, sacrificing in the Temple in their own special area.

εἰς δὲ τὸ ἱερὸν ἀναθήματα στέλλοντες θυσίας [οὐκ] ἐπιτελοῦσιν διαφορότητι
ἀγνειῶν ἃ νομίζοιεν καὶ δι'αὐτὸ εἰργόμενοι τοῦ κοινοῦ τεμενίσματος
ἐφ᾿ αὑτῶν τὰς θυσίας ἐπιτελοῦσιν

They send votive offerings (ἀναθήματα) to the Temple, but they [do not] offer sacrifices, using different rites of purification. Because of this they [were] excluded [themselves] (εἰργόμενοι) from the common court (τοῦ κοινοῦ τεμενίσματος),[182] and offer their sacrifices by themselves.[183]

Josephus' account might mean that the Essenes sent *both* votive offerings *and* performed (animal) sacrifices.[184] Yet there is no clear indication that the Essenes sacrificed within their own communities and no clear indication that a specific area of the Temple was reserved for their use. It is possible to read στέλλοντες as meaning that it is *through* sending votive offerings that they sacrifice because their sacrifices were different. Josephus clearly describes several Essenes *teaching* in the Temple courts, so they presumably revered the Temple.[185] It is likely, however, that Josephus' description of the Essenes is based on Philo's *earlier* account (c. 20–40 CE), which *denies* that the Essenes practiced animal sacrifice:

ἐπειδὴ κἂν τοῖς μάλιστα θεραπευταὶ θεοῦ γεγόνασιν, οὐ ζῷα καταθύντες, ἀλλ᾿ ἱεροπρεπεῖς τὰς ἑαυτῶν διανοίας κατασκευάζειν ἀξιοῦντες.

---

[182] Translating εἰργόμενοι as a middle participle results in the Essenes separating themselves whereas a passive signifies that the Essenes were excluded from the Temple. On Josephus' Essenes corresponding to Philo's Essenes offering "spiritual" sacrifices as in the Qumran texts (CD 11.18–21; 1QS 9.3–5; 4QFlorilegium), see Jamal-Dominique Hopkins, "The Dead Sea Scrolls and the Greco-Roman World: Examining the Essenes' View of Sacrifice in Relation to the Scrolls," in A. Lange, E. Tov, M. Weigold, and B. Reynolds III (eds.), *The Dead Sea Scrolls in Context: Integrating the Dead Sea Scrolls in the Study of Ancient Texts, Languages, and Cultures* (2 vols; VTSup 140; Leiden: Brill, 2011), 367–83.

[183] *A.J.* 18.1.5.

[184] The problem hinges on whether οὐκ is original. It is present in the Latin and the Epitome of Josephus, our two earliest manuscripts, but absent in the Greek manuscripts.

[185] *B.J.* 1.3, 5 §78; *A.J.* 15.10, 5 § 373; *B.J.* 2.20, 4 § 562–7.

Since they are men utterly dedicated to the service of God; they do *not* offer animal sacrifice, judging it more fitting to render their minds truly holy.[186]

Philo's report on the Essenes suggests that voluntary nonparticipation in the Temple cult was not unprecedented in the Second Temple period. We could dismiss Philo's Εσσαῖοι as an invention of the Hellenized philosopher,[187] and his criticism of animal sacrifice as kin to that of the Neoplatonic and Pythagorean Porphyry,[188] but Philo certainly seems to have preferred *bloodless* sacrifices.[189] Philo saw sacrifice as stemming from and meeting "a basic human desire, an aspiration to relationship with the Divine."[190] The slaughtered animal represents symbolic aspects of the one sacrificing. The sacrifice of an animal symbolizes and represents "*self*-sacrifice."[191] Philo also describes the idealized and Essene-like Therapeutae of Alexandria as philosophical vegetarians, emphasizing their "table kept pure from the animal food" (τρά ιιεζα καθαρὰ τῶν ἐνσίμων),[192] At Qumran, as in Josephus and Philo's accounts of the Essenes and Therapeutae, the *principle* of sacrifice has been preserved, although sacrificial *practices* have changed.

The Qumran community, the Essenes, and the Dead Sea Scrolls provide us with counter-Temple traditions contemporary to the Jesus movement. By 30 CE, the Qumran community had not participated in Temple worship for over a century. They had long since come to see themselves as an effective – and rival – temple to the Temple based in

[186] *Quod Omnis Probus Liber Sit* 75. Geza Vermes and Martin Goodman, *The Essenes according to the classical sources* (Sheffield: JSOT, 1989), 21. Taylor, *The Essenes*, 29–30, asserts that Philo is contrasting "two types of service" and that the idea that Philo is "indicating that the Essenes spurned animal sacrifices in the Temple is simply wrong." For Philo's critique of symbolic as opposed to literal observance, see *On the migration of Abraham* 89–93.

[187] See Baumgarten, "Josephus on Essene Sacrifice"; Todd S. Beal, *Josephus' Description of the Essenes Illustrated by the Dead Sea Scrolls* (Cambridge University Press, 1988), 118.

[188] *On Abstinence from Killing Animals.*

[189] Jutta Leonhardt, *Jewish Worship in Philo of Alexandria* (TSAJ 84; Tübingen: Mohr Siebeck, 2001), 276. See *Spec. Laws* 1.275.

[190] William K. Gilders, "Jewish Sacrifice: Its Nature and Function (According to Philo)," in *Ancient Mediterranean Sacrifice*, 94–105, here 97. See Philo, *On the Special Laws* 1.66–67, 1.195.

[191] Gilders, "Jewish Sacrifice" 98.

[192] *De vita contemplativa* 73–4. On the Therapeutae, see Joan E. Taylor, *Jewish Women Philosophers of First-Century Alexandria: Philo's "Therapeutae" Reconsidered* (New York: Oxford University Press, 2003).

Jerusalem and this was certainly a source of tension with other Jews, most probably the high priesthood. The Qumran texts illustrate that the community's relationship to the Torah was rigorous and reverent, but open to new revelation. The Torah and Temple were divine (i.e., eternal) ideals that changed over time. The Essenes sought to fulfill the priestly function of atonement through *alternative* forms and expressions, envisioning its own community as a substitute for the corrupted Temple.

John the Baptist also seems to have withdrawn from and criticized the Temple's current administration. Scholars have, of course, long noted a number of remarkable correspondences between John and the (Qumran) Essenes. The fact that these two movements overlapped, both chronologically and geographically, is striking. John's baptism has even been interpreted as a quasi-priestly rite of purification and atonement for sin intended as an alternative to the Temple cult in Jerusalem. John seems to have insisted that his baptism was not only for proselytes, but for *all of Israel*, implying that the entire nation needed repentance and purification, a position characteristic of the Qumran community.[193] By encouraging Jews to "come together" for baptism, John seems to have been calling his audience to form a cohesive group and using baptism as the means by which the group could identify itself.[194] John's baptism may have functioned as a kind of initiation into "true Israel,"[195] a creative adaptation of ritual purification.[196] John preached and conducted baptisms in the Judean wilderness by the Jordan river, a location highly symbolic of the Exodus and Conquest narratives.[197] Whereas traditional ritual bathing tended to be self-administered, *John's* baptisms are *mediatorial*.[198] His role as ὁ Βαπτιστής parallels the mediating role of "a priest

---

[193] Leonard F. Badia, *The Qumran Baptism and John the Baptist's Baptism* (Lanham: University Press of America, 1980), 37.

[194] Robert L. Webb, "John the Baptist and His Relationship to Jesus," in B. D. Chilton and C. A. Evans (eds.), *Studying the Historical Jesus: Evaluations of the State of Current Research* (NTTS 19; Leiden: Brill, 1994), 196.

[195] Webb, "John the Baptist and His Relationship to Jesus," 194.

[196] Bruce D. Chilton, *Judaic Approaches to the Gospels* (Atlanta: Scholars, 1994), 26–7.

[197] Robert L. Webb, *John the Baptizer and Prophet: A Socio-Historical Study* (JSNT Sup 62; Sheffield: JSOT, 1991), 181–3, 360–6.

[198] Webb, "Jesus' Baptism by John: Its Historicity and Significance," 114. See also Leonhard Goppelt, *Theology of the New Testament*, 2 vols. (trans. J. E. Alsup; Grand Rapids: Eerdmans, 1981–1982), 1:36; Jürgen Becker, *Johannes der Täufer und Jesus von Nazareth* (BibS[N] 63; Neukirchen-Vluyn: Neukirchener, 1972), 38–40.

in performing a sacrifice to mediate forgiveness in the sacrificial system."[199] He exhorts the people of Israel to repent for their sins and be purified.[200] Anyone offering baptism for the "forgiveness of sins" could have been seen as offering a substitute for the Temple cult while issuing "a protest against the Temple establishment."[201] We may not be sure that John's baptism was *actually* perceived as facilitating the "*forgiveness* of sins" in his lifetime,[202] but the sudden appearance of a charismatic preacher in the Jordan wilderness would certainly have alarmed the religious authorities in Jerusalem. Josephus explicitly portrays John as a *political* figure whose arrest and execution were calculated political decisions made by Herod Antipas out of fear of John's growing authority over the people.[203]

The relationship between John the Baptist and Jesus suggests that Jesus picked up some of John's antipathy toward the Temple. While the precise nature of the Jesus movement's relationship to the Essenes continues to be debated, John and Jesus can be located along a social *continuum* of alternative-temple movements marked by deep undercurrents of suspicion and hostility toward the Temple's current administration. It is within this conflicted political atmosphere that the apocalyptic communities of Qumran, the Essenes, John, and Jesus re-imagined the eschatological Temple and its role in Israel.[204] Let us proceed, then, by carefully surveying the New Testament sources on Jesus' relationship to the Temple.

---

[199]   Webb, "John the Baptist," 191–2.

[200]   Webb, *John the Baptizer and Prophet*, 203–5.

[201]   Webb, "Jesus' Baptism by John: Its Historicity and Significance," 120.

[202]   Mark 1:4.

[203]   See Richard Horsley, "Popular Messianic Movements Around the Time of Jesus," *CBQ*, 46 (1984), 471–95; Richard Horsley and John S. Hanson, *Bandits, Prophets, and Messiahs: Popular Movements in the Time of Jesus* (NVBS; Minneapolis: Winston, 1985), 88–134; Webb, *John the Baptizer and Prophet*, 310–12, 333–48.

[204]   On temple-imagery, see Georg Klinzing, *Die Umdeutung des Kultus in der Qumrangemeinde und im Neuen Testament* (SUNT 7; Göttingen: Vandenhoeck & Ruprecht, 1971); Elisabeth Schüssler Fiorenza, "Cultic Language in Qumran and in the NT," *CBQ*, 38 (1976), 159–77.

4

THE TEMPLE CONTROVERSY

A Chronological Inventory of Sources

To state the matter somewhat provocatively, one could call the Gospels passion narratives with extended introductions.[1]

Martin Kähler, *The So-Called Historical Jesus*

There is no narrative account of the Temple incident in Q. As we have seen, Q 11:49–51 and Q 13:34–35 represent a serious indictment of the Temple. Jesus declares Jerusalem's "house" (οἶκος), that is, the Temple, to be "forsaken."[2] The city of Jerusalem and its leaders must repent before they ever see Jesus again:

> O Jerusalem, Jerusalem, who kills the prophets and stones those sent to her!
>
> How often I wanted to gather your children together, as a hen gathers her nestlings under her wings, and you were not willing!
>
> Look, your House (οἶκος) is forsaken! I tell you: You will not see me until you say: 'Blessed is the one who comes in the name of the Lord!'

A "forsaken" Temple is not one in which sacrifices are either efficacious or capable of reconciling Israel and God. The Temple is a place where the prophets are killed.[3] Jerusalem has rejected Jesus, and its Temple is now "forsaken." These Q passages, like Q 14:27 (the cross saying), seem to reflect a *post*-30 CE awareness of Jesus' death;

---

[1] Martin Kähler, *The So-Called Historical Jesus and the Historic Biblical Christ* (Philadelphia: Fortress, 1964), 80, n. 11.

[2] Schulz, *Spruchquelle*, 356.

[3] Kloppenborg, "The Sayings Gospel Q: Recent Opinion," 25.

hence, it is not clear how we should use them in reconstructing the historical Jesus' attitude toward the Temple. The Q tradition has its own ideological and theological agenda in pronouncing judgment on "this generation," but we may infer, at the very least, that Q properly identifies *who* was responsible for Jesus' death as much as it confirms the nature of his death by crucifixion.

The earliest narrative account of Jesus' action in the Temple is found in the Gospel of Mark. Interpreting Mark is complicated, however, by the fact that Mark represents a conflation of earlier Jesus traditions in a new narrativized form. There are theological elements in Mark consistent with the atonement theology contained in Paul's letters. Indeed, a central theme in Mark is the representation of Jesus' death as a divine imperative: Jesus' mission is to sacrifice himself.[4] At the same time, Mark's Jesus also promotes the ideal of *self-sacrifice* as the primary mark of the true disciple: Jesus' disciple must "deny himself" (ἀπαρνησάσθω ἑαυτὸν),[5] and take up the cross. Self-sacrifice is the characteristic hallmark of a follower of Jesus. The disciple must "deny" the self, pick up the cross, and follow Jesus. Sacrifice becomes the central theme and dominant characteristic of discipleship, the complete renunciation of one's personal identity and separate will. The true disciple must be willing to renounce (i.e., sacrifice) everything,[6] and face death.

Like sacrifice and the cross, the Temple plays a "vital role in the plot of Mark's gospel ... It serves as the stage for the Markan Jesus' conflict with the Jewish authorities, and moreover it is the vital reference point for the narrative portrait of Jesus' identity, mission, and eschatological message."[7] We first encounter Jesus' criticism of the Temple in Mark 13:1–2, where Jesus predicts, but does not threaten, its destruction.[8] Here Mark uses ἱερόν to refer to the Temple complex,[9] but when Jesus' accusers give their false testimony during his

---

[4] Mark 8:27–37. See Lamar Williamson, *Mark: Interpretation: A Biblical Commentary for Teaching and Preaching* (Louisville: Westminster John Knox, 1983), 150; Ben Witherington III, *The Gospel of Mark: A Socio-rhetorical Commentary* (Grand Rapids: Eerdmans, 2001), 239.

[5] Mark 8:34.

[6] Mark 1:18, 20; 2:14, 10:28–30.

[7] Timothy C. Gray, *The Temple in the Gospel of Mark: A Study in Its Narrative Role* (Grand Rapids: Baker Academic, 2010), 198, 199.

[8] Sanders, *Jesus and Judaism*, 71.

[9] The term ἱερόν is used for the temple of Artemis in Acts 19:27; for the Jerusalem Temple in LXX Ezek. 45:19; 1 Chron. 29:4, but also for the entire Temple complex in Matt 12:6, 24:1; Mark 13:3; Luke 21:5, 22:52; Acts 4:1, 24:6, 25:8; 1 Cor 9:13. It also

trial, Mark uses ναὸν to refer to the Temple (14:58). While ἱερόν generally refers to the Temple's entire enclosure, including the buildings, courts, balconies, and porticoes, the word ναός refers to either the inner sanctuary or the Holy of Holies, where the high priest was allowed to enter once a year on the Day of Atonement. Mark also differentiates between the present Temple "made with human hands" (χειροποίητον) and another (ἄλλον) Temple, "not made with human hands" (ἀχειροποίητον), yet to be built, a destruction-and-rebuilding which Mark indicates has already begun with the rending of the veil (15:38).[10] The author of Mark seems to be "expressing contempt" for the present Temple.[11] The new Temple – "not made with human hands" and to be built "after three days" – is most likely a reference either to Jesus' resurrection and/or to the new community-as-Temple, a theme already present in Second Temple literature.[12] There is no reason to think that Jesus expected a new *physical* Temple "made with human hands" would be built three days after the destruction of the present (Herodian) Temple.

As we will see, there is also little reason to think that Jesus threatened to destroy the Temple himself. Mark emphatically states that this accusation was *false testimony* (14:56, 57). The testimony is not only insufficient to convict Jesus; it is also inconsistent: the witnesses do not agree. Moreover, Jesus is never reported as having actually made such a threat.[13] On the other hand, the fact that the Temple saying is multiply attested in the tradition strongly suggests that Jesus said and did *something* highly offensive about the Temple. Mark envisions Jesus *truly* predicting, foreseeing, and even inaugurating the Temple's destruction (15:38–39), but the witnesses were giving "false testimony" in misrepresenting Jesus as the agent of destruction.[14] In other words, Jesus may have *predicted* the Temple's destruction, but did not threaten its destruction nor represent himself as the *agent* of

refers to certain parts, i.e., courts, of the Temple complex (Matt 21:12, 14, 26:55; Mark 14:49; Luke 19:47, 21:37, 22:53, 24:53; John 5:14, 7:14, 28, 8:20, 18:20; Acts 3:2, 5:20).

[10] Cf. Acts 7:48; 17:24, where Stephen insists that God does not dwell in houses or sanctuaries "made by hands." In Hebrews 9:11 and 9:24, where Christ (as high priest) enters into the heavenly Temple through the perfect tabernacle "not made by hands" (οὐ χειροποιήτου).

[11] Brown, *The Death of the Messiah*, 1: 440.

[12] 1QS 9.6; CD 3.19; 4Q177/4QFlorilegium.

[13] Dieter Lührmann, "Markus 14, 55–64: Christologie und Zerstörung des Tempels im Markusevangelium," *NTS*, 27 (1981), 459–60, argues that the threat is a fabrication.

[14] Brown, *The Death of the Messiah*, 447.

its destruction, which is why the accusation is false.[15] It is clear from Mark's account of the rending of the veil (15:38), the Parable of the Wicked Tenants (12:1–12), and the cursing of the fig tree, however, that its author *did* see Jesus' death as inaugurating the destruction of the Temple.[16] The Temple incident is located between the story of the cursing and withering of the fig tree and represents "a prophetic gesture foretelling the eschatological end of the temple."[17] Why does Jesus curse the fig tree in Mark? The Markan context seems clear: the fig tree symbolizes the Temple; it is only after the Temple incident that the fig tree is found to be withered.[18] The story serves as a prophetic act.[19] The withering of the fig tree represents God's judgment.[20] The

[15] Matthew emphasizes Jesus' ability and power to destroy the Temple (Matt 27:39–40), but does not make Jesus the *agent* of destruction and drops the charge of falsity.

[16] Jostein Ådna, "Jesus' Symbolic Act in the Temple (Mark 11:15–17): The Replacement of the Sacrificial Cult by his Atoning Death," in B. Ego, A. Lange, and P. Pilhofer (eds.), *Gemeinde ohne Tempel: Zur Substituierung und Transformation des Jerusalemer Tempels und seines Kults im Alten Testament, antiken Judentum und frühen Christentum* (WUNT 118; Tübingen: Mohr Siebeck, 1999), 461–75, regards the Temple act and sayings as Jesus' "messianische Sendung." On Mark as anti-Temple, see Burton L. Mack, *A Myth of Innocence: Mark and Christian Origins* (Philadelphia: Fortress, 1988), 292; Paula Fredriksen, "Jesus and the Temple, Mark and the War," in *SBL Seminar Papers, 1990* (SBLSP 29; Atlanta: Scholars, 1990), 293–310, 297.

[17] Gray, *The Temple in the Gospel of Mark*, 29. See also John P. Heil, "The Narrative Strategy and Pragmatics of the Temple Theme in Mark," *CBQ*, 59.1 (1997), 76–100, here 78.

[18] Mark 11.20–25.

[19] See Gerhard Münderlein, "Die Verfluchung Des Feigenbaumes (Mk. XI.12–14)," *NTS*, 10/1 (1963), 89–104, esp. 94–5; H. Giesen, "Der verdorrte Feigenbaum – Eine symbolische Aussage? Zu Mk 11,12–14.20f," *BZ*, 20 (1976), 95–111; Witherington, *The Gospel of Mark*, 312; J. R. Edwards, "Markan Sandwiches: The Significance of Interpolations in Markan Narratives," *NovT*, 31 (1989), 193–216; Painter, M*ark's Gospel*, 159; Meier, *A Marginal Jew*, vol. 2: *Mentor, Message, and Miracles*, 887; C. Böttrich, "Jesus und der Feigenbaum. Mk 11:12–14, 20–25 in der Diskussion," *NovT*, 39 (1997), 328–59; E. Schweizer, *The Good News According to Mark* (trans. D. H. Madvig; Atlanta: John Knox, 1970), 230; G. Gnilka, *Das Evangelium nach Markus* (EKKNT 11/2; Zürich: Benzinger, 1979), 125; W. R. Telford, *The Barren Temple and the Withered Tree* (JSNTSup 1; Sheffield: JSOT, 1980), 49; L. H. Hurtado, *Mark* (NIBC; Peabody: Hendrickson, 1983), 181; D. J. Harrington, *The Gospel of Matthew* (SP 1; Collegeville: Liturgical Press, 1991), 297; M. A. Hooker, *A Commentary on the Gospel According to St. Mark* (BNTC; London: Black, 1991), 262; T. Söding, "Die Tempelaktion Jesu," *TTZ*, 101 (1992), 36–64, esp. 40; B. Kinman, *Jesus' Entry into Jerusalem: In the Context of Lukan Theology and the Politics of His Day* (AGJU 28: Leiden: Brill, 1995), 125–6; Theissen and Merz, *The Historical Jesus*, 293; C. A. Evans, *Mark 8:27–16:20* (WBC 34B; Nashville: Thomas Nelson, 2001), 160.

[20] Jr. 5:17; 8:13; Hos 2:12; 9:10, 16; Am 4:9.

fig tree thus represents either the Jewish people, Israel as a whole,[21] the Jewish religious leaders in Jerusalem,[22] the Temple, and/or the sacrificial cult. The dead fig tree foretells "the destruction of the sacrificial system."[23] Mark envisions Jesus as symbolically inaugurating the end of the Temple cult.[24] The Temple incident represents Jesus' judgment against the Temple. Mark has no interest in *retaining* the Temple.[25] Jesus *replaces* the Temple.

The Parable of the Wicked Tenants (Mark 12:1–12)

The Parable of the Wicked Tenants can be found in the Synoptics and the *Gospel of Thomas*.[26] The dominant theory regarding its provenance is that Mark either created or transmitted the parable, and that Matthew and Luke both took it from Mark.[27] The parable is generally recognized as referring to the death of Jesus as a polemic against the high priests and religious leaders of Israel. Most scholars agree that the parable can be said to be an allegory in which the

---

[21] Hooker, *The Gospel According to St. Mark*, 267.

[22] Evans, *Mark*, 154,

[23] R. G. Hamerton-Kelly, "Sacred Violence and the Messiah: The Markan Passion Narrative as a Redefinition of Messianology," in J. H. Charlesworth (ed.), *The Messiah: Developments in Earliest Judaism and Christianity* (Philadelphia: Fortress, 1992), 461–93, esp. 467, proposes that the tree is a symbol of the sacrificial system "whose time is now passed." Similarly, Telford, *The Barren Temple and the Withered Tree*, 137. See also W. W. Watty, "Jesus and the Temple - Cleansing or Cursing?" *ExpT*, 93 (1982), 235–9, esp. 237; E. L. Schnellbächer, "The Temple as Focus of Mark's Theology," *HBT*, 5 (1983), 95–113, esp. 101–02; C. Myers, *Binding the Strong Man: A Political Reading of Mark's Story of Jesus* (Maryknoll: Orbis, 1988), 304; Edwards, "Markan Sandwiches," 208; Kinman, *Jesus' Entry into Jerusalem*, 125–6; Böttrich, "Jesus und der Feigenbaum," 353; Evans, *Mark*, 155; J-M. Sevrin, "Mark's Use of Isaiah 56:7 and the Announcement of the Temple Destruction," in A. Niccacci (ed.), *Jerusalem: House of Prayer for All Peoples in the Three Monotheistic Religions: Proceedings of a Symposium Held in Jerusalem, February 17–18, 1997* (SBFA, 52; Jerusalem: Franciscan Printing Press, 2001), 45–57, esp. 50.

[24] See Juel, *Messiah and Temple*, 130; W. H. Kelber, *Mark's Story of Jesus* (Philadelphia: Fortress, 1979), 62; Telford, *The Barren Temple and the Withered Tree*, 49, 262; Myers, *Binding the Strong Man*, 193–6; Painter, *Mark*, 157; Evans, *Mark*, 151. Seeley, "Jesus' Temple Act," 274, sees the cursing of the fig tree as "the symbolization of the end of the temple service itself."

[25] Loader, *Jesus' Attitude*, 107, 111–12: "Mark is not interested in cleansing the Jerusalem temple; it is too late for that." Evans, "Cleansing or Portent," 248–56, argues for Temple *reform*.

[26] Mark 12:1–12; Matt 21:33–46; Luke 20:9–19; *Thomas* L. 65, 66.

[27] Snodgrass, *Parable of the Wicked Tenants*, 56–71.

"vineyard" is Israel, the owner of the vineyard is God, the wicked tenants are the religious leaders, the persecuted servants/slaves are the prophets, and the "beloved son" is Jesus.[28] While these allegorical symbols appear fairly obvious in the text, much of the discussion has centered on the fact that the parable contains two citations from the Septuagint: Isaiah 5's "Song of the Vineyard" and Psalm 117's "cornerstone" motif. A close comparison of these texts with Mark 12:1–12 confirms that these citations are taken directly from the Septuagint.[29] Mark uses the LXX version of Isa 5:2 in four distinct phrases. He describes a man that "planted a vineyard," "put a fence around it," "dug a pit," and "built a tower." In Isaiah, the "Song of the Vineyard" describes the vineyard's destruction by God.[30] In Jer 2:21 and Ezek 15:6, the people of Israel are also referred to as a vineyard. Ezekiel describes how the "inhabitants of Jerusalem" will be burned like the "wood of the vine."[31] A first-century Jewish audience could have inferred that allegorical references to a "vineyard," "fence," "pit," and "watchtower" signified the idea of Israel's judgment and destruction. The fact that Mark uses the Septuagint suggests a secondary development.[32] Furthermore, there is evidence of an allegorical use of Isaiah 5 at Qumran,[33] therefore, it is possible that Mark could have inherited this citation from Isa. 5 in a collection of "proof-texts" circulated by the early Jesus movement. After

[28] John S. Kloppenborg Verbin, "Egyptian Viticultural Practices and the Citation of Isa 5:1–7 in Mark 12:1–9," *NovT*, 44 (2002), 134; John S. Kloppenborg, *The Tenants in the Vineyard: Ideology, Economics, and Agrarian Conflict in Jewish Palestine* (WUNT 195; Tübingen: Mohr Siebeck, 2006).

[29] Kloppenborg Verbin, "Egyptian Viticultural Practices," 138; "Isa 5:1–7 LXX and Mark 12:1, 9, Again," *NovT*, 46 (2004), 12–19. See Craig A. Evans, "How Septuagintal is Isa 5:1–7 in Mark 12:1–9?," *NovT*, 45 (2003), 110; W. J. C. Weren, "The Use of Isaiah 5,1–7 in the Parable of the Tenants (Mark 12, 1–12; Matthew 21,33–46)," *Bib*, 79 (1998), 26.

[30] Isa 5:5–6.

[31] Jer. 2:21; Ezekiel 15:6.

[32] J. Jeremias, *The Parables of Jesus* (London: SCM, 1955), 56. See also John S. Kloppenborg Verbin, "Isaiah 5:1–7, the Parable of the Tenants, and Vineyard Leases on Papyrus," in S. G. Wilson and M. Desjardins (eds.), *Text and Artifact: Religions in Mediterranean Antiquity: Essays in Honor of Peter Richardson* (SCJ 9; Waterloo, Ontario: Wilfrid Laurier University Press, 2000), 111–34; John Dominic Crossan, *In Parables: The Challenge of the Historical Jesus* (New York: Harper San Francisco, 1973), 91–5.

[33] See J. M. Baumgarten, "4Q500 and the Ancient Conceptions of the Lord's Vineyard," *JJS*, 40 (1989), 1–6; G. J. Brooke, "4Q500 1 and the Use of Scripture in the Parable of the Vineyard," *DSD*, 2 (1995), 268–94.

all, Mark 12:1–12 includes Ps. 117:22–23, which also seems to have been used in the early Jesus movement:

Ps 117:22–23 (LXX)	**Mark 12:10–11**
The very stone which the builders rejected has become the head of the corner.	The very stone which the builders rejected has become the head of the corner.

Mark cites the Septuagint verbatim. Yet the use of Ps. 117 turns the parable from being a pronouncement of judgment on the leaders of Israel into a declaration of Jesus' vindication.[34] It would seem that this citation was attached to the end of the parable to lend the story a triumphal ending. The fact that these verses from Ps. 117 were used in the early Jesus movement suggests that it was regarded as a proof-text of Jesus as the (rejected) "cornerstone" of the new Temple.[35] The symbolism of the "cornerstone" can also be found in 1QS 8.4: the community is the Temple and the "Holy of Holies," the "tested wall," and "precious cornerstone." The precise verbal correspondence in Mark's use of Isa. 5 and Ps. 117 does not seem to be a result of oral tradition but rather evidence of intertextuality. Consequently, it seems justified to attribute these citations to secondary development of the parable's transmission, that is, as a creation of the early Church.[36]

On the other hand, a number of scholars believe that there is an historical core to the parable and that if we could peel back the secondary layers, the parable would appear as a relatively simple story about a man's vineyard, his servants, son, and tenants.[37] Pheme Perkins argues that the vineyard owner's reticence to inflict punishment on the tenants accurately reflects Jesus' own program of forgiveness and nonviolence, a reading of the parable that the evangelists later

[34] Arland J. Hultgren, *The Parables of Jesus: A Commentary* (Grand Rapids: Eerdmans, 2000), 363–4.

[35] Acts 4:11; 1 Pet 2:6–8.

[36] Bultmann, *History*, 177; C. H. Dodd, *The Parables of the Kingdom* (New York: Charles Scribner's Sons, 1961), 124–32.

[37] See Dodd, *The Parables of the Kingdom*, 96–102; A. T. Cadoux, *The Parables of Jesus: Their Art and Use* (New York: Macmillan, 1931), 41; C. A. Evans, "Jesus' Parable of the Tenant Farmers in Light of Lease Agreements in Antiquity," *JSP*, 14 (1996), 25–83; Crossan, *In Parables*, 86–96; Jan Lambrecht, *Once More Astonished: The Parables of Jesus* (New York: Crossroad, 1981), 130; Hultgren, *The Parables of Jesus*, 361.

misrepresented to suggest a judgmental and punishing God.[38] John
Dominic Crossan also holds that the theme of violent judgment is a
secondary development in the parable's transmission.[39] It is not clear,
however, that the theme of judgment can so easily be excised from
the parable. Mark clearly inserted the parable alongside Jesus' triumphal entry and cursing of the fig-tree, two events that foreshadow
Jesus' conflict with the Temple authorities.[40]

There are also elements of the parable as we have it in Mark that
present us with peculiar features.[41] The motif of the "beloved son"
shows clear signs of Markan redaction as a narrative foreshadowing
of Jesus' death. Mark's reference to the "beloved son" in 12:6 also
seems like a clear allusion to his earlier description of Jesus as the
"beloved son" after his baptism in 1:11, which is itself a partial quotation from Ps. 2. Mark's "beloved son" motif is redactional, as is the
son's identification as the *"rejected"* cornerstone (Ps. 118:22). There
is also the enigmatic Semitic wordplay between the "son" (בֵּן) and
the "stone" (אֶבֶן) that the builders "rejected" (Ps. 118:22–23), a verbal
clue that this passage did not originate in Greek, but in an earlier
Hebrew and/or Aramaic source.[42]

There are also intriguing similarities between the parable and
Q. In Q 12:42–46 ("The Faithful and Unfaithful Slave"), we have a
story/parable about an "unfaithful" servant who is punished after his
master returns from a long journey. Like the "wicked tenants," this
unfaithful slave was put in charge over his household to produce food
on time yet beat his fellow servants, and abused his position by eating and drinking. Consequently, his "inheritance" will be taken away
from him. Similarly, in Q 19:12, 13, 15–24, 26 ("Entrusted Money"),
we have a Q parable that describes a master going on a long journey and leaving his estate to be cared for by his servants. When he
returns he inquires over his *three* servants in succession, and the last
one, the "wicked" servant, is punished, and his portion is taken away
from him. In Q 14:16–18, 21, 23 ("The Invited Dinner Guests"), the
invitation to a "large dinner" prepared for the guests is ignored or
rejected and, in response, the invitation is withdrawn and given to

[38] Pheme Perkins, *Hearing the Parables of Jesus* (New York: Paulist, 1981), 184.
[39] Crossan, *In Parables*, 71.
[40] Gärtner, *The Temple and the Community in Qumran and the New Testament*, 106.
[41] Kloppenborg Verbin, "Egyptian Viticultural Practices," 136, points out that "the
scenario presented in Mark is economically and legally incoherent."
[42] See Snodgrass, *The Parable of the Wicked Tenants*, 63–5, 113–18.

others. In each of the three pericopae, there is a (1) parable/story about a (2) master, his (3) servant(s), (4) property, and (5) judgment for the master's expectations not being met. These stories certainly seem to be cryptic allusions to the salvation history of Israel.

Mark 12:1–12 provides us with a story about a number of "servants" sent by the owner of the vineyard who were treated badly, beaten, wounded, and killed. The idea that Israel repeatedly killed the prophets sent to her is found in several places in the Hebrew Bible.[43] According to Q, Jesus stood in this successive line of prophets. In Q 11:47, Jesus pronounces woes against the "exegetes of the law" who kill the prophets. In Q 13:34–35, Jesus identifies Jerusalem as the city that kills the prophets sent to her and states that its house is "forsaken." In Q 11:49, Wisdom says "I will send them prophets and sages, and some of them they will kill and persecute." Q and Mark also both portray Jesus as the "son" of God.

There continues to be considerable discussion over whether *Thomas'* version of the tradition is dependent or independent of the Synoptics.[44] Some scholars maintain that the *Thomas* version represents an independent, if not earlier, version of the Synoptic parable.[45] Several Fellows of the Jesus Seminar hold that *Thomas* preserves an early version which lacks any reference to Isaiah 5. Crossan claims that L. 65 is "an independent version" of the Synoptic parable.[46] Similarly, Stephen Patterson argues that the *Thomas* version agrees in a number of features with Matthew or Luke against Mark.[47] He concludes that L. 65 represents an earlier, more primitive version of the Synoptic parable:[48] Mark took a simple story about "absentee landlords and rebellious tenants" and transformed it into an allegory about the death of Jesus. Since the *Thomas* version contains

[43] 2 Chron. 24:20–21; Jer 37:15; Neh 9:26.

[44] Kloppenborg Verbin, "Egyptian Viticultural Practices," 135.

[45] Gilles Quispel, "The Gospel of Thomas and the New Testament," *VC*, 11 (1957), 205–6; Hugh Montefiore, "A Comparison of the Parables of the Gospel according to Thomas and the Synoptic Gospels," in H. E. W. Turner and H. Montefiore (eds.), *Thomas and the Evangelists* (SBT 35; Naperville: Alec R. Allenson, 1962), 455–65; J. D. Crossan, "The Parable of the Wicked Husbandmen," *JBL*, 90 (1971), 451–65; Helmut Koester, "Three Thomas Parables," in A. H. B. Logan and A. J. M. Wedderburn (eds.), *The New Testament and Gnosis: Essays in Honor of Robert McL. Wilson* (Edinburgh: T & T Clark, 1983), 199–200.

[46] Crossan, *In Parables*, 92, 95.

[47] Stephen J. Patterson, *The Gospel of Thomas and Jesus* (Sonoma: Polebridge, 1993), 48–51.

[48] Patterson, *The Gospel of Thomas and Jesus*, 51.

no "secondary" allegorical elements, it must be the earlier version.[49] L. 66 is simply "a loose paraphrase" of Ps. 117, and this *also* points toward *Thomas'* independence.[50] Like Crossan, Patterson concedes that the order of the two logia cannot be accidental. This admission should settle the matter. The fact that logia 65 and 66 are found in precisely the same order as in Mark strongly suggests that these two sayings were already linked. This argues *against* an independent *Thomas* tradition for these two sayings. The simpler, less allegorical version found in *Thomas* is dependent on a Synoptic version.[51] In other words, the Markan version of the parable is the earliest form of this allegory and its narrative purpose is clearly to indict the religious authorities of the Temple. The idea that Jesus "cleanses" the Temple in Mark, therefore, is not a cleansing leading to renewal, restoration, or reformation. Rather, the Temple seems devoted to destruction.

The Markan Passion Narrative and Zechariah 9–14

The destruction of the Temple foreshadowed in Mark 12:1–12 represents the culmination of a combination of passages that appeal, in multiple instances, to Zech 9–14, particularly in reference to the "triumphal entry" and Temple incident.[52] Zech 9–14 looks forward to the Day of the Lord, envisioned as an eschatological war culminating in divine victory "on that day" and the restoration of Jerusalem. The author foresees several battles between Israel and the nations (9:13; 12:2–3; 14:1–2), but in the end a "fountain will be opened for the house of David and the inhabitants of Jerusalem" will be "cleansed" of "sin and impurity" (לחטאת ולנדה) (13:1). There will no longer be "traders in the house of the Lord" (14:21), and all the nations will come to serve God in Jerusalem (14:16–21):

---

[49] Patterson, *The Gospel of Thomas and Jesus*, 228–9.

[50] Patterson, *The Gospel of Thomas and Jesus*, 50.

[51] Robert M. Grant and David N. Freedman, *The Secret Sayings of Jesus* (Garden City: Doubleday, 1960), 172; Klyne Snodgrass, "The Parable of the Wicked Husbandmen: Is the Gospel of Thomas Version the Original?," *NTS*, 21 (1975), 142–4; *The Parable of the Wicked Tenants*, 1983, 52–4. Sariola, *Markus*, 217, argues that the pre-Markan tradition should be understood as Jesus attacking the Temple, particularly the sacrificial cult. See also Gnilka, *Markus II*, 129; F. Hahn, *Der urchristliche Gottesdienst* (SBS 41; Stuttgart: KBW, 1970), 29–30.

[52] Henk Jan de Jonge, "The Cleansing of the Temple in Mark 11:15 and Zechariah 14:21," in C. Tuckett (ed.), *The Book of Zechariah and its Influence* (Burlington: Ashgate, 2003), 87–100.

Zech 9:9–10 "Rejoice greatly, O daughter Zion! Shout aloud, O daughter of Jerusalem! Look, your king comes to you, triumphant and victorious is he, humble, and mounted on a donkey, and on a colt, the foal of a donkey ... he will command peace to the nations."

Zech 14:20 "on that day ... the vessels in the house of the Lord will be like the bowls before the altar."

Zech 14:21 "There shall no longer be traders in the house of the Lord of hosts on that day."

It is not difficult to find echoes and allusions to Zech 9–14 in the Markan passion narrative. The author of Mark utilized Zech 9–14 to illustrate how Jesus' visit to Jerusalem fulfilled eschatological prophecies of the Day of the Lord. Zech 9–14 was a particularly fitting text for this purpose as it envisions the eschatological restoration of Jerusalem and Judea. In Mark 11:1–11, Jesus enters Jerusalem "triumphantly" on a colt, which Matthew understands as fulfilling Zech 9:9.[53] In Mark 11, Jesus cleanses the Temple, which seems to allude to Zech 14:21. The author supplements his implicit condemnation of the Temple by portraying Jesus as refusing to allow "anyone to carry a vessel (σκεῦος/כלי) through the Temple," alluding to Zech 14:20.[54] Jesus not allowing anyone to carry "anything" (σκεῦος) through the Temple seems to refer to sacred vessels, suggesting that Jesus was forbidding the practice of sacrifice.[55] Mark's Jesus puts an end to the Temple's sacrificial service – even if only for an afternoon. Mark's Gospel also contains an additional criticism of Israel's particularity, citing Isa. 56:7 to signify that the Temple's destruction is a result of its failure to include the Gentiles.[56]

---

[53] See Zech 9:9/Matt 21:5; Zech 13:7/Matt 26:31; Zech 11:12–13/Matt 27:9–10; Zech 10:2/Matt 9:36; Zech 9:11/Matt 26:28. For other Matthean allusions, see John Nolland, "The King as Shepherd: The Role of Deutero-Zechariah in Matthew," in Thomas R. Hatina (ed.), *Biblical Interpretation in Early Christian Gospels*, vol. 2: *The Gospel of Matthew* (London: T & T Clark International, 2008), 133–46; C. A. Ham, *The Coming King and the Rejected Shepherd: Matthew's Reading of Zechariah's Messianic Hope* (Sheffield Phoenix Press, 2005).

[54] Mark 11:6.

[55] Telford, *The Barren Temple and the Withered Tree*, 92–3, n. 102.

[56] Juel, *Messiah and Temple*, 135; Kelber, *Mark's Story of Jesus*, 62. Isaiah foresaw "all nations" coming to the Temple to worship the God of Israel (Mark 11.16. Isa 2.2–4; Mic 4.1–3; Zech 14.16). It is only Mark that uses "for all the nations"/πᾶσιν τοῖς ἔθνεσιν, although none of the Gospels quote the *preceding* verses describing God *accepting* burnt offerings (Isa 56.6–7 (LXX). Paesler, *Das Tempelwort Jesu*, 242, doubts

Henk Jan de Jonge has suggested that the triumphal entry and Temple incident were once linked in a *pre*-Markan literary unit, and that Mark subsequently placed the Temple incident scene within the framework provided by the story of the fig tree in order to symbolize its imminent destruction. Mark, however, was no longer aware that the cleansing of the Temple was related to Zech 14:21. Therefore, whereas the prophecy in Zechariah speaks of a removal of traders from the Temple as "a sign of the *holiness* of the temple," the author of Mark reads this expulsion as "symbolic of the *condemnation* of the Jewish cult."[57] Mark thus portrays Jesus as abolishing the Temple cult by driving out those who bought and sold, and not allowing anyone to carry anything through the Temple.

According to de Jonge, an early (pre-Markan) link between the triumphal entry and Temple incident would have been associated with royal cultic authority,[58] but there is no good reason to "trace this tradition back to an historical event in Jesus' lifetime."[59] It is a purely theological reading of Jesus' significance in light of Zechariah's prophecy of the "Day of the Lord." Mark's redaction of this pre-Markan tradition radically changed the meaning of the Temple incident from a purified Temple on the Day of the Lord to a Temple destined for destruction because it was "fruitless." For Mark, the Temple incident represents, albeit in symbolic form, "a divine punishment for Israel's disobedience."[60] The Temple incident in Mark symbolizes the Temple's imminent destruction.[61]

De Jonge's insights are significant. If Mark inherited pre-Markan traditions that identified the Temple incident as a symbolic enactment of the "Day of the Lord," this not only helps explain the conflated themes in the tradition, but supports the idea that what we have here are redactional layers and/or levels of meaning, with earlier traditions pointing not to Jesus' symbolic destruction or replacement of the Temple, but an objection to its administration and an

---

the authenticity of Mark 11:17b's citation of Isa 56:7, suggesting that it is an editorial addition, a "judenchristliche Neuinterpretation," in light of the Gentile mission.

[57] De Jonge, "The Cleansing of the Temple," 95 (emphasis added).

[58] De Jonge, "The Cleansing of the Temple," 91; cf. 1 Macc 4:36–61; 2 Macc 10:1–8; *Psalms of Solomon* 17.

[59] De Jonge, "The Cleansing of the Temple," 92.

[60] De Jonge, "The Cleansing of the Temple," 95.

[61] Hooker, *The Gospel According to St. Mark*, 266.

attempt to re-sanctify it as an enactment of eschatologically realized prophecy.

The destruction of the Temple and Jerusalem began to be seen, not as God punishing Israel for its corrupt leaders and illegitimate high priests, but rather as part of a pre-ordained plan to substitute Jewish sacrificial worship at the Temple with a new form of worship: Jesus' "sacrifice" and "body" replacing the Temple's sacrificial system. The association of Jesus with the Passover lamb – a truly pure, innocent, and "unblemished" sacrifice – led to the ideological replacement of a Jewish sacrificial system, ethnicity, and Israel.[62] While the Markan Jesus' condemnation of the Temple may have been edifying to a community that regarded itself as a new Temple,[63] this motif should probably be seen as secondary to the historical Jesus' own interests in challenging the Temple's administration. Early supersessionism was already in place by 70 CE. In other words, by the time of Mark, Jesus' own interests in "restoring" the Temple (or challenging its administration) had already been replaced by a replacement theology that saw his *death*, *body*, and *followers* as a new symbolic temple-system.[64] The Temple was *redefined* in the post-Easter period to represent the new community: *Jesus* is the cornerstone (κεφαλὴ γωνίας), the foundation of a new Temple, one not made with hands, "a house of prayer for all nations."[65] The *community* is the new Temple "which fulfils the temple's *original* purpose of being a house of prayer for all nations."[66]

The Markan Jesus consistently challenges the Temple. Even Mark 1:40–44 – where Jesus heals a leper and instructs him to go to the priest, and "offer for your cleansing what Moses commanded, as a testimony *to* them" (μαρτύριον αὐτοῖς) – is not a polite deference to priestly authority or a vestige of early pre-Markan pro-Temple Jesus tradition. According to Leviticus, a priest would pronounce

---

[62] Mark's setting of Jesus' crucifixion during Passover explicitly associates Jesus' death with the atonement mediated through sacrifice. Jesus cries out at the ninth hour shortly before he dies (15:34–37), the same time that the Passover lamb was sacrificed (see Josephus, *B.J.* 6.9.3).

[63] Gray, *The Temple in the Gospel of Mark*, 91.

[64] Gray, *The Temple in the Gospel of Mark*, 179.

[65] Evans, "Cleansing or Portent," 240; Morna D. Hooker, "Traditions about the Temple in the Sayings of Jesus," *BJRL*, 70 (1988), 9; Joel Marcus, *The Way of the Lord: Christological Exegesis of the Old Testament in the Gospel of Mark* (Louisville: John Knox Westminster, 1992), 119–29.

[66] Loader, *Jesus' Attitude*, 135 (emphasis added).

whether leprosy had been removed and purity regained, which would require the sacrifice of two birds.[67] It would seem that here Jesus upheld "what Moses commanded." But Mark's Jesus is not deferring to priestly authority; he is indirectly *challenging* it: μαρτύριον αὐτοῖς is better translated "as a testimony *against* them."[68] This has been aptly described as an "infringement of priestly prerogative" that reveals "a *tension* arising within the ministry of the historical Jesus."[69] James Crossley suggests that Mark 1:40–44 is "[o]ne of the clearest examples of Jesus upholding the Temple system,"[70] but acknowledges that εἰς μαρτύριον αὐτοῖς *can* be read "in the sense of a witness against the priests." He protests, however, that "this can hardly be taken in the sense of a direct confrontation with the purity system."[71] Rather, "Jesus is sending the man to the priest to show that he really is clean, or it may be Mark's anticipation of priestly opposition to Jesus," but this deference to priestly authority is quite peculiar in the Markan narrative. The passage is more plausibly read as an early narrative foreshadowing of the Temple conflict that climaxes later in Mark's Gospel. In any case, Mark does *not* tell us that the man actually went to the priests or performed any sacrifices. All we are told is that the man "went out and began to proclaim it freely, and to spread the word."[72] This passage thus conforms to Mark's "messianic secret" motif and sets the stage for Jesus' later confrontation with the Temple authorities. Jesus is not deferring to priestly

[67] Lev. 14.2–4, 4–8; 13.17, 50.

[68] See Emilio G. Chávez, *The Theological Significance of Jesus' Temple Action in Mark's Gospel* (TST 87; Lewiston: Edwin Mellen, 2002). See also Mark 6:11. Sanders, *The Historical Figure of Jesus*, 224, sees Jesus as being in agreement with "standard Jewish advice, which reflects endorsement of the sacrificial system." On the healed leper as a witness intended to confront the priests, see E. K. Broadhead, "Mark 1,44: The Witness of the Leper," *ZNW*, 83 (1992), 257–65, here 260–3; "Christology as Polemic and Apologetic: The Priestly Portrait of Jesus in the Gospel of Mark," *JSNT*, 47 (1992), 21–34, esp. 24–5; Jarmo Kiilunen, *Die Vollmacht im Widerstreit: Untersuchungen zum Werdegang von Mk 2,1–3,6* (ASFDHL 40; Helsinki: Suomalainen Tiedeakatemia, 1985), 33, n. 17; Banks, *Law*, 103. Myers, *Binding the Strong Man*, 153; H. C. Cave, "The Leper: Mk 1:40–45," *NTS*, 25 (1979), 245–50, esp. 249–50; Hurtado, *Mark*, 31; C. R. Kazmierski, "Evangelist and Leper: A Socio-Cultural Study of Mk 1.40–45," *NTS*, 38 (1992), 37–50, esp. 46–8. Holmén, *Jesus and Jewish Covenant Thinking*, 329 n. 316. Loader, *Jesus' Attitude*, 22, sees Jesus' act as affirming priestly authority.

[69] Robert L. Webb, "Jesus Heals a Leper: Mark 1.40–45 and *Egerton Gospel* 35–47," *JSHJ*, 4.2 (2006), 177–202, here 200–1.

[70] Crossley, *Date*, 87–8.

[71] Crossley, *Date*, 88.

[72] Mark 1:45.

authority nor should we assume that Jesus was trying to facilitate the leper's official re-admission into polite Israelite society. On the contrary, the Markan Jesus is issuing a challenge to priestly authority.[73] Mark 1:40–44 does not provide us with historical evidence of Jesus' support for or participation in the Temple cult.

The Markan Jesus does *not* participate in the Temple's sacrificial system. Given the hostility that the Markan Jesus displays toward the priests and the Temple, it seems highly unlikely that Jesus ever deferred to their authority; similarly, the idea that here Jesus is simply trying to facilitate the leper's ritual re-entry into the Jewish community by having the priests authorize it seems like a strained way to avoid an anti-Temple interpretation of this passage. The Markan Jesus delivers the Greatest Commandment, loving God and loving one's neighbor,[74] and announces that observing *these* commandments is "more important than all burnt offerings and sacrifices."[75] For Mark, this is more than "prioritizing" Torah; rather, these commandments announce "the abandonment of the temple as a sacrificial system … the temple, like its laws governing externals, belongs in the earthly realm of things made by human hands."[76] For Mark, the Temple was meant to be "a house of *prayer*," not sacrifice.

Mark's appeal to Isa. 56 is paralleled by Matthew's citation of Hos. 6:6, where the prophet declares that God wants "mercy, not sacrifice."[77]

> Mark 11:17 (Isa. 56:7) "my house shall be called *a house of prayer* for all nations"
>
> Matt 9:13 (Hos. 6:6) "I desire *mercy*, and not sacrifice"

The Gospel of Matthew usually follows Mark, but when it comes to the Temple and Torah, Matthew tends to be more conservative, suggesting that Jesus' attitude toward the Temple was more nuanced. Matthew omits Mark's detail about Jesus forbidding people to carry vessels in the courtyard (Mark 11:16), omits Mark's "for all nations" (thereby downplaying Jesus' interest in a Gentile mission), removes

---

[73] Gaston, *No Stone on Another*, 91: "When here the leper is not only healed but cleansed, then the prescribed sacrifice no longer makes any sense. That the man is nevertheless told to go to the priest and offer his sacrifice does not contradict this."

[74] Mark 12:28–34; Deut 6:4–5; Lev 19:18

[75] Mark 12:33.

[76] Loader, *Jesus' Attitude*, 101.

[77] Isa 56; Hos 6:6.

the juxtaposition of the cursed fig tree with the Temple incident (21:10–19; cf. Mark 11:11–21), and downplays the Markan identification of Jesus' community as the new Temple (21:12–13; cf. Mark 11:15–25). Matthew's redaction of Mark suggests a more positive attitude toward the Temple. According to Matt. 17:24–27, Jesus willingly pays the Temple tax (τὸ δίδραχμον),[78] and, in Matt. 5:23–24, instructs a disciple about offering a "gift" (δῶρόν) at the altar, implying that it is not sacrifice that requires criticism, only those sacrificing with the wrong attitude. Yet here Matthew's Jesus does not explicitly refer to animal sacrifice; he only mentions a "gift." This could theoretically refer to grain or cereal offerings. In any case, the historical authenticity of the passage is dubious.[79] Many interpreters are inclined to take Matt 5:23 as evidence for Jesus' affirmation of animal/blood sacrifice, but it should first be recalled that this is special "M" material not found in Mark or Luke. We must also recall that Matthew is writing after the destruction of the Temple and that this allegedly pro-Temple passage can also be read against the grain, that is, as an argument that "the demands of reconciliation take precedence over the action of sacrifice."[80] If the Matthean Jesus' instruction to "go back and make your offering" is redactional,[81] a gloss to "soften" the blow of Jesus' far more radical re-prioritizing of sacrifice, then this passage would have been "a particularly shocking statement for the hearers of Jesus because it reverses an established and accepted primacy of order – that God should be honoured above all else ... a dismissal of one of the most sacred images" of Judaism: "the Israelite engaged in the very act of sacrifice."[82] A more conservative view of the Temple is also found in Jesus' saying that

---

[78] Eric Ottenheijm, "'So the Sons are Free': The Temple Tax in the Matthean Community," in A. Houtman, M. Poorthuis, J. Schwartz, and Y. Turner (eds.), *The Actuality of Sacrifice: Past and Present* (Jewish and Christian Perspectives 28; Leiden: Brill, 2014), 71–88.

[79] The Jesus Seminar rejects the authenticity of the passage. Loader, *Jesus' Attitude*, 173–4.

[80] J. A. McGuckin, "Sacrifice and Atonement: An Investigation into the Attitude of Jesus of Nazareth towards Cultic Sacrifice," in Yehuda Bauer et al. (eds.), 3 vols., *Remembering for the Future: Working Papers and Addenda; Volume 1: Jews and Christians During and After the Holocaust*, (Oxford: Pergamon, 1989), 1:648–61, here 651.

[81] McGuckin, "Sacrifice and Atonement," 652.

[82] Gaston, *No Stone on Another*, 94: "The passage Mt 5:23f can not in any case be used to demonstrate that the early church participated in the temple sacrifices, for the main thrust of the passage does not concern sacrifice at all."

"whoever swears by the Temple swears by it and by Him who dwells in it," which contrasts sharply with Jesus declaring the Temple to be "forsaken."[83] Matthew tells us that Jesus healed the blind and lame in the Temple,[84] signifying Hosea 6.6's emphasis on "mercy, not sacrifice,"[85] as a kind of *messianic* cleansing."[86] Matthew's representation of Jesus as the Davidic king also symbolizes his ability to "build" a Temple while Peter's confession of Jesus as the Davidic king represents further cultic themes, with Peter as the "rock" or foundation stone "upon" which Jesus will "build" his church.[87] Matthew represents a more nuanced supersessionistic interpretation of Jesus as the new Temple-community-builder, but Matthew nonetheless still replaces the current Temple with the Temple of Jesus' followers.[88]

Many exegetes have rightly noted Matthew's relatively "positive" view of the Temple.[89] Yet Matthew's attitude to the Temple is more complex than that. In Matthew's narrative world, the positive Temple-sayings are set within a larger framework in which Jesus' death represents a *transference* of the soteriological efficacy of atoning sacrifice (Matt 1:21; 20:28; 26:28). In other words, Matthew's "positive" view of the Temple is temporary in so far as it represents a corrupted divine institution which is now being *replaced* by Jesus, abandoned by God, and re-instituted as the new "temple" of Jesus'

---

[83] See Matt. 23:21.

[84] Matt. 21.14.

[85] D. Patte, *The Gospel According to Matthew: A Structural Commentary on Matthew's Faith* (Philadelphia: Fortress, 1987), 287; W. Weren, "Jesus' Entry into Jeruasalem: Mt 21, 1–17 in the Light of the Hebrew Bible and the Septuagint," in C. M. Tuckett (ed.), *The Scriptures in the Gospels* (BETL 131; Leuven University Press, 1997), 117–41, esp. 136–7.

[86] Roloff, *Das Kerygma und der irdische Jesus*, 101; Harrington, *Matthew*, 295; D. Runnalls, "The King as Temple Builder: A Messianic Typology," in E. J. Furcha (ed.), *Spirit within Structure: Essays in Honor of George Johnston* (Allison Park: Pickwick Publications, 1983), 15–37, esp. 30; Söding, "Die Tempelaktion Jesu," 42; Trautman, *Zeichenhafte*, 97–8.

[87] See Michael Patrick Barber, "Jesus as the Davidic Temple Builder and Peter's Priestly Role in Matthew 16:16–19," *JBL*, 132.4 (2013), 935–53.

[88] Contra Crossley, *Date*, 108. On the theme of replacement in Matthew, see K. M. Campbell, "The New Jerusalem in Matthew 5:14," *SJT*, 31 (1978), 335–63; W. J. Dumbrell, "The Logic of the Law in Matthew V 1–20," *NovT*, 23.1 (1981), 1–21; T. L. Donaldson, *Jesus on the Mountain: A Study in Matthean Typology* (Sheffield: JSOT, 1985).

[89] Daniel M. Gurtner, *The Torn Veil: Matthew's Exposition of the Death of Jesus* (SNTSMS 139; Cambridge University Press, 2007), 100, argues that Matthew presents a "remarkably consistent and positive portrayal of the temple."

eschatological community. In this light, it is difficult to affirm the idea that Matthew's view of the Temple unproblematically reflects Jesus' "positive" view of the Temple cult.

Like Mark and Matthew, the Gospel of Luke also tells the story of Jesus in relationship to the Temple. Luke highlights the birth of John announced by Zechariah, a *priest in the Temple* (Luke 1:8-23). Jesus is brought *to the Temple* to be consecrated (Luke 2:22). He is recognized *in the Temple* by Simeon and Anna (2:25-26, 26-38). His parents offer *sacrifices* in the Temple (2:25, 39). It is in Luke's Gospel that Jesus *visits* the Temple – his "Father's house" – as a twelve year old boy (Luke 2:49). The Lukan narrative highlights Jerusalem as the place of Jesus' death (Luke 9:51; 13:22; 17:11). It is Luke's Gospel that narrates Jesus' appearances and ascension in Jerusalem (Luke 24:50) as well as the gift of the Holy Spirit (Luke 24:29; Acts 1:4). And it is Luke who describes the disciples as teaching and praying *in the Temple*. Luke portrays the Temple and the city of Jerusalem as the symbolic center to and from which salvation comes (Luke 24:47; Acts 1:8). Luke clearly wanted to illustrate the continuity between Jesus and Judaism by affirming the sanctity of the Temple. But if Jesus and the early Jesus movement participated in the Temple cult – as Luke seems to suggest – then why did they receive so much hostility and opposition from the Temple leadership?

In a recent study, Eyal Regev points out that the early Jesus movement and the Sadducean priesthood were in direct conflict between 30 and 62 CE, a time when "the early Christian leaders in Jerusalem were also brought to trial before the Temple's high priests."[90] He notes that the "major charges" brought against Peter, Stephen, Paul, and James were "violations of the Temple's sacredness, both by means of statements about and actions within it." He further suggests that the Jerusalem community "sought to partake in the Temple worship *in its own way.*" The book of Acts, therefore, accurately represents "the conviction of Jewish leaders that Jesus posed a threat to the Temple" and "the extreme sensitivity of the Sadducean high priests ... to any possible violation of the cultic order."[91] Early Christian activities in the Temple were understood as "sacrilegious threats" and their offenses

---

[90] See Regev, "Temple Concerns," 64; "Moral Impurity and the Temple in Early Christianity in Light of Qumranic Ideology and Ancient Greek Practice," *HTR*, 79 (2004), 383–411.

[91] Regev, "Temple Concerns," 65.

ranged from blasphemy to healing, teaching, and proclaiming Jesus' resurrection in the Temple to criticizing the Temple as "made by human hands,"[92] and bringing Gentiles into the Temple.[93] At the same time, Regev recognizes that "Luke portrays *Paul* as devoted to the Temple cult."[94] According to Acts 22:17, Paul "prays" in the Temple and comes to Jerusalem "to offer sacrifices."[95] Regev claims that Luke's account is tendentious,[96] or "*biased*, but not fictitious," arguing that since Luke failed to take advantage of several opportunities "to condemn the Temple and rebuke its high priests,"[97] he did "not wish to condemn the leaders of the Temple or the high priests … On the contrary, he confirms the credibility of the Temple."[98]

It is true that Luke affirms continuity between the Temple and early Christians, but it is equally true that Luke has not entirely redacted early Christian criticism of the Temple cult and its administration either. It is ironic, therefore, that Regev affirms the historicity and "originality" of the destruction-saying (with Jesus as the agent of destruction), but wonders why "the authors of the gospels downplay Jesus' anti-Temple stance."[99] Regev proposes that the evangelists were "reacting" to "accusations" that Jesus and his followers were enemies of the Temple. Regev concludes that Peter, Paul, James, and "the earliest traditions concerning the early Jerusalem Church largely regarded the Temple in a favorable fashion" and that "the actual attitude toward the Temple displayed by Peter, Paul, and James was not very different from that of their fellow Jews."[100]

Were the earliest Christians really "not very different" from their fellow Jews? To what extent should we allow the evangelists' representations of the Jesus movement to determine the *historical* accuracy of their representations? The author of Luke-Acts provides us with what is perhaps the most extensive, but ambiguous and paradoxical evidence of the Jesus movement's relationship to the Temple.[101]

---

[92] Acts 7:48; cf. Mark 14:58.
[93] Acts 21:18–26.
[94] Regev, "Temple Concerns," 69 (emphasis added).
[95] Acts 24:17–18.
[96] Regev, "Temple Concerns," 71.
[97] Regev, "Temple Concerns," 72.
[98] Regev, "Temple Concerns," 73–4.
[99] Regev, "Temple Concerns," 83–4.
[100] Regev, "Temple Concerns," 88.
[101] C. Bretytenbach and J. Schröter (eds.), *Die Apostelgeschichte und die hellenistiche Geschichtsschreibung: Festschrift für Eckhard Plümacher zu seinem 65. Geburtstag* (AJEC 57; Leiden: Brill, 2004).

Despite Acts' idyllic scene of the disciples meeting "in the Temple courts" (2:46), early Christian tradition clearly contains explicit criticism of the Temple.[102] Acts 3:1 describes Peter and John "going up to the Temple at the time of *prayer*" but it does not mention anything about them *sacrificing*.[103] Acts 21:26–27 describes Paul attempting to support and fulfill a Nazirite vow, but he never does.[104] Acts 6:14 reports that Jesus said that he wanted to "change the customs" of Moses, but then describes these accusers as "false witnesses":

> we have heard him say that this Jesus of Nazareth will destroy this place and will *change the customs* (ἀλλάξει τὰ ἔθη) that Moses handed down to us.

In Acts 7, Stephen is directly questioned by the high priest. Stephen responds by delivering a speech of Israel's salvation history, which includes an explicit criticism of the idolatrous Temple, emphasizing that

> the Most High does not dwell in houses made with human hands (Acts 7:48).

Despite the fact that there is a long-standing tradition in Early Judaism of criticizing the Temple's administration, Acts 7, like Q 13:35,

---

[102] Acts 6.13, 7. Hegesippus reports that James "went alone *into* the Temple and *prayed* in behalf of the people," but James does not sacrifice (Jerome, *De Viris Illustribus* 2). Ananus murders James (*Eccl. Hist.* 2.23.8–9; *A.J.* 20.9.1), illustrating a continuing conflict between the Jesus movement and the Temple. Josephus indicates that some Jews believed that Jerusalem was destroyed as a punishment for the murder of James (*Against Celsus* 1.47; *Eccl. Hist.* 2.23.19–20). For the Temple in Luke, see P. M. Head, "The Temple in Luke's Gospel," in T. D. Alexander and S. Gathercole (eds.), *Heaven on Earth: The Temple in Biblical Theology* (Carlisle: Paternoster, 2004), 102–19. T. Desmond Alexander, *From Eden to the New Jerusalem: An Introduction to Biblical Theology* (Grand Rapids: Kregel, 2008), 68, notes that "as Luke's account of the early church progresses [in Acts], the Jerusalem temple becomes less and less significant."

[103] Horsley, *Jesus and the Spiral of Violence*, 291–2: "there is no clear indication ... that the early apostles in Jerusalem were in the Temple to bring sacrifices."

[104] Matti Myllykoski, "James the Just in History and Tradition: Perspectives of Past and Present Scholarship (Part II)," *CBR*, 6 (2007), 11–98, esp. 19, notes that Luke's information about the purification rites is problematic and concludes that "it was only Luke who made Paul a Nazirite." Gaston, *No Stone on Another*, 97-98, suggests that "Luke's own uninformed interest tends to emphasize the fact that the church before him was not concerned with sacrifices at all ... it is likely that the church from the very beginning abstained from any cultic activities within the temple."

questions the soteriological efficacy of the present Temple.[105] Stephen's speech may not call for an abolition of the Temple cult, but it does seem to call for the reformation of Temple worship, perhaps suggesting that the Temple should be turned into "a sort of synagogue prayer/worship which also granted access to Gentiles."[106] Not only does Stephen (like the Jesus of Q) deny that God dwells in the Jerusalem Temple, he also quotes Amos 5:25–27, a prophetic passage which describes how Israel did *not* offer sacrifices to God during their forty years of wandering in the desert:

> Did you offer to me slain victims and sacrifices forty years in the wilderness, O house of Israel? No ...

Is the author of Acts suggesting that "sacrifices might not be necessary for God"?[107] This *appears* to be an early Christian apology for *not* sacrificing.[108] Stephen, in other words, is challenging the validity of the Temple cult.[109] Let us recall that the author of Luke narrates the Temple incident to illustrate Jesus' conflict with the Temple's administration but transfers the "false witnesses" to Acts in order to emphasize the parallels in the two trials, suggesting that Stephen was "indebted to Jesus for his views on the subject of the sanctuary in Jerusalem."[110]

---

[105] Hans Joachim Schoeps, *Theologie und Geschichte des Judenchristentums* (Tübingen: Mohr Siebeck, 1949), 7.

[106] Tiwald, "Jewish-Christian Trajectories in Torah and Temple Theology," 395–6. On the Temple in Acts, see Geir Otto Holmås, '"My House Shall Be a House of Prayer," Regarding the Temple as a Place of Prayer in Acts within the Context of Luke's Apologetic Objective,' *JSNT*, 27 (2005), 394–416, here 416. Although see Dennis Sylva, "The Meaning and Function of Acts 7.46–50," *JBL*, 106 (1987), 261–75; J. J. Kilgallen, "The Function of Stephen's Speech (Acts 2–53)," *Bib*, 70 (1989), 177–81; Edvin Larsson, "Temple-Criticism and the Jewish Heritage: Some Reflections on Acts 6–7," *NTS*, 39 (1993), 379–95.

[107] Tiwald, "Jewish-Christian Trajectories," 397: "sacrifices in the temple are not necessary 1) because God did not wish for them in the forty years of wandering in the desert and 2) because God does not even dwell in a handmade temple."

[108] Tiwald, "Jewish-Christian Trajectories," 397: "the 'Hellenists' were convinced already in their pre-Christian period that ritual laws – like temple sacrifices and circumcision – should be interpreted in a spiritual way and not be practiced as a cultic reality."

[109] Rudolf Pesch, *Die Apostelgeschichte I* (EKK 5; Zürich: Benziger, 1986), 238; Gerhard Schneider, *Die Apostelgeschichte: I. Teil: Einleitung, Kommentar zu Kap. 1,1–8, 40* (HTKNT 5.1; Freiburg: Herder, 1980), 439.

[110] Martin Henry Scharlemann, *Stephen: A Singular Saint* (AB 34; Rome: Pontifical Biblical Institute, 1968), 87. Scharlemann argues that Stephen was influenced by Samaritan criticism of and polemical hostility towards the Temple in Jerusalem.

Moreover, Acts affirms that Stephen was filled with the Holy Spirit, so Stephen's speech certainly seems to have Luke's blessing.[111] The fact, therefore, that Luke simultaneously takes special pains to emphasize Jesus and his earliest followers' faithfulness to the Temple amounts to an ambiguous and inconsistent approach to this topic.[112] In Acts 7:7, Stephen seems to affirm "this place" (the Temple), circumcision (7:8), and the "living oracles" at Sinai (7:38), but then charges the Israelites with idolatry (7:39–41), arguing that "the Most High does not dwell in what is made by human hands" (χειροποίητος) (7:49), a word used in the LXX to attack *idolatry*.[113] Is Stephen both upholding and attacking the Temple?[114] Or has the role and function of the Temple been misunderstood?[115] Stephen affirms that it is fitting to have a place to worship God and does not so much criticize the existence of the Temple as the *use* to which it was put, that is, the idolatry that surrounded it.[116] In other words, Luke has an *agenda* in portraying Jesus and the earliest Christians as faithful to the Torah and Temple cult,[117] but that agenda could not conceal a vigorous anti-cultic component in the tradition characterized by criticism of the Temple cult.[118] Luke-Acts affirms the Temple as the proper place for prayer, worship, miracle-working, and teaching, but never portrays or describes any early Christian performance of animal sacrifice.[119] In fact, Stephen's speech seems to draw a sharp contrast between the "authentic" Torah and "the ordinances concerning sacrifices and Temple, which were invented by Jews."[120] What came before the golden calf was divine; what came after was not. Stephen's opposition to the Temple seems "absolute and unrestricted."[121] The question

---

[111] Acts 6:3; 7:55.

[112] Marcel Simon, *St. Stephen and the Hellenists in the Primitive Church: The Haskell Lectures Delivered at the Graduate School of Theology Oberlin College, 1956* (London: Longmans, Green, and Co., 1958), 24.

[113] Isa 2:18; 10:11; 31:7; 46:6.

[114] Barrett, *Acts*, 337–9.

[115] Salo, *Law*, 172–89.

[116] See Schneider, *Apostelgeschichte I*, 467–8; J. Bradley Chance, *Jerusalem, the Temple, and the New Age in Luke-Acts* (Macon: Mercer, 1988), 40; Brawley, *Luke-Acts*, 118–20.

[117] See S. Arai, "Zum 'Tempelwort' Jesu in Apostelgeschichte 6.14," *NTS*, 34 (1988), 403–10.

[118] Klinghardt, *Gesetz*, 284–303, here 303.

[119] Acts 21 does not count because Paul never fulfills the vow or offers animal sacrifices.

[120] Simon, *St. Stephen*, 48.

[121] Simon, *St. Stephen*, 53. For Stephen, the Temple seems to be equated with idolatrous worship (51). Simon links Stephen's speech with Justin Martyr's *Dialogue*

before us, then, is: how could the Stephen of Acts consider the Temple to be a place of idolatrous worship while the author of Acts simultaneously portrays the earliest Christians as "worshipping" in the Temple, a portrait not unlike Hegesippus' description of James also praying in the Temple on behalf of Israel?[122]

Stephen's speech *appears* to be the record of an intra-Jewish critique, but it can more plausibly be read as a post-Pauline historicization of a Christian critique of Judaism. That, in any case, is how it *functions* in Acts, where Stephen's speech delineates how Israel has been unfaithful to God. Stephen is brought before the Sanhedrin, which includes the high priest, the elders, and scribes, and proceeds to recount how "our ancestors" refused to obey Moses (7:39), "opposed" the Holy Spirit (7:51), persecuted the prophets (7:52), became "betrayers and murderers," and failed to keep the law (7:53). This list represents far more than a simple critique of the Temple, but it is not Stephen's critique of the Temple that leads to his stoning. It is only after Stephen claims to have a vision of Jesus in heaven (7:55–57) that he is murdered. Nonetheless, the case against Stephen is cumulative. He is introduced as one who calls the Torah into question, although Luke is at great pains to dismiss this as the testimony of "false witnesses:

> [The] "synagogue of the Freedmen … Cyrenians, Alexandrians, and others of those from Cilicia and Asia … secretly instigated some men to say 'We have heard him speak blasphemous words against Moses and God.'"[123]
>
> "This man never stops saying things against this holy place and the law; for we have heard him say that this Jesus of Nazareth will destroy this place and will change the customs that Moses handed on to us."[124]

Stephen's speech is a skillfully crafted literary work that nonetheless betrays its artifice by subtly shifting its rhetorical focus from "*our* ancestors" (οἱ πατέρες ἡμῶν) to "*your* ancestors" (οἱ πατέρες ἡμῶν).[125]

(22:2–6), where Amos 5:25–27 with Jer 7:21–22 are linked, with Justin interpreting the sacrificial system as not originally desired by God but accepted them in order to divert the Jews into proper worship. For Justin, the sacrificial system was divinely inspired but not because God wanted or needed sacrifices.

[122] Eusebius, *Eccl. Hist.* 2.23.6.

[123] Acts 6:11.

[124] Acts 6:13–15.

[125] Luke 7:2, 15, 19, 38, 44, 45; cf. 7:51, 52, 53.

This shift represents a transitional moment in Luke's larger narrative, distancing Stephen from the Jews, and illustrating how an intra-Jewish conflict became a conflict *between* Jews and Christians. This serves Luke's larger purpose of explaining how the Gospel was proclaimed to the Gentiles *after* it had been rejected by the Jews.

The Temple Incident in the Gospel of John

The Gospel of John represents a relatively distinctive approach to Jesus' relationship to the Temple.[126] The most conspicuous example of this is that John locates the Temple incident at the *beginning* of his ministry, rather than during Jesus' last week.[127] There are indications, both in vocabulary and in plot, that John's version may be based on Mark.[128] Jesus' action at the very beginning of his three-year ministry disrupts the Temple's commerce, drives out the buyers and sellers, turns over the tables of the money-changers, and the seats of those who sold doves:[129]

> In the Temple he found people selling cattle, sheep, and doves, and the money changers seated at their tables. Making a whip of cords, *he drove all of them out of* (πάντας

---

[126] On the Temple incident, see G. Selong, "The Cleansing of the Temple in Jn 2,13–22 with a Reconsideration of the Dependence of the Fourth Gospel upon the Synoptics," Ph.D. diss., Faculty of Theology, Leuven, 1971; and J. Rahner, *Er aber sprach vom Tempel seines Leibes. Jesus von Nazaret als Ort der Offenbarung Gottes im vierten Evangelium* (BBB, 117; Bodenheim: Philo, 1998); M. L. Coloe, *God Dwells with Us: Temple Symbolism in the Fourth Gospel* (Collegeville: Liturgical Press, 2001); A. R. Kerr, *The Temple of Jesus' Body: The Temple Theme in the Gospel of John* (JSNTSup, 220; Sheffield Academic Press, 2002).

[127] John Muddiman, "The Triumphal Entry and Cleansing of the Temple (Mark 11.1–17 and Parallels): a Jewish Festival Setting?," in C. M. Tuckett (ed.), *Feast and Festivals* (CBET 53; Leuven: Peeters, 2009), 77–86, dissociates the "Triumphal Entry" and "Cleansing" from any particular festival setting (especially Passover) and suggests that these events could have taken place at *any* time during Jesus' ministry when he might have visited Jerusalem (cf. John 2).

[128] For common vocabulary, see Ἱεροσόλυμα, ἱερόν, πωλέω, περιστερά, ἐκβάλλω, κολλυβιστής, τράπεζα, ἀνα/καταστρέφω, and οἶκος. Both Mark and John describe Jesus' arrival, his overturning the tables of the money-changers, driving out the dovesellers, and both provide an explanation following a scriptural citation (Mark's citation of Isa 56:7/Jer 7:11, and John's use of Zech 14:21 and Ps 69:10). See Davies and Allison, *Matthew*, 3.134–35.

[129] Mark 11.15.

ἐξέβαλεν ἐκ) the Temple, *both* the sheep *and* the cattle (τά τε πρόβατα καὶ τοὺς βόας). He also poured out the coins of the money changers and overturned their tables. He told those who were selling the doves, 'Take these things out of here! Stop making my Father's house a marketplace! His disciples remembered that it was written, 'Zeal for your house will consume me.'[130]

As in Mark, John's Jesus also objects to the Temple being "a house of trade" (or marketplace) (ἐμπορίου), possibly alluding to Zech. 14:21 ("In that day there shall be no more a trader in the house of the Lord").[131] Jesus' action is directly against the commercial activity taking place in the Temple court. John's narrative has Jesus remove the sacrificial animals from the Temple.[132] As in Mark, Jesus' action symbolizes the abolition of sacrifice.[133] In fact, the expulsion of "traders *in animals*" is "the single point of consensus" in the four Gospels about what Jesus actually did.[134] The author cites Ps. 69:10 to emphasize Jesus' "zeal" for the Temple as the house of God and provides us with Jesus' prediction of the Temple's destruction ("Destroy this sanctuary and in three days I will raise it up"),

[130] John 2:14–17.

[131] John 2:16. See Cecil Roth, "The Cleansing of the Temple and Zecharia xiv.21," *NovT*, 4 (1960), 174–81.

[132] On the authenticity of John's account, see D. Moody Smith, "Jesus Traditions in the Gospel of John," in S. E. Porter and T. Holmén (eds.), 4 vols., *Handbook for the Study of the Historical Jesus* (Leiden: Brill, 2011), 3: 1997–2039, 2036.

[133] C. K. Barrett, *The Gospel According to St. John* (London: SPCK, 1955), 198; R. Schnackenburg, *The Gospel According to John*, 2 vols. (New York: Crossroad, 1987), 356: "The cleansing of the temple is meant to portray the abrogation of the Jewish cult by Jesus." See also Jacob Neusner, "Money-Changers in the Temple: The Mishnah's Explanation," *NTS*, 35 (1989), 287–90, esp., 290; Coloe, *God Dwells with Us*, 73. Kenneth A. Matthews, "John, Jesus and the Essenes: Trouble at the Temple," *CTR*, 3.1 (1988), 101–26, here 120–21, interprets John's version as Jesus calling for "a disjuncture between the old and new orders of worship." The Mosaic system is "displaced as a result of its being superseded by the presence of Jesus" (125). The eschatological Temple "had no sacrificial system." On Johannine temple-symbolism, see Kåre Sigvald Fuglseth, *Johannine Sectarianism in Perspective: A Sociological, Historical, and Comparative Analysis of Temple and Social Relationships in the Gospel of John, Philo and Qumran* (NovT Sup 119; Leiden: Brill, 2005); Paul M. Hoskins, *Jesus as the Fulfillment of the Temple in the Gospel of John* (Milton Keynes: Paternoster, 2006).

[134] Chilton, *The Temple of Jesus*, 100 (emphasis added).

instructing us to identify Jesus' body as the replacement of the Temple.[135] The Johannine Jesus sees himself as the new Temple.[136] It is difficult not to see Jesus as here expressing a "fundamental opposition to the temple itself,"[137] announcing that "the time is coming *and now is,* when the true worshippers will worship the Father in spirit and in truth" (4:23), an explicitly anti-cultic and anti-Temple orientation. This reading is further supported by the fact that Jesus "found" the sellers and the money-changers and "threw *all* of them," that is, *the sheep and cattle,* out of the Temple.[138] He overturns the tables of the money-changers, but he tells the sellers to *remove* the doves.[139] Does John's πάντας ἐξέβαλεν refer *only* to the animals?[140] Or does it refer to the animals *and* the traders?[141] The gender of πάντας is masculine, but 2:14 contains all three possible antecedent genders for πάντας – those selling (m); cattle (m); sheep (n); doves (f); and money-changers (m) and they could all theoretically have provided

[135] Harold W. Attridge, "The Temple and Jesus the High Priest in the New Testament," in *Jesus and the Temple*, 213–37, here 215, asserts that "The most primitive form of the saying threatening the Temple is that of the Gospel of John." Paesler, *Das Tempelwort Jesu,* proposes *two* layers of tradition for John 2:19: an original form referring to destruction and rebuilding, and a redactional layer which added "in three days."

[136] Wright, *Jesus and the Victory of God,* 426. Jacob Chanikuzhy, *Jesus, The Eschatological Temple: An Exegetical Study of Jn 2,13–22 in the Light of the Pre-70 C.E. Eschatological Temple Hopes and the Synoptic Temple Action* (CBET; Leuven: Peeters, 2012).

[137] G. A. Yee, *Jewish Feasts and the Gospel of John* (Wilmington: Glazier, 1989), 62.

[138] John 2.15.

[139] John 2.16.

[140] E. Haenchen, *John,* 1, 2 (Hermeneia; Philadelphia: Fortress, 1984), 183; E. C. Hoskyns, *The Fourth Gospel* (London: Faber and Faber, 1947), 194; M. A. Matson, "The Contribution to the Temple Cleansing by the Fourth Gospel," in E. H. Lovering (ed.), *Society of Biblical Literature 1992 Seminar Papers* (SBLSP 31; Atlanta: Scholars, 1992), 489–506, esp. 499.

[141] John Henry Bernard, *A Critical and Exegetical Commentary on the Gospel According to St. John,* 2 vols., (Edinburgh: T & T Clark, 1928), 1, 90–1; Barrett, *John,* 197–8; B. Lindars, *The Gospel of John* (NCBC 25; London: Oliphants, 1972), 138; Ben Witherington III, *John's Wisdom* (Cambridge: Lutterworth Press, 1995), 87. G. R. Beasley-Murray, *John* (WBC 36; Waco: Word Books, 1987), 38. John McHugh, *A Critical and Exegetical Commentary on John 1–4* (ICCHSONT; London: Continuum, 2009), 203, argues that the term refers to the merchants in v. 14 and secondarily to the sheep and cattle in vol. 15 since John cannot be referring to the animals only (which would have used the neuter πάντα). On this reading, πάντας takes its gender from the masculine τους πωλουντας (those selling) and τους κερματιστας (money-changers) in vol. 14.

the pronoun's gender.[142] The question is whether the masculine pronoun πάντας covers τους πωλουωτας as well. The masculine form can be used when different genders are combined in one grouping.[143] Here John uses a partitive–appositive construction (τε … καί) to define the parts of the pronoun πάντας.[144] Consequently, τά τε πρόβατα καὶ τοὺς βόας stands in apposition and clarifies the constituent parts of the whole (πάντας). The phrase is rightly translated in the New Revised Standard Version (NRSV) and other translations as "he drove them all, *both* the sheep *and* the cattle, from the Temple."[145] Normal Greek grammar suggests that the term refers to the *animals*, not the traders.[146] The fact that the Gospel of John explicitly portrays Jesus as expelling the sacrificial *animals* out of the Temple (but not the traders) is a significant detail: Jesus' prophetic action signifies the end of *animal* sacrifice.

The New Testament Gospels present us with four distinctive narrative portraits of Jesus' relationship to the Temple,[147] no particular one of which can simply be called "historical" or "most primitive." They are all "tendentious."[148] There is no reliable historical evidence about Jesus' relationship to the Temple outside of the Gospels and Acts. The letter to the Hebrews and the book of Revelation illustrate the direction that the early Christian movement was heading: away from traditional Temple practices and toward an explicitly "antitemple

[142] If John had used the neuter πάντα, this would suggest that Jesus only drove out the sheep yet since it was the Passover, the sacrificial sheep had to be male (Exod. 12:5). The masculine pronoun covers both sheep and cattle. If John had used the feminine pronoun πασας, this would suggest he drove out the doves with a whip. The narrative excludes the possibility that the dove sellers were driven out of the Temple with the whip because v. 15 says that Jesus addressed them, saying "Take these out of here!" This suggests that the vendors continued to be present inside the court even after he drove "all" out. John used the masculine pronoun because he did not want to repeat the pronoun in the relevant gender before each word in the subsequent phrase.

[143] Matson, "The Contribution to the Temple Cleansing," 499, n. 55; Haenchen, *John*, 1, 183.

[144] This construction connects concepts of the same kind or corresponding as opposites. When the two terms are combined, the conjunctions signal a closer connection between two sentence parts.

[145] Andy Alexis-Baker, "Violence, Nonviolence and the Temple Incident in John 2:13–15," *BI*, 20 (2012), 73–96, here 88–92.

[146] Thomas R. Yoder Neufeld, *Killing Enmity: Violence and the New Testament* (Grand Rapids: Baker Academic, 2011), 60–1.

[147] Chilton, *The Temple of Jesus*, 115.

[148] Chilton, *The Temple of Jesus*, 119.

polemic."[149] The letter to the Hebrews, in particular – perhaps the most explicitly "sacrificial" text in the New Testament,[150] replaces the physical Temple in Jerusalem – an institution that did not offer an effective atonement, with a heavenly Temple.[151] Instead of bloody sacrifices, Jesus is both the high priest and the final sacrifice,[152] the one who provides true atonement in a sanctuary *not* made by human hands.[153] Finally, the book of Revelation envisions a future *without* the cultic Temple:

> I saw no Temple (ναὸν) in the city, for its Temple is the Lord God the Almighty and the Lamb (Rev. 21:22).

The new age will not need a physical Temple because the New Jerusalem will be transformed into a Temple, and God will live *among* His people.[154]

The New Testament evidence for the historical Jesus' relationship to the Temple is inconsistent and ambiguous. Despite a number of pro-Temple sayings in the Gospels of Mark, Matthew, and Luke-Acts, the Gospels emphasize Jesus' tension with the Temple authorities and his predicting, if not threatening, the destruction of the Temple. Pauline themes and motifs were adopted by Mark and subsequently absorbed by Matthew, Luke, and John. The book of Acts, the letter to the Hebrews, and the book of Revelation provide further evidence of subversive anti-Temple themes in the early Christian tradition. It remains for us now to evaluate whether our sources support, confirm, or further problematize the traditional models of Jesus' "cleansing" or symbolic "destruction" of the Temple.

---

[149] Klawans, *Purity*, 242.

[150] Girard, *Things Hidden*, 228.

[151] Heb 9:9–10, 10:4, 11; 8:1–5.

[152] Heb 7:22, 24–26.

[153] Heb 9:11, 14.

[154] See 1 Cor. 3:16–17; Eph. 2:21; cf. 1 Pet. 2:5–11. For the Temple-symbolism in Revelation, see T. Desmond Alexander, *From Eden to the New Jerusalem: An Introduction to Biblical Theology* (Grand Rapids: Kregel, 2008), 18–20.

5

THE TEMPLE INCIDENT: TOWARD A NEW
MODEL OF ESCHATOLOGICAL RESTORATION

The Symbolic Destruction of the Temple

Since the publication of E. P. Sanders's seminal *Jesus and Judaism*, the idea that the Temple incident should be read as a prophetic and symbolic destruction of the Temple has gained considerable support and popularity. Sanders emphasized the Temple incident as the central causal factor in Jesus' arrest, trial, and crucifixion, and linked the Temple incident with Jesus' destruction sayings, although it is still not clear *why* Jesus (or God) thought this was necessary. We are only told that Jesus expected that "a new temple would be given by God from heaven."[1] But did he? Despite the fact that *some* Early Jewish texts seem to envision the eschatological renewal or restoration of the Temple,[2] there is not much evidence for any widespread expectation that a new *physical* Temple would be built in Jerusalem during Jesus' lifetime.[3] Sanders does not attempt to adjudicate between whether Jesus personally *threatened* or simply *predicted* the Temple's destruction, although he seems to favor the former.[4] This ambivalence is both problematic and significant, for if the original form of the destruction-saying was *predictive*, but not *threatening*, then the incident itself may have had more to do with the particulars of *what* Jesus was criticizing than with the Temple as a doomed institution.

---

[1] Richard Bauckham, "Jesus' Demonstration in the Temple," in B. Lindards (ed.), *Law and Religion: Essays on the Place of the Law in Israel and Early Christianity* (Cambridge: James Clarke & Co., 1988), 86–7, points out that many of Jesus' contemporaries hoped for the replacement of the Herodian Temple with a new Temple.

[2] See *1 En.* 90.28–30; Zech. 14:21; *Shemoneh Esre*, benediction 12.

[3] Horsley, *Jesus and the Spiral of Violence*, 293, 289: "there is little or no textual evidence for a rebuilt Temple as part of some supposed Jewish apocalyptic scheme into which Jesus' saying might have fit." See also Klawans, *Purity, Sacrifice, and the Temple*, 233, 236.

[4] Sanders, *Jesus and Judaism*, 73.

Are there good grounds for thinking that the prediction-saying is earlier and/or more authentic?[5] Mark 13:1–2 is set during Jesus' last week with his disciples. On the other hand, Mark 14:57–58 occurs during Jesus' trial, when none of his disciples were present. Here the threatening-saying is dismissed as *hearsay* and "false witness" ("We *heard* him say, '*I* will destroy.'"). Mark 14:57 and Matt. 26:60–61 both spiritualize the tradition, with covert references to Jesus' body and resurrection. John 2:19–22 takes this metaphorical interpretation further, claiming for Jesus only the power to restore, not destroy, and "raise" (ἐγερῶ), not "rebuild" (οἰκοδομεῖν), removing the accusation of destruction from Jesus while affirming the authenticity of the prediction. The most primitive version of the tradition, therefore, seems to be Mark 13:1–2, where the predictive form is more reminiscent of a warning, as in Q 13:34–35, where Jesus laments over the fate of Jerusalem, the city that "kills the prophets":

> Mark 13:2: "Not one stone will be left on another."
>
> Q 13:34–35: "Jerusalem ... how often I wanted to gather your children together ... And you were not willing. Look! Your House is forsaken" (ἀφίεται).

In Q 11:50–51, this judgment on Israel is envisioned as a "settling of accounts" for "this generation," a divine punishment brought on Jerusalem for killing the prophets. There will be judgment on those who do not pay heed to Jesus' warning.[6] If the earliest form of the saying is *predictive*-prophetic, supplemented by additional *threatening* sayings, then the *Sitz im Leben* of the threatening sayings may be the perceived rejection of the post-Easter Jesus movement. This

---

[5] Paesler, *Das Tempelwort Jesu*, 76–92, 256, 259–60. Paesler argues that Mark 13:2 is an authentic (Aramaic) saying of Jesus (based on an unfulfilled prophecy) and that Mark 14:58 is dependent on Mark 13:2. Mark 14:58, however, influenced other passages (cf. Matt 26:61; Mark 15:29; acts 6:14) (189-193). Jostein Ådna, *Jesu Stellung zum Tempel: die Tempelaktion und das Tempelwort als Ausdruck seiner messianischen Sendung* (WUNT II.119; Tübingen: Mohr Siebeck, 2000), 440–2, argues that Mark 13:2 and Mark 14:58 are both authentic and independent. Wedderburn, "Jesus' Action in the Temple," 15–20, also regards Mark 13:2 as possibly authentic.

[6] O. H. Steck, *Israel und das gewaltsame Geschick der Propheten: Untersuchungen zur Überlieferung des deuteronomistischen Geschichtsbildes im Alten Testament, Spätjudentum und Urchristentum* (WMANT 23; Neukirchen-Vluyn: Neukirchener, 1967); Lührmann, *Die Redaktion*. Han, *Jerusalem and the Early Jesus Movement*, 183, suggests that while Q 13:34–35 declares the Temple "forsaken," Q 11:49–51 announces "the total rejection of the Temple."

may be why Mark calls those who accused Jesus of *threatening* the Temple "*false* witnesses" –because Jesus only *predicted* the Temple's destruction. Finally, if Jesus did *not* threaten to destroy the Temple, then there is no direct link between the destruction-sayings and the Temple incident. The incident may not have been an act of symbolic destruction, but could point in an altogether different direction.[7] It is also difficult to reconcile Jesus' alleged prophecy of the Temple's imminent destruction with Jesus' alleged *participation* in the Temple cult. It is difficult to imagine him condemning the Temple to destruction one day and eating the sacrificial Passover lamb the next. Indeed, Theissen and Merz have rightly called into question Sanders's assumption that Jesus' participation in the Temple's purification rites before Passover can be taken "for granted."[8]

Despite this apparent incongruity, the symbolic-destruction model has a significant following. In *Who Killed Jesus?*, John Dominic Crossan offers his own reconstruction, identifying both John the Baptist and Jesus as "engaged in a program of social revolution and political subversion in the name of the Jewish God."[9] Locating John and Jesus within the larger social, economic, and political contexts in which "peasant attitudes" toward the Temple were "ambiguous," Crossan reviews several episodes relating to the Temple: the turmoil over Caligula's statue,[10] the Zealot attack on the high priesthood during the Revolt,[11] the general atmosphere of upheaval during festival days,[12] and the prophetic "oracle" against the Temple pronounced by another peasant "Jesus" in 62 CE.[13] Crossan concludes that the Jewish people could be both "for and against their Temple," with the high holy days such as Passover always being occasions of potential conflict and violence. Words and actions, "even symbolic actions against the Temple could get you killed."[14] In this context, John the Baptist's provision of "a radical alternative to the Temple cult as an apocalyptic visionary announcing the cataclysmic advent of God," a

---

[7] Sanders, *Jesus and Judaism*, 76, appeals to Acts' narrative accounts of early Christian activity in the Temple (2.46; 3.1; 21.26) as an "added advantage" in his case for the historicity of the Temple incident as an act of symbolic destruction.

[8] Theissen and Merz, *The Historical Jesus*, 432.

[9] Crossan, *Who Killed Jesus?*, 58.

[10] *A.J.* 18.263–72; *B.J.* 2.192–197; Philo, *Embassy to Gaius* 222–49.

[11] *B.J.* 4.147–8, 153–7.

[12] *B.J.* 2.10–13; *A.J.* 17.204–5; *B.J.* 2.224–7; *A.J.* 20.106–12.

[13] *B.J.* 6.300–309.

[14] Crossan, *Who Killed Jesus?*, 58.

"free and populist alternative to the Temple's purification process for sin,"[15] naturally had dangerous implications. Like Sanders, Crossan sees Jesus' death as linked to the Temple and holds that Jesus must have done or said something against it.[16] Crossan also holds *Thomas'* saying on the Temple to be early and independent:

> Jesus said, 'I will destroy this house (ϯⲛⲁϣⲟⲣ[ϣⲣ ⲙ̅ⲡⲉⲉⲓⲏ] ⲉⲓ), and no one will be able to build it again' (L. 71).

Jesus' reference to the Temple as "this house" is clearly a reference to the Jerusalem Temple, not an esoteric metaphor for the world.[17] This reading is confirmed not only by the Coptic grammar, but by early Christian tradition.[18] Many scholars see this as a form of the Temple saying, not unlike Q 13:35, where Jesus proclaims "your *house* is forsaken." "House" here is not a covert reference to "body," as in the Gospel of John.[19] The Thomasine Jesus insists that the Temple will *not be rebuilt.*[20] We should be cautious about assuming that *Thomas'* version of the saying is early when the exact opposite is more likely.[21] Crossan's case hinges on the dating of this *Thomas*-saying, for it sets the stage for his reconstruction of Jesus declaring "*I* will destroy this house." Consequently, when Crossan turns to the Gospel of John (which he also takes to be an *independent* saying), he proposes that John "is very careful to protect Jesus against saying 'I will destroy,'"[22] implying that we now have two independent sources of Jesus threatening to destroy the Temple. It is more likely, however, that Jesus only issued a prophetic *warning* of destruction, which was then misrepresented as an eschatological *threat* before it became an *imperative* (John) and, finally, in *Thomas*, a free-floating, first-person representation of Jesus claiming to be the *agent* of destruction. The fact that *Thomas* does not appeal to the motif of the rebuilt Temple, replaced Temple, or the community-as-Temple also argues against an early date. *Thomas* simply asserts that the Temple, that is, *the sacrificial*

---

[15] Crossan, *Who Killed Jesus?*, 43.

[16] Crossan, *Who Killed Jesus?*, 59.

[17] Gerd Lüdemann, *Jesus After 2000 Years: What He Really Said and Did* (Amherst: Prometheus, 2001), 626.

[18] Q 13:34–35; Mark 11:17; John 2:16–17.

[19] There are also instances in *Thomas* where "house" just means "house." See L. 16, 97.

[20] McL. Wilson, *Studies in the Gospel of Thomas*, 115.

[21] Crossan, *Who Killed Jesus?*, 59; Crossan, *The Historical Jesus*, 356.

[22] Crossan, *Who Killed Jesus?*, 61.

system, will *never* be restored. The *Gospel of Thomas* does not associate or identify the end of the Temple with Jesus' death as a sacrifice. Unlike Mark, *Thomas* does not protest that Jesus' destruction-saying is "false testimony." Unlike John, *Thomas* does not attempt to explain it as a reference to Jesus' body. *Thomas* does not portray Jesus as anticipating a new *physical* Temple nor does it redefine the Temple as the community of believers. *Thomas* simply sees an irrevocable end to the Temple and its sacrificial system with no hint of Christian supersessionism or any suggestion that Jesus' sacrificial death replaced the need for the sacrificial system. We must conclude that L. 71 is neither early nor dominical.

Mark's version of the saying remains the *first* and *earliest* version of the tradition, and the Markan Jesus is clearly portrayed as "symbolically destroying the Temple, just as he had destroyed the fig tree."[23] Mark's Jesus "does not cleanse or purify the Temple," he destroys it. For Crossan, however, cleansing and purification are "very misleading terms for what Jesus was doing, namely, an *attack* on the Temple's very existence," a "symbolic negation of all that office or Temple stands for."[24] Crossan denies that anything being done in the Temple was "invalid or illegitimate,"[25] but nonetheless seems to accept Mark's account as more or less *historical*: Jesus *actually* threatened the destruction of the Temple and the evangelists, embarrassed, downplayed the saying and deed so as to signify a "cleansing." According to Crossan, Mark's insistence (during Jesus' trial-scene) that Jesus' word against the Temple was *false* testimony is misleading: Mark knows that Jesus "destroyed the Temple," not only because he juxtaposes the Temple incident with the cursed fig tree, but also because he explicitly portrays the Temple veil being rent in two.[26] Considering that the symbolic destruction of the Temple is *precisely* the image that Mark *wants* his readers to imagine and envision, I am reluctant to reinscribe Jesus' Temple action as a historical memory of symbolic destruction, not only because it would fall all too neatly in line with Mark's agenda of Jesus *replacing* the Temple,

---

[23] Crossan, *Who Killed Jesus?*, 63.
[24] Crossan, *Who Killed Jesus?*, 65 (emphasis added).
[25] Crossan, *Who Killed Jesus?*, 64.
[26] Crossan, *Who Killed Jesus?*, 109–10. Crossan concludes "*something* about destroying the Temple, however misunderstood, was constitutive for the accusation against Jesus. But if there was a historical link between Jesus' Temple action and his subsequent execution, it is now fast disappearing from the tradition."

but because Mark repeatedly uses symbolic actions and motifs in his narrative. Jesus' *symbolic* destruction of the Temple, like the *symbolic* fig tree and the *symbolic* Temple curtain, are coherent motifs in his larger project of Temple-supersessionism. We must be cautious in portraying the historical *Jesus* in such terms, not only because a violent destruction of the Temple seems inconsistent with Jesus' larger program of love, compassion, and nonviolence, but more so because Jesus was a first-century Jew and it is very difficult to picture him threatening to destroy the Temple *himself*. It is far more likely that Jesus issued a predictive, prophetic *warning* of destruction and that the Markan tradition developed this warning into a full scale *threat* of destruction. This is why no reliable witnesses could be found at Jesus' trial: because Jesus *never said* that *he* would destroy the Temple.

Jesus' prophetic warning of the Temple's destruction should not be viewed as a *threat*. Jesus' warning was predictive; we should not identify Jesus as an agent of destruction.[27] The incident itself was not a symbolic act of destruction.[28] Overturning a few tables would have been an exceptionally weak symbol of eschatological destruction.[29] Moreover, if Jesus only temporarily interrupted business and demonstrated concern about the sanctity of the Temple, there is no good reason to describe the event as an act of symbolic destruction. The texts that anticipate or hope for a new or rebuilt Temple – and that presumably support the idea that Jesus expected a new Temple – are pre-Herodian, pre-Christian, and do not reflect *Jesus*' own position.[30] Jewish reverence for the Temple as the house of God could clearly be combined with criticism of its administration and warnings of its possibly imminent destruction. Here we must proceed with caution, for the common interpretation of the Temple incident as a

---

[27] N. H. Taylor, "Jerusalem and the Temple in Early Christian Life and Teaching," *Neot*, 33 (1999), 445–61 (456), sees Jesus' symbolic act as a corrective measure.

[28] Contra Sanders, *Jesus and Judaism*, 61–76; Holmén, *Jesus and Jewish Covenant Thinking*, 323–9; Matson, "The Contribution to the Temple Cleansing," 489–506; Theissen and Merz, *The Historical Jesus*, 433; Wright, *Jesus and the Victory of God*, 334.

[29] Peter Richardson, *Building Jewish in the Roman East* (JSJSup 92; Waco: Baylor, 2004), 242; "Why Turn the Tables? Jesus' Protest in the Temple Precincts," in E. H. Lovering (ed.), *SBL 1992 Seminar Papers* (SBLSP 31; Atlanta: Scholars), 508. For criticism of Sanders's suggestion, see Ådna, *Jesu Stellung zum Tempel*, 354–7.

[30] For the rebuilding or restoration of the Temple, see 4Q174; 11QTemple 29.8–10; *1 En.* 90.28–29; 91.13; *Tob.* 13.16–17; 14.4–7; *Jub.* 1.15–17; *SibOr* 3.286–294; *2 Bar.* 68.5–6.

prophetic act of symbolic destruction all too easily lends itself to supersessionist theologies in which the Temple is replaced by Jesus, with God favoring the "new covenant" by eliminating, punishing, and judging the old covenant.[31] N. T. Wright, for example, affirms Sanders's proposal that the Temple incident represents a symbolic destruction of the Temple, but goes several steps further in asserting that Jesus not only *replaced* the Temple with his own followers,[32] but believed his death had atoning, redemptive significance:[33] Jesus was, in fact, the living embodiment of the "return of YHWH to Zion."[34] Consequently, God could now "inhabit his people, turning them individually into walking temples and corporately into a single body designed for praise, holiness and sacrifice."[35] This supersessionistic reading of the Temple incident is certainly consistent with post-Easter theological developments, but it does not adequately address the inner-religious conflicts that led to Jesus' arrest and trial before Jewish authorities.

While the "Third Quest" rightly focuses on "restoration eschatology" as the key to understanding Jesus' program of renewal, there is a pervasive idea in the literature that an eschatological judgment or "tribulation" precedes or accompanies this restoration. Since Schweitzer, the idea that Jesus viewed his death as inaugurating this "tribulation" and providing atonement for Israel has proven attractive to many.[36] According to Schweitzer, Jesus died a tragic figure, a messianic failure broken on the wheel of history, waiting for an End that never came. Yet this model also portrays Jesus in historical continuity with Christian atonement theology. Moreover, according to this model, the destruction of the Temple fits quite neatly into the "eschatological" timetable, with the "symbolic destruction" of the Temple paralleling the emergence of an eschatological "remnant" now identifiable as "Christianity." It is ironic, therefore, that Sanders

---

[31] For criticism of this tendency, as well as anachronistic views of sacrifice, see Klawans, *Purity, Sacrifice, and the Temple* ; Ullucci, *The Christian Rejection of Animal Sacrifice*.

[32] N. T. Wright, *Simply Jesus: A New Vision of Who He Was, What He Did, and Why He Matters* (New York: HarperOne, 2011), 175.

[33] Wright, *Jesus and the Victory of God*, 591–603; Dunn, *Jesus Remembered*, 824; McKnight, *Jesus and His Death*, esp. 336–9.

[34] Wright, *Paul and the Faithfulness of God*, 1041–2.

[35] Wright, *Paul and the Faithfulness of God*, 1074.

[36] Albert Schweitzer, *The Mystery of the Kingdom of God* (New York: Macmillan, 1950). See also Meyer, *The Aims of Jesus*; Wright, *Jesus and the Victory of God*.

criticized Schweitzer for imposing ideas of an eschatological "tribulation" onto his portrait of Jesus,[37] when Sanders himself posits that Jesus was an apocalyptic prophet who demonstrated the "symbolic destruction" of the Temple.

Brant Pitre suggests that the historical Jesus adopted "the common Jewish expectation of a final time of suffering and trial that will take place at the end of the age."[38] Like Schweitzer, Pitre affirms that Jesus saw himself as the "messianic son of man" whose suffering and death would atone for the sins of Israel.[39] There is no denying that the themes of eschatological "judgment" and "restoration" are frequently paired together in some extant Second Temple Jewish sources,[40] and Pitre certainly builds an impressive cumulative case of a kind of pan-apocalypticism. But that is precisely the problem: *the Gospels were written to tell the story of the suffering and dying messianic son of man whose death atoned for the sins of "many."* There is no denying that Paul and the Gospels *portray* Jesus' death as inaugurating a great day of "judgment" or "tribulation" soon to come. The question is: What did the historical *Jesus* think about such things? Here we are trying to navigate a complex nexus between the historical Jesus, the post-Easter proclamations of soteriological and sacrificial views of Jesus' messianic death, and the post-70 CE milieu of gospel-composition. If we are not careful, we run the risk of superimposing both post-30 CE and post-70 CE developments onto the life of the historical Jesus rather than locating Jesus' kingdom-vision within the actual social, economic, political, and religious context(s) of his contemporaries. So while it seems virtually certain that the historical Jesus should be located within a cultural context of eschatological restoration, it is by no means clear precisely how we should relate the "judgment" and "restoration" themes in his life.

---

[37] Sanders, *Jesus and Judaism*, 23: "his hypothesis does not arise naturally from the study of the texts but seems to be imposed upon them, and the dogma which he ascribes to Jesus may not in fact even be thoroughly grounded in the contemporary Jewish expectation. The expectation of sufferings before the Messiah comes, for example ... may not precede the two wars with Rome."

[38] Brant Pitre, *Jesus, the Tribulation, and the End of the Exile: Restoration Eschatology and the Origin of the Atonement* (WUNT II. 204; Tübingen: Mohr Siebeck, 2005), 29.

[39] Pitre, *Jesus, the Tribulation, and the End of the Exile*, 382–507.

[40] Pitre cites *1 Enoch*, the book of Daniel, the book of *Jubilees*, the Third Sibylline Oracle, the Psalms of Solomon, the Testament of Moses, the *Parables of Enoch*, and the sectarian Qumran texts (1QH, 4Q171, 4Q174, 4Q177, 1QS, CD, 1QM, 4Q246).

Steven Bryan has argued that Jesus' eschatological program must be understood in terms of *both* judgment and restoration, that is, as an enactment of "realized" eschatological restoration. Bryan appeals to Jesus' miracle-working, his welcoming of sinners, calling of the Twelve, subordination of purity laws, and criticism of the Temple tax as indications that Israel was not only being judged and found wanting, but had also lost its special election.[41] The Temple was to be destroyed because it was not the eschatological Temple.[42] Jesus symbolically destroyed the Temple and promised to build a new non-physical Temple.[43] For Bryan, the historical Jesus did not object to any specific aspect of the Temple's administration because Jesus' action was directed "*against the operation of the Temple as a whole.*"[44]

There is much to be commended in Bryan's reconstruction, in particular his proposal that "Jesus' use of traditions of national judgment . . . forced a reconception of national restoration,"[45] and that this reconception meant that "Dramatic changes were expected, changes which would alter Israel's social structures and institutions."[46] There are difficulties, however, involved in reinscribing the Temple incident as an act of symbolic destruction, especially if one assumes that Jesus also visited the Temple for teaching, prayer, and observing the sacrificial rites of Passover. Apart from the fact that it is not entirely clear whether Jesus' commotion in the Royal Stoa *would* have been perceived as a symbolic act of the Temple's destruction, Jesus' allegedly symbolic destruction of the Temple is only attested in *post*-70 CE sources that deploy it theologically. Moreover, there is no evidence that a "messianic" figure would destroy the Temple.[47] There is

---

[41] Bryan, *Jesus and Israel's Traditions of Judgement and Restoration*, 6.

[42] Bryan, *Jesus and Israel's Traditions of Judgement and Restoration*, 189.

[43] Contra Sanders, Bryan argues that Jesus did *not* expect "a material Temple in the eschaton" (232), but rather "some kind of non-physical Temple" (235), and that "he himself would build a temple of another kind, a non-physical Temple."

[44] Bryan, *Jesus and Israel's Traditions of Judgement and Restoration*, 217.

[45] Bryan, *Jesus and Israel's Traditions of Judgement and Restoration*, 6.

[46] Bryan, *Jesus and Israel's Traditions of Judgement and Restoration*, 130: "the judgement and restoration of Israel were to be experienced as simultaneous realities."

[47] Evans, "Jesus' action in the Temple: Cleansing or Portent of Destruction?," 409-10; cf. Adela Yarbro Collins, *Mark: A Commentary* (Minneapolis: Fortress, 2007), 600. Le Donne, *The Historiographical Jesus*, 252, argues that Mark 14:58 and John 2 both represent "refraction trajectories that share the same mnemonic point of departure." Consequently, "we may positively assert that Jesus was remembered . . . to have made such a claim" (to destroy and rebuild the Temple). But even if Jesus was "remembered" as making such a claim in the Gospel of Mark, that does not mean the historical Jesus made such a claim.

no evidence that Jesus expected to rebuild a new physical Temple. The idea that Jesus sought to *replace* a (destroyed) Temple with himself ("in three days") seems unmistakably *post*-30 CE in its signification of Jesus' death and resurrection.[48] This would have been especially true when read in light of the Temple's destruction in 70 CE.

It is often thought that the apocalyptic judgment language in the Jesus tradition is an unproblematic aspect of Jesus' apocalyptic continuity with John the Baptist and the post-Easter Jesus movement, both of which seem to have anticipated an end-time agent of divine judgment.[49] This conclusion, however, must be more nuanced. There are serious difficulties in determining precisely what the historical Jesus may have meant by divine eschatological "judgment."[50] Unfortunately, Bryan's primary focus on the *national* restoration of Israel misses the more utopian and universal aspects of the prophetic and apocalyptic traditions, aspects which correspond to and complement the *Urzeit/Endzeit* themes of a renewal of creation. This is especially pertinent, given Jesus' *halakhic* stance on divorce. We might also question whether Mark's use of Isaiah 56:7, which appeals to an "eschatological ingathering of the Gentiles,"[51] is more likely a Markan reflection on the Pauline mission than an historical memory of Jesus' Temple action.

Bryan rightly notes that some scholars have suggested that Jesus' "repudiation of the cult" may represent an important key to understanding the Temple incident,[52] but dismisses this possibility because "only a relatively small proportion of sacrifices would have been offered to expiate sin."[53] Bryan suggests that "one of the controlling assumptions" of critics who think that Jesus rejected the Temple cult is because he anticipated his own

---

[48] Paula Fredriksen, "Gospel Chronologies, the Scene in the Temple, and the Crucifixion of Jesus," in F.E. Udoh (ed.) *Redefining First-Century Jewish and Christian Identities: Essays in Honor of Ed Parish Sanders* (CJA 16; Notre Dame: Universityof Notre Dame, 2008), 246-82, here 259; F. Siegert, "Zerstört diesen Tempel ...!" Jesus als 'Tempel' in den Passionsüberlieferungen," in J. Hahn (ed.) *Zerstörungen des Jerusalemer Tempels: Geschehen-Wahrnehmung-Bewältigung* (WUNT 147; Mohr Siebeck: Tübingen, 2002), 108-39, here 111.

[49] Dale C. Allison, "John and Jesus: Continuity and Discontinuity," *JSHJ*, 1.1 (2002), 6-27.

[50] For a discussion of the issues in terms of violence, see Joseph, *The Nonviolent Messiah*, 71-89.

[51] Bryan, *Jesus and Israel's Traditions of Judgement and Restoration*, 221.

[52] Bryan, *Jesus and Israel's Traditions of Judgement and Restoration*, 211.

[53] Bryan, *Jesus and Israel's Traditions of Judgement and Restoration*, 212.

atoning death,[54] but argues that early Jewish Christians *"could have believed that Jesus' death obviated other forms of expiatory sacrifice and yet see no contradiction between this belief and continued participation in the rest of the cultic system."*[55] Bryan, in other words, affirms Acts' accounts of early Christian participation in the Temple cult, except perhaps for the purposes of *atonement.* If this were the case, then how do we explain Jesus condemning the Temple to destruction – presumably because its sacrificial system was no longer efficacious – but failing to communicate this rather important datum to his followers? Did Jesus perform an act of animal sacrifice on Passover – or not? If Jesus believed that the eschatological Temple was not functioning properly, *should* we really assume that he participated in the Temple cult? Conversely, if Jesus communicated to his followers that the present Temple was under imminent judgment, would they still have continued offering sacrifices there? Unfortunately, Bryan does not fully address the early sacrificial interpretation of Jesus' death inscribed in Paul's letters nor how this conviction (may have) influenced the composition and redaction of the Gospels. Nor does he explain how later "Jewish Christians," who revered the Temple and Jerusalem, but rejected animal sacrifice, fit into this picture. Bryan's portrait of a Jesus who condemns the Temple and the "nation" to judgment and destruction while promising to build a new Temple "not made by hands" is certainly a plausible construction within Second Temple Judaism, but it it also sounds very much like the Markan/Pauline model of the new "Christian" community-as-temple *replacing* the physical Temple of nationalistic, ethnic Israel. The subtle supersessionism inherent in such a reading suggests that we should continue to seek alternative ways of understanding Jesus' realized eschatological program *within* Judaism. It seems far more likely that Jesus, as a faithful Jew, revered the Temple as the house of God but sought its reformation, which put him in conflict with its administrators.[56] In short, it seems far more likely that Jesus sought to *re-form* the Temple, not destroy it.

[54] Bryan, *Jesus and Israel's Traditions of Judgement and Restoration*, 212.

[55] Bryan, *Jesus and Israel's Traditions of Judgement and Restoration*, 234.

[56] The Qumran community idealized an eschatological Temple, but they did not seek the present Temple's destruction. Rather, they hoped to reclaim their rightful place at its center. Philo praises "spiritual" worship, but denies that physical Temple rites can be ignored.

The Cleansing of the Temple

In response to Sanders's proposal of symbolic destruction, a number of scholars have reaffirmed the traditional interpretation of Jesus' action in the Temple as its eschatological "cleansing."[57] Craig Evans, in particular, has argued persuasively against the symbolic destruction model, pointing out that while there is *no* evidence that the early Church was "embarrassed" about Jesus' criticism of the Temple, there *is* evidence of Jesus' conflict with the Temple's administration. Moreover, there is no evidence that a messiah or prophet was expected to destroy the Temple before building a new one. Finally, ancient sources suggest that many first-century Jews thought the Temple was corrupt and in need of purification. A number of "cleansing proposals" have been made, ranging from Jesus being seen as critical of the economic trade in the Temple precincts,[58] to his indignation over how the Court of the Gentiles was being used,[59] to unethical worship,[60] and priestly corruption.[61] These

[57] Hans Dieter Betz, "Jesus and the Purity of the Temple (Mark 11:15–18): A Comparative Religion Approach," *JBL*, 116 (1997), 455–72; Evans, "Jesus' Action in the Temple," 237–70; "Jesus and the "Cave of Robbers," 92–110; "Opposition to the Temple: Jesus and the Dead Sea Scrolls," 235–53; P. Maurice Casey, "Culture and Historicity: The Cleansing of the Temple," *CBQ*, 59 (1997), 306–32; Chilton, *The Temple of Jesus*, 135–6; V. Eppstein "The Historicity of the Gospel Account of the Cleansing of the Temple," 42–58; Derrett, "The Zeal of thy House and the Cleansing of the Temple," 79–94. On the incident as anachronistic, see Sanders, *Jesus and Judaism*, 67–8; Bauckham, "Jesus' Demonstration in the Temple," 72–3; Betz, "Jesus and the Purity," 459.

[58] Trautmann, *Zeichenhafte Handlungen Jesu*, 115; M. Davies, *Matthew* (R/ANBC; Sheffield: JSOT, 1993), 145; Jerome Murphy-O'Connor, "Jesus and the Money Changers (Mark 11:15–17; John 2:13–17)," *RB*, 107 (2000), 42–55 (44); Ådna, "Jesus' Symbolic Acts in the Temple," 461–75, esp. 463. For Jesus' criticism of trade, see Eppstein, "The Historicity of the Cleansing of the Temple," 42–58. But see E. P. Sanders, *Judaism: Practice and Belief, 63 BCE – 66 CE* (London: SCM, 1992), 87; Haenchen, *John*, 1, 2. See also Betz, "Jesus and the Purity," 461–2; Evans, *Mark*, 173; F. F. Bruce, *The Gospel of John* (Grand Rapids: Eerdmans, 1983), 74; Seeley, "Jesus' Temple Act," 268.

[59] Davies, *The Gospel and the Land*, 350–1; C. A. Evans, "From 'House of Prayer' to 'Cave of Robbers': Jesus' Prophetic Criticism of the Temple Establishment," in C. A. Evans and S. Talmon (eds.), *The Quest for Context and Meaning: Studies in Biblical Intertextuality in Honor of James A. Sanders* (Leiden: Brill, 1997), 417–42, esp. 441–2. But see Sanders, *Jesus and Judaism*, 68; A. E. Harvey, *Jesus and the Constraints of History* (London: Duckworth, 1982), 132; C. S. Mann, *Mark* (AB; Garden City: Doubleday, 1986), 419; Seeley, "Jesus' Temple Act," 269.

[60] Morna Hooker, *The Signs of a Prophet: The Prophetic Actions of Jesus* (London: SCM, 1997), 45–8.

[61] S. G. F. Brandon, *Jesus and the Zealots: A Study of the Political Factor in Primitive Christianity* (New York: Scribners, 1967), 326–56; Martin Hengel, *The*

variations on the theme of an eschatological cleansing have the merit of allowing us to recognize Jesus' high regard for the Temple while permitting him to critique its administration.

The Gospels agree that Jesus' offense in Jerusalem was registered primarily by the Jewish Temple priests. It seems fitting, therefore, to consider whether *economic* motives lay behind Jesus' action in the Temple and a high priestly plot against him. Some scholars have suggested that Jesus objected to the annual half-shekel Temple tax, but this particular tax is mentioned only once in the New Testament (Matt 17:24–27),[62] and here Jesus is depicted as dutifully *paying* the tax. Although Jesus seems to suggest that the people of Israel *should* be exempt from payment, he goes on to say that the tax should be paid *so as not to cause offense*. Many scholars regard this as a late saying and inauthentic.[63] The Jesus Seminar dismisses Matt 17:24–27 as redactional.[64] On the other hand, David Flusser argues that the tradition *could* be early and that Jesus' opposition to the tax is similar to Qumran texts that also oppose the Temple tax.[65] It is not clear, however, that this tax-debate has anything to do with the Temple incident. The relationship, if any, may be more thematic and textual.[66] Textually, the reference to the tables of the money-changers (τῶν κολλυβιστῶν) may reflect a Mishnaic tradition describing their location near the Temple shortly before Passover to collect the Temple

---

Zealots: Investigations into the Jewish Freedom Movement in the Period from Herod I Until 70 A. D. (trans. D. Smith; Edinburgh: T & T Clark, 1989), 213–17. But see Sanders, *Jesus and Judaism*, 68; Chilton, *Temple of Jesus*, 96; Fredriksen, *Jesus of Nazareth*, 234. On Jesus' criticism of priestly corruption, see C. A. Evans, "Jesus' Action in the Temple: Cleansing or Portent of Destruction?," in B. Chilton and C. A. Evans (eds.), *Jesus in Context: Temple, Purity and Restoration* (AGJU, 39; Leiden: Brill, 1997), 395–439, esp. 421–6. Perrin, *Jesus the Temple*, argues that Jesus thought of himself and his community as the new Temple.

[62] See Richard Bauckham, "The Coin in the Fish's Mouth," in D. Wenham and C. Blomberg (eds.), *Gospel Perspectives VI: The Miracles of Jesus* (Sheffield: JSOT, 1986), 219–52; Bruce Chilton, "A Coin of Three Realms (Matthew 17.24–27)," in D. J. A. Clines, S. E. Fowl, and S. E. Porter (eds.), *The Bible in Three Dimensions: Essays in Celebration of Forty Years of Biblical Studies in the University of Sheffield* (JSOT Sup 87; Sheffield Academic Press, 1990), 269–82, and William Horbury, "The Temple Tax," in E. Bammel and C. F. D. Moule (eds.), *Jesus and the Politics of His Day* (Cambridge University Press, 1984), 265–86.

[63] Collins, "Jesus' Action in the Temple," 50–1.

[64] Funk, *The Five Gospels*, 212–13.

[65] David Flusser, "Matthew XVII, 24–27 and the Dead Sea Sect," *Tarbiz*, 31 (1961), 150–6. See also Bauckham, "Coin in the Fish's Mouth."

[66] Bauckham, "Jesus' Demonstration in the Temple," 73–4; Richardson, "Why Turn the Tables."

tax.[67] The problem, however, as many interpreters have noted, is that the money-changers were a practical necessity in the Temple. They exchanged foreign monies into the silver coinage of Tyre.[68] The Mishnah refers to a certain "surcharge" (קלבון), or fee, consisting of a small fraction of a shekel, for the service.[69] It has been suggested that Jesus objected to the Temple tax, the "surcharge" fee, and/or the money-changers who collected the funds. Thematically, it has been suggested that the priests' corruption, focused perhaps on this "surcharge," angered Jesus.[70] Nonetheless, there does not seem to be anything particularly scandalous about a "surcharge" being added as part of an officially sanctioned economic transaction.[71] People needed to purchase sacrificial items and money-changers exchanged monies; we never hear anything in the Gospels about Jesus objecting to these services. Moreover, even if he did object to the "surcharge," why did Jesus also object to the merchants?

Did Jesus think that *he* should be exempt from the tax?[72] Some priests were thought to be exempt from paying the tax,[73] although some sources only exempt priests from the surcharge.[74] But Jesus never claims to be a priest exempt from the tax. It has also been suggested that Jesus rejected the idea that the poor should have to pay the Temple tax,[75] that Jesus thought that the sacrifices should be paid for by everyone through the Temple tax, and that Jesus' rejection of the tax was equivalent to his rejection of the Temple.[76] The Qumran community, for example, opposed the *annual* collection of the tax,

[67] Matt 21:12; Mark 11:15; John 2:15; Mishnah Tractate *Sheqalim*. See Richardson, "Why Turn the Tables," 512–13; Neusner, "Money-Changers in the Temple," 287–90.

[68] Yaakov Meshorer, "One Hundred Ninety Years of Tyrian Shekels," in Arthur Houghton, et al. (eds.), *Festschrift für/Studies in Honor of Leo Mildenberg* (Wetteren: Editions NR, 1984), 171–91. According to rabbinic sources (*m. Sheqalim* 2.4; *m. Bekhorot* 8.7), the Temple tax was to be paid in the form of Tyrian coins.

[69] Samuel Tobias Lachs, *A Rabbinic Commentary on the New Testament: The Gospels of Matthew, Mark and Luke* (Hoboken: Ktav; New York: Anti-Defamation League of B'Nai Brith, 1987), 347.

[70] Casey, "Culture and Historicity," 313–16.

[71] Sanders, *Jesus and Judaism*, 63–4.

[72] Chilton, "A Coin of Three Realms," 350; David Daube, "Temple Tax," in E. P. Sanders (ed.), *Jesus, the Gospels and the Church* (Macon: Mercer University Press, 1987), 121–34.

[73] *m. Sheqalim* 1.4.

[74] *m. Sheqalim* 1.3, 6.

[75] Hugh Montefiore, "Jesus and the Temple Tax," *NTS*, 10 (1965), 70–1.

[76] Neusner, "Money-Changers," 289–90; Wright, *Jesus and the Victory of God*, 423.

holding that the tax should only be paid *once*, when a man reached the age of 20.[77] Did Jesus, then, oppose an *annual* Temple tax or the tax in general, as suggested by Matthew?[78] Alternatively, it has been suggested that Jesus objected to the pagan iconography on Tyrian shekels, coins that featured an eagle on one side and the head of Hercules/Melqart on the other,[79] but there is not much evidence for this theory. There is no evidence that Jesus objected to pagan symbols on the coinage.[80] Collections of coins with such images have also been found at Qumran.[81]

Did Jesus object to the actual physical *location* of commerce in the Temple? If so, this could be seen as zealously defending the sanctity of the Temple and/or as a cleansing of the Temple.[82] After all, Jesus does seem to have "thrown out" traders from the Temple,[83] and, according to Mark, prevented anyone from carrying anything in the Temple.[84] Some scholars have also suggested that Herod's expanded Temple Mount led to changes regarding wherein economic transactions were conducted.[85] But if Jesus objected to the commercialization of sacrifice,[86] or reminisced about some golden age when sacrifice was pure and free of commerce,[87] such sentiments have not left much of a mark in the tradition.[88] Jonathan Klawans suggests that Jesus'

[77] 4Q159 fr. 1, II.6–7.

[78] G. Dautzenberg, "Jesus und der Temple. Beobachtungen zur Exegese der Perikope von der Tempelsteuer (Mt 17,24–27)," in I. Oberlinner and P. Fiedler (eds.), *Salz der Erde – Licht der Welt: Exegetische Studien zum Matthäusevangelium. FS für Anton Vögtle zum 80. Geburtstag* (Stuttgart: KBW, 1991), 223–38, here 236–8, proposes that Matthew reflects criticism of the sacrificial system, an attempt on Jesus' part to prepare his followers for abandoning sacrifice.

[79] Richardson, "Why Turn the Tables"; Collins, "Jesus' Action," 58–60. But see Chilton, *Feast of Meanings*, 172–6.

[80] Chilton, *Feast of Meanings*, 174.

[81] See Magness, *Archaeology of Qumran*, 188–93, 206–7.

[82] Eppstein, "Historicity"; David Flusser, *Jesus* (New York: Herder and Herder, 1969), 138; Shmuel Safrai, *Pilgrimage at the Time of the Second Temple* (Jerusalem: Akademon, 1985), 148; Betz, "Jesus and the Purity," 461–2, 467–9; Collins, "Jesus' Action," 53–8.

[83] Matt 21:12; Mark 11:15; Luke 19:45; John 2:15.

[84] Mark 11:16.

[85] Collins, "Jesus' Action," 57–8.

[86] Betz, "Jesus and the Purity," 461, 465, 467.

[87] Sanders, *Jesus and Judaism*, 63.

[88] Loader, *Jesus' Attitude*, 113–14. Chilton, *The Temple of Jesus*, 110, suggests that Jesus could not have interrupted the collection for long, and second, the tax was not only used to support sacrifice but also maintained the Temple as an institution.

Temple-action focused on "the moral issues at the nexus between sacrifice and property," taking his cue from the tradition that Jesus *expelled* ("threw out") the money-changers *and* animal-merchants.[89] For Klawans, these two proprietors had "a marked impact" on the poor, not only because of the Temple-tax surcharge, but more so because the Temple habitually exploited the plight of the poor who could not afford to sacrifice.[90] Jesus thus opposed the idea that "the poor should be required to pay for their own offerings," and believed that the poor "should not have to pay what they could not easily afford."[91] The Temple incident is therefore consistent with Jesus' overarching concern for the poor demonstrated throughout his ministry.[92]

While Klawans is surely correct to focus on the *economic* aspects of Jesus' critique of the Temple's administration, the fact that these proposals tend to assume that Jesus fully accepted the Temple's sacrificial system in light of the tradition's questioning this very assumption is troubling. The fact that Jesus' death is represented as a sacrifice in each of the Gospels may indeed reflect secondary theological interpretation, but this still indicates a relatively radical dissociation between Jesus and the Temple. It is difficult to picture the earliest Jewish Christians simultaneously regarding Jesus' death *and* the Temple cult as equally efficacious and divinely sanctioned sacrifices. Furthermore, Jesus' demonstrated hostility toward the Temple, the high priest's response to his critique, and early Christian non-participation in the Temple cult are all data that must be accounted for in any reconstruction. In comparison, Jesus' objection to service charges, the location of economic transactions, and the occasional exploitation germane to such activity seem – while perfectly plausible – relatively mundane.[93]

---

[89] Klawans, *Purity, Sacrifice, and the Temple*, 237.

[90] Klawans, *Purity, Sacrifice, and the Temple*, 237.

[91] Klawans, *Purity, Sacrifice, and the Temple*, 239.

[92] Klawans, *Purity, Sacrifice, and the Temple*, 239. See also Q 6:20; Matt 19:23–24; Mark 10:23–25; Luke 18:24–25; Matt 6:24; Luke 16:13; Matt 19:27; Mark 10:28; Matt 19:16–22; Mark 10:17–22; Luke 18:18–23; Mark 12:41–44; Luke 21:1–4.

[93] There is not much evidence of any *particular* exploitative practices taking place in Jesus' day. Bryan, *Jesus and Israel's Traditions*, 219-220, challenges the idea that Jesus was simply criticizing economic corruption and suggests that "Jesus' objections may have been broader and aimed more widely." Jesus' act was not simply directed toward the priests, but "would have been perceived to be directed against worshippers making use of the Temple commerce as well."

If Jesus endorsed the sacrificial system, he would have had to have accepted the need for commerce, the Temple tax, and the surcharge for money-changing. If Jesus did not object to the Roman tribute – at least not to the point of sedition – then it seems even less likely that a disagreement about the annual or once-only Temple tax would have led to his death. While any attack on the Temple system – especially its finances – would not have been taken lightly, and Jesus' offense was obviously serious enough to alarm the priests, it was not uncommon for Jews to disagree with each other. If it is also true that Jesus' challenge to the Temple climactically surfaced within the inner chambers of the high priest's palace, we must not trivialize the offense, for even if it is *possible* that Jesus was executed for a relatively minor or even accidental matter, this seems unlikely. Why? Because Jesus seems to have known what he was doing. He could have avoided appearing in public. He could have left Jerusalem. He knew he was antagonizing his opponents. He seems to have had at least several opportunities to deny any wrong-doing. But no, he seems to have intentionally moved forward with some secret plan that only he knew or understood, trusting in God's providence despite all appearances to the contrary. So while one can hardly deny that commercialism, economic exploitation, corruption, impurity, and priestly illegitimacy were valid concerns and common criticisms in Second Temple Judaism (and probably bothered Jesus, too), the fact that none of these stands out as distinctively characteristic of *Jesus* is noteworthy. Let us recall, in other words, that the Jewish religious leadership's accusations against Jesus centered on such charges as *blasphemy* and *leading Israel "astray,"* accusations that suggest that Jesus' ministry represented a controversial *religious* scandal, not – as they would soon claim – political revolt against the Roman state.

Richard Bauckham rightly notes that interpreters "disagree on what it was that Jesus saw as objectionable" within the Temple,[94] and suggests that Jesus' demonstration was not a symbolic destruction of the Temple, but a "symbolic denunciation of the activities" in the Temple.[95] According to Bauckham, Jesus objected to the commercial corruption of the sacrificial system that had distorted its "real purpose … as a vehicle of prayer."[96] Bauckham suggests that Jesus

---

[94] Bauckham, "Jesus' Demonstration in the Temple," 73.

[95] Bauckham, "Jesus' Demonstration in the Temple," 86.

[96] Richard Bauckham, *Living with Other Creatures: Green Exegesis and Theology* (Waco: Baylor University Press, 2011). 99. See also Richard Bauckham, "The Coin in

objected to paying the Temple tax (Matt 17:24–27), yet "approved of voluntary giving" to the Temple (Mark 12:41–44).[97] Bauckham also argues that Jesus was "protesting against the way in which the temple treasury had turned the sacrificial system into a profit-making business."[98] The Temple was being run "for the benefit of the temple treasury," instead of fulfilling its true function as a "vehicle of the people's worship." While Bauckham maintains that Jesus' protest was "primarily against commercialism rather than corruption," he does not discount the possibility that the Temple's officials were also prone to corruption.[99] Bauckham's proposal certainly has its merits. His model explains, in part, why Jesus would have been viewed as a threat to Temple officials – one, because he was attacking the Temple's "financial arrangements"; two, because he was challenging their authority; three, because he was undermining the Jewish/Roman political/collaborative status quo; four, because he was threatening the destruction of the Temple; and five, because Jesus' triumphal entry and Temple incident could be used to indict Jesus' alleged messianic pretensions.[100]

Nonetheless, Bauckham's proposal is undermined by the fact that Jesus apparently endorsed paying the Roman tribute (Mark 12:13–17), but objected to paying the Temple tax (Matt 17:24–27), which he nonethless pays. Bauckham's thesis allows for Jesus to object both to commercialism *and* corruption, but it is not entirely clear on these grounds whether Jesus sought to condemn or reform the Temple. It is also difficult to accept Bauckham's proposal that Jesus did not object to the sacrificial system but sought to drive out the money-changers, buyers, sellers, and animals. Why would Jesus object to commerce when the purchasing of animals was an integral part of the sacrificial process and the exchange of monies a necessary prerequisite?[101]

Rejecting the idea that the Temple incident was a revolutionary act, a prophetic demonstration of symbolic destruction, or an eschatological "cleansing,"[102] K. H. Tan suggests that the Temple act was a "prophetic protest" against the "profiteering racket" of the Temple

the Fish's Mouth," in D. Wenham and C. Blomberg (eds.), *Gospel Perspectives VI: The Miracles of Jesus* (Sheffield: JSOT, 1986), 219–52.

[97] Bauckham, "Jesus' Demonstration in the Temple," 74.

[98] Bauckham, "Jesus' Demonstration in the Temple," 78.

[99] Bauckham, "Jesus' Demonstration in the Temple," 79.

[100] Bauckham, "Jesus' Demonstration in the Temple," 88–9.

[101] Holmén, *Jesus and Jewish Covenant Thinking*, 316.

[102] K. H. Tan, *The Zion Traditions and the Aims of Jesus* (SNTSMS 91; Cambridge University Press, 1997), 174-187.

establishment.[103] Tan analyzes Mark 11:15-17 in light of Jewish "Zion traditions" and argues that Jesus objected to the Temple tax and the Temple's current administration, but never criticized the Temple cult itself. According to Tan, it was the failure of the Temple and its rejection of Jesus' message that condemned it to destruction, which is why Jesus' sacrificial death was "intended to ratify a 'new' covenant for a 'new' people of God through the shedding of his blood."[104] While there is no question that this reconstruction conforms to the passion narratives' representation of Jesus' last week – with Jesus' sacrificial death replacing the need for the Temple cult and its sacrificial system of atonement – it is less clear that the Markan narrative of the Temple incident can so easily be interpreted solely as an economic critique. The narrative context may be better read as a *symbolic* abolition of the animal sacrifices of the Temple cult.

The Gospel of Mark narrates four distinctive acts performed by Jesus: (1) driving out "those who bought and sold"; (2) overturning the tables of the money-changers; (3) overturning the seats of whose who sold pigeons; and (4) prohibiting anyone from carrying a vessel through the Temple. Rabbinical traditions suggest that the Temple tax was to be used to pay for the daily whole-offerings.[105] This has been interpreted as evidence that Jesus sought to abolish the Temple cult.[106] Second, Mark portrays Jesus as overturning the seats of those who sold doves, which is tantamount to Jesus (temporarily) prohibiting sacrifice.[107] Third, Mark 11:15 tells us that Jesus drove out "those who bought and sold" (τοὺς πωλοῦντας καὶ τοὺς ἀγοράζοντας). The implication here, again, is that Jesus (temporarily) stopped the buying and selling of sacrificial animals.[108] Fourth, Mark's reference to the "vessel" is obscure, which is presumably why both Matthew and Luke drop it, but is best read as a reference to the sacred vessels used for sacrificial offerings.[109] It would seem to follow, therefore, that

---

[103] Tan, *The Zion Traditions*, 181.

[104] Tan, *The Zion Traditions*, 198.

[105] *t.Shek.* 1.6.

[106] Neusner, "Money-changers," 287-90.

[107] Tan, *The Zion Traditions*, 178, suggests that this is Jesus' condemnation of the Temple exploiting the poor (Lev 15:14; 15:29; *m. Ker.* 6.8. *A.J.* 3.230).

[108] Tan, *The Zion Traditions*, 179, suggests that this refers to "the people who were trading with the temple staff … selling supplies … and merchants who were buying valuable items which the people had donated to the temple."

[109] Telford, *Temple*, 93, n. 102. Tan, *The Zion Traditions*, 181, reads this as an attempt "to stop the carriage with these sacred vessels … into the storehouses in the Court of Women by the temple staff of sacred supplies."

what Mark consistently has in mind is Jesus' *symbolic* abolition of the Temple cult.

James Crossley has argued that the Markan Jesus does not oppose the sacrificial system but "implicitly accepts its validity."[110] Rather, it was the economic corruption of the Temple system that "required [its] destruction."[111] It is difficult, again, to imagine Jesus *participating* in the sacrificial system while criticizing its corruption, participating in anti-Temple polemic, and threatening its destruction. The Gospel authors may hold these views in tension, but *we* must ask: Did Jesus participate in the sacrificial system (because sacrifices were efficacious) or not? It is *Mark*, after all, who sees Jesus inaugurating the Temple's destruction, withering the fig tree, and calling out the "wicked tenants." While Jesus almost certainly perceived the Temple to be economically corrupt, this would make Jesus' critique similar to many of his contemporaries who were also disgruntled with the Temple's administration. If Jesus was simply complaining about economic corruption, then Mark has radically and skillfully re-worked Jesus' interests into a rather elaborate supersessionistic theological scheme of sacrificial atonement.

Here Crossley raises the argument from silence: if Jesus rejected the sacrificial system, then why is there no such conflict in the narrative, especially where "we might legitimately expect an explicit legal dispute over something as revolutionary as rejecting the whole sacrificial system in the Temple?"[112] It is a good question, but there are good reasons for this apparent absence. The central theme of Mark's theological narrative is to identify Jesus as the suffering son of man who dies a sacrificial death ("ransom") for all nations and thereby inaugurates the destruction (and, implicitly, the replacement) of the Temple system. For Mark, the Temple has not lived up to its true purpose ("a house of prayer for all nations"), the fig tree has not produced fruit, and the vineyard has now been given to another.

---

[110] James G. Crossley, "Mark's Christology and a Scholarly Creation of a Non-Jewish Christ of Faith," in *Judaism, Jewish Identities and the Gospel Tradition: Essays in Honour of Maurice Casey* (London: Equinox, 2010), 118–51, here 129.

[111] Crossley, "Mark's Christology," 12. See also Crossley, *Date*, 62–74.

[112] James Crossley, *Why Christianity Happened: A Sociohistorical Account of Christian Origins (26–50 CE)* (Louisville: Westminster John Knox, 2006), 94–5 (emphases added), discounts Sanders's suggestion that Jesus "bypassed the Temple system" by asserting that "no such sentiments are advocated in the Synoptic tradition and nowhere is Jesus ever criticized for saying such a thing, *something for which we would surely have some evidence if it were the case.*"

The Markan Jesus has a Pauline agenda. The Markan Jesus does not attack the *ideology* of blood sacrifice because the Markan Jesus *is* a blood sacrifice. Mark shifts the soteriological center of gravity from the Temple to Jesus by affirming the sacrificial interpretation of Jesus' death. Mark's Jesus may not refer to his death as a replacement of the Temple, but that is precisely what *Mark* has in mind. Neither Mark nor the Markan Jesus is particularly interested in affirming Jewish legal minutiae. Mark, like Matthew and Luke, situates "Jesus" within Jewish conflicts in order to illustrate why Jesus was rejected by his people, how he "abrogated" the law, challenged Jewish religious authority, and became the savior for the Gentiles, the audience for whom Mark is writing (Mark 7:3; 13:10; 14:9). That is, after all, why Mark must explain numerous Aramaic terms. We must not confuse Mark's *literary*-narrative construction of "Jesus" with the historical Jesus or his historical ministry.

One of the most innovative solutions to the significance of the Temple incident in light of Jesus' first-century Jewish context has been proposed by Bruce Chilton. According to Chilton, Jesus objected to the way in which Temple officials were conducting the sacrifices, arguing that the poor should be able to bring their own animals instead of being required to purchase them in Jerusalem.[113] After the failure of his Temple occupation, however, Jesus "instituted" the Eucharist as an anti-sacrificial "mimetic surrogate" for the Temple cult.[114] This subversive substitute for the Temple cult was perceived as a direct threat by the high priesthood.[115] This was the "generative moment" in which Christianity emerged as "a religion separate from Judaism."

---

[113] Chilton, *Temple of Jesus*, 91–136, esp. 108–11; *A Feast of Meanings: Eucharistic Theologies from Jesus through Johannine Circles* (Leiden: Brill, 1994), 57–63; *Pure Kingdom*, 115–23; *Rabbi Jesus*, 213–30. Chilton suggests that there was a debate between the houses of Hillel and Shammai (*m. Betzah* 2.4; *b. Betzah* 20a-b). The debate revolved around the permissibility of "laying hands" (Lev. 1:4) on certain sacrifices. According to Chilton, the Hillelites advocated the position that sacrifices could be purchased on site and that ownership was effected when the individual "laid hands" on the animal before offering it. The Shammaites (and Jesus!) rejected this view.

[114] Bruce Chilton, "The Eucharist and the Mimesis of Sacrifice," in A. W. Astell and S. Goodhart (eds.), *Sacrifice, Scripture, & Substitution* (CJA 18; University of Notre Dame Press, 2011), 140–54, here 141, 145. But see Robert J. Daly, "Eucharistic Origins: From the New Testament to the Liturgies of the Golden Age," *TS*, 66 (2005), 3–22.

[115] Chilton, *The Temple of Jesus*, 150–54. See also *A Feast of Meanings*; Bruce Chilton and Craig A. Evans, *Jesus in Context: Temple, Purity, and Restoration* (Leiden: Brill, 1997);

Jesus identified the wine and bread of his Last Supper as a new form of sacrificial worship that replaced animal sacrifices in the Temple. Jesus' shared meal became "a rival altar." Jesus' original intention was then misunderstood when Paul identified the "blood of the covenant" with Jesus' own blood.[116] Jesus' original intention was to replace animal sacrifice with a shared sacred meal; Jesus' "substitute" for animal sacrifice was transformed when *Jesus* became the (substitute) sacrifice. Chilton's innovative model has the merit of placing Jesus "firmly within the Judaism of his period and the final dispute of his life," accounts for "the opposition of the authorities to him," and explains the chronological development of the Eucharist in early Christianity.[117] Chilton's model is not *anti*-sacrificial, however, for he denies that Jesus found anything objectionable about the Temple cult itself. His disagreement with the authorities simply "concerned purity within the Temple."[118]

Chilton is to be commended for constructing a hypothesis in which Jesus' objections to the Temple cult are firmly located within a plausible cultural and historical context, especially one in which ethical and ritual *purity* were his foremost concerns. It is difficult, however, not to perceive the seeds of a kind of covert Christian supersessionism in Jesus' substitution or *replacement* of the sacrificial system with the Eucharistic meal. Jesus' concerns may have indeed been focused on *purity*, but Jesus' critique of the Temple system was far more radical than reforming ritual procedure. Chilton's model forces us to accept that the traditional meaning(s) associated with the Pauline Eucharist – repeated in the Synoptics – were misunderstandings of Jesus' original substitutionary intention (which safeguards Jesus from supersessionism), but leaves unanswered the questions of whether Jesus actually sought to replace the Temple rites indefinitely, and whether Jesus thought that the Temple system was soon to be destroyed, along with its traditional ability to mediate the forgiveness or atonement of sins.

Like Chilton,[119] Bernhard Lang proposes that after Jesus "failed to reform the animal sacrifices" in the Temple, he "practiced a substitute

---

[116] 1 Cor 11:25.
[117] Chilton, *The Temple of Jesus*, 146.
[118] Chilton, *The Temple of Jesus*, 145.
[119] Hartmut Gese, *Essays on Biblical Theology* (trans. Keith Crim; Minneapolis: Augsburg, 1981).

sacrifice in which bread and wine represented the animal's body and blood."[120] During his life, Jesus and his followers typically "went to the Temple to offer their sacrifices" but during his last visit to Jerusalem, Jesus objected to the way the sacrificial system was organized.[121] The Temple's sacrificial procedures had been reduced to "a financial transaction" whereas "in ancient times the actual slaughtering had been the task of the offering person himself." Jesus "wanted people to participate more in their offering."[122] In response to his rejection by the priests, Jesus designed a new form of sacrifice and "reduced the Temple ritual to its unbloody part," although it "still served the same purpose of honoring God with a present and giving him thanks for benefits received."[123] The priests, however, were "so enraged with Jesus that they wanted to kill him" because he performed "an act that threatened their very existence."[124] Jesus "never thought of himself as a source of sacrificial blood."[125] Jesus simply introduced bread and wine as a substitute for blood and flesh. At first, early Christians participated in Temple-worship,[126] but when certain "Christian intellectuals" began to argue that Christ had abolished sacrifice and identified him as a kind of scapegoat that took away their sins, "the entire system of sacrifice" became superfluous. By the time Paul arrived on the scene and "received" the tradition of the Lord's Supper in Antioch in the 30s CE, Jesus' Temple reform was now transformed to mean that "his own death would be a sacrifice."[127] We do not know who "devised the Antiochene Eucharist," but it must have been "a man of Jewish background."

The sacrificial-reform model proposed by Lang and Chilton is an innovative solution that not only takes Jesus' subversion of the Temple system seriously but also reconstructs the Temple incident, and Jesus'

[120] See Bernhard Lang, *Sacred Games: A History of Christian Worship* (New Haven: Yale University Press, 1997), esp. 207–81, here 3.

[121] Lang, *Sacred Games*, 223, cites Mark 1:44 and Matt 5:24–25 as evidence that Jesus "accepted the institution of animal sacrifice" and the "biblical legislation regulating it."

[122] Lang, *Sacred Games*, 225–6.

[123] Lang, *Sacred Games*, 220, 221.

[124] Lang, *Sacred Games*, 226.

[125] Lang, *Sacred Games*, 230.

[126] Lang, *Sacred Games*, 228, proposes that eventually "Christians gave up killing animal victims in a ritual context and felt that this should never be restored. Nevertheless, they continued the practice of material (but non-animal) offerings" (278).

[127] Lang, *Sacred Games*, 230.

arrest and trial within a plausible Jewish context. It also has the merit of tracing the historical development of the Lord's Supper from being a *substitute* for animal/blood sacrifice to its subsequent representation of Jesus' death *as* a blood sacrifice. The flaw in this proposal, however, is the idea that Jesus focused his ministry and risked his life on objecting to a particular ritual procedure in the sacrificial administration. Jesus' substitution was thus a "temporary measure" of reform that became, by mere "accident," the prototype that created "a new, nonsacrificial religion."[128]

If it is reasonable to conclude that Jesus must have said or done something *serious* enough to get the high priests involved and request Pilate to execute Jesus despite the fact that they knew that he was *not* a military leader, then it is also reasonable to suppose that they knew they needed a charge that would do the job. It is difficult to see Jesus' offense as anything less than directly challenging the authority, efficacy, and legitimacy of the Temple system itself. We may conclude, therefore, that there is indeed a sense in which Jesus sought to "cleanse" the Temple and restore its sanctity, but this motif was and is subject to multiple conflicting interpretations, few of which are directly supported by the literary, narrative, and theological representations of the Gospels.

The Rejection of Animal Sacrifice

Jesus affirmed the Temple's function as the house of God but criticized its current administration. His predictive *warning* of the Temple's destruction was secondarily reinterpreted as an eschatological *threat*.[129] Nonetheless, Jesus' actions may be best understood as restorative – a kind of eschatological cleansing – intended to affirm and correct the sanctity of the Temple.[130] Jesus' critique of the Temple

---

[128] Lang, *Sacred Games*, 278.

[129] Gaston, *No Stone on Another*, 161, suggests that the threat to destroy the Temple was Stephen's position, not Jesus.'

[130] Ådna, "Jesus and the Temple," in T. Holmén (ed.), *Handbook for the Study of the Historical Jesus*, 4 vols., (Leiden: Brill, 2011), 2668, affirms that Jesus "accepted and endorsed the Zion tradition" while simultaneously symbolically "abolishing" and replacing Temple sacrifice with his own blood sacrifice. Ådna, *Jesu Stellung*, 136-142, sees the Temple act as a call to repentance (cf. 405) combined with a "messianic" self-understanding of his own mission. Jesus not only sought to demonstrate the end of the Temple cult and the beginning of a new worship of God in a Temple dedicated to prayer, but also understood his own death as an atoning sacrifice that replaced the

does not make him "an isolated figure in his own time."[131] On the contrary, he stands within the Jewish tradition of internal cultural critique. Jesus' affirmation of the Temple's sanctity as the house of God, however, does not *require* his participation in or endorsement of the Temple cult. We must differentiate Jesus' high regard for the Temple from his critical stance toward its administration. Despite its virtually ubiquitous presence in antiquity, it is a methodological fallacy – and a pernicious one at that – to pre-suppose or assume that "sacrifice" or the Temple is to be equated solely with the performance of blood or animal sacrifice as if that were its only possible function and purpose.

Jesus visited the Temple on multiple occasions. He seems to have taught (and even healed) in the Temple courts. He may have disrupted business in the Royal Stoa, but the strong probability that Jesus predicted the Temple's destruction suggests that Jesus did *not* participate in the Temple cult. Whether we hold that Jesus *predicted* the destruction of the Temple or *threatened* the destruction of the Temple, it is difficult to imagine Jesus participating in a cultic system he foresaw as destined for immediate destruction.[132] It is "hard to imagine Jesus taking a Passover lamb a few days later from the temple which he criticized so sharply, in order to eat it with the disciples."[133] The Temple no longer provided atonement, its administration was corrupt, and it was soon to be destroyed. Jesus' apparent lack of participation must be interpreted. If Jesus did not threaten to destroy the Temple (Mark insists that this was the testimony of "false

need for its sacrificial system. Ådna does not always succeed in avoiding Christian anachronism, especially in the way he describes the Temple authorities as "clinging to the traditional temple cult instead of obediently answering Jesus' call" (2669). See also Ulrich Wilckens, *Theologie des Neuen Testaments*, vol. I.2 (Neukirchen-Vluyn: Neukirchener, 2003), 62–5.

[131] Gerd Theissen and Dagmar Winter, *The Quest for the Plausible Jesus: The Question of Criteria* (trans. M. Eugene Boring; Louisville: Wesminster John Knox, 2002), 182.

[132] Neusner, "Money-Changers in the Temple," 290.

[133] Theissen and Merz, *The Historical Jesus*, 434. On the absence of lamb in the Synoptics, Martin, "Jesus in Jerusalem: Armed and Not Dangerous," 17, suggests that Jesus simply did not "participate in the sacrificial cult." Fredriksen, "Arms and The Man," 321, insists that the Markan Jesus *does* eat lamb ("*the* Passover") (τὸ πάσχα) (Mark 14:14), but reads this *into* the text. Moreover, this oblique reference symbolizes Jesus' sacrificial death *as* the Passover lamb (cf. 1 Cor 5:7). Martin, "Response to Downing and Fredriksen," *JSNT*, 37.3 (2015), 337, rightly notes that "we have no hint in our sources that Jesus or the disciples participated in sacrifices."

witnesses"), then it seems that Jesus' sayings and deeds were intended to point to the Temple's administration being under imminent divine judgment. Yet there is no reason to think that Jesus expected a new physical Temple that would replace the current Temple nor does he seem to seek to overthrow or replace the Temple's current administration. This may be how Jesus was *seen* by the religious authorities. By word and deed, Jesus violated the Temple's sanctity. This is why the high priest acted the way he did, conspiring with a wayward disciple, convening an impromptu "council," condemning Jesus to death for blasphemy, and transforming the charge into an offense punishable by Rome.

If Jesus did not participate in the Temple cult yet revered the Temple as the house of God, we must account for this data with a hypothesis of sufficient explanatory power to reconcile this apparent paradox and clarify precisely why the early Jesus tradition contains both pro- and anti-Temple materials.[134] Why does Q, for example, declare the Temple to be "forsaken"? Why does Mark see the Temple as immediately destined for destruction? Why does Luke go to such lengths to portray Paul, Peter, and the earliest Christians as worshipping (but not sacrificing) in the Temple yet construct an elaborate narrative in which Stephen rejects the validity of the Temple altogether? If Jesus offered sacrifices in the Temple would that not have undermined his identity as the ultimate sacrifice? Did Jesus, then, stand in the line of the prophets in critiquing the Temple cult?[135] Did Jesus reject the central institution of Judean religious practice?[136]

Jacob Neusner has suggested that Jesus' overturning the tables of the money-changers in the Temple signified Jesus' rejection of the Torah's "explicit teaching concerning the daily whole offering."[137] Jesus saw the cult as essentially useless and introduced a new "means

---

[134] Gaston, *No Stone on Another*, 101-2, concludes that the early church's abstention from the Temple cult "can only be explained if it corresponds to the attitude of Jesus himself." For Gaston, Jesus' attitude to the cult was one of "sublime indifference."

[135] On Jesus as a prophet critiquing the Temple administration, but not the cult itself, see Young, "Temple Cult and Law in Early Christianity," 336.

[136] Horsley, *Jesus and the Spiral of Violence*, 285–317, here 325, proposes that Jesus "rejected the institutions themselves." See also *The Prophet Jesus and the Renewal of Israel: Moving Beyond a Diversionary Debate* (Grand Rapids: Eerdmans, 2012), 138–49, esp. 143.

[137] Neusner, "Money-Changers in the Temple," 289.

of atonement," the Eucharist. Alternatively, Frances Young argues
that Jesus did not reject the Temple cult, but emphasized the prophetic point of view on *morality*.[138] It was not Jesus, but "[a] group
of Hellenized Jews" who interpreted Jesus' prophetic saying against
the Temple to mean that "they should reject the Temple-worship."[139]
It was not long, however, before Christianity spread while the
importance of sacrifice and the Temple "naturally decreased." The
Christian rejection of the Temple proceeded in stages, first because
Stephen and other converts rejected the Temple and subsequently in
"light of Christ's death on the cross."[140] The Temple incident was then
"reinterpreted as a rejection of the Jewish cult" in the Gospels.[141] The
new movement adopted the language and symbolism of sacrifice but
transformed it so that the new "cult" was the offering of prayers, the
new altar was the minds and hearts of believers, and the new Temple,
sacrifice, and high priest was Christ.[142]

Tom Holmén has also proposed that the "common denominator"
in Jesus' anti-Temple sayings and the Temple incident is the sacrificial cult.[143] According to Holmén, "Jesus' attitude to the Temple was
somehow negatively shaped," and the Temple incident was directed
against the Temple cult.[144] Jesus was not trying to reform the cult nor
did he envision a new Temple to be built in its place. On the contrary,

[138] Young, *Sacrifice and the Death of Christ*, 47; "Temple Cult and Law in Early
Christianity," 325–38; *The Use of Sacrificial Ideas in Greek and Christian Writers
from the New Testament to John Chrysostom* (Cambridge: Philadelphia Patristic
Foundation, 1979).

[139] Young, *Sacrifice and the Death of Christ*, 49.

[140] Young, *Sacrifice and the Death of Christ*, 50. Young sees two "elements" in the
"Jewish background" of atonement theology: "the idea that the death of a righteous
martyr was expiatory" and "the search for prophecies" of the crucified messiah (64), a
search that culminated in the discovery of Isaiah 53.

[141] Young, *Sacrifice and the Death of Christ*, 51.

[142] Young, *Sacrifice and the Death of Christ*, admits that Paul adopted the *language*
of sacrifice to *interpret* the death of Jesus while the author of Hebrews asserted that
Jesus' sacrifice *replaced* the need for sacrifice.

[143] Holmén, *Jesus and Jewish Covenant Thinking*, 275–328. See also Idem, "The
Temple Action of Jesus (Mark 11:15–17) in Historical Context," in K J. Illman et al.
(eds.), *A Bouquet of Wisdom: Essays in Honour of Karl-Gustav Sandelin* (Åbo: Åbo
Akademi, 2000): 118–24.

[144] Holmén, *Jesus and Jewish Covenant Thinking*, 289. As H. Merklein, *Jesu
Botschaft von de Gottesherrschaft. Eine Skizze* (3rd edn.; Stuttgart: Katholisches
Bibelwerk, 1989), 135–6, puts it: "Affront gegen die Sinnhaftigkeit des Kultbetriebes
überhaupt."

Jesus wanted to "put forward the idea that the Temple with its cult should (and would) disappear."[145] Appealing to the prophets' critique of the Temple,[146] Jesus indicated that the Temple would be destroyed because of Israel's "persistence in a sinful way of life."[147] The cult was "futile and expendable."[148] It had not fulfilled its Isaianic destiny as "a house of prayer for all nations." For Holmén, the divine destruction of the Temple was "a secondary theme" because Jesus was "particularly concerned with the Temple's sacrificial system."[149] The cult was "meaningless" and was soon to be "abolished."[150]

Similarly, John McGuckin proposes that Jesus "adapted the prophetic criticism of the cult that called for its *purification* by *ethical* involvement."[151] Jesus, however, did not just echo the prophetic critique, but "sharpened" it "in a radical way by what he saw to be the implications of the End-Time."[152] For McGuckin, Jesus' vision of the kingdom centered on "reconciliation ... without any recourse to the notion of cultic sacrifice." In short, "Jesus had no place for the cult in his theological schema."[153] Jesus did "nothing to encourage the use of sacrificial concepts to illuminate the relationship of God to Israel."[154] But Jesus' relationship to the Temple was theologically "(re)interpreted" by the author of Mark, the first evangelist who initiated "the long tradition that sees it as a 'purification'" of the Temple. Mark appeals to Zech 14:21 ("there shall be no more traders in the Temple") and Isa 56:7 ("my house will be a house of prayer for all nations") to interpret the event, but the original meaning of the event was not a symbolic destruction of the Temple, but a prophetic demonstration that the Temple was now rendered obsolete in light of the imminent kingdom.[155] Nonetheless, Jesus' own disciples used

---

[145] Holmén, *Jesus and Jewish Covenant Thinking*, 321.

[146] Amos 5:21–24; Isa 1:11, 13–15; Prov 21:27; Jer 6:19–21.

[147] Holmén, *Jesus and Jewish Covenant Thinking*, 322.

[148] Holmén, *Jesus and Jewish Covenant Thinking*, 323.

[149] Holmén, *Jesus and Jewish Covenant Thinking*, 328, 326: "the cult should and would cease, and was accompanied by the implied idea of the demolition of the Temple."

[150] Holmén, *Jesus and Jewish Covenant Thinking*, 328, 329.

[151] McGuckin, "Sacrifice and Atonement," 648 (emphases added).

[152] McGuckin, "Sacrifice and Atonement," 649.

[153] McGuckin, "Sacrifice and Atonement," 649, argues that Jesus' kingdom vision "effectively rendered the sacrificial cult superfluous for him."

[154] McGuckin, "Sacrifice and Atonement," 649.

[155] McGuckin, "Sacrifice and Atonement," 655: "the entire substance of Jesus' words during the Temple incident has been supplied by the evangelist by proof texts ...

the language of sacrifice "as a synopsis of his work and theological significance."[156]

Jesus' teaching focused on the kingdom of God. The central ethic of the earliest Jesus traditions preserved in Q is an instructional body of wisdom advocating a lifestyle of radical eschatological nonviolence:[157]

Q 6:20–21:	Beatitudes for the Poor, Hungry, and Mourning
Q 6:22–23:	Beatitude for the Persecuted
Q 6:27–28:	Love Your Enemies
Q 6:29:	Renouncing One's Own Rights
Q 6:31:	The Golden Rule
Q 6:32, 34:	Impartial Love
Q 6:36:	Being Full of Compassion like Your Father
Q 6:37–38:	Not Judging

Nonviolence is a distinctive and characteristic aspect of the historical Jesus' sayings and deeds.[158] Jesus' uncompromising imperative to love one's enemies not only contradicts our normal human tendencies, but also undermines the biblical tradition of divine violence that repeatedly describes God as annihilating Israel's enemies. It is difficult not to conclude that Jesus extended this imperative – based on his vision of God's compassionate nature and unconditional love – to the Temple's administration. The Temple cult trafficked in violence; the sacrificial system required an incessant supply of blood from the marketplace to the altar. Jesus' radical imperative collided with and undermined the most obvious site of violence in his world. If Jesus concluded that God did not want, let alone need violence, and if Jesus believed, as most specialists agree, that the end-time had arrived – and with it the promised fulfillment of the Isaianic age of peace – then the violence of the Temple cult would need to come to an end. Jesus, like most Jews, knew that God had created an Edenic garden of peace "in the beginning" and that violence was not God's

---

This leaves us to ask what else could have been the significance of the act if 'spiritual purification' and 'renewal' emerge as secondary."

[156] McGuckin, "Sacrifice and Atonement," 655.

[157] John S. Kloppenborg, "The Function of Apocalyptic Language in Q," *SBLASP*, 25 (1986), 224–35, at 235, citing Q 6:27–28. See also idem, "Symbolic Eschatology and the Apocalypticism of Q," *HTR*, 80.3 (1987), 287–306, at 305. See also Martin Hengel, *Was Jesus a Revolutionist?* (trans. William Klassen; Philadelphia: Fortress, 1971), 26.

[158] Joseph, *The Nonviolent Messiah*, 23–50, 197–228.

will at creation. Nor was violence God's will in the world to come. Jesus did not reject "Judaism," "sacrifice," or the "Temple." Jesus did not reject the Torah as God's will or the Temple as God's house. His objections need not even have signified an attempt to abolish or reform the cultic system, but may have simply been expressed as an ethical and eschatological conviction. Nonetheless, such a conviction *would* have been perceived as scandalous and offensive in light of the inherited tradition.

The "cleansing" of the Temple was indeed symbolic in its restoration of the original creation in the "place" that had been corrupted. The Temple – as a new eschatological Eden – represented the "place" of creation, the *axis mundi* where God was supposed to "rest."[159] Jesus' action in the Temple sought to restore this "place" in alignment with the original creation. That is why early Jewish Christians continued worshipping, teaching, and praying in the Temple: because Jesus had sought to "restore" it to its original purpose as the house of God and it was still contested sacred ground in first-century sectarian Judaism. Jesus interpreted the Torah as the law of God revealed at creation and the Temple as the house of God, the holy "place" of worship and prayer. If, as we have seen, sacrifice is not inherently violent and is more properly understood as an act of sanctification, then Jesus, like the Qumran community before him, could indeed have envisioned bloodless sacrifice, including prayer, righteous acts, and the "(self-) sacrifice/sanctification" of one's life as valid "sacrifices." Despite the conflicts it engendered and the price he would pay for his commitment, Jesus' creative interpretation of scripture – his eschatological re-signification of the Torah and Temple – represents a distinctive voice *within* Early Judaism.

We find further support for our proposal in Jesus' emphasis on the forgiveness of sins. Either directly or indirectly, Jesus mediates forgiveness and assumes the authority to pronounce the forgiveness of sins whether or not "sinners" met their obligatory sacrificial rites. Jesus advocated a way of life that did not need the Temple

---

[159] On Eden as sanctuary or Temple, see G. J. Wenham, "Sanctuary Symbolism in the Garden of Eden Story," in *PWCJS* 9 (1986), 19–25; T. D. Alexander and S. Gathercole (eds.), *Heaven on Earth: The Temple in Biblical Theology* (Carlisle: Paternoster, 2004). On the *Urzeit/Endzeit* theme, see also Jon D. Levenson, "The Temple and the World," *JR*, 64 (1984), 275–98; Barker, *The Gate of Heaven*, 68. On the Isaianic "new creation" in Jerusalem, see B. G. Webb, "Zion in Transformation: A Literary Approach to Isaiah," in D. J. A. Clines, S. E. Fowl, and S. E. Porter (eds.), *The Bible in Three Dimensions* (JSOT Sup 87; Sheffield: JSOT, 1990), 65–84, here 71.

cult.[160] Jesus did not require traditional repentance from "sinners." This was an offense to "normal piety," for it found Mosaic Law inadequate.[161] This forgiveness of sins was also a direct threat to the priesthood, whose *business* was atonement.[162] Jesus' admission of "sinners" into the kingdom without sacrifice again points to an implied criticism: *God did not require blood sacrifice.*[163]

Jesus was not critical of the Temple.[164] Jesus criticized the practice of blood sacrifice.[165] The Gospel of Matthew, of course, identifies Jesus as something "*greater* (μεῖζόν) than the Temple,"[166] but places this statement immediately before a *second* allusion to Hosea 6:6 ("mercy and not sacrifice"): Jesus' compassionate interpretation of the Torah is greater than what happens in the Temple, that is, mercy and compassion are superior to the Temple sacrifices. The Matthean Jesus quotes Hosea and Micah's radical critiques, and Jeremiah's anti-Temple saying.[167] Jesus, in other words, did not seek to *replace* the Temple or "abrogate" the Torah. Jesus'

---

[160] Sanders, *Jesus and Judaism*, 61–76. See D. J. Antwi, "Did Jesus Consider His Death to be an Atoning Sacrifice?" *Int*, 45 (1991), 17–28.

[161] Sanders, *Jesus and Judaism*, 207–11, esp. 271.

[162] See Tobias Hägerland, *Jesus and the Forgiveness of Sins: An Aspect of His Prophetic Mission* (SNTSMS 150; Cambridge University Press, 2011).

[163] Sanders, *Jesus and Judaism*, 269, maintains that Jesus' action meant "that the Mosaic legislation of sacrifices was neither 'final' nor 'adequate.'" See also Theissen and Winter, *The Quest for the Plausible Jesus*, 182: "For Jesus, God offers salvation without any ritual act." On the other hand, Sanders argues that "the principal function of any temple is to serve as a place for sacrifice, and that sacrifices *require* the supply of suitable animals" (63). Here Sanders *conflates* animal *and* vegetable sacrifice, that is, the *principle* of sacrificial ritual with a particular *practice* or form of sacrifice. In *The Historical Figure of Jesus*, 255–6, n. 92, Sanders claims that Jesus could not have attacked the Temple because it "was central to Palestinian Judaism and important to all Jews everywhere. To be against it would be to oppose Judaism as a religion. It would also be an attack on the main unifying symbol of the Jewish people ... If Jesus really assailed this central institution, we would have some evidence of this apart from the incident."

[164] Snodgrass, "The Temple Incident," 432, claims that Jesus' act was "a prophetic protest that pointed to future eschatological hope" (464).

[165] Ådna, "Jesus and the Temple," 3: 2635–75, esp. 2670, proposes that "the old atonement cult must be brought to an end because it is inappropriate in the eschatological era." Bernard, *John*, 87–8, proposed that Jesus "directed public attention ... to the futility of animal sacrifices ... This it was which set the Temple officials against Him." On Jesus intending to "replace" the cult, see Trautmann, *Zeichenhafte Handlungen Jesu*, 121; Paesler, *Das Tempelwort Jesu*, 244.

[166] Matt. 12.6.

[167] Matt. 9:13; 12:7; 23:23; and Matt 21:13, respectively.

Torah-interpretation is eschatologically restorative. As we have seen, Jesus' prohibition of divorce provides us with a hermeneutical key to understanding Jesus' *halakhah*. This key also explains why Jesus objected to animal sacrifice: because animal sacrifice, like divorce, was not God's original intention.[168] It is reasonable to suppose that Jesus found God's original intention for creation worth restoring.[169] The messianic prophecies of Isa. 2:2–4 and 11:1–9 envision a time of universal peace.[170] Similarly, compassion and nonviolence are characteristic themes of Jesus' sayings and deeds.[171] The Torah prohibits inflicting unnecessary suffering and stresses compassion for animals (צער בעלי חיים).[172] Jesus was not transgressing Torah by advocating a higher ideal than the Torah allowed. The principle of *Lifnim Mishurat Hadin* (לפנים משורת הדין), literally "between the lines of the law," holds that going "beyond the letter of the law" can fulfill the pursuit of higher ethical ideals.[173] Jesus affirmed what God originally *intended*, not what the Mosaic Law subsequently *allowed*.

Jesus' rejection of animal sacrifice was an historical enactment of eschatological Temple restoration and a radical challenge to

---

[168] The Talmud describes Adam as not allowed to eat meat (*B. Sanh.* 59b). It is not until Gen. 9:2–3 that God permits meat-eating. Animal sacrifice, however, is *post-Edenic*.

[169] H. Stegemann, "Some Aspects of Eschatology in Texts from the Qumran community and in the Teachings of Jesus," *Biblical Archaeology Today: Proceedings of the International Congress on Biblical Archaeology, Jerusalem, April 1984* (Jerusalem: Israel Exploration Society, Israel Academy of Sciences and Humanities, American Schools of Oriental Research, 1985), 412–16, esp. 417. Stegemann suggests that Jesus believed that the sacrificial system ended with the arrival of the messianic era and the restoration of "paradise." A. I. Baumgarten, *The Flourishing of Jewish Sects in the Maccabean Era: An Interpretation* (JSJ Sup 55; Leiden: Brill, 1997), 155: "Apocalypses are revelations concerned with ... the achievement of the ideal humanity."

[170] See Jonathan Huddleston, *Eschatology in Genesis* (FAT 2/57; Tübingen: Mohr Siebeck, 2012).

[171] On Jesus' compassion, see Matt 9:36; 14:14; 15:32, 20:34, Luke 7:12–15; cf. Mark 1:40–42, where Jesus is "filled with compassion" (σπλαγχνισθείς).

[172] Num. 22:32; Deut. 25:4; 22:10; Exod. 20:8–10; Lev 22:27; 22:28; Deut. 22:6–7; 14:21; Exod. 23:19; 34:26. On צער בעלי חיים, see *Bava Metzia* 32b, based on Exod. 23:5, 20:10; Deut. 25:4.

[173] Richard A. Davis, "*Lifnim Mishurat Hadin: The Rabbinic Concept*," Ph.D. diss., Hebrew Union College – Jewish Institute of Religion, New York, 1972; Saul J. Berman, "Lifnim Mishurat Hadin," *JJS*, 26 (1975), 86–104; 28 (1977), 181–93; Louis E. Newman, "Law, Virtue and Supererogation in the Halakha: The Problem of '*Lifnim Mishurat Hadin*' Reconsidered," *JJS*, 40(1) (1989), 61–88.

sacrificial legislation. Jesus claimed the authority and power to be able to mediate God's forgiveness and compassion without blood sacrifice:

> When Jesus saw their faith, he said to the paralytic, "Son, your sins are forgiven."[174]
> "Friend, your sins are forgiven you."[175]
> "Your faith has made you well."[176]
> "he touched their eyes and said, 'According to your faith let it be done to you.'
> And their eyes were opened."[177]

The Gospels elevate Jesus and his teachings over the traditional sacrificial system. The Markan Jesus declares that love of God and neighbor is *"greater than all burnt offerings and sacrifices"* (περισσότερόν ἐστιν πάντων τῶν ὁλοκαυστωμάτων καὶ θυσιῶν).[178] The Matthean Jesus quotes Hosea: "I desire mercy, *not* sacrifice"' (θέλω καὶ οὐ θυσίαν).[179] It would seem to follow, therefore, that Jesus developed the insight that God does not *require* blood sacrifice even further: God does not *desire* blood sacrifice.[180] It is this radicalization of the prophetic critique of the sacrificial system that offended the priestly authorities. Jesus was not just gaining a popular following. He was also challenging the authority of the Mosaic Law.[181] He was asserting that the

---

[174] Mark 2:5.

[175] Luke 5:20.

[176] Matt 9:22; Mark 5:34; 10:52; Luke 8:48.

[177] Matt 9:28–30.

[178] Mark 12:33. Gray, *The Temple*, 107, n. 39: Mark "suggests that animal sacrifice is rendered obsolete."

[179] Matt 9:13; 12:7.

[180] For the Temple incident as an attack on the sacrificial system, see Snodgrass, "The Temple Incident," 466–7. See Ådna, *Jesu Stellung zum Tempel*, 383–7, 412–13, 429–48; Neusner, "Money-Changers in the Temple," 287–90; Holmén, *Jesus and Jewish Covenant Thinking*, 326–7; William R. Herzog II, *Jesus, Justice, and the Reign of God* (Louisville: Westminster John Knox, 2000), 142; Christopher M. Tuckett, *The Contemporary Revival of the Griesbach Hypothesis* (SNTSMS 44; Cambridge University Press, 1983), 116; Theissen and Merz, *The Historical Jesus*, 433. Telford, *The Barren Temple and the Withered Tree*, 92–3, n. 102; Chilton, *The Temple of Jesus*, 150–4.

[181] Sanders, *Jesus and Judaism*, 293.

animal sacrifices were objectionable.[182] The gravity of this perceived offense to traditional norms of priestly piety and authority was more than sufficient to result in his death.

Conclusion

The relationship between Jesus and the Temple can now be better understood in light of Jesus' radicalized eschatology. There is good reason to think that early Jewish Christians both inherited and developed the idea of the community-as-temple in light of Jesus' ministry. The New Testament attests to a Palestinian Jewish origin of this concept, particularly in Paul's letters.[183] It is also possible to trace a Christological trajectory of this developing theme from theoretically earlier expressions identifying the *community* as a temple to identifying *Jesus* as the (new) temple.[184] The question, of course, is whether this temple-imagery derives from the historical Jesus or from the post-30 CE Jesus movement. But if Jesus did not participate in the Temple cult, did not seek to destroy the Temple, and did not seek to "abolish" animal sacrifice – *but opposed it in principle* – then Jesus may indeed have envisioned himself "building" a new temple-community in co-existence and competition with the present Temple. This need not be seen as an attempt to *replace* the Temple, but that is certainly how it could have been *perceived* by his contemporaries. It is this combination of opposition to the Temple's economic adminstration, criticism of the Temple cult (and, by definition, Mosaic Law and priestly authority), in conjunction with the formation of a new temple-community, which made Jesus' ministry a direct threat to the Temple establishment. Consequently, there would be a direct

---

[182] Contra Sanders, *Jesus and Judaism*, 269: Jesus' Temple "action was not construed to mean, and probably did not mean, that Jesus objected to the sacrifices instituted by God."

[183] On the early Christian community as a temple, see 2 Cor 6:16 ("we are the temple of the living God"). As an "Essene" interpolation, see Joseph A. Fitzmyer, "Qumran and the Interpolated Paragraph in 2 Cor 6,14-7,1," *CBQ* 23 (1961), 271-80. In 1 Cor 6:19, it is the *individual* body that is a "temple of the Holy Spirit within you." Similarly, in 1 Cor 3:16, Paul says "Do you not know that you are the temple of God and that the Spirit of God dwells in you?" See also 1 Peter 2:4-9; Eph 2:19-22; Rev 21:10; 1 Tim 3:15; 2 Tim 2:19; Heb 3:1-6.

[184] Gaston, *No Stone on Another*, 226, 241, 243, suggests that Jesus used the language of "rebuilding" a temple in reference to the eschatological community as a "temple of God."

line of continuity between Jesus' (new) temple-community and the early Palestinian Jesus tradition of envisioning the (non-sacrificing) Jerusalem community as a new temple with its leaders as "pillars," James the "rampart," Peter/Cephas the "rock,"[185] and Jesus the "*rejected* cornerstone." This would also explain why Jesus' Jewish followers "remembered" him as opposing animal sacrifice and created a complex body of traditions that emphatically assert that Jesus criticized the practice of animal sacrifice.[186]

---

[185] Paul's reference to the "pillars" in Gal 2:9 suggests that the Jerusalem leaders were thought of as "the foundations of the new temple" (Gaston, *No Stone on Another*, 195). This language seems to *precede* Paul and may have been foundational to the self-conception of the nascent Jewish Christian community (200). On Simon/Peter as the "rock," see Matt 16:18.

[186] See especially *The Book of Elchasai* (c. 117 CE); *The Gospel of the Ebionites* (c. 180 CE); the *Grundschrift* or Basic Writing, the source of *Rec.* 1.27–71 (c. 200 CE); the Pseudo-Clementine *Homilies* and *Recognitions* (c. 400 CE); and Epiphanius' *Panarion* (390 CE).

6

THE JEWISH CHRISTIAN REJECTION
OF ANIMAL SACRIFICE

[T]he common assumption that "canonical" works must be chronologically prior to extracanonical works should be rejected as theologically freighted and historiographically fallacious.

John S. Kloppenborg, "A New Synoptic Problem."

What Is "Jewish Christianity"?

The term *Jewish Christianity* refers to members of the Jesus movement who maintained and combined loyalty toward Jewish law with reverence for Jesus.[1] The term has recently come under fire as definitionally imprecise,[2] with accusations of it facilitating "a modernist heresiology,"[3] and reinscribing a discourse that attempted to expel

---

[1] Matt Jackson-McCabe (ed.), *Jewish Christianity Reconsidered: Rethinking Ancient Groups and Texts* (Minneapolis: Fortress, 2007); Petri Luomanen, *Recovering Jewish Christian Sects and Gospels* (VCSup 110; Leiden: Brill, 2012); Edwin K. Broadhead, *Jewish Ways of Following Jesus: Redrawing the Religious Map of Antiquity* (WUNT 266; Tübingen: Mohr Siebeck, 2010); James Carleton Paget, *Jews, Christians, and Jewish Christians in Antiquity* (WUNT 251; Tübingen: Mohr Siebeck, 2010); Oskar Skarsaune and Reidar Hvalvik (eds.), *Jewish Believers in Jesus: The Early Centuries* (Peabody: Hendrickson, 2007); Simon C. Mimouni, *Le Judéo-christianisme ancien: Essais historiques* (Paris: Cerf, 1998); *Early Judaeo-Christianity: Historical Essays* (ISACR 13; trans. R. Fréchet; Leuven: Peeters, 2012); S. C. Mimouni and F. S. Jones (eds.), *Le Judéo-Christianisme dans tous ses états: acts du colloque de Jérusalem 6–10 Juillet 1998* (Paris: Cerf, 2001); Jean Danielou, *The Theology of Jewish Christianity* (trans. J. A. Baker, London: Darton, Longman, and Todd, 1964); Georg Strecker; *Das Judenchristentum in den Pseudoclementinen* (Berlin: Akademie, 1958); Hans-Joachim Schoeps, *Jewish Christianity: Factional Disputes in the Early Church* (trans. D. R. A. Hare; Fortress, 1969).

[2] Daniel Boyarin, "Rethinking Jewish Christianity: An Argument for Dismantling a Dubious Category (to which is Appended a Correction of my *Border Lines*)," *JQR*, 99.1 (2009), 7–36.

[3] Karen L. King, *What Is Gnosticism?* (Cambridge, MA: Harvard University Press, 2003); Michael Allen Williams, *Rethinking "Gnosticism": An Argument for Dismantling a Dubious Category* (Princeton University Press, 1996).

Jewish influences from Christianity by constructing Judaism as separate and distinct from Christianity.[4] The term is admittedly problematic, both because it is a modern scholarly category (the term is never used by ancient Jewish believers in Jesus) and because it is linked to heresiological discourse. Moreover, there is little agreement on precisely what the *Jewishness* in "Jewish Christianity" is supposed to refer to.[5] Is Jewish Christianity a type or subclass of *Christianity*? Or a form of *Judaism* suppressed and marginalized by proto-orthodox Christianity? Does the term represent *Jewish* ethnic individuals and groups holding on to Jewish beliefs and practices while accommodating their belief in Jesus as messiah? Or does it refer to "*Christians*" covertly exploiting Jewish ideals to advance Christian supersessionism? As long as these categorical identifications remain unclear, there will be more than enough room for misunderstanding. So our problem is partly one of definition. We could well be talking past each other unless we have a common, mutual understanding of *who* these folks were and *to whom* this term refers. Fortunately, we do have the ability to limit our definitional imprecision by appealing to the criteria of ethnic identity.

Ancient (and contemporary) Jewish identity is complex and multi-faceted, based on birth, religion, culture, and geographical location, that is, a nexus of multiple inter-related components, no single one of which is determinative. Each of these elements should play a role in differentiating ancient "Jews" and "Jewish Christians" from non-Jews. For example, if Jewish identity is based on *ethnicity*, how are we to define Jewish ethnicity in the first century? If by birth, then by matrilineal descent,[6] patrilineal descent, or both? There is no reason to think that rabbinical *halakhah* was normative for all Jews at the time of Jesus. If at least one parent was Jewish, it would have been possible to identify a child as Jewish. In this context, ethnicity alone

[4]   Boyarin, "Rethinking Jewish Christianity," 23.

[5]   On Ἰουδαῖος as "Jew" or "Judean," see Daniel R. Schwartz, "'Judean' or 'Jew'? How Should We Translate *Ioudaios* in Josephus?" in J. Frey, D. R. Schwartz and S. Gripentrog (eds.), *Jewish Identity in the Greco-Roman World: Jüdische Identität in der griechisch-römischen Welt* (AJEC 71; Leiden: Brill, 2007), 3–27; John H. Elliott, "Jesus the Israelite was neither a 'Jew' nor a 'Christian': On Correcting Misleading Nomenclature," *JSHJ*, 5/2 (2007), 119–54; Graham Harvey, *The True Israel: Uses of the Name Jew, Hebrew and Israel in Ancient Jewish and Early Christian Literature* (Leiden: Brill, 1996); David Goodblatt, "From Judeans to Israel: Names of Jewish States in Antiquity," *JSJ*, 29 (1998), 1–36.

[6]   *M. Qidd.* 4.1.

was a lifelong guarantor of Jewish identity. Jewish identity could be compromised by apostasy, but even an apostate Jew is still a Jew. The socio-rhetorical exclusion of Jewish Christians as either מינים or נוצרים from rabbinical Jewish communities is well known.[7] The *Birkat ha-minim* (ברכת המינים) may refer both to various Jewish "heresies" (מינים) *and* to *Jewish* Christians (נוצרים). Justin tells us that Jews pronounced "curses against those who believe in Christ" (*Dial.* 16). Epiphanius also tells us that "the Jews … pronounce curses and maledictions over them when they say prayer in the synagogues. Three times a day, they anathematize crying: "May God curse the Nazoreans" (ἐπικαταράσαι ὁ Θεὸς τοῦς ναζωραίους)" (*Pan.* 29.9.2). Epiphanius identifies the Nazoreans (Ναζωραίους) and the נוצרים. Jerome also reports that Jewish Christians are both Ναζωραίους and מינים (Letter 112).

If Jewish identity is understood as based on *practice*, then which specific practices qualify? Circumcision? Keeping the Sabbath? Attending Jewish festivals? Observance of the food laws? Reverence for Jerusalem? If *praxis* is determinative, then what about those Jews who lived Jewish lives without the Temple? What about those who presumed the scribal authority and freedom to "rewrite" the Torah?[8] If Christology is a defining factor, then what kinds of messianic beliefs qualify? Davidic? Prophetic? Angelic? How far can a "Jewish Christian" stray from "Judaism" and/or "Christianity" and still maintain ethnic and Christological alliances and loyalties to both? According to Justin (c. 150 CE) there was room in the

---

[7] See S. C. Mimouni, "La 'Birkat ha-minim': Une prière juive contre les judéo-chrétiens," *RSR*, 71 (1997), 275–98; P. S. Alexander, "Jewish Believers in Early Rabbinic Literature (2nd to 5th Centuries)," in O. Skarsaune and R. Hvalvik (eds.), *Jewish Believers in Jesus: The Early Centuries* (Peabody: Hendrickson, 2007), 659–709; W. Horbury, "The Benediction of the Minim and Early Jewish-Christian Controversy," *JTS*, 33 (1982), 19–61; T. C. G. Thornton, "Christian Understandings of the Birkat ha-Minim in the Eastern Roman Empire," *JTS*, 38 (1987), 419–31; Yaakov Y. Teppler, *Birkat haMinim: Jews and Christians in Conflict in the Ancient World* (trans. S. Weingarten; TSAJ 120; Tübingen: Mohr Siebeck, 2007); R. Kalmin, "Christians and Heretics in Rabbinic Literature of Late Antiquity," *HTR*, 87 (1994), 155–69; Martin Goodman, "The Function of Minim in early Rabbinic Judaism," in P. Schäfer (ed.), *Tradition – Reflexion. Festschrift für Martin Hengel zum 70. Geburtstag, I* (Tübingen: Mohr Siebeck, 1996), 501–10.

[8] Mimouni, *Le judéo-christianisme ancien*, 70; "Pour une définition nouvelle du judéo-christianisme ancien," *NTS*, 38 (1992), 161–86; Carleton Paget, "Definition of the Terms Jewish Christian and Jewish Christianity," 740.

church for both Jewish and Gentile Christians. This relative toler-ance and inclusivism changed by the fourth century when heresi-ologists such as Epiphanius began to dismissively describe Jewish Christians as

> different from Jews, and different from Christians, only in the following. They disagree with Jews because they have come to faith in Christ; but since they are still fettered by the Law – circumcision, the Sabbath, and the rest – they are not in accord with Christians.[9]

Note here that Epiphanius' *definition* of "Christian" *excludes* Jewish practice. Jerome gives us a similarly exclusive description of Jewish Christians:

> They believe in Christ, the Son of God ... but since they want to be Jews and Christians, they are neither Jews nor Christians.[10]

If Jewish identity is based, in part, on being recognized as Jewish by other Jews, then *which* Jews authorize this recognition? Based on the complex nature of Jewish identity, it would seem that Jewish or Christian denials of Jewish Christian "Jewishness" were more the result of losing socio-cultural recognition by other Jews or Christians than matters of ethnicity, observance, or messianism. While most Jews, especially rabbinic Jews, commemorated Temple practices in the Mishnah, this does *not* mean that *all* Jews did the same.[11] Just as we cannot assume that Jesus or his first followers practiced animal

---

[9] *Pan.* 29.7.5–6.

[10] *Letter* 112, 13.

[11] Naftali S. Cohn, *The Memory of the Temple and the Making of the Rabbis* (Divinations: RLAR; Philadelphia: University of Pennsylvania Press, 2013). Alexander Guttmann, "The End of the Jewish Sacrificial Cult," *HUCA*, 38 (1969), 138, notes that the rabbis did *not* prohibit the sacrificial cult after the destruction of the Temple but also did not call for its continuation, suggesting that post-70 CE sacrifice may have been considered "*optional*" (*M. 'Eduyyoth* 8.6; *B. Megillah* 10a. The rabbbis *halakhically* pre-supposed the end of *public* sacrifice (*M. Sheqalim* 8.8; *M. Ta'anith* 4.6; *B. Rosh Ha-Shanah* 21b). Yohanan ben Zakkai asserted that deeds of loving-kindness (נמילות חסדים) were just as effective as sacrifices (*Avoth de-Rabbi Nathan*, version I, ch. 4). R. Eleazar said that charity was more important than sacri-fice (*B. Sukkah* 49b).

sacrifice – since there is no clear or compelling evidence for this[12] – so too we cannot simply assume that all Jewish Christians were uniformly faithful to the Mosaic Law.[13] Judaism and Jewish Christianity were not uniform, monolithic systems.

The term "Jewish Christianity" may be problematic, but it should be retained not only because it actively discourages supersessionistic readings of the (Jewish) Christian tradition, the Pseudo-Clementine tradition, and the early Church Fathers, but because it represents a historically significant wing of the Jesus movement.[14] The Pseudo-Clementines, for example, emphasize Jesus' identity as the "True Prophet" predicted by Moses, emphasize baptism and food regulation,[15] presuppose a Jewish *and* Gentile mission, regard James and Peter as the leaders of the community, and criticize Paul (as "the enemy"). Peter is identified with the Jews.[16] Hebrew is the original language of humanity.[17] The blame for killing Jesus is attributed to a number of wicked Jews, but not to "the Jews" as a whole.[18] The difference between the law-observant believers and nonbelievers is belief in Jesus' messianic identity.[19] Identifying these identity-markers as "Jewish" should not be particularly controversial or problematic.

It is by no means easy, however, identifying ideological, genealogical, and archaeological continuities between *early* and *later* "Jewish

[12] Robert Daly, *Christian Sacrifice: The Judaeo-Christian Background Before Origen* (Washington: Catholic University of America, 1978), 214.

[13] W. Petersen, "Constructing the Matrix of Judaic Christianity from Texts," in *Le Judéo-Christianisme*, 136–137, notes that Jewish Christianity regarded "some parts of it as obsolete or corrupt ... the Judaic-Christian gospel fragment ... requires violating the Jewish Law, not obeying it."

[14] For the *"Jewish* Christian" identity of the Pseudo-Clementines, see Daniel Boyarin, "Justin Martyr Invents Judaism," *CH*, 70 (2001), 459; Annette Yoshiko Reed, "'Jewish Christianity' as Counter-history?: The Apostolic Past in Eusebius' Ecclesiastical History and the Pseudo-Clementine Homilies," in G. Gardner and K. Osterloh (eds.), *Antiquity in Antiquity: Jewish and Christian Pasts in the Greco-Roman World* (TSAJ 123; Tübingen: Mohr Siebeck, 2008), 204–13. Jewish Christian traditions might even be likened to Foucault's concept of "counter-memory," that is, alternative ways of representing and constructing the past. See Michel Foucault, *Language, Counter-Memory, Practice: Selected Essays and Interviews* (Ithaca: Cornell University Press, 1977).

[15] *Rec.* 4.36.4.

[16] *Rec.* 1.32.1.

[17] *Rec.* 1.30.5.

[18] *Rec.* 1.41.2.

[19] *Rec.* 1.43.2; 1.50.5; 1.44.2; 1.60; 1.62.4.

Christianity." *Jewish*-Christianity incorporates ethnicity, ideology,[20] practice,[21] geography, Christology,[22] and socio-cultural recognition by other Jews,[23] a complex of different kinds of Jewish reverence for Jesus.[24] Yet we must still attempt to differentiate between *early* Jewish Christianity, a category that properly includes Jesus' family (the δεσπόσυνοι),[25] the Twelve, Peter, James, Jude, Q, and Matthew, and *later* Jewish Christianity, an equally complex spectrum of ethnically Jewish groups identified as Nazoreans, Ebionites, and Elchasaites by the early Church Fathers.[26] F. Stanley Jones identifies the earliest Jewish Christians as Jews who "confessed Jesus as the Messiah" whereas "Early Jewish Christianity" was characterized by belief in Jesus as messiah, Jewish observances, and ethnic-genetic relationship(s) to Jesus' first Jewish followers. Similarly, Petri Luomanen identifies a nexus of ethnic identity markers, or "indicators," including Jewish observances, ideas, ethnicity, and sociological relationship(s) to other Jewish groups,

---

[20] Schoeps, *Theologie und Geschichte*; Daniélou, *Theology of Jewish Christianity*.

[21] F. J. A. Hort, *Judaistic Christianity* (Cambridge University Press, 1894); Marcel Simon, *Verus Israel: Étude sur les relations entre Chrétiens et Juifs dans l'Empire Romain (135–425)* (Paris: Editions de Boccard, 1948).

[22] R. N. Longenecker, *The Christology of Early Jewish Christianity* (SBT 2/17; London: SCM, 1970).

[23] Alan F. Segal, "Jewish Christianity," in H. W. Attridge and G. Hata (eds.), *Eusebius, Christianity, and Judaism* (Leiden: Brill, 1992), 326–51, here 348.

[24] On the different types of "Jewish Christianity," see Raymond E. Brown, "Not Jewish Christianity and Gentile Christianity but Types of Jewish/Gentile Christianity," *CBQ*, 45 (1983), 74–9; A. F. J. Klijn, "The Study of Jewish Christianity," *NTS*, 20 (1974), 419–31; R. A. Kraft, "In Search of 'Jewish Christianity' and Its 'Theology'": Problems of Definition and Methodology," *RSR*, 60 (1972), 81–92; R. Longenecker, "Jews, Hebrews and Christians: Some Needed Distinctions," *NovT*, 24 (1983), 194–208; Burton L. Visotzky, "Prolegomenon to the Study of Jewish-Christianities," *AJSR*, 14 (1989), 47–70; B. J. Malina, "Jewish Christianity or Christian Judaism: Toward a Hypothetical Definition," *JSJ*, 7 (1976), 46–57; S. K. Riegel, "Jewish Christianity: Definitions and Terminology," *NTS*, 24 (1978), 46–57; R. Murry, "Defining Judaeo-Christianity," *Heythrop*, 15 (1974), 303–10; "Jews, Hebrews and Christians: Some Needed Distinctions," *NovT*, 24 (1982), 194–208; Joan E. Taylor, "The Phenomenon of Early Jewish Christianity: Reality or Scholarly Invention?," *VC*, 44 (1990), 313–34.

[25] Eusebius, *Hist. Eccl.* 1.7.14; 3.11–12, 19–20; 32.5–6; 4.22.4. See Richard Bauckham, *Jude and the Relatives of Jesus in the Early Church* (Edinburgh: T & T Clark, 1990).

[26] F. Stanley Jones, *An Ancient Jewish Christian Source On the History of Christianity: Pseudo-Clementine Recognitions I.27–71* (Atlanta: Scholars, 1995), 164, n. 21. See also J. Munck, "Primitive Jewish Christianity and Later Jewish Christianity: Continuation or Rupture?" in *Aspects du judéo-christianisme: Colloque de Strasbourg, 23–25 avril 1964* (Paris: Presses Universitaires de France, 1965), 77–93.

that facilitate the construction of "Jewish Christian profiles."[27] So despite our ongoing debates on definition and categorization, the term "Jewish Christianity" adequately refers to a wide spectrum of *ethnically and ideologically Jewish individuals and groups who maintained Jewish observances and religious loyalties toward Jesus.*

A number of second- and third-century Jewish Christian texts and traditions alleged that Jesus rejected and opposed animal sacrifice.[28] The two most prominent examples of this tradition can be found in the *Gospel of the Ebionites* cited by Epiphanius and the Jewish Christian source underlying *Rec.* 1.27–71,[29] the latter of which can be dated to c. 200 CE.[30] How far back does this tradition go? The prevailing assumption in contemporary scholarship is that this Jewish Christian tradition represents a second-century response to the destruction of the Temple,[31] and that such Jewish Christian traditions are late, harmonizing, corrupt, syncretistic, and *post*-Synoptic developments.[32] The problem is that *non*-Synoptic material is also

---

[27] Luomanen, *Recovering Jewish Christian Sects*, 8–13.

[28] Schoeps, *Theologie und Geschichte*, 241.

[29] Richard Bauckham, "The Origin of the Ebionites," in P. J. Tomson and D. Lambers-Petry (eds.), *The Image of the Judaeo-Christians in Ancient Jewish and Christian Literature* (WUNT 158; Tübingen: Mohr Siebeck, 2003), 165, 168.

[30] Graham Stanton, "Jewish Christian Elements in the Pseudo-Clementine Writings," in Oskar Skarsaune and Reidar Hvalvik (eds.), *Jewish Believers in Jesus: The Early Centuries* (Peabody: Hendrickson, 2007), 324, as there seems to be an allusion to Hadrian's decree at 135 CE (39.3) and similarities with Justin's *Dialogue with Trypho*. See also Strecker, *Judenchristentum*, 253–54; Skarsaune, *Proof from Prophecy*, 252–53. James M. Scott, *Geography in Early Judaism and Christianity: The Book of Jubilees* (SNTSMS 113; Cambridge University Press, 2002), 97–125, dates the source to 100–115 CE.

[31] Reed, '"Jewish Christianity,"' 211. Bauckham, "The Origin of the Ebionites," 167; Ron Cameron, *The Other Gospels: Non-Canonical Gospel Texts* (Philadelphia: Westminster, 1982), 103–6. For the tendency to date Jewish Christianity to the second or third centuries, see Johannes Munck, "Jewish Christianity in Post-Apostolic Times," *NTS*, 6 (1960), 103–16; "Primitive Jewish Christianity and Later Jewish Christianity: Continuation or Rupture?" 77–93. For critique, see Hyam Maccoby, *The Mythmaker: Paul and the Invention of Christianity* (New York: Harper & Row, 1987); John Painter, *Just James: The Brother of Jesus in History and Tradition* (Columbia: University of South Carolina Press, 1997), 229; Gerd Lüdemann, *Heretics: The Other Side of Early Christianity* (trans. John Bowden; Louisville: Westminster John Knox, 1996), 52–3; Michael Goulder, *St. Paul versus St. Peter: A Tale of Two Missions* (Louisville: Westminster John Knox, 1995), 134.

[32] Jonathan Bourgel, "*Reconnaissances* 1.27-71, ou la réponse d'un groupe judéo-chrétien de Judée au désastre du soulèvement de Bar-Kokhba," *NTS*, 61.1

present in these texts. It is all too easy for New Testament specialists to assume that noncanonical gospel literature is inauthentic and
that there is no good reason to even consider it.[33] Francis Watson,
however, has recently argued that "Gospel writing" must now be
understood in a wider context of post- and non-Synoptic gospel
compositions,[34] recognizing that canonical limits have all too often
over-determined scholarly interest in early Christianity.[35] Christopher
M. Tuckett – in his 2013 Presidential Address to the Society for New
Testament Studies – also affirmed the study of noncanonical texts in
the context of New Testament studies, suggesting that our discipline
needs to move beyond canonical boundaries and reflect this broader
perspective.[36]

Despite these methodological advances, the study of Jewish
Christianity is fraught with assumptions about its "late" and secondary status.[37] Some scholars think that it would have been
"unthinkable" for pre-70 CE Jews to reject the sacrificial system,[38]
and so the anti-cultic tradition must reflect (Christian?) "opposition to second-century Jewish hopes to rebuild the temple."[39] Yet
the assumption that Jewish Christians only changed their attitude

(2015): 30-49, here 41, for example, argues that the author of *Rec.* 1.27-71's "opposition farouche aux sacrifices sanglants" can be attributed to a post-135 CE Jewish
Christian response to Bar Kokhba's failed attempt to restore the Temple cult. *Rec.*
1.27-71 was composed "à expliquer les raisons de cette catastrophe" and "à apporter
une réponse aux difficultés qu'elle engendra."

[33] Francis Watson, *Gospel Writing: A Canonical Perspective* (Grand Rapids:
Eerdmans, 2013), 217. But see John S. Kloppenborg, "A New Synoptic Problem:
Mark Goodacre and Simon Gathercole on Thomas," *JSNT*, 36/3 (2014), 199–239,
here 202–3.

[34] Watson, *Gospel Writing*.

[35] Kloppenborg, "A New Synoptic Problem," 202–203.

[36] Christopher M. Tuckett, "What is 'New Testament Study'? The New Testament
and Early Christianity," NTS, 60/2 (2014), 157–184.

[37] Adam H. Becker and Annette Yoshiko Reed (eds.), *The Ways that Never Parted:
Jews and Christians in Late Antiquity and the Early Middle Ages* (TSAJ 95; Tübingen:
Mohr Siebeck, 2003).

[38] Craig A. Evans, "The Jewish Christian Gospel Tradition," in O. Skarsaune and R.
Hvalvik (eds.), *Jewish Believers in Jesus: The Early Centuries* (Peabody: Hendrickson,
2007), 241–77, here 252–53; Snodgrass, "The Temple Incident," 432. Casey, "Culture
and Historicity: The Cleansing of the Temple," 322, dismisses the idea as "culturally inappropriate." So also Helen K. Bond, *The Historical Jesus: A Guide for the
Perplexed* (London: T & T Clark, 2012), 139–40.

[39] G. A. Koch, "A Critical Investigation of Epiphanius' Knowledge of the
Ebionites: A Translation and Critical Discussion of Panarion 30," Ph.D. dissertation,
University of Pennsylvania, 1976, 344, and *Rec.* 1.39, 64.

to the Temple *after* the destruction of the Temple is not particularly compelling.[40] The hostility between the earliest Jewish Christians and the Sadducees – illustrated by James' assassination – suggests that Jesus' Jewish followers quickly detached themselves from participation in the Temple cult.[41] Marcel Simon, for example, suggests that an early anti-Temple view associated with the "Ebionites" and the Pseudo-Clementine literature may have ultimately originated with the anti-cultic traditions associated with Stephen.[42] According to Simon, Stephen's speech suggests that Jesus' role was "to re-establish the genuine Mosaic Law" that had been distorted by Jewish idolatry "ever since they have worshipped the golden calf."[43] Jesus was "the restorer of Mosaic religion." It is this interpretation of Jesus that seems "on the way" toward the "Ebionite conception of the True Prophet."

The idea that the Ebionites represent an early and original form of Christianity has a long history in New Testament scholarship.[44] This identification seems to have begun with John Toland, a British scholar whose work *Nazarenus* (1718) influenced F. C. Baur and the Tübingen

---

[40] Luomanen, *Recovering Jewish Christian Sects*, 164, n. 40: "it seems (likely) that those who had a positive attitude towards the worship usually ended up reinterpreting its significance, instead of starting to think that the whole thing was misconstrued from the very beginning."

[41] Hengel, *The Atonement*, 56–7, notes that "The death of Jesus was presumably one of the causes of the Ebionite criticism of sacrifice ... from the beginning the Jewish Christians adopted a fundamentally detached attitude to the cult ... This rejection of the traditional cult must have had very early roots."

[42] Simon, *St. Stephen*, esp. 94.

[43] Simon, *St. Stephen*, 63.

[44] Mimouni, *Early Judaeo-Christianity*, 66, proposes that the Ebionites originated "in a rupture within the community of Jerusalem." James Robinson suggests that the "Q movement" may have "faded from history as the heresy of the Ebionites." See James M. Robinson, *The Sayings Gospel Q*, 184; "The Sayings Gospel Q," in F. Van Segbroek (ed.), *The Four Gospels 1992: Festschrift Frans Neirynck* (BETL 100; Leuven: Peeters, 1992), 382; "The Jesus of the Sayings Gospel Q," 10. For older research, see John Noland, *Nazarenus: Or, Jewish, Gentile, and Mahometan Christianity*, 2nd edn. (London: J. Brotherton, J. Roberts, and A. Dodd, 1718), 76; F. C. Baur, *Über den Ursprung des Episcopats in der christlichen Kirche* (Tübingen: Ludwig Friedrich Fues, 1838), 123; *Das Christentum und die christliche Kirche der drei ersten Jahrhunderte*, 2nd edn. (Tübingen: Ludwig Friedrich Fues, 1860), 174; Albert Schwegler, *Das nachapostolische Zeitalter in den Hauptmomenten seiner Entwicklung*, 2 vols. (Tübingen: Ludwig Friedrich Fues, 1846), 1:179; Johann Karl Ludwig Gieseler, "Über die Nazaräer und Ebioniten," *AANKG*, 4 (1820), 279–330, here 298. Gregory C. Finley, "The Ebionites and 'Jewish Christianity': Examining Heresy and the Attitudes of Church Fathers," Ph.D. dissertation, Catholic University of America, 290, notes "some kind of connection between the Ebionites and the Pseudo-Clementines."

School.[45] A particularly vocal proponent of this view is Hans-Joachim Schoeps, a German Jewish scholar who reconstructed a full history and theology of an "Ebionite" movement, "a conservative, early form of primitive Christianity … excluded from the tradition of the Great Church."[46] Schoeps's theory of direct continuity between Jesus, the Jerusalem community, and the "Ebionites" did not convince many. It also illustrated the dangers involved with uncritically conflating the Pseudo-Clementine literature with Epiphanius' Jewish-Christian gospel fragments in order to construct a pan-Ebionite movement, although some of his insights still carry some weight. For example, if Jewish Christians did attempt "to reform the law," this would certainly have alienated them from their fellow Jews.[47] It is Schoeps's most provocative proposal, however, – that the "Ebionite" rejection of the Temple cult had its origin in the historical Jesus[48] – that still requires our careful consideration.[49]

The "Ebionites" ('Ἐβιωναῖοι) are first mentioned c. 175 CE by Irenaeus.[50] They are also mentioned by Hippolytus,[51] Tertullian, Origen,[52] Eusebius,[53] and Epiphanius.[54] The early church fathers came

[45] F. Stanley Jones, "The Genesis, Purpose, and Significance of John Toland's *Nazarenus*," in F. Stanley Jones (ed.), *The Rediscovery of Jewish Christianity: From Toland to Baur* (HBS 5; Atlanta: Society of Biblical Literature, 2012), 91–104, here 95-96.

[46] Schoeps, *Jewish Christianity*, 108.

[47] Schoeps, *Jewish Christianity*, 130.

[48] Schoeps, *Jewish Christianity*, 74–5.

[49] Lang, *Sacred Games*, 229, refers to this saying as "a prophetic dictum" that circulated in "the early community." Skarsaune, *In the Shadow of the Temple*, 156, dates *Rec.* 1.27–71 to c. 150 CE and suggests that "the view of the sacrifices held by the author of *Recognitions* 1.27–71 is actually much older than the document itself … [and] does not differ radically in its view of the temple from that of the pre-70 Jerusalem community."

[50] *Adv. haer.* 1.26.2; 3.11.7. See also Tertullian, *Praescr.* 30.11; Origen, *Hom. Luc.* 17; *In epist. Ad Titum*; *Hom. Gen.* 3.5; *Comm. Ser. Matt.* 79; *Hom. Jer.* 19.12; Origen, *Cels.* 2.1; *Princ.* 4.3.8; *Contra Celsum* 5.65; Eusebius, *Eccl. Hist.* 3.27.1–6. On the *Gospel of the Ebionites*, see M.-E. Boismard, "Evangile des Ebionites et problème synoptique (Mc 1, 2–6 and par.)," *RB*, 73 (1966), 321–52; D. A. Bertrand, "L'Evangile des Ebionites: une harmonie évangélique antérieure au Diatessaron," *NTS*, 26 (1980), 548–63. Skarsaune, "The Ebionites," in *Jewish Believers in Jesus*, 423, 457, argues that Epiphanius' citations are not "Ebionite." See also S. Häkkinen, "Ebionites," in A. Marjanen and P. Luomanen (eds.), *A Companion to Second-Century Christian "Heretics"* (Leiden: Brill, 2005), 247–78.

[51] *Haer.* 7.34.1–2; 10.22.

[52] *Cels.* 5.65; *Hom. Gen.* 3.5; *Hom. Jer.* 19.12.2.

[53] *Hist. eccl.* 3.27.1–6; 6.17.

[54] Epiphanius conflated this material with quotations from the *GosEb* and Pseudo-Clementine literature, claiming that Clement's work was modified by Ebionites (*Pan.* 30.16.7; 3.2–6; 18.4–5).

up with a number of ways to ridicule "Ebionites" for their apparent self-identification as "the Poor" (אביונים/אביון).[55] Today, scholars question the utility of the term *Ebionite* as it is unclear whether there was one or more *Ebionite* groups and whether the Church fathers were accurate in their representation of these groups. The term may not refer to a mono-lithic group but rather to several diverse groups.[56] The problem is further complicated in that Ebionites may have been influenced by Cerinthus and the Elchasaites.[57] The Elchasaites, in particular, appear to have originated as a Jewish Christian movement in the early second century.[58] We can be reasonably confident of Elchasai's Jewish (Christian) background because circumcision was presupposed,[59] Sabbath obser-vance was affirmed,[60] and Elchasai directed prayer toward Jerusalem. Epiphanius also reports that Elchasai (Ἠλχασαΐ/Ἠλξαΐ) combined this reverence for Jerusalem with criticism of animal sacrifice:[61]

> For he hinders praying toward the east, saying one should not turn in this manner but rather should face Jerusalem … For on the one hand he condemns sacrifices and rites as for-eign to God and as never at all having been offered to God by the fathers and the law, and yet there he says it is necessary to pray toward Jerusalem, where there was the altar and the sac-rifices. While he rejects the eating of meat as practiced by the

---

[55] Origen, *De Principiis* IV, 22; *Contra Celsum* II, 1; Eusebius, *Hist. Eccl.* 3, 27; Origen, *De Princ.* 4, 22; *Hom. in Gen.* 3, 5; Eusebius, *Hist. Eccl.* 3, 27; Epiphanius, *Pan.* 30, 17.

[56] Mimouni, *Early Judaeo-Christianity*, 220–1, refers to "a plurality of Ebionite movements."

[57] Joseph A. Fitzmyer, "The Qumran Scrolls, the Ebionites and their Literature," *TS*, 16 (1955), 335–72. Skarsaune, "The Ebionites," 451, argues that Epiphanius trans-fered to "Ebion" attributes of Cerinthus and confused Ebionites with Elchasaite tradi-tions. See J. Thomas, *Le mouvement baptiste en Palestine et Syrie (150 v.J.C. - 300 apr. J.C.)* (Gembloux: Duculot, 1935), 171–83.

[58] On the Elchasaites, see G. Bareille, "Elcésaites," in *Dictionnaire de théologie catholique*, 4/2 (1911), 2233–9; W. Brandt, "Elkesaites," *Encyclopedia of Religion and Ethics V* (1912), 262–9; G. Strecker, "Elkesai," *Reallexikon für Antike und Christentum*, 4 (1959), 1171–86; W. Brandt, *Elchasai, ein Religionsstifter und sein Werk. Beiträge zur jüdischen, christlichen und allgemeinen Religionsgeschichte* (Leipzig: J. C. Hinrichs, 1912); Skarsaune, "Cerinthus, Elxai, and Other Alleged Jewish Christian Teachers or Groups," in *Jewish Believers in Jesus*, 488–502.

[59] Hippolytus, *Ref.* 9.14.1; Pseudo-Clementine *Adjuration* 1.1; *Pan.* 19.5.1; 30.17.5.

[60] *Ref.* 19.16.3.

[61] *Pan.* 19.3.5–7. On the *Book of Elchasai*, see F. Stanley Jones, "The *Book of Elchasai* in its Relevance for Manichaean Institutions with a Supplement: The *Book of Elchasai* Reconstructed and Translated," *ARAM*, 16 (2004), 179–215.

Jews as well as the other things, both the altar and the fire as foreign to God, he says that water is proper and fire is foreign.

Epiphanius states that Elchasai directed prayer toward Jerusalem, discouraged meat-eating,[62] and condemned sacrifices and the Temple.[63] This pushes back our earliest attestation of an antisacrifice tradition to c. 116–117 CE,[64] that is, within the timeframe of the composition of the books of the New Testament.

The Jewish Christian Rejection of Animal Sacrifice

The *Gospel of the Ebionites* can be dated between the middle and the end of the second century,[65] and seems to have been written in Greek, related to Matthew and Luke,[66] and perhaps composed in Syria.[67] There are seven fragmentary passages contained in Epiphanius'

---

[62] *Pan.* 19.3.6; 53.1.4.

[63] *Pan.* 19.3.3–7.

[64] J. Irmscher, "The Book of Elchasai," in W. Schneelmelcher (ed.), *New Testament Apocrypha II: Writings Relating to the Apostles, Apocalypses and Related Subjects* (trans. R. McL. Wilson; Louisville; John Knox Press, 1992) 685–90; Gerard P. Luttikhuizen, *The Revelation of Elchasai: Investigations into the Evidence for a Mesopotamian Jewish Apocalypse of the Second Century and Its Reception by Judeo-Christian Propagandists* (TSAJ 8; Tübingen: Mohr Siebeck, 1985); A. F. J. Klijn and G. J. Reinink, "Elchasai and Mani," *VC*, 28 (1974), 277–89.

[65] Bauckham, "The Origin of the Ebionites," 163: there is "good reason to think that this Gospel of the Ebionites was used by the Ebionites of whom Irenaeus knew." A. F. J. Klijn, *Jewish-Christian Gospel Tradition* (VC Sup 17; Leiden: Brill, 1992). Mimouni, *Early Judaeo-Christianity*, 223, dates it "between the year ca 100 and the year ca 135."

[66] On the *Gospel of the Ebionites* as a post-Synoptic harmony, see Bertrand, "L'évangile des Ébionites," 550–1, 562; W. L. Petersen, "From Justin to Pepys: The History of the Harminonised Gospel Tradition," *StPatr*, 30 (1997), 71–96, here 73. See also Howard, "Gospel of the Ebionites," 4037–44; Édouard Massaux, *Influence de l'Évangile de saint Matthieu sur la littérature chrétienne avant saint Irénée* (UCL 2.42; Leuven University Press, 1950), 347–357; P. Henne, "L'Evangile des Ebionites. Une fausse harmonie. Une vraie supercherie," in D. Van Damme, et al. (eds.), *Peregrina curiositas. eine Reise durch den Orbis antiquus: zu Ehren von Dirk van Damme* (Göttingen: Vandenhoeck & Ruprecht, 1994), 57–75, argues that the gospel rewrites Matthew in particular; E. Schlarb and D. Lührmann, *Fragmente apokryph gewordener Evangelien in griechischer und lateinischer Sprache* (Marburg: N. G. Elwert, 2000), 32; P. Vielhauer and G. Strecker, "The Gospel of the Ebionites," in W. Schneemelcher (ed.), *New Testament Apocrypha*, vol. 1 (Cambridge: James Clarke and Co., 1991), 167–68.

[67] Mimouni, *Early Judaeo-Christianity*, 223, also proposes its use in Palestine and Arabia.

Panarion.[68] Irenaeus' account also supports the existence of a "gospel" used by Ebionites in the late second century. Irenaeus' Ebionites seem to have used a version of Matthew. Epiphanius' quotations also appear to depend on Matthew and Luke,[69] although Epiphanius calls this "*Gospel of the Ebionites*" a corruption of Matthew and a "Hebrew Gospel."[70] Nonetheless, both Irenaeus and Epiphanius claim that the Ebionites used a version of Matthew (εὐαγγελίῳ κατὰ Ματθαῖον). The title, however, is a modern scholarly invention derived from Epiphanius' claim that Ebionites used a "forged and mutilated" (νενοθευμένῳ καὶ ἠκρωτηριασμένῳ) version of Matthew.[71]

The seventh fragment of this *Gospel* represents its most distinctive and controversial feature: Jesus' rejection of animal sacrifice:

> ἦλθον καταλῦσαι τὰς θυσίας, καὶ ἐὰν μὴ παύσησθε τοῦ θύειν
> οὐ παύσεται ἀφ'ὑμῶν ἡ ὀργή.[72]

I have come to abolish sacrifices, and if you do not cease from sacrificing, the wrath (of God) will not cease from you.

This passage appears to be an indirect allusion to Matt 5:17–18:[73]

> Μὴ νομίσητε ὅτι ἦλθον καταλῦσαι τὸν νόμον ἢ τοὺς προφήτας
> οὐκ ἦλθον καταλῦσαι ἀλλὰ πληρῶσαι

Do *not* think that I have come to abolish the law or the prophets, I have come not to abolish but to fulfill.[74]

---

[68] *Pan.* 30.13.1–8; 30.14.5; 30.16.4–5; 30.22.4.

[69] Andrew Gregory, "Prior or Posterior? *The Gospel of the Ebionites* and the Gospel of Luke," *NTS*, 51 (2005), 344–60; Bertrand, "L'Évangile des Ébionites," 548–63. But see J. R. Edwards, "The Gospel of the Ebionites and the Gospel of Luke," *NTS*, 48 (2002), 568–86; C.-B. Amphoux, "L'Évangile selon les Hébreux: Source de L'Évangile de Luc," *Apocrypha*, 6 (1995), 67–77.

[70] *Pan.* 13.2–3.

[71] See Koch, "A Critical Investigation of Epiphanius' Knowledge of the Ebionites," 316–58; Finley, "The Ebionites and 'Jewish Christianity'; Mimouni, *Le judéo-christianisme ancien*, 258–72; Schoeps, *Theologie und Geschichte*; Bauckham, "The Origin of the Ebionites," 172.

[72] *Pan.* 30.16.4–5, in Karl Holl (ed.), *Ancoratus und Panarion*, 3 vols. (Leipzig: J. C. Hinrichs, [1915] 1933).

[73] Edwards, "The Gospel of the Ebionites and the Gospel of Luke," 579.

[74] Verheyden, "Epiphanius on the Ebionites," 191.

The use of ἦλθον καταλῦσαι in Matt 5:17 and a similar ἦλθον καταλῦσαι construction in the *Gospel of the Ebionites* suggests literary dependence. In Q and the canonical Gospels, the "I have come" sayings are widely regarded as secondary traditions summarizing the *purpose* of Jesus' mission:[75]

> *I have come* to hurl fire on the earth, and how I wish it had already blazed up.[76]
> Do you think that *I have come* to hurl peace on earth? I did not *come* to hurl peace, but a sword![77]
> For *I have come* to divide son against father, daughter against her mother, daughter-in-law against her mother-in-law.[78]

The fact that the *Gospel of the Ebionites* uses this traditional Christological formula further suggests that this saying is a secondary development.

Is the *Gospel of the Ebionites* a post-Synoptic Jewish Christian harmonizing gospel?[79] Or an independent tradition *preceding* the Synoptics? While this saying certainly *could* "have originated at a time when the temple still stood," we simply do not know its original historical context. The author sees Jesus either as "condemning sacrifices as no longer valid or as never having been valid."[80] The saying against animal sacrifice represents a *non*-Synoptic tradition, but this tradition cannot be dated simply by appealing to *post*-Synoptic sayings.[81] The *Gospel of the Ebionites* may *be* a harmony, but we cannot

---

[75] Theissen and Merz, *The Historical Jesus*, 525. See E. Arens, *The ΗΛΘΟΝ-Sayings in the Synoptic Tradition* (OBO 10; Göttingen: Vandenhoeck and Ruprecht, 1976).

[76] Q 12:49.

[77] Q 12:51.

[78] Q 12:53.

[79] Mimouni, *Early Judaeo-Christianity*, 224, proposes that the *Gospel of the Ebionites* and the Synoptics "have drawn on a common tradition (oral or written)." In *Les fragments évangéliques Judéo-chrétiens "apocryphisés": Recherches et perspectives* (CahRB 66; Paris: Gabalda, 2006), Mimouni attributes the Synoptic similarities to a common set of older traditions and proposes an early date of composition for the work, between 60 and 80 CE

[80] Loader, *Jesus' Attitude towards the Law*, 507, 516. Hans Dieter Betz notes that Matthew 5:17's affirmation of the law may be responding to this anti-sacrificial saying-tradition. See H. D. Betz, *The Sermon on the Mount* (Minneapolis: Fortress, 1995), 175–176.

[81] James Edwards argues that Epiphanius' citations from the *Gospel of the Ebionites* represent a Greek translation of a "Hebrew Gospel" described by the early church

rule out the possibility that it is *also* using *pre*-Synoptic sources or traditions.

One of the most remarkable aspects of the Ebionite tradition is that the *Gospel of the Ebionites* explicitly characterizes Jesus as *refusing* to eat meat:[82]

μὴ ἐπιθυμίᾳ ἐπεθύμησα κρέας τοῦτο τὸ Πάσχα φαγεῖν μεθ᾽ ὑμῶν

I did *not* earnestly desire to eat meat this Passover with you.[83]

Like the *Gospel of the Ebionites'* use of Matt. 5:17, this saying also alludes to a Synoptic parallel, in this case Luke 22:15:

Ἐπιθυμίᾳ ἐπεθύμησα τοῦτο τὸ πάσχα φαγεῖν μεθ᾽ὑμῶν

I *have* earnestly desired to eat this Passover (before I suffer) (πρὸ τοῦ με παθεῖν).

The *Gospel of the Ebionites* inserts the word "not" (μὴ) before "this Passover," suggesting literary dependency on Luke 22:15, where Jesus declares "I *have* earnestly desired to eat this Passover." The Synoptic Last Supper traditions suggest that Jesus ate the Passover meal with his disciples, but they do not mention a Passover lamb: the Gospels only mention bread and wine. Neither the Synoptics nor the Gospel of John describe Jesus eating meat.

The Jewish Christian rejection of animal sacrifice is part of a broader tradition of Jewish Christian vegetarianism.[84] This tradition can be found in the Pseudo-Clementine literature, the *Gospel of the Ebionites*, Epiphanius' reports on the "Ebionites," Elchasaite traditions, Hegesippus's references to James, and the *Didascalia*.

---

fathers and used by Luke. See Edwards, "The Gospel of the Ebionites and the Gospel of Luke," 584. Gregory, "Prior or Posterior?" argues that the *Gospel of the Ebionites* derives from a Synoptic harmony, yet leaves open the possibility that the *Gospel of the Ebionites* draws on pre-Lukan material.

[82] *Pan.* 30. See also 30.18.9.

[83] *Pan.* 30.22.4. On κρέας as animal flesh or meat, see *Od.* 3.65; *Ar. Pl.* 1137; *Zen.* 4.85.

[84] F. Stanley Jones, "Jewish Christianity of the Pseudo-Clementines," in A. Marjanen and P. Luomanen (eds.), *A Companion to Second Century Christian "Heretics"* (Leiden: Brill, 2005), 322, refers to the "latent vegetarianism in the *Circuits of Peter"* (*Rec.* 7.6.4 par. *Hom.* 12.6.4), its rejection of sacrifices (*Hom.* 3.45.2; *Rec.* 1.36–37), the vegetarian diet of James according to Hegesippus (Eusebius, *Hist. eccl.* 2.23.5), and the vegetarians of the Jewish Christians of the *Didascalia* 23, as well as the *Gospel of the Ebionites* and *Pan.* 30.16.7; 30.15.3; 19.3.6.

According to Epiphanius, Ebionites held that Peter's diet consisted of "bread alone, with olives and rarely vegetables."[85] According to Clement of Alexandria, the apostle Matthew was a vegetarian:[86]

Matthew the apostle used to take seeds, and nuts, and vegetables, without animal flesh.

Ματθαῖος ... ὁ ἀπόστολος σπερμάτων καὶ ἀκροδρύων καὶ λαχάνων ἄνευ κρεῶν μετελάμβανεν.

The *Gospel of the Ebionites* implicitly identifies John the Baptist as a vegetarian.[87] The Synoptic Gospels of Mark and Matthew both describe John as eating "locusts" (ἀκρίδες).[88] The *Gospel of the Ebionites*, however, refers to John's diet as "wild honey," which tasted like "manna, *like cakes* (ὡς ἔγκρις) in olive oil." The author of the Ebionite gospel seems to have changed the Synoptic ἀκρίς to ἐγκρίς, associating John's diet with the "manna" in the Exodus narratives: "its taste like a cake in honey" (ὡς ἐγκρὶς ἐν μέλιτι), "like the taste of a cake from olive oil" (ὡσεὶ γεῦμα ἐγκρὶς ἐξ ἐλαίου).[89] Vegetarian interpretations of John's diet can also be found in several Syriac witnesses to Tatian's *Diatessaron*, where a substitution of "locusts" for "milk" make John appear to be a vegetarian.[90]

According to Eusebius, Hegesippus' *Hypomnemata* (*Memoirs*) explicitly referred to Jesus' brother James as a vegetarian:

He was holy from his mother's womb, and he drank neither wine nor strong drink, *nor did he eat animal flesh*.

[85] See *Rec.* 7.6.4; *Hom.* 12.6.4. See also *Hom.* 8.15.2–16.2; *Rec.* 1.30.1. See also *Pan.* 30.15

[86] Clement of Alexandria, *The Instructor* (*Paedagogus*) 2.1.16.1.

[87] For John's diet, see James A. Kelhoffer, *The Diet of John the Baptist: 'Locusts and Wild Honey' in Synoptic and Patristic Interpretation* (WUNT 176; Tübingen: Mohr Siebeck, 2005).

[88] Mark 1:6; Matt. 3:4.

[89] Exod. 16:31; Num. 11:8 LXX.

[90] See Theodor Zahn, *Das Evangelium des Matthäus* (Leipzig: A. Deichert, 1922), 133, n. 33. See also Alexandros Pallis, *A Few Notes on the Gospels according to St. Mark and St. Matthew: Based Chiefly on Modern Greek* (Liverpool: Liverpool Booksellers, 1903), 3–6; Philipp Kieferndorf, "Seine Speise war Heuschrecken?" *VW*, 54 (1921), 188–9; Robert Eisler, "The Baptist's Food and Clothing," in *The Messiah Jesus and John the Baptist according to Flavius Josephus' Recently Rediscovered 'Capture of Jerusalem' and Other Jewish and Christian Sources* (New York: L. MacVeagh [Dial], 1931 [1929–1930]), 235–40.

οὗτος δὲ ἐκ κοιλίας μητρὸς αὐτοῦ ἅγιος ἦν, οἶνον καὶ σίκερα οὐκ ἔπιεν οὐδὲ ἔμψυχον ἔφαγεν.[91]

The historical reliability of this tradition has been highly debated.[92] It is striking that while Hegesippus portrays James as a life-long Nazirite like Samson, Samuel, and John the Baptist,[93] we cannot explain James' vegetarianism as part of a Nazirite vow because meat-eating was not part of that tradition. Matti Myllykoski finds this particular detail "peculiar" and proposes that "Refusing to drink wine and eat meat indicate general fasting habits" or "an ascetic avoidance of pleasant food."[94] This proposal, however, does not *resolve* or explain the tradition, not only because James' vegetarianism stands in tension with his assumed Torah observance, sacrificial practice, and (hagiographical) role as a "high priest," but more so because there is a multiply attested Jewish Christian tradition of vegetarianism that still has yet to be explained.[95]

The Synoptic Gospels, of course, portray Jesus as multiplying fish, but it is only the *resurrected* Jesus who eats fish. Indeed, Luke 24:40–43 is the *only* passage in the entire New Testament that clearly states that Jesus ate meat. Moreover, this Lukan passage portraying the risen Jesus eating fish may be better understood as an attempt to deny early docetic views of Jesus' resurrection body. In the Gospel of John, the risen Jesus only *serves* fish.[96] In the Gospel accounts of the miraculous feeding(s) of the multitudes, Jesus, again, only *serves* fish.[97] Moreover, Jesus' feeding of the multitudes serves a *symbolic* function. The idea of Jesus serving and/or multiplying fish may have more to do with early Christological symbolism than with Jesus' own

[91] Eusebius, *Eccl. History* 2.23.5, citing Hegesippus' *Hypomnemata* (c. 180 CE).
[92] Lüdemann, *Opposition to Paul in Jewish Christianity*, 298 n. 24.
[93] Judg 13:4–5, 7, 14; 1 Sam 1:11, 15 LXX; and Luke 1:15, 35, respectively.
[94] Myllykoski, "James the Just in History and Tradition," 34, citing W. Pratscher, *Der Herrenbruder Jakobus und die Jakobustradition* (FRLANT 139; Göttingen: Vandenhoeck & Ruprecht, 1987), 111, who proposed that James' vegetarianism could be explained as an avoidance of impure food, and Painter, *Just James*, 126, who connects it to various Jewish sects mentioned by Irenaeus (*Adv. Haer.* 1.28.1) and Epiphanius (*Pan.* 30.15).
[95] F. Stanley Jones, "Hegesippus as a Source for the History of Jewish Christianity," in Mimouni and Jones (eds.), *Le judéo-christianisme*, 209–10.
[96] John 21:4–13. Many scholars view Luke's account of the risen Jesus (24:43) as a polemic demonstrating that the post-Easter Jesus had a real, physical human body.
[97] Matt. 14:7–21; 15:32–38; Mark 6:38–44; Luke 9:12–17; John 6:9–14.

dietary habits.[98] Sharing fish and bread are symbols of communion with Jesus.[99] The miraculous feeding(s) of the four and five thousand symbolize the spiritual fellowship of the Eucharist,[100] just as "three thousand" and "five thousand" new members joined the early Church in the days following Pentecost (Acts 2:41; 4:4). If the multiplication of "Fish" symbolically represents the multiplication of new members of the body of Christ in and through the acronym produced by the confession of "Jesus Christ, Son of God, Savior" (ΙΧΘΥΣ) and the Eucharistic formula, the multiplication of bread further signifies Jesus' teaching, in contrast with the "leaven" of the Pharisees.[101]

Food conflicts were a contentious and divisive issue in the early Jesus movement. We know that contrary to Paul and Mark's parenthetical comment (Mark 7:19b), Jesus probably did not declare "all foods clean." If he did, his earliest disciples, not to mention Paul, certainly didn't know anything about it.[102] Yet Paul seems to be quite aware of "weak" vegetarians in the early Church:

> Welcome those who are weak in faith, but not for the purpose of quarreling over opinions. Some believe in eating anything, while the weak eat only *vegetables* (λάχανα).[103]

Many interpreters see this passage as referring to meat sacrificed to idols.[104] E. P. Sanders suggests that early (Jewish) Christian vegetarianism began as an attempt to maintain table fellowship with Gentiles by eating either "their own food or only vegetables."[105] This

---

[98] Crossan, *The Historical Jesus*, 398–404, esp. 404, sees the fish motif, whether as Nature miracle or as proof of Jesus' resurrection, as "credal statements about ecclesiastical authority."

[99] Crossan, *The Historical Jesus*, 401. Theissen and Merz, *The Historical Jesus*, 302–3, point out that "The miraculous feeding is narrated in such a way (especially in Mark 8.6f.) that primitive Christian listeners were involuntarily reminded of the words of institution in the eucharist."

[100] Chilton, "The Eucharist and the Mimesis of Sacrifice," 148.

[101] Loader, *Jesus' Attitude*, 84.

[102] In Acts 10:1–15, Peter receives a vision from God declaring all foods clean.

[103] Rom 14:1–2.

[104] 1 Cor 8; 10:19–33.

[105] E. P. Sanders, "Jewish Association with Gentiles and Galatians 2:11–14," in R. T. Forna and B. R. Gaventa (eds.), *The Conversation Continues: Studies in Paul and John in Honor of J. Louis Martyn* (Nashville: Abingdon, 1990), 170–88, here 177. Ulrich Wilckens suggests that Jewish Christian vegetarianism in Romans was the result of purity concerns. See *Der Brief an die Römer* (EKK 6; 3 vols.; Neukirchen-Vluyn: Neukirchener, 1982), 3:113–15.

is reminiscent of Daniel choosing a vegetarian diet of "seeds" (זרעים) instead of Gentile food in order to avoid violating the food laws.[106] This would suggest that (Jewish) Christian vegetarianism began as an avoidance of Gentile meat and its potential impurities in order to maintain table fellowship and *kashrut*. Indeed, since the time of Origen, it has been widely held that the "weak" were Jewish Christian vegetarians who abstained from meat entirely in order to avoid any possible contamination from impure meat.[107] It should be noted, however, that the Jewish population of Rome would probably have been able to provide a steady supply of kosher meat most of the time.[108] It should also be noted that Paul's references to Christian abstention from idol-meat in 1 Corinthians are *not* repeated in Romans 14–15. It is possible, therefore, that some of the "weak" in Rome – whether Jewish or Gentile Christian – were attracted to a vegetarian diet not so much because they were trying to be faithful to the dietary laws, but because they were influenced by Greco-Roman philosophical and ascetic ideals, the original antediluvian diet prescribed in Genesis 1, and heightened eschatological convictions.[109] Mark Reasoner outlines three philosophical "rationales" for vegetarianism current in first-century Rome: "(1) arguments based on the metaphysical order of nature ... (2) arguments based on various forms of primitivism, that vegetarianism is the preferable diet; and (3) arguments based on the spiritual value of purity."[110] This philosophical discourse on vegetarianism – particularly its appeal to the "chronological primitivism" of a Golden Age – parallels the biblical account of creation, where the original diet of humankind (Adam) is vegetarian. While Paul was almost certainly aware of this discourse, his "strength" in being able to eat whatever he wanted seems to be primarily motivated by his characteristic relaxation of Torah observance:

---

[106] Dan 1:3–17. See also Jdt. 12:17–19; Add. Esth. C. 14:17; Tobit 1:11; 1 Macc 1:65; 2 Macc 5:27; Josephus, *Vita* 14.

[107] Origen, *Commentaria in epistolam beati Pauli ad Romanos* 9.35. For the literature, see Mark Reasoner, *The Strong and the Weak: Romans 14.1–15.13 in Context* (SNTSMS 103; Cambridge University Press, 1999), 6–16, 18–20.

[108] Claudius expelled (some) Jews from Rome c. 49 CE (Acts 18:2; Seutonius, *Divus Claudius* 25; Cassius Dio, *History* 60.6.6–7), although they returned under Nero (54 CE).

[109] Reasoner, *The Strong and the Weak*, 102–31, 219. Reasoner suggests that the "weak" are (mostly) Jewish (Christian) vegetarians motivated by concern for the laws of *kashrut* and attracted by Greco-Roman philosophical traditions of vegetarianism.

[110] Reasoner, *The Strong and the Weak*, 103–36.

Some judge one day to be better than another, while others judge all days to be alike. Let all be fully convinced in their own minds. Those who observe the day, observe it in honor of the Lord. Also those who eat (meat) (ἐσθίων), eat in honor of the Lord, since they give thanks to God; while those who abstain, abstain in honor of the Lord and give thanks to God.[111]

Paul seeks to maintain unity within the community by not "offending" the "weak" and was willing to renounce meat-eating, even though he personally identified himself as one of the "strong" for whom all foods were "clean":

It is good not to eat meat [*flesh*] (κρέα) or drink wine or do anything that makes your brother or sister stumble (Rom. 14:21).

If food (βρῶμα) is a cause of their falling, I will never eat meat [*flesh*] (κρέα), so that I may not cause one of them to fall (1 Cor. 8:13).

While Paul certainly *acknowledges* first-century "Christian" vegetarianism, the apostle is relatively indifferent to the issue and does not attribute it to a saying of the Lord, let alone represent it as an ethical imperative. This would seem to suggest that there was no such tradition, since Paul had no problem disagreeing with "the Lord" when it came to clarifying his own particular views on divorce, although he is obviously aware of Jewish Christian colleagues who hold this view. For Paul, the unity of the *ekklesia* "in Christ" superseded dietary convictions. This relativizing of dietary concerns ultimately came to inform the composition of Mark 7:19, Peter's "vision" in Acts 10, and the Apostolic "decree" of Acts 15. Yet *Jewish* Christian traditions, which appeal to *"Jesus'"* interpretation of Torah as their authoritative center, could both promote vegetarianism *and* stay faithful to the Torah because humanity (Adam) was *created vegetarian*:[112]

God said, "See, I have given you *every plant yielding seed* (את כל עשב זרע זרע) that is upon the face of all the earth, *and every tree with seed in its fruit* (כל העץ אשר בו פרי עץ זרע ואת); you will have them for *food/meat* (לאכלה) ... And to

[111] Rom 14:5–6.
[112] Stegemann, "Some Aspects of Eschatology," 412–16.

> every animal ... I have given *every green herb for food/meat*
> (כל ירק עשב לאכלה)."[113]

We should not dismiss the symbolic power of this Adamic ideal. The prophet Isaiah certainly didn't. Isaiah envisioned the messianic age as a time of cosmic *dietary* transformation – that is, universal vegetarianism – on earth:

> The wolf and the lamb will eat together; And *the lion will eat straw* like the ox ...
> They will not hurt or destroy on all my holy mountain.[114]

> The Spirit of the Lord will rest on him, the Spirit of Wisdom and understanding ... *and the lion will eat straw* like the ox.[115]

Adam, or humanity, was created vegetarian and the messianic prophecies of Isa 2:2–4 and 11:1–9 envision a time of universal peace and vegetarianism,[116] forming an *Urzeit/Endzeit* unit. As we have seen, the Enoch tradition of the *Animal Apocalypse* also looked forward to the appearance of a new "Adam,"[117] as did the Qumran Essenes who composed and collected the Dead Sea Scrolls.[118] An Adamic identification of Jesus is a major feature in Paul's Christology.[119] The early rabbinic tradition was also well aware of the vegetarian Adam:

> Rabbi Judah stated in the name of Rav: Adam was not permitted meat for purposes of eating as it is written "for you shall it be for food and to all beasts of the earth," but not beasts of the earth for you.[120]

> אמר רב יהודה אמר רב אדם הראשון לא הותר לו בשר לאכילה
> דכתיב לכם יהיה לאכלה ולכל חית הארץ ולא חית הארץ לכם

Pesachim 109a suggests that since the destruction of the Temple, Jews are not *required* to eat meat:

[113] Gen 1:29–30.
[114] Isa. 65:25.
[115] Isa. 11:2–9.
[116] See Huddleston, *Eschatology in Genesis*.
[117] *An. Apoc.* 90.37–38.
[118] 1QS 4.22–23, CD 3.20, and 1QH 4.15.
[119] 1 Cor 15:45–49; Rom 5:12–21.
[120] *Sanh.* 59b.

It was taught, R'Yehuda b. Beteira says, "while the Temple is standing, there is no joy unless there is meat, as it says (Deut. 27)," "And you shall sacrifice peace-offerings and eat them there, and you will be joyful before the Lord, your God." Now that the Temple is not standing, there is no joy without wine (שאין בית המקדש קיים אין שמחה אלא ביין ועכשיו).

The Torah clearly prohibits inflicting unnecessary suffering on any animal and stresses compassion for animals (צער בעלי חיים).[121]

Although our ancient sources suggest that Jewish Christians remembered Jesus as advocating vegetarianism, contemporary scholars are somewhat at a loss to explain the emergence of this tradition. Consequently, it has been variously explained by positing "ascetic impulses," "a strongly Hellenized (Pythagorean) mentality,"[122] a "safety measure in a pagan environment,"[123] a "reaction to the destruction of the temple," or an "intensification of purity regulations."[124] These are reasonable conjectures, but they do not necessarily identify the primary reason why the Jewish Christian Jesus rejected animal sacrifices and promoted vegetarianism. Jörg Frey, for example, rightly notes that the *Gospel of the Ebionites* reflects a strict *halakhic* practice ("eine rigide halachische Praxis"), but it is less clear that this apparently "complete renunciation of meat" ("völligen Fleischverzicht") can so easily be explained as Jewish Christian adaptation to a non-Jewish environment, especially when *many*

---

[121] Num. 22:32; Deut. 25:4; 22:10; Exod. 20:8–10; Lev 22:27; 22:28; Deut. 22:6–7; 14:21; Exod. 23:19; 34:26. On צער בעלי חיים, see *Bava Metzia* 32b (cf. Exod. 23:5, 20:10, and Deut. 25:4).

[122] Jones, "Jewish Christianity of the Pseudo-Clementines," 322.

[123] John T. Townsend, "The Date of Luke-Acts," in C. H. Talbert (ed.), *Luke-Acts: New Perspectives from the Society of Biblical Literature* (New York: Crossroad, 1984), 51–2, suggests that Jewish Christian vegetarianism stems from their difficulty in obtaining kosher meat.

[124] Gregory, "Jewish-Christian Gospels," 65. After 70 CE, some Jews may have renounced meat-eating in commemoration of the destruction of the Temple. Charlotte Elisheva Fonrobert, "*The Didascalia Apostolorum: A Mishnah for the Disciples of Jesus*," *JECS*, 9 (2001), 483–509, esp. 493–94, argues that the vegetarianism of the *Didascalia* "makes sense in a Jewish context," but the *Didascalia* is an attack on those who "abstained from flesh and from wine," (DA 24; CSCO 408:214); its author counters that its readers should "make use of all His creatures with thanksgiving" (DA 24; CSCO 407:214).

Diasporic Jews adapted to non-Jewish urban life for centuries without ever needing to adopt a vegetarian diet.[125]

The fact that Jewish Christian traditions portray Jesus as rejecting animal sacrifice and abstaining from animal flesh – two relatively common features of Second Temple Jewish life – suggests that Jewish Christians could not have justified such renunciation if it did not make *halakhic* sense in an eschatological context. A plain reading of Gen 1:29, however, shows that God intended a vegetarian diet for humanity: Adam was created vegetarian. The first ten generations of Adam were vegetarian. It is only in Gen. 9:3 that *permission* is given to eat meat; animal sacrifices are not legislated until the time of Moses.[126] William Hallo suggests that the Israelite sacrificial cult developed from Mesopotamian traditions where animal sacrifices served as a means of justifying meat consumption,[127] which was generally reserved for elite members of society.[128] The prophetic tradition, however, envisioned the ideal diet in the world to come as the restoration of the original creation. Similarly, in the Pseudo-Clementines, the true law was given by God *at the time of creation.*[129] There are no explicit connections linking the rejection of animal sacrifice to vegetarianism in "Jewish Christian" literature and we certainly cannot conclude that *all* Jewish Christians were vegetarian. Nonetheless, there is good reason to think these themes are related. The eschatological logic of an *Endzeit* restoration of Edenic conditions would warrant, if not require, a radical commitment to the nonviolent, nonsacrificial, and vegetarian conditions of the *Urzeit*.

If Jesus was a devout Jewish "charismatic" prophet, he would undoubtedly have seen Isaiah's prophecy as "emanating from God

---

[125] Jörg Frey, "Die Fragmente des Ebionäerevangeliums," in C. Markschies and J. Schröter, (eds.), *Antike christliche Apokryphen in deutscher Übersetzung 1: Evangelien und Verwandtes 1* (Tübingen: Mohr Siebeck, 2012), 615–16.

[126] Klawans, *Purity*, 61, citing Gen. 4:1–5, 8:20, and 9:1–3, argues that the idea that animal sacrifice was not "originally intended" by God is a "misconception" because animals were sacrificed by Abel and Noah. Animal sacrifice, however, like meat-eating, is *post-Edenic*: it is not until Adam leaves Eden that animal sacrifice is first practiced; it is not until the time of Noah that meat-*eating* is permitted.

[127] Maimonides identified meat-eating as a temporary concession: God understood that the people of Israel were accustomed to animal sacrifices from their pagan neighbors and allowed sacrifices, although God prohibited *human* sacrifice and centralized worship in Jerusalem. See Maimonides, *Guide to the Perplexed* (trans. M. Friedlander; Dover Publications, 1956), 3.32.

[128] Hallo, "The Origin of Israelite Sacrifice," 59–71.

[129] *Hom.* 8.10.

and therefore bound to come to pass at the end of days."[130] Indeed, highly idealized radical imperatives are *characteristic* of the historical Jesus, a man who challenged Mosaic Law, commanded love of enemies, encouraged celibacy, renounced traditional burial customs, and demanded unswerving loyalty to his ministry and person. While the historical evidence is inconclusive, it is certainly possible – given its multiple attestation in the Jewish Christian tradition – that Jesus affirmed God's will by advocating vegetarianism as a return to or restoration of the ideal Edenic diet. This radical interpretation of divine will – in conjunction with his rejection of blood sacrifice – would have deeply offended traditional Jewish customs. It would also explain why Jesus' Jewish followers insisted that he rejected eating meat on Passover and how this tradition found its way into the Pseudo-Clementine literature,[131] along with Jesus' explicit rejection of the practice of animal sacrifice.[132]

Animal Sacrifice, Vegetarianism, and the Torah of Creation

The Pseudo-Clementine writings represent a literary puzzle with formidable problems.[133] Four sets of writings drawing on earlier sources interpolated by later hands have been preserved in eight languages.[134] It is widely held that the *Homilies* and the *Recognitions* are based on an earlier source, the *Grundschrift*, or Basic Writing, which contained Jewish Christian traditions.[135] The *Grundschrift* can be dated to c. 220 CE in Syria.[136] This *Grundschrift* in turn drew on earlier source

---

[130] Rivkin, *What Crucified Jesus?* 75, citing Isa 11:6–9.

[131] Jones, *An Ancient Jewish Christian Source*, 148, proposes that the author of *Rec.* 1.27–71 used the *Gospel of the Ebionites* because they both affirm Jesus' abolition of sacrifices.

[132] See Boustan and Reed, "Blood and Atonement," 333–64; Annette Yoshiko Reed, "'Jewish Christianity' after the 'Parting of the Ways,'" in *The Ways that Never Parted*, 189–231; "'Jewish Christianity' as Counter-history? 173–216.

[133] Stanton, "Jewish Christian Elements in the Pseudo-Clementine Writings," 305.

[134] The Greek *Homilies* is extant in two manuscripts (*Parisinus Graecus* 930 (P) and *Vaticanus Ottobonianus* 443 (O). There are Syriac fragments of the *Homilies* (Add. 12150) (c. 411 CE). The *Recognitions* is preserved in a Latin translation made by Rufinus of Aquileia (c. 406 CE), in Syriac, in fragmentary form (Add. 14609), and in Armenian, also in fragmentary form.

[135] Stanton, "Jewish Christian Elements," 311.

[136] Jones, *An Ancient Jewish Christian Source*, 164–66, dates the source underlying *Rec.* 1.27–71 to c. 200 CE. J. L. Martyn, "Clementine Recognitions 1,33–71, Jewish Christianity, and the Fourth Gospel," in J. Jervell and W. A. Meeks (eds.), *God's Christ*

material.[137] A Jewish Christian source behind *Rec.* 1.27–71 has been isolated by a number of scholars,[138] pre-dating the *Homilies* by over a century. The historical value of the Pseudo-Clementine literature is a matter of intense debate. The general tendency today is to shy away from constructing models that apply a specific group-marker to the source, although some continue to identify *Rec.* 1.27–71 as Ebionite.[139] Graham Stanton, on the other hand, calls it "an Apologia for Jewish believers in Jesus" and dates it to the "middle of the second century."[140] Oskar Skarsaune argues that its antisacrificial polemic is a more primitive version of the antisacrificial material in Justin and Barnabas.[141] F. Stanley Jones simply calls it an "Ancient Jewish Christian Source," a work of apologetic historiography dependent on Luke-Acts as a rival account of Christian origins,[142] and dates the source underlying *Rec.* 1.27–71 to c. 200 CE.[143] A number of

and His People: Studies in Honour of Nils Alstrup Dahl (Oslo: Universitetsforlaget, 1977), 265–95, 274, affirms Strecker's dating of *Rec.* 1.33–71 to "the mid-point of the second century."

[137] The author of *Rec.* 1.27–71 knew *Jubilees* and maybe Justin's *Dialogue with Trypho*.

[138] Jones, *An Ancient Jewish Christian Source*; "An Ancient Jewish Christian Rejoinder to Luke's Acts of the Apostles: Pseudo-Clementine Recognitions 1.27–71," in R. Stoops (ed.), *Semeia 80: The Apocryphal Acts of the Apostles in Intertextual Perspectives* (Atlanta: Scholars, 1990) 239–40. See also Stanton, "Jewish Christian Elements in the Pseudo-Clementine Writings," 312, 323; Boustan and Reed, "Blood and Atonement," 340, n. 21.

[139] See especially Bauckham, "The Origin of the Ebionites," 163. James Carleton Paget, "The Ebionites in Recent Research," in *Jews, Christians, and Jewish Christians in Antiquity* (WUNT 251; Tübingen: Mohr Siebeck, 2010), 338–9. Fitzmyer, "The Qumran Scrolls," 451, notes that it is "quite generally held" that the Pseudo-Clementine literature is "Ebionite in origin." For positive assessments of Epiphanius' association of the Pseudo-Clementines and the Ebionites, see also J. Magnin, "Notes sur l'Ébionitisme," *Proche-Orient Chrétien*, 23 (1973), 233–65; Martyn, "Clementine Recognitions I, 33–71," 265–95; Häkkinen, "Ebionites," 257.

[140] Stanton, "Jewish Christian Elements in the Pseudo-Clementine Writings," 312, 322. So also Strecker, *Judenchristentum*, 253–4; Skarsaune, *Proof from Prophecy*, 252–3.

[141] Skarsaune, *Proof from Prophecy*, 296–8, 316–18.

[142] Jones, "An Ancient Jewish Christian Rejoinder," 239–40.

[143] Jones, *An Ancient Jewish Christian Source*, 164–6. Martyn, "Clementine Recognitions," 265–95, 274, affirms Strecker's dating of *Rec.* 1.33–71 to "the mid-point of the second century." F. Stanley Jones, "The Genesis of Pseudo-Clementine Christianity," a paper presented for the Construction of Christian Identities Section at the 2009 Annual Meeting of the Society of Biblical Literature, New Orleans, in *Pseudoclementina Elchasaiticaque inter Judaeochristiana: Collected Studies* (OL 203; Leuven: Peeters, 2012), 204–6, cautions against the uncritical use of the term

scholars now emphasize the fourth-century context(s) of these texts' final redactions.[144] This does not mean that earlier sources need be denied.[145] We must take care not to reinscribe the marginalization of a distinctive Jewish Christian source that does not conform to our preconceptions of what is normatively "Jewish" or "Christian."[146] We need not deny that a literary character from a fourth-century novel that utilizes second-century sources is problematic. At the same time, let us not relegate Jewish Christianity to historical and theological oblivion, irrelevancy, or as mere source material for the rhetorical goals of a fourth-century redactor.

The *Homilies* and the *Recognitions* share a number of elements in common, but represent two distinct approaches to animal sacrifice. In the *Homilies*, the motif is linked to the Enochic motif of the fallen angels: blood sacrifice is demonic, a form of pagan worship; God neither commanded nor required them. The Mosaic sacrificial legislation is a punishment for disobedience as well as a way to protect Israel from pagan idolatry. In the *Recognitions*, sacrifice is linked to pagan idolatry, but animal sacrifice was allowed by Moses as a *temporary* concession in order to prevent Israel from further idolatry. Moses allowed sacrifice, but only to God, so that when Jesus came, sacrifice was replaced by baptism. The destruction of the Temple is linked to Israel's failure to heed Jesus' warning and instruction. In both texts, God never intended Israel to sacrifice; animal sacrifice originated in imitation of pagan practices. The Homilist further associates sacrifice and sacrificial meat-eating with the "table of demons."[147] According to the Homilist, sacrifice was a divine punishment for disobedience,

---

"Ebionite," arguing that its author simply saw him/herself as a legitimate heir of the early Jerusalem community.

[144] Nicole Kelley, *Knowledge and Religious Authority in the Pseudo-Clementines: Situating the Recognition in Fourth-Century Syria* (WUNT II.213; Tübingen: Mohr Siebeck, 2006), 1–26; "Problems of Knowledge and Authority in the Pseudo-Clementine Romance of Recognitions," *JECS*, 13.3 (2005), 315–48; D. Coté, *Le thème de l'opposition entre Pierre et Simon dans les Pseudo-Clémentines* (Paris: Institut d'Études Augustiniennes, 2001); William Robins, "Romance and Renunciation at the Turn of the Fifth Century," *JECS*, 8 (2000), 531–7; Frédéric Amsler, "Les Reconnaissances du Pseudo-Clément comme catéchèse romaneque," in D. Marguerat (ed.), *La Bible en récits: L'exégèse biblique à l'heure du lecteur* (Geneva: Labor et Fides, 2003), 443.

[145] Kelley, *Knowledge and Religious Authority*, 179.

[146] Boustan and Reed, "Blood and Atonement," 362.

[147] 1 Cor. 8:1–13; 10:28–29; Acts 15:29; 21:25; Porphyry, *On Abstinence* 2.36–37, 42–43, 49.

a motif the author shares with Justin,[148] and the Torah's prescriptions of animal sacrifice are understood as "false pericopes."[149] In the *Recognitions*, God allows sacrifice, but only as a temporary concession. The author of the *Recognitions* sees animal sacrifice as divinely prescribed only in so far as sacrifice would be directed toward God. In neither case do our sources represent the death of Jesus as an atoning sacrifice that replaces animal sacrifice.[150]

The most distinctive feature of the *Homilies* is that the Torah's prescription of sacrifices are "false pericopes."[151] According to the Homilist, certain scriptural passages are "false" (ψευδής) or "spurious" (νόθος). The interpretive principle at work is that "everything spoken or written *against God* is false" (πᾶν λεχθὲν ἤ γραφὲν κατὰ τοῦ θεοῦ ψεῦδός ἐστιν).[152] The divorce saying is one example of contrast between the "true things of the law" (τὰληθῆ τοῦ νόμου)[153] and the Mosaic Law as an example of a false scriptural passage. Another example relates to Adam. According to the Homilist, Adam did not sin or "transgress" (οὔτε Ἀδὰμ παραβάτης ἦν).[154] The origin of sin is to be found as a result of the fallen angels.[155] The *Homilies* associate "blood with 'pagan' worship, demons, and impurity, while making no reference either to the atonement effected by Jesus' death or to its ritual memorialization."[156] Animal sacrifice is "degraded and demonic, and they apply this idea of sacrifice *both* to the practices of their 'pagan' contemporaries *and* to the past acts of Jewish priests."[157] Animal sacrifice "originated as a result of the fallen angels and their demonic sons"; to offer sacrifices was to "enslave oneself to

---

[148] *Dial.* 19, 22; 92.

[149] In his *Syllogisms* (c. 160–170 CE), the Marcionite Apelles also taught that many passages in the Old Testament were contradictory, inconsistent, or untrue, and so not from God. See Ambrosius, *De Paradiso* 8.38; 5.28; Origen, *In Genesim Homilia* 2.2; Pseudo-Tertullian, *Adv. Omn. Haer.* 6.6; Hippolytus, *Ref.* 10.20.2; 7.38.2. See also *Hom.* 3.45.2.

[150] Bart D. Ehrman, *The New Testament: A Historical Introduction to the Early Christian Writings* (5th edn.; Oxford University Press, 2012), 3, asserts, without further qualification, that Jewish Christians/Ebionites believed that Jesus "fulfilled his divine commission by dying as a willing sacrifice on the cross for the sins of the world, a sacrifice that put an end to all sacrifices."

[151] *Hom.* 3.45, 51–52, 56.

[152] *Hom.* 2.40.1.

[153] *Hom.* 3.54.2.

[154] *Hom.* 2.52.2.

[155] *Hom.* 8.10.20.

[156] Boustan and Reed, "Blood and Atonement," 335.

[157] Boustan and Reed, "Blood and Atonement," 338.

demons."[158] The Homilist's rejection of animal sacrifices is linked to the Enochic myth of the fallen angels,[159] a tradition connecting early Jewish apocalypticism, the early Jesus movement, and early Jewish Christianity.[160] *1 Enoch* describes the Watchers wrongly revealing heavenly secrets to humanity, the results of which are violence, bloodshed, and sexual misconduct.[161] The fallen angels enslaved humanity "by teaching them to offer sacrifices and incense and libation."[162] The fallen angels' spirits led humanity astray "to sacrifice to demons" (ἐπιθύειν τοῖς δαιμονίοις). It is the giants, the offspring of the Watchers, that introduced eating flesh and blood.[163] After the Flood, the fallen angels' offspring are bound by divine and angelic law.[164] The *Homilies* emphatically state that God did not command animal sacrifice.[165] The author links the prophetic critique of sacrifice to Jesus' rejection of animal sacrifice, appealing again to the "true things of the law."[166] A major exegetical-theoretical tool of the Homilist is the "harmony criterion," a principle that proposes that Scripture is valid only in so far as it is in "harmony" with creation.[167] This criterion

[158] *Hom.* 8.13–19; *Rec.* 1.29; 4.29. Boustan and Reed, "Blood and Atonement," 339.

[159] John J. Collins, "Creation and the Origin of Evil," in *Apocalypticism in the Dead Sea Scrolls* (London: Routledge, 1997), 30–51; Paolo Sacchi, *Jewish Apocalyptic and Its History* (trans. W. J. Short; JSP Sup 20; Sheffield Academic Press, 1997). George W. E. Nickelsburg, *1 Enoch: A Commentary on the Book of 1 Enoch* (Hermeneia; Philadelphia: Fortress, 2001), 46.

[160] Nickelsburg, *1 Enoch*, 1. Gabriele Boccaccini, *Beyond the Essene Hypothesis: The Parting of the Ways between Qumran and Enochic Judaism* (Grand Rapids: Eerdmans, 1998), 12. For the ongoing influence of Enoch traditions on early Jewish Christianity, see Eibert Tigchelaar, "Manna-Eaters and Man-Eaters: Food of Giants and Men in the Pseudo-Clementine Homilies 8," in Jan B. Bremmer (ed.), *The Pseudo-Clementines* (SECA 10; Leuven: Peeters, 2010), 92–114, esp. 97; Nickelsburg, *1 Enoch*, 97–8. F. Stanley Jones, "Pseudo-Clementine Literature," in L. H. Schiffman and James C. VanderKam (eds.), *Encyclopedia of the Dead Sea Scrolls* (New York: Oxford University Press, 2000), 718; James C. VanderKam, *Enoch: A Man For All Generations* (Columbia: University of South Carolina Press, 1995), 179–80.

[161] *1 En.* 8.1; 9.6; 10:4–8.

[162] Annette Yoshiko Reed, *Fallen Angels and the History of Judaism and Christianity: The Reception of Enochic Literature* (Cambridge University Press, 2005), 164. For sorcery, spells, and divination, see *1 En.* 7:1, 8:3, 9:7. For idolatry and pagan sacrifices, see *1 En.* 19:1.

[163] *Hom.* 8.15.

[164] *Hom.* 8.19–20.

[165] *Hom.* 3.45.2.

[166] *Hom.* 3.51–52.

[167] Donald H. Carlson, *Jewish-Christian Interpretation of the Pentateuch in the Pseudo-Clementine Homilies* (Minneapolis: Fortress, 2013), 137–213.

represents a kind of "philosophical" rationalism, whereby the Homilist declares certain passages false because they are "censured by creation" (ὑπὸ τῆς κτίσεως ἐλέγχονται).[168] God did not order animal sacrifices (ὡς οὐκ ὄντα θεοῦ προστάγματα),[169] God has no desire for sacrifices,[170] and does not need blood sacrifice. Animal sacrifice is "contrary to nature" (παρὰ φύσιν).[171]

The rejection of animal sacrifice is a distinctive theme in *Rec.* 1.27–71.[172] The animal sacrifices legislated in the Torah were a temporary concession now abolished by the True Prophet.[173] The people of Israel suffered misfortunes so that "they might be taught that a people who offer sacrifices are driven away and delivered up into the hands of the enemy." The Prophet instituted baptism in place of sacrifices.[174] Animal sacrifice was never intended by God.[175] The practice of sacrifice was the result of Israel being influenced by pagan rites, a concession to Israel's weakness,[176] but God desires "mercy, not sacrifice."[177] Jesus' mission was to replace sacrifice with baptism as a means of atonement.[178] This rejection of animal sacrifice appeals to a Torah (or law) of creation. This appeal culminates in a prophetic warning, not a threat: the *time* for animal sacrifice is over and the Temple will be destroyed *if* the law of (creation) is not restored. Here restoration is correction. In this context, what appears to be the rejection of Torah is the correction of Torah. The rejection of animal sacrifice is not "unthinkable"; it is *eschatological*. It is not an abrogation of Torah; it is the "fulfillment" of Torah. This is not Christian supersessionism; this is Jewish Christian restorationism.[179]

The Pseudo-Clementine literature, although contemporaneous with Marcion and Justin, is not supersessionistic. Justin affirmed the mission to the Jews (as long as they didn't Judaize), but the rhetorical

---

[168] *Hom.* 3.46.
[169] *Hom.* 3.52.1.
[170] *Hom.* 3.45.
[171] *Hom.* 8.15.2–4.
[172] Jones, *An Ancient Jewish Christian Source*, 65–66. *Rec.* 1.36.1.
[173] *Rec.* 1.37.
[174] Jones, *An Ancient Jewish Christian Source*, 68–69. *Rec.* 1.39.1–2.
[175] *Rec.* 1.54.
[176] *Rec.* 1.36
[177] *Rec.* 1.37. See also *Rec.* 1.36; *Hom.* 3.47; 48, 51, 52.
[178] *Rec.* 1.39.
[179] Boustan and Reed, "Blood and Atonement," 38.

thrust of Justin's *Dialogue* is to transfer the covenantal privileges from Jews to Christians (especially the "sacrifice" of the Eucharist); the Jews are cursed. The rhetorical goals of the Pseudo-Clementine texts are not Gentile Christian; they promote the Jewish Christian mission to Jews *and* Gentiles. The Jewish Christian agenda is to affirm the continuity of the Jesus movement *within Judaism* while correcting problematic misinterpretations of the tradition. Since the Jewish Christian rejection of animal sacrifice pre-dates Justin, Justin is not an obvious explanation as the original *source* for the Jewish Christian rejection of animal sacrifice.[180] While some might say that virtually every known form of Christianity contains supersessionistic elements in so far as Christianity is regarded as the ideological replacement of Judaism, it would be a categorical error to identify *Jewish* Christianity as *Christian* supersessionism. *Christian* supersessionism was the result of the progressive marginalization of Jesus' Jewish followers, Jewish ritual practices, the Jewish contexts within which Jesus' critiques were registered, and the transference of these critiques to Christian critiques of Jews and Judaism. The original agreement of two missions reached in Jerusalem collapsed into supersessionism. Subsequently, the Gospel of Mark portrayed Jesus as inaugurating the destruction of the Temple and its religious leadership; the Gospel of John portrayed Jesus *as* the new Temple.

The Jewish Christianity of the Pseudo-Clementines *does not* claim that Jesus' death was a sacrifice to end all sacrifices, nor that Jesus' body replaced the Temple, nor does Jesus' death have salvific value.[181] In other words, the *classic* components of *Christian* supersessionism are curiously *absent* here. Why would Jewish Christians, presumably influenced by Justin and Christian supersessionism, not affirm Jesus' death as an atoning sacrifice? If we saw the rejection of animal sacrifice *alongside* explicit references to Jesus' death as a sacrifice, Pauline atonement theology, a sacrificial Eucharist, and references to Jesus' death atoning for Adam's sin, *then* we would be rightly inclined to call this traditional Christian supersessionism, but these features are strikingly absent. Instead, we see the rejection of animal sacrifice, vegetarianism, a sinless Adam, and the absence of any reference to

---

[180] Skarsaune, *Proof from Prophecy*, 173, proposes that Justin used a Jewish Christian source which contained the idea of "the New Law," combined with "a polemic concerning the ceremonial components of the Mosaic law, and substituting baptism for animal sacrifices."

[181] Schoeps, *Theologie und Geschichte*, 76, 157.

Jesus' sacrificial and atoning death.[182] Jesus' death is not envisioned as an atoning sacrifice, let alone the ultimate sacrifice that replaces animal sacrifice. Rather, it is Jesus' teaching – especially his proscription of animal sacrifice – that "holds the power to save."[183]

The assumption that the *Jewish Christian* rejection of animal sacrifice is simply late *Christian* supersessionism erases a distinctively *Jewish* response to Second Temple culture, reinscribes a heresiological discourse that denied social and theological legitimacy to being both Jewish *and* Christian, and marginalizes an already marginalized group even further out of existence. Here we are dealing with normative definitions of Jewish identity, definitions that attempt to dictate what is (and what is not) possible for an ancient Jew to think, do, or believe.[184]

The *Homilies* and the *Recognitions* – like the *Gospel of the Ebionites* and the *Book of Elchasai* – suggest that Jesus rejected animal sacrifice. These texts may be chronologically later than the New Testament Gospels, but this has little to do with their authenticity as traditions. The chronological privileging of *canonical* sources is "historiographically fallacious."[185] The New Testament Gospels do not provide us with a clear or consistent explanation of Jesus' conflict with the Temple authorities. It is time for us to reconsider these traditions as late *textual* vestiges of the historical Jesus' actual relationship to the sacrificial system.

Animal Sacrifice, the Absence of Evidence, and the Argument from Silence

New Testament scholarship has given "virtually no attention" to Jesus' relationship to animals.[186] In a rare exception, Richard Bauckham has recently discussed the relationship between Jesus, sacrifice, vegetarianism, and the Temple. He affirms what he calls "creation theology" in Jesus' life and teaching,[187] a vision of the renewal of creation,"[188] and a "return to paradisal conditions,"[189] envisioning

---

[182] Carlson, *Jewish-Christian Interpretation*, 101; Schoeps, *Jewish Christianity*, 83.
[183] Boustan and Reed, "Blood and Atonement," 344.
[184] See Arnal, *The Symbolic Jesus.*
[185] Kloppenborg, "A New Synoptic Problem," 202–3.
[186] Bauckham, *Living with Other Creatures*, 79.
[187] Bauckham, *Living with Other Creatures*, 64.
[188] Bauckham, *Living with Other Creatures*, 72.
[189] Bauckham, *Living with Other Creatures*, 75.

not only a world of "peace between animals," but one in which there is a highly idealized "peace between the human world ... [and] wild animals."[190] Yet despite Bauckham's obvious sympathies with Jesus' kingdom-vision, restoration eschatology, creation-theology, and Jewish Christianity, he concludes that Jesus sacrificed animals and ate meat.[191] According to Bauckham, Jesus' loyalty to Old Testament traditions included killing animals for sacrifices and food.[192] Moreover, if Jesus had rejected either practice, "then the Gospels ... would surely have recorded it."[193] Bauckham appeals to Matt 5:23–24, where Jesus seems to take it for granted that his hearers make offerings in the Temple, although as we have seen, Matthew does not specify what is being offered and is retroactively portraying Jesus as pro-Temple in a post-Temple era. More significantly, there is simply no evidence supporting the idea that Jesus ever performed animal sacrifice. Consequently, we cannot *assume* he did so. Bauckham is well aware that Jesus' warning to stop sacrificing was a view held by Jewish Christians, but he regards this as a view "*adopted* by the *later* Jewish Christian *sect* of the Ebionites" developed "*doubtless in reaction* to the destruction of the temple and the end of the temple cult in 70 CE."[194] As such, it is "of no historical value."[195] The problem is that just as there is *no* evidence that Jesus ever performed animal sacrifice, there are also *no* explicit references to Jesus eating meat or fish *during his ministry*.[196] Bauckham knows that some pre-Christian Jews (like the Therapeutae) abstained from meat,[197] but identifies their motives as either being an attempt to avoid the impurity of meat sacrificed to idols,[198] because vegetarianism was "an ascetic practice of self-denial,"[199] or because meat was a "luxury."[200] But while some post-70 CE Jews may have abstained from meat out of mourning

[190] Bauckham, *Living with Other Creatures*, 75.

[191] Bauckham, *Living with Other Creatures*, 99–104.

[192] Bauckham, *Living*, 99–100. On Jesus eating meat, see Bauckham, *Living*, 101.

[193] Bauckham, *Living*, 99.

[194] Bauckham, *Living*, 100 (emphases added).

[195] Bauckham, *Living*, 101.

[196] The only exception is Luke 24:42–43, where the post-Easter Jesus eats a piece of fish, and this is widely held to be an anti-Docetic illustration of Jesus' genuine corporeality.

[197] On vegetarianism, see Roger T. Beckwith, "The Vegeterianism of the Therapeutae, and the Motives for Vegetarianism in Early Jewish and Christian Circles," *RevQ*, 13 (1988), 407–10.

[198] Bauckham, *Living*, 102, citing Dan. 1:5–16; Tob. 1:10–13; Jdt. 10:5; 12:2).

[199] Bauckham, *Living*, 102.

[200] Bauckham, *Living*, 102.

for the Temple's loss, it is less plausible to suggest that James did so *before* the Temple was destroyed.[201]

Despite Bauckham's idealized vision of Jesus' kingdom-message as the "renewal of creation" – including a notable affirmation that *human beings will be vegetarian "in the messianic age"* – Jesus apparently did not inaugurate this age.[202] Bauckham concedes that his objections to a vegetarian, nonsacrificing Jesus are theologically informed,[203] but if Jesus inaugurated the messianic age, renewed creation, and restored paradisal conditions, it is difficult to see why Jesus would not also have re-established the vegetarian diet established by God at creation and predicted by Isaiah, which is precisely how his Jewish Christian followers remembered him. Bauckham's appeal to the argument from silence fails to persuade. The eschatological ethics of Jesus should not be reduced to problematic assumptions of non-eschatological normative interpretations of "Judaism":

> Most Jews ate meat.
> Jesus was Jewish.
> Jesus ate meat.

> Most Jews sacrificed animals.
> Jesus was Jewish.
> Jesus sacrificed animals.

These simplistic equations not only disregard the complex sectarian variety within Second Temple Judaism, they also undermine Jesus' radical ethic of eschatological nonviolence. These appeal(s) to silence, the absence of evidence, and the argument from normative Judaism simply fail to convince.

An argument from silence (*argumentum ex silentio*) is a conclusion based on the *absence* of textual evidence.[204] It is "a pattern of

---

[201] Bauckham, *Living*, 103.

[202] Bauckham, *Living*, 103 n. 63.

[203] Bauckham is concerned that if Jesus ate meat, and meat-eating is "absolutely wrong," this would "clearly contradict the Christian belief in the sinlessness of Jesus" *and* "cut Christianity's roots in the Jewish tradition of faith to which Jesus so clearly belonged."

[204] See C. A. Briggs, "The Argument *E Silentio*: With Special Relation to the Religion of Israel," *JSBLE*, 3 (1883), 3–21; Andrew Constantinides Zenos, *The Elements of the Higher Criticism* (New York: Funk and Wagnalls, 1895), 74–94; Charles Victor Langlois and Charles Seignobos, *Introduction to the Study of History* (trans. G. G. Berry; New York: Henry Holt and Co., 1904), ch. 3; John Lange, "The

reasoning in which the failure of a known source to mention a particular fact or event is used as the ground of an inference ... that the supposed fact is untrue."[205] While arguments from silence are fairly common in historiographical work, they are often unreliable and difficult to establish in cases of ancient historiography. Arguments from silence thus bear a formidable burden of proof.[206] Timothy McGrew has recently identified three conditions that such arguments must meet:

(R₁)   If the disputed event had actually transpired, then the author whose silence is being invoked could not have been ignorant of it.

(R₂)   If the author had not been ignorant of the event, he could not have failed to mention it.

(R₃)   If the author had mentioned it, we would be aware of that today.[207]

Despite the difficulties in meeting these conditions, the argument from silence is commonly used to cast doubt on the possibility that Jesus rejected blood sacrifice. In many cases, such arguments from silence could be framed like this:

> If Jesus rejected animal sacrifice, the canonical Gospel authors would and should have mentioned it. The authors of the canonical Gospels did not mention it. Therefore, Jesus did not reject animal sacrifice.

The question here, however, is this: *Should* we expect the authors of the Gospels to have mentioned this? I do not think that we can simply assume this. And this means that we must make a case for why the authors would have done so – or not. We must begin, in other words, with a historical argument. In this light, a restructured argument from silence could look something like this:

> The canonical Gospels contain no explicit references to Jesus rejecting animal sacrifice.

Argument from Silence," *HT*, 5 (1966), 288–301; David P. Henige, *Historical Evidence and Argument* (Madison: University of Wisconsin Press, 2005), ch. 16.

[205] Timothy J. McGrew, "The Argument from Silence," *Acta Analytica*, 29.2 (2013), 215–28.

[206] McGrew, "The Argument from Silence," 223.

[207] McGrew, "Argument from Silence," 219–20, citing Charles de Smedt, *Principes de la critique historique* (Paris: Librarie de la Societe Bibliographique, 1883), 227.

The authors of the canonical Gospels intended to provide a complete list of everything Jesus said, did, or thought, and be perfectly clear about what Jesus objected to in the Temple.

The authors of the canonical Gospels would not have neglected to mention that Jesus objected to animal/blood sacrifice and it was something they would and/or should have known about.

Therefore, Jesus did not reject animal sacrifice.

If the above statements are all true, the argument from silence would succeed and we could be virtually certain that Jesus did not criticize or reject animal sacrifice. The argument, however, fails. We cannot know if the authors of the canonical Gospels intended to provide their readers with a complete list of everything Jesus said, thought, or did. We cannot know that they wanted to tell us exactly what Jesus objected to in the Temple. And so we cannot reasonably conclude that they would *not* have withheld Jesus' criticism of animal sacrifice (if they had known of it) or even that they *could* have known it. For the argument from silence to succeed, the authors would need to have been in a position to know this information, found it interesting and significant, *and* to have intended to provide a complete account of Jesus' thoughts about the Temple, but these conditions cannot be met. Moreover, the authors of the Gospels each had their own particular authorial and redactional interests and their own individual theological goals. They were most definitely *not* interested in providing us "just the facts," let alone a *complete* rendering of them. The argument from silence is properly regarded as fallacious. So while it is indeed odd that the New Testament never mentions Jesus' rejection of animal sacrifice (assuming, for the moment, that it is historically correct), there may be very good reasons for this apparent omission.

First, it is a commonplace in scholarship that the Gospels do not contain a great deal of information that we would like to know about Jesus. The final author/redactor of the Gospel of John is quite aware of this (John 21:25). Second, the Gospels – indeed the entire New Testament – was collected, edited, and canonized to serve the needs of the predominantly Gentile wing of the Jesus movement that regarded itself as a substitute for the Temple cult. The Gospels (and Paul's letters) share this theme in common. They also affirm Jesus' identity as the suffering son of man/messiah who must die as a sacrifice for humanity, thereby replacing the Temple, with Jesus' spilled blood serving to save his followers from the "wrath" of God. Given that the sacrificial interpretation of Jesus' death is a major, if not the dominant theological and soteriological theme underlying the New Testament canon, it is not very likely that we would find any explicit references to theologies that undermine that very theme. It may not have served Luke's interests, for example, to *explicitly* identify Jesus' death as a sacrifice. Luke certainly emphasizes the *necessity* (δεῖ) of Jesus' suffering and death and his role in bringing salvation to Israel (Luke 24:26, 44-47), but conspicuously omits Mark's "ransom" saying (10:45). But just as Luke re-presents Paul as conforming to traditional Jewish norms of piety (and downplays Paul's more radical polemic against the Torah), so, too, does he highlight the role of the Temple in the salvation history of Israel while downplaying the soteriological and sacrificial functions of Jesus' death.[208] Nonetheless, Luke does not *object* to the sacrificial interpretation of Jesus' death as much as he *obscures* it.

Third, the Temple incident is a common feature in all four Gospels yet no one seems to have really known precisely what Jesus was upset about. True, the authors cite scriptural passages to make up the difference – including citations that seem to undermine the efficacy of "sacrifice" in relation to mercy (Hosea 6:6) – but all most seem sure about is that there were ambiguous historical tensions between Jesus and the Temple administration. A surface reading of the four Gospels does not provide us with a clear picture of what Jesus objected to in the Temple, although the common theme seems to be a symbolic abolition of animal sacrifice. At the same time, we are indeed encouraged to think that Jesus' death was a divinely preordained sacrifice and that Jesus predicted both his death and the Temple's destruction. This tension – between an ambiguous Temple incident that *leads* to the historical Jesus' death and a theological prediction of the Temple's destruction that *coincides* with Jesus' death – is never resolved. The Gospels narrate a supersessionist vision in which Jesus and his sacrifice replaces the Temple, but do not do so in a way that properly locates Jesus within a plausible first-century Jewish context and conflict. We must look elsewhere.

---

[208] Conzelmann, *The Theology of St. Luke*, 201: "there is no trace of any Passion mysticism, nor is any direct soteriological significance drawn from Jesus' suffering or death." Peter Doble, *The Paradox of Salvation: Luke's Theology of the Cross* (SNTSMS 87; Cambridge University Press, 1996), 234, notes that "Luke distanced himself from sacrificial or vicarial strands of thought."

Fourth, another possible reason for the apparent omission of Jesus' rejection of *animal* sacrifice in the New Testament is that Jesus did *not* reject sacrifice or the Temple *per se*, but rather the *violence* of *blood* sacrifice. Jesus rejected violence; there is no good evidence that he ever used violence to cause anyone harm, whether man or animal. It would therefore have been consistent of Jesus to have objected to the violence of blood sacrifice. There is no explicit evidence that Jesus ever performed animal sacrifice, or even ate meat, not even at Passover. The idea that Jesus ate a Passover lamb at the Last Supper must be *read into* or inferred from the Gospels. If the authors of the canonical Gospels identified Jesus as a blood sacrifice, it would not have served them to portray Jesus criticizing that very institution and practice. The destruction of the Temple in 70 CE served to confirm that Jesus was the ultimate sacrifice and true Temple. One might argue (again, from silence) that it would have served the evangelists (and Paul) if Jesus had actually rejected sacrifice because that would have made their job – to promote Jesus as a sacrifice – easier. If this is true, then there would have been no good reason for them to omit this, presuming they knew about it. But this argument fails. It is difficult to conceive of how "Jesus" could both criticize the violence of blood sacrifice and simultaneously *be* a violent blood sacrifice.

Fifth, while it is true that the New Testament does not mention Jesus' criticism of blood sacrifice, this *is* mentioned in multiple Jewish Christian sources and traditions. These sources may not be *canonical*, but they are *ancient*. If the dogmatic rejection of canonical sources is historiographically fallacious, then we can now acknowledge that the early Church certainly had good reason to suppress what was in them, whether or not their contents corresponded to anything in the canonical Gospels.

Sixth, the authors of the canonical Gospels were not consistently or primarily interested in preserving Jesus' distinctive hermeneutic of Torah. They do preserve it on occasion, but their overarching interests involved affirming Jesus' role in the history of salvation, not simply preserving what Jesus taught. Consequently, Jesus' approach to the Torah is sometimes conflated with the interests of the evangelists, which is why we know so much less about Jesus than we would like. The evangelists report that Jesus proscribed divorce and affirmed the Sabbath (appealing to arguments from creation), but not everything derived from such an argument served the theological interests of the evangelists.

The central theme of the Gospels is the "good news" of Jesus' death and resurrection, the efficacy of his blood sacrifice and the salvation it mediates. These themes are based on Jesus' relationship to the Torah and the Temple, but interpreted in such a way as to imply replacement theology rather than internal cultural criticism. If we want to relocate Jesus *within* Judaism, we must correct for these interpretations by recognizing that the eschatological rejection of animal sacrifice is perfectly consistent (if not an inevitable conclusion) of a radically realized vision of a restored creation, which Jesus called the kingdom of God.

Conclusion

The Temple incident was the primary causal factor that led to Jesus' death. Jesus' death, however, was quickly interpreted within a salvation-history that came to see his blood as being spilled for the "new covenant."[209] The idea that Jesus' death was a blood-sacrifice – modeled in part after the Suffering Servant of Isaiah 53 – was rapidly associated with the idea that Jesus' sacrificial death replaced the need for any further participation in the sacrificial system. The Gospels subsequently represented the Temple incident as an eschatological "cleansing" of the Temple and/or a prophetic demonstration of the Temple's imminent destruction, but these narrative portrayals of Jesus' offense were developed in tension with the overarching theological motif of Jesus' sacrificial death.

The historical Jesus was a first-century Jewish healer, teacher, prophet, and messianic figure who affirmed and sought to restore God's original intention of creation – which he called the "kingdom of God" – among the people of Israel. Several converging lines of evidence point to this conclusion. First, Jesus' saying on divorce appeals to the principle of creation and assumes the authority to reinterpret Mosaic Law. Second, Jesus' kingdom-vision of divine providence promises a paradisal restoration.[210] Third, Jesus' conflicts with Jewish religious authorities – culminating in accusations of blasphemy – indicate a powerfully counter-cultural orientation vis-a-vis the Temple and Torah. Fourth, Jesus' radical stance on nonviolence – and its implicit critique of the Torah – strongly suggest that Jesus did not endorse the biblical tradition of divine violence. It is equally unlikely that Jesus envisioned his imminent death as a blood sacrifice.

---

[209] Rom. 3:25–26.
[210] See esp. Joseph, " 'Seek His Kingdom.' "

Jesus criticized animal/blood sacrifice because it was not what God originally intended for humanity. A Temple without blood sacrifices would have transformed the sanctuary into a kind of new Eden.[211] This was the implicit meaning underlying the traditional theme of the *"cleansing* of the Temple." The critique and rejection of animal sacrifice is a central theme of – and multiply attested in – the Jewish Christian gospel tradition. This criticism was *embarrassing* to an early Church that had quickly come to view Jesus' death *as* a (Paschal) sacrifice.[212] Jesus' critique of animal/blood sacrifice therefore meets the criteria of rejection, execution/crucifixion,[213] ambiguity,[214] and a Palestinian cultural environment. The rejection of blood sacrifice is indeed sufficiently "dissimilar" to both Second Temple Judaism" and early (non-Jewish) Christianity. Although the criterion of (double) dissimilarity was first formulated to isolate authentic traditions based on the assumption that the historical Jesus was "different" from both Judaism and the early Church,[215] it has rightly come in for severe criticism.[216] Nonetheless, the rejection of blood sacrifice is relatively rare or "dissimilar" within Second Temple Judaism and sufficiently rare in early Christianity (given that Jesus is predominantly represented *as* a blood sacrifice) that its relegation to the heretical margins of Jewish Christianity can now be better understood. The rejection of violence is also characteristic of Jesus. Furthermore, the rejection of blood sacrifice conforms to N. T. Wright's *criterion of double similarity/dissmilarity*, which proposes

---

[211] See Wenham, "Sanctuary Symbolism in the Garden of Eden Story," 19–25; *Heaven on Earth*. On the Isaianic "new creation" in Jerusalem, see Webb, "Zion in Transformation," 71.

[212] Schoeps, *Theologie und Geschichte*, 76.

[213] Meier, *A Marginal Jew: Roots of the Problem*, 177. On the criterion of crucifixion, see now Brian Pounds, "The Crucifiable Jesus," Ph.D. dissertation, University of Cambridge, 2015.

[214] See Robert L. Webb, "The Historical Enterprise and Historical Jesus Research," in D. L. Bock and R. L. Webb (eds.), *Key Events in the Life of the Historical Jesus: A Collaborative Exploration of Context and Coherence* (Grand Rapids: Eerdmans, 2009), 71.

[215] Norman Perrin, *Rediscovering the Teaching of Jesus* (New York: Harper & Row, 1967), 39; *The New Testament: An Introduction: Proclamation and Parenesis, Myth and History* (New York: Harcourt Brace Jovanovich, 1974), 281; Käsemann, "The Problem of the Historical Jesus," 37.

[216] For criticism, see Morna D. Hooker, "On Using the Wrong Tool," *Th*, 75 (1972), 570–81; David L. Mealand, "The Dissimilarity Test," *SJT*, 31 (1978), 41–50; Sanders, *Jesus and Judaism*, 16–17, 252–55.

that "when something can be seen to be credible (though perhaps deeply subversive) within first-century Judaism, *and* credible as the implied starting point (although not the exact replica) of something in later Christianity, there is a strong plausibility of our being in touch with the genuine history of Jesus."[217] The rejection of blood sacrifice is contextually *plausible* within Second Temple Judaism and its rapid marginalization in early Christianity (and preservation in *Jewish* Christianity) is explainable by its subversive *effects*.[218] It also fits a continuum approach, producing "a Jesus who is both fitting within his Jewish context and in a comprehensible relation to early Christian attitudes."[219]

One might object that Jesus' criticism of animal/blood sacrifice is not recorded in the New Testament Gospels and/or that it is "inconceivable," "unthinkable," or "culturally inappropriate" to suggest such a thing, but it seems unwise to predetermine what a first-century Jew could or could not have thought or done based on allegedly normative assumptions of what constituted first-century "Jewishness." The second objection – that our proposal is not represented in the New Testament Gospels – is a more weighty criticism. It is true – the New Testament does not openly or explicitly preserve this criticism – but we cannot dismiss numerous second and third century Jewish Christian traditions simply by appealing to their apparently late date. These sources might well represent authentic traditions. Nor should canonical considerations play a role in reconstructing history.

The cumulative weight of the converging lines of evidence for our proposal *is* substantial. Is it possible, then, to affirm a first-century setting for Jesus' rejection of animal/blood sacrifice? The short answer is Yes. Let us review.

First, a significant number of second-century Jewish Christians were opposed to animal sacrifice and attributed this opposition to Jesus. The fragmentary antisacrifice traditions present in the *Book of Elchasai*, the *Gospel of the Ebionites* (*Pan.* 30.16.5), the second-century source underlying *Recognitions* 1.27–71 and its derivatives (the *Grundschrift*, *Recognitions*, and *Homilies*) represent a multiply attested interpretive lens through which Jewish Christians

---

[217] Wright, *Jesus and the Victory of God*, 132, see 131–33.

[218] Theissen and Winter, *The Quest for the Plausible Jesus*, 211.

[219] Tom Holmén, "An Introduction to the Continuum Approach," in Tom Holmén (ed.), *Jesus from Judaism to Christianity: Continuum Approaches to the Historical Jesus* (LNTS 352; London: T & T Clark, 2007), 1–2.

"remembered" Jesus.[220] These traditions are too widely ignored, disregarded, explained away, and/or assigned to heretical repositories as late, bizarre post-Synoptic derivatives. The Jewish Christian roots of Christianity may continue to be an embarrassment to New Testament scholarship, exposing the ideological biases, problematic disciplinary boundaries, and faith-commitments of our guild, but it is a simple, incontestable historical fact that Jesus' first followers were Jews.

Second, the assumption that Jesus was simply a faithful Mosaic Law-abiding Jew fails to explain why Jesus was regarded as such a threat by religious leaders in Jerusalem and why Jewish Christian followers of Jesus were so adamant that he rejected animal sacrifice.[221] Jesus is remembered for his provocative challenges to tradition and for offending his contemporaries, particularly the priestly leadership of the Temple who conspired in instigating his execution. The antisacrifice tradition provides a remarkably cogent and compelling explanation for the conflict underlying the Temple incident and has the greatest explanatory power in its ability to reconcile conflicting accounts and multi-valent data.

Third, the Temple incident is one of the most perplexing puzzles of the Jesus tradition, which supports its historicity and explains early Christian embarrassment about both the incident and the Temple-saying. The anti-Temple saying is multiply attested and our earliest Jesus/Temple traditions, Q 11:49–51 and Q 13:34–35, unambiguously declare the Temple to be "forsaken." There is no evidence of Jesus' participation in animal sacrifice (despite his interest in the Temple and his active teaching and healing in the Temple precincts), and no unambiguous evidence that Jesus expected, desired, or anticipated a new physical Temple. On the contrary, each of the Gospels presuppose a supersessionist theology in which the Temple and its sacrifices are symbolically redefined in order to signify Jesus, his body, and/or his followers as the new Temple, with Jesus' sacrificially efficacious death replacing the need for further Temple sacrifices.

Fourth, Jesus' opposition to the violence of animal sacrifice is consistent with and a logical extension of Jesus' radical nonviolence, a distinctive, characteristic, and well-attested aspect of Jesus' life, teachings, ministry, and death.

---

[220] Skarsaune, *In the Shadow of the Temple*, 156.

[221] Donald A. Hagner, "Jesus and the Synoptic Sabbath Controversies," in *Key Events*, 283, notes that "Jesus penetrates to the essence of the Sabbath, by going back to its foundation in Genesis."

Fifth, Jesus' criticism of animal sacrifice is consistent with a prophetic tradition that critiqued the institution and asserted that God did not originally desire, require, or legislate animal sacrifice.

The Jewish Christian rejection of animal sacrifice stands in ideological continuity with earlier Jesus traditions. These texts may be dated to the second and third centuries, but their most distinctive feature – the rejection of animal sacrifice – represents not only an *ideological* continuity with the Jesus tradition, but a *genealogical* continuity with the life, ministry, and death of the historical Jesus, a compelling counter-narrative and ideological corrective to the historical and theological representation of Jesus as a dying savior sacrificed by God to vicariously atone for the sins of all humankind. The idea that Jesus criticized animal sacrifice – and died defying the very practice he would himself be most commemorated for – was scandalous to Jews and Christians for whom sacrifice served as the central core of their traditions. In response, the Jesus of the Gospels does not abolish the Torah; he fulfills it. Similarly, Jesus does not only destroy the Temple; he *replaces* it with his own body and death as the ultimate sacrifice. In response, sacrificial theology became even more pronounced in Christianity as it became a religion "centered on" – and ultimately defined by – sacrifice.[222]

---

[222] Stroumsa, *The End of Sacrifice*, 72.

7

THE DYING SAVIOR

> The universal soteriological interpretation of the death of
> Jesus ... necessarily led to a break with the sacrificial cult.
>
> Martin Hengel, *The Atonement*[1]

"For Our Sins": The Vocabulary of Sacrifice in
1 Corinthians 15:3–8

The earliest historical references to the concept of Jesus' sacrificial
death are found in the letters of Paul. Paul uses a wide variety of
images and metaphors to describe Jesus' death.[2] It initiates reconciliation between humanity and God.[3] It is "a stumbling block to Jews
and foolishness to Gentiles,"[4] a cosmic turning point,[5] and the defeat
of the Powers.[6] Jesus is "our Passover lamb." Jesus died *"for us"* (ὑπὲρ
ἡμῶν) and/or "for our sins,"[7] "according to the Scriptures."[8] Paul uses
this expression so frequently that it has been described as "the most
important confessional statement in the Pauline epistles."[9] Jesus' followers are "justified by his blood" and "reconciled to God" because
Jesus was "given up (ὃς παρεδόθη) for (διὰ) our trespasses and raised
for (διὰ) our justification."[10] This is language deeply indebted to the

---

[1] Hengel, *The Atonement*, 47.
[2] John T. Carroll and Joel B. Green, "Paul's Theology of the Cross," in J. T. Carroll
and J. B. Green (eds.), *The Death of Jesus in Early Christianity* (Peabody: Hendrickson,
1995), 125.
[3] 2 Cor. 5:18–20.
[4] 1 Cor. 1:22–23.
[5] 2 Cor. 5:17; Gal. 6:15.
[6] Gal. 3:10–14; Col. 2:15.
[7] 1 Cor. 15:3; Rom. 5:6, 8, 14:9; 2 Cor. 5:14, 15; Gal. 2:21, 1 Thess. 5:10. See
Christina Eschner, *Gestorben und hingegeben "für" die Sünder. Die griechische
Konzeption des Unheil abwendenden Sterbens und deren paulinische Aufnahme für die
Deutung des Todes Jesu Christi* (WMANT 122; Neukirchen-Vluyn: Neukirchener,
2010), 107–29.
[8] 1 Cor. 15:3.
[9] Rom. 5:6–8; 2 Cor. 5:14; 1 Thess. 5:10. Hengel, *Crucifixion in the Ancient World*, 37.
[10] Rom 5:9, 5:10, 4:25.

Temple cult.[11] While there continues to be debate about whether Paul refers to Jesus' death as a sin- or guilt-offering,[12] it is clearly identified *as* a sacrifice.[13] Jesus' death as "a *sacrifice* (ἱλαστήριον) *of atonement*" by God seems to refer to the Day of Atonement,[14] when the high priest entered the Holy of Holies: Jesus is now the *place* where atonement occurs (the ἱλαστήριον was the place where the sins of Israel were cleansed on the Day of Atonement). Jesus' sacrificial death lies at the very heart of Paul's theology.[15] But how did Paul "receive" this tradition?

The origin of the sacrificial interpretation of Jesus' death is one of the great historical and theological "mysteries" of the Christian faith. I have argued in previous chapters that the earliest Jewish Christians, like Jesus himself, did not participate in the animal sacrifices of the Temple cult yet maintained their reverence for Jerusalem and the Temple as the house of God. I have also suggested that the early Jerusalem community came to see itself – not unlike the Qumran community before them – as an eschatological temple. The language and vocabulary of sacrifice would still have been meaningful, even integral, to their self-conception, especially considering the wider discourse on sacrifice in antiquity. Following Jesus' death, early Christians came to adopt a variety of sacrificial and soteriological ideas about him. As we will see, Paul's first letter to the Corinthians,

[11] On Paul's temple-imagery, see John R. Lanci, *A New Temple for Corinth: Rhetorical and Archaeological Approaches to Pauline Imagery* (New York: Peter Lang, 1997). On Paul's use of (non-atonement) cultic metaphors, see Nijay K. Gupta, *Worship That Makes Sense to Paul: A New Approach to the Theology and Ethics of Paul's Cultic Metaphors* (New York and Berlin: de Gruyter, 2010). See also Albert L.A. Hogeterp, *Paul and God's Temple: A Historical Interpretation of Cultic Imagery in the Corinthian Correspondence* (BTS 2; Leuven: Peeters, 2006), esp. 271-377.

[12] Rom 8:3; 2 Cor 5:21.

[13] 2 Cor. 5:21. See J. D. G. Dunn, "Paul's Understanding of the Death of Jesus as Sacrifice," in S. Sykes (ed.), *Sacrifice and Redemption: Durham Essays in Theology* (Cambridge University Press, 1991), 35–56.

[14] Rom. 3:24–25. On Paul, see H. N. Ridderbos, "The Earliest Confession of the Atonement in Paul," in R. Banks (ed.), *Reconciliation and Hope* (Grand Rapids: Eerdmans, 1974), 76–89; Dunn, *The Theology of Paul*, 207–33. McLean, "The Absence of an Atoning Sacrifice in Paul's Soteriology," 531–53. T. R. Schreiner, "Sacrifices and Offerings in the NT," in G. W. Bromiley (ed.), *The International Standard Bible Encyclopedia* (Grand Rapids: Eerdmans, 1988), 274; Stephen Finlan, *The Background and Content of Paul's Cultic Atonement Metaphors* (AB 19; Atlanta: Society of Biblical Literature, 2004); Dunn, "Paul's Understanding of the Death of Jesus as Sacrifice," 35–56.

[15] Wright, *Paul and the Faithfulness of God*, 1:1071.

the Last Supper tradition, Adamic Christology, Isaiah's Servant Songs, and the "Hellenistic" Jewish martyrological tradition all coalesced in this development. While we may not be able to reconstruct the precise process in and through which Jesus' death was first envisioned as a "sacrifice," I have suggested that Jesus' instructional program of "self-sacrifice," or ascetic renunciation, informed his own ministry as a prophetic witness ("martyr") and provided the earliest model of discipleship and emulation. Jesus' instructions were thus part of a wider philosophical discourse on sacrifice in antiquity and served as the foundation upon which subsequent themes of martyrological atonement could be further developed and ritually commemorated in the tradition underlying 1 Cor 15:3-8.

1 Cor 15:3–8 is one of the most important passages in the New Testament.[16] It is our earliest evidence for the atoning death and bodily resurrection of Jesus. The passage is also crucial in so far as it confirms Paul's continuity with the earliest apostolic traditions. It is widely held that 1 Cor 15:3–8 "incorporates ... a pre-Pauline formula."[17] There are several converging lines of evidence and argument that combine to make a strong case for this judgment.

First, the passage appears to be part of a formulaic tradition. There is no denying that traditions were important to Paul. He even claims to have been more zealous than others "of the traditions (παραδόσεων) of my fathers" (Gal 1:14). There is also no doubt that Paul received and transmitted traditions,[18] and could be careful in distinguishing his teaching from tradition.[19] Paul, on one occasion, explicitly refers to the teaching *of the Lord* on marriage. He also uses the term ἱστορῆσαι to describe what he did with Peter in Jerusalem, a term which means "to get information from" or "to

---

[16] Theissen and Merz, *The Historical Jesus*, 487–90.

[17] Allison, *Resurrecting Jesus*, 233–4. See A. Seeberg, *Der Katechismus der Urchristenheit* (Leipzig: Deichert, 1906); P. Winter, "1 Corinthians XV, 3b-7," *NovT*, 2 (1958), 142–50; H. Conzelmann, "On the Analysis of the Confessional Formula in 1 Corinthians 15:3–5," *Int* 20 (1965): 15–25; W. Kramer, *Christ, Lord, Son of God* (SBT 50; London: SCM, 1966), 19–21. As tradition, see P. Barnett, *Jesus and the Rise of Early Christianity: A History of New Testament Times* (Downers Grove: InterVarsity, 1999), 181; Robert W. Funk and the Jesus Seminar, *The Five Gospels*, 454; Craig S. Keener, *1–2 Corinthians* (NCBC; Cambridge University Press, 2005), 123; Helmut Koester, *History and Literature of Early Christianity*, 2nd edn. (New York: Walter de Gruyter, 2000), 91.

[18] 1 Cor 7:10; 9:14; 11:23; 15:1–3, 12; cf. 1 Cor 11:2; Phil 4:9; 2 Thess 2:15.

[19] 1 Cor 7:10–13, 25. Meier, *A Marginal Jew* (1991), 46.

inquire into a thing, to learn by inquiry." Elsewhere, Paul reminds his community-members about "the teaching which you learned"[20] and "the things you have learned and received."[21] It is widely thought that Paul uses two technical terms here that refer to inherited traditions "delivered" and "received" in his use of παρέδωκα ... ὃ καὶ παρέλαβον ("I handed on what I also received").[22] Appeals have been made to link these terms to parallel terms in rabbinic literature.[23] Paul identifies his teaching with that which the apostles preached. In 1 Cor 15:11, he writes that "whether it was I or they, so we preach (κηρύσσομεν) and so you believed."

Second, 1 Cor 15:3–8 uses language relatively uncharacteristic of Paul. In fact, vocabularic analysis of this passage appears to be decisive. Paul uses words and expressions here that he does not use elsewhere:

> For I handed on to you what I in turn had received:
> that Christ died for our sins (ἁμαρτιῶν)
> according to the scriptures (κατὰ τὰς γραφὰς) ...
> and that he was raised (ἐγήγερται) ...
> and that he appeared (ὤφθη) ...
> then to the Twelve (τοῖς δώδεκα).

A number of non-Pauline traits have been identified. For example, except for Gal 1:4, the expression "for our *sins*" (ὑπὲρ ἁμαρτιῶν ἡμῶν) in the plural is absent in Paul as he prefers the singular.[24] The phrase "according to the Scriptures" is absent in the Pauline letters as Paul prefers the expression "it is written" (γέγραπται).[25] Paul uses the perfect passive "he has been raised" instead of the aorist.[26] The use of

---

[20] Rom 16:17.

[21] Phil 4:9.

[22] John Kloppenborg, "An Analysis of the Pre-Pauline Formula in 1 Cor 15:3b-5 in Light of Some Recent Literature," *CBQ*, 40.3 (1978), 351–7, esp. 351; John P. Meier, *A Marginal Jew: Rethinking the Historical Jesus, Vol. 3: Companions and Competitors* (New York: Doubleday, 2001), 139; Alan F. Segal, *Life After Death: A History of the Afterlife in Western Religion* (New York: Doubleday, 2004), 400.

[23] *'Abot* 1.1; *Pe'a* 2.6; *'Abot* 1.3; *Zebah* 1.3.

[24] Although "sin" appears sixty-four times in Paul, fifty use "sin" in the singular. In the six occurrences where the plural occurs, tradition may be present (1 Cor 15:3; 1 Cor 15:17; Gal 1:4; Rom 7:5; Eph 2:1; Col 1:14). Allison, *Resurrecting Jesus*, 234; Theissen and Merz, *The Historical Jesus*, 487, although περὶ τῶν ἁμαρτιῶν ἡμῶν appears in 1 Jn 2:2; 4:10; cf. Luke 11:4; 1 Pet 2:24.

[25] Allison, *Resurrecting Jesus*, 234; Theissen and Merz, *The Historical Jesus*, 487.

[26] The former is found only in 1 Cor 15:12–14, 16, 20, 2 Tim 2:8. See Allison, *Resurrecting Jesus*, 234; Theissen and Merz, *The Historical Jesus*, 487.

"on the third day" is also only here in Paul; the term "appeared to/was seen" (ὤφθη) is found only in 1 Cor 15:5–8 and 1 Tim 3:16. Finally, "the Twelve" is only here in Paul; elsewhere he uses "the apostles."[27]

The combination of unusual and uncharacteristic terms in conjunction with Paul's explicit claim to have "received" tradition synonymous with that preached by the apostles (1 Cor 15:11) is compelling. It is certainly true that Paul introduces new phrases (15:6b, 8) ("most of whom are still living, though some have fallen asleep" and "and last of all he appeared to me also, as to one untimely born"),[28] but it is far less clear whether the phrases "for our sins" and "according to the scriptures" are secondary additions to the tradition.

A strong case can be made for Jerusalem as the source of this tradition.[29] Paul explicitly states that teachings came from that community.[30] There is also no doubt that many of Jesus' first disciples were located in Jerusalem.[31] It is possible that Paul inherited this tradition from the Greek-speaking Jewish Christian "Hellenists" described in Acts, but this is uncertain [32] Other possibilities include Damascus, Arabia, and Antioch. The truth is that we do not know where – or from whom – Paul "received" this tradition. We know that Paul may have been in accord with the Jerusalem community on Jesus' identity as messiah (Χριστός/משיחא), Son of God, the general resurrection of the dead, the new creation, baptism, thanksgiving meals, and a Gentile mission, but we also know that Paul received his own private revelations.[33] What we seem to have here, therefore, is a charismatic movement of remarkably prolific exegetical creativity and ingenuity, a movement in which Paul "receives" both apostolic traditions and

---

[27] Allison, *Resurrecting Jesus*, 234; Theissen and Merz, *The Historical Jesus*, 487.

[28] Allison, *Resurrecting Jesus*, 234; Jerome Murphy O' Connor, "Tradition and Redaction in 1 Cor 15:3–7," *CBQ*, 43.4 (1981), 582–9.

[29] Larry H. Hurtado, *Lord Jesus Christ: Devotion to Jesus in Earliest Christianity* (Grand Rapids: Eerdmans, 2003), 168–9.

[30] Rom 15:25–27; cf. 1 Cor 9:11.

[31] Gal 1:17–18; 2:1–10; Acts 1:8; 4:16; 5:28; 6:7; 8:1, 14; 9:26; 11:27; 12:25; 13:13; 15:2, 4–6; 16:4; 21:17–18.

[32] Hans Conzelmann, "Zur Analyse der Bekenntnisformel I. Kor 15,3–5," *EvTh*, 25 (1965), 1–11.

[33] Paul tells us that he received traditions "from the Lord" (1 Cor 11:23). Paul may be referring to additional oral traditions he received from the apostles, but he uses the same formulaic language of παρέλαβον-παρέδωκα ("received-passed on") both to cite known Jesus sayings-traditions *and* to describe his own private *revelations* from Jesus ("the Lord") (Gal 1:12); cf. (1 Cor. 11:23; 1 Cor. 15:1; Gal. 1:11. See Funk and the Jesus Seminar, *The Five Gospels*, 458.

divine revelations.[34] We do not know where – or from whom – Paul first "received" the tradition that Jesus' death was foretold in the scriptures, but it is so deeply (and polyvalently) embedded in Paul's own thought that it is difficult not to conclude that it is a pre-Pauline tradition appealing – like Paul himself – to exegetical traditions identifying Jesus as the Servant of Isaiah 53.

For Paul, the significance of Jesus' sacrificial death is that it *saves*. The language of sacrifice complements the language of salvation. Christ's followers are "saved from the wrath to come."[35] The phrase ἡ ὀργὴ εἰς τέλος has been interpreted both as the eschatological "birth pangs" of the messianic woes and the eschatological inauguration of the Deuteronomistic "curses." In 1 Thess. 2:16, Paul speaks of God's wrath falling upon the Judeans/Jews of his day. Similarly, Romans 1:10 and 5:9 refer to Christ's followers being "delivered" or "saved" from the divine wrath. Christ's followers have been "saved" from the eschatological wrath because Christ's death "atoned" for them.[36] Christ went to the cross "in place" of his followers. Here the language of ὑπὲρ indicates Jesus' vicariously atoning death.[37] Jesus "saves" by protecting his followers from God's wrath. We find a similar protecting or "saving" (salvific) function and power in Paul's identification of Jesus as "our Passover lamb, Christ, (who) has been sacrificed (ἐτύθη)" (1 Cor. 5:7). Paul uses θύω, a term usually used for animal sacrifice.[38] This identification of Jesus-as-Passover (lamb) is "the original and controlling sacrificial

---

[34] McKnight, *Jesus and His Death*, 341. For the Lord's Supper as Pauline, see H. Lietzmann, *Mass and Lord's Supper: A Study in the History of the Liturgy* (Leiden: Brill, 1953–1979 [1926]).

[35] Ben F. Witherington III, *Paul's Narrative Thought World: The Tapestry of Tragedy and Triumph* (Louisville: Westminster John Knox, 1994), 162. See G. H. C. MacGreggor, "The Concept of the Wrath of God in the New Testament," *NTS*, 7 (1961), 101–9. See also Rom. 1:18; 2:5; 2:8; 3:5; 4:15; 5:9; 9:22; 12:19.

[36] Rom 5:9–10.

[37] Gal 1:4; 2:20; Rom. 5:6; 1 Cor 11:24. See Tibor Horvath, *The Sacrificial Interpretation of Jesus' Achievement in the New Testament: Historical Development and its Reasons* (New York: Philosophical Library, Inc., 1979), 47–65; Ernst Käsemann, "The Pauline Theology of the Cross," *Int*, 24 (1970), 151–77; Ralph Martin, *Carmen Christi: Philippians ii.5–11 in Recent Interpretation and in the Setting of Early Christian Worship* (SNTSMS 4; Cambridge University Press, 1967), 84–8; Leon Morris, *The Cross in the New Testament* (Grand Rapids: Eerdmans, 1962), 55–9, 320–2.

[38] Dean O. Wenthe, "An Exegetical Study of 1 Corinthians 5:7b," *Sp*, 38 (1974), 134–40.

image for the death of Jesus."[39] Jesus' death functioned as a scapegoat, carrying away the sins of the people,[40] and a Passover Lamb
saving "us" from God's wrath and judgment.

Jesus' sacrificial death is implicit as the sub-text in the shared sacred
meal of the Eucharist.[41] The symbolic motifs of the sacrificial lamb,
the atoning value of Jesus' "sacrifice" given "for you" (Luke 22:19,
20; 1 Cor. 11:24) or "for many" (Matt. 26:28; Mark 14:24), the conjunction of blood with covenant-language (Matt. 26:28; Mark 14:24;
Luke 22:20; 1 Cor. 11:25), and Jesus' alleged command to ritually
re-perform the act in remembrance of his self-offering (Luke 22:19;
1 Cor. 11:24), suggest that the participatory nature of the Eucharist
refers to Jesus' sacrificial death.[42] Christians have life "in him."[43]

Paul also associates Jesus' suffering with his own,[44] an association
that would develop into the martyrological tradition.[45] Following
Jesus requires cross-bearing.[46] Paul's interpretation of Jesus' death
as a sacrifice inspired a martyrological paradigm of offering up oneself "in sacrifice"[47] as a way of "following" Jesus.[48] Variations on this
theme can be found throughout the New Testament.[49] Those who follow Christ are taught to "offer (παραστῆσαι) your bodies as a living

---

[39] Wright, *Paul and the Faithfulness of God*, 2:1343.

[40] A. Andrew Das, *Paul, the Law, and the Covenant* (Peabody: Hendrickson, 2001),
143, identifies this as an "apotropaic ritual."

[41] On the Septuagint's semantic range of θυσία (referring to nonanimal offerings)
as a possible explanation for the identification of the Eucharist as a "sacrifice," see
Andrew McGowan, "Eucharist and Sacrifice: Cultic Tradition and Transformation in
Early Christian Ritual Meals," in Matthias Klinghardt and Hal Taussig (eds.), *Mahl
und religiöse Identität im frühen Christentum. Meals and Religious Identity in Early
Christianity* (Tübingen: Francke, 2012), 191–206.

[42] On ὑπὲρ ἡμῶν as a reference to Jesus' sacrificial death, see Daly, *Christian
Sacrifice*, 237.

[43] 1 Thess. 4:13–5:11; 5:9–10. See also Rom. 8:3–4, 14:9; 2 Cor. 5:15, 21.

[44] Carroll and Green, "Paul's Theology of the Cross," 130; John S. Pobee, *Persecution
and Martyrdom in the Theology of Paul* (JSNTSup 6; Sheffield: JSOT, 1985), 102–6.

[45] Carroll and Green, "Paul's Theology of the Cross," 155. On Christian martyr-
dom as the imitation of Christ by demonstrating fearlessness in the face of death, see
Tertullian, *Apol.* 50.13. See also Daniel Boyarin *Dying for God: Martyrdom and the
Making of Christianity and Judaism* (Stanford University Press, 1999) 94.

[46] Senior, "The Death of Jesus," 242–5. See also Seeley, *The Noble Death*.

[47] Rom. 12:1.

[48] In the LXX, it generally refers to the כפרת, the golden lid or "mercy seat" over the
ark of the covenant in the Holy of Holies. On the Day of Atonement, the high priest
would sprinkle the blood of the sacrifice onto its lid for the forgiveness of the people's
sins (Exod 25:10–22; Lev 16).

[49] Rom. 12:1; 1 Pet. 2:5; Rev. 5:8, 8:3; Heb. 13:15.

sacrifice (θυσίαν ζῶσαν), holy and acceptable to God."[50] Jesus' sacrifice was *communal* and participatory.[51] Paul compares converts to the "first fruits" offered to the Temple (Rom 16:5; 1 Cor 16:15) and the "offering" of Christians to the contributions made by Jews to the Temple (Rom 15:25–32; 2 Cor 9:13–14; Phil 4:18). Paul compares "Christian" worship to sacrificial service (Rom 12:1; 1 Cor 10–11) and proclaims himself as "working in the *priestly service* of God's good news, so that the *offering* of the nations may be *acceptable*, sanctified in the Holy Spirit" (Rom 15:15). He also sees himself being *"poured ou*t like a *drink-offering* on the *sacrifice* and service of your faith" (Phil. 2:17). The new community is a new Temple.[52] According to 2 Cor. 6:16, Paul proclaims that "we are the temple of the living God."[53]

Paul's role in disseminating the sacrificial interpretation of Jesus' death can clearly be seen in the Gospels of Mark, Matthew, and Luke.[54] Mark's Gospel contains clear echoes of the Pauline Last Supper: Jesus is the Son of God, an obedient, suffering, sacrificial figure.[55] He comes *to call* sinners.[56] As the suffering son of man,[57] he gives "his life a *ransom* for many."[58] The *wine* of the Last Supper meal is "the *blood* of the covenant ... poured out for many."[59] Matthew echoes Mark's predictions,[60] repeats the Markan saying that the son of man came to give his life as "a ransom for many,"[61] and *adds* "for the forgiveness of sins,"[62] associating the Eucharist with Jesus' atoning sacrifice with echoes of Isaiah's Servant bearing "the sins

---

[50] Rom. 12:1.

[51] Wright, *Paul*, 1339.

[52] 1 Cor. 3:16–17; 1 Cor. 6:19; 2 Cor 6:16. See also Eph. 2; 1 Pet. 2:4–6. On Qumranic parallels, see R. J. McKelvey, *New Temple: The Church in the New Testament* (OTM; Oxford University Press, 1969), 95; David Peterson, "The New Temple: Christology and Ecclesiology in Ephesians and 1 Peter," in T. D. Alexander and S. Gathercole (eds.), *Heaven on Earth: The Temple in Biblical Theology* (Carlisle: Paternoster, 2004), 161–76, here 162.

[53] Wright, *Paul*, 2:1039.

[54] Matt. 8:17 explicitly quotes Isa. 53:4, and Acts 8:26–40.

[55] See Joel B. Green, *The Way of the Cross: Following Jesus in the Gospel of Mark* (Nashville, Tn: Discipleship Resources, 1991); Marcus, *The Way of the Lord*.

[56] Mark 2:17.

[57] Mark 8:31, 9:12, 9:31–32.

[58] Mark 10:45.

[59] Mark 14:22–24.

[60] Matt. 16:21, 17:12, 17:22, 20:18–19, 26:2.

[61] Matt. 20:28.

[62] Matt. 26:28.

of many."[63] The Gospel of John associates Jesus' death with the
Passover lamb, with Jesus handed over to death when the lambs are
slaughtered.[64] John the Baptist refers to Jesus as the "Lamb of God
who takes away the sins of the world."[65] Jesus is the Shepherd who
lays down his life for his sheep.[66]

There seems to be no particularly compelling reason to doubt that
Jesus shared a final meal with his disciples on the night of his arrest.
He may well have even anticipated his death, took a loaf of bread,
a cup of wine, and given thanks, sharing this meal with his companions. It is reasonable to suppose that his disciples "remembered" this
event ritually, communally, and consistently in fellowship meals and
that Paul inherited a meal-tradition from the Jerusalem community's leadership. Does this mean that the historical Jesus identified the
bread and wine with his body and blood and imbued the rite with
sacrificial imagery? Here there is no consensus. Some scholars would
argue for a harmonious correspondence between the historical Jesus,
Paul's letters, and the Synoptics. Others would disagree. Still others
would admit that they simply do not know. We can only establish
probabilities based on the evidence at hand. What we can surmise,
however, is that the Last Supper was probably *not* an official Passover
meal. There is no reference to a paschal lamb and a Passover meal
would have required the slaughter of a lamb. Mark seems to have
embellished the Passover association, but for particular theological
purposes.[67] The Synoptic account also diverges from John's account.
According to the Gospel of John, after all, the Last Supper was
not a Passover meal, although the death of Jesus is again synchro-
nized with the slaughtering of the lambs.[68] John's account also omits
any Eucharistic features in the meal. Paul identified Christ as "our
Passover,"[69] but this only requires a *proximity* to Passover. Paul does
not actually mention Passover in his account of the Last Supper.
We can surmise that the meal took place *around* Passover, but that
is all. We simply don't know how the pre-70 CE. Passover meal was
celebrated nor do the Gospels refer to unleavened bread, a visit to

[63] Isa. 53:12.
[64] John 19:14–16.
[65] John 1:29.
[66] John 10:7–8; 15:12–13.
[67] McKnight, *Jesus and His Death*, 271–3.
[68] John 18:28.
[69] 1 Cor. 5:7.

the Temple, a lamb, or bitter herbs. The Synoptic passion narratives
re-present the meal as a Passover meal.[70] The covenant saying is secondary,[71] added to support the Passover association due to its connotations with Exodus, the lamb, and the "*blood* of the covenant."[72]

In the Synoptics, it is the blood that connects the wine of the Last
Supper with Jesus' death and the language of sacrifice. In the Gospel
of John, however, the "last supper" is simply a Jewish meal where
Jesus washes the feet of his disciples. John thus detaches the Temple
incident from the Last Supper and the Last Supper from Passover
and the theme of a sacrificial cultic ritual. In contrast, the Synoptics
collapse the Last Supper and Temple incident, encouraging us to
read the Last Supper accounts in light of Jesus' criticism and "symbolic destruction" of the Temple, suggesting that Jesus' Last Supper
is a *replacement* of the Temple sacrificial system, a new "rite" of sacrifice. The Synoptics want us to see the Last Supper and Jesus' death
as sacrificial rites that rival and/or replace the Temple.

For early Christians, the death of Jesus was understood and represented as a cosmic turning point, the "end of the ages" heralding
both a "new creation" and the transformation of ancestral religious
traditions. Jesus' death – as an atoning sacrifice – would soon come
to signify the replacement of the Temple, its sacrificial system, and
the Torah itself.[73] Humanity was now being restored according to
God's original divine intention:

> So if anyone is in Christ, then (he) is *a new creation* (καινὴ
> κτίσις): everything old has passed away: see, everything has
> become new![74]
>
> For neither circumcision nor uncircumcision is anything;
> but *a new creation* (καινὴ κτίσις) is everything![75]

According to Paul, Jesus renewed the *Adamic* covenant between
God and humanity. It is only in and through Jesus' identification as

[70] Rudolf Pesch, *Das Markusevangelium*, 2 vols. (HTKNT 2; Freiburg im
Breisgau: Herder, 1977), 2:1–27; Brown, *The Death of the Messiah*, 1:46–57.

[71] Jens Schröter, *Das Abendmahl: Frühchristliche Deutungen und Impulse für die
Gegenwart* (SBS 210; Stuttgart: Katholisches Bibelwerk 2006), 132–3; McKnight,
Jesus and His Death, 304–12.

[72] Exod 24:18.

[73] Das, *Paul, the Law, and the Covenant*, 122. See also Rosner, *Paul and the Law*,
217–18.

[74] 2 Cor 5:17. Cf. 2 Cor 3:6.

[75] Gal 6:15.

a new Adam that Paul could envision Christ incorporating but also transcending Abraham, Israel, Mosaic Torah, and Davidic ancestry. The symbiotic, corporate, and mystical relationship between humanity and Christ is based on an Adamic identification of Christ: Jesus' death restoring humanity from its fallen, sinful, and mortal state inherited from Adam.[76] Christ is a new Adam,[77] the herald of the "new creation,"[78] and the "image of God,"[79] having given "himself for our sins to set us free from the present evil age."[80] He has "disarmed the rulers and authorities ... triumphing over them,"[81] setting us free "from the law of sin and of death."[82] Paul's idea of salvation is the restoration of humanity according to the "image of God" in which Adam had been created.[83] God has now called all those "predestined to be conformed to the image of his Son."[84] Christ received the "glory" intended for Adam that now enables believers to be transformed according to his likeness.[85] Adam was "the first man" and Christ "the last Adam."[86] Jesus' death was the *sacrifice* of the sinless, obedient Son that restored the original covenant between God and humanity (Adam), inaugurating a new creation, and the regeneration of humanity.

"A Light to the Nations": Jesus and the Suffering Servant

How can the guilt of one man be expiated by the death of another who is sinless?

Rudolf Bultmann, *Kerygma and Myth*[87]

Jesus' Jewish followers located Jesus' death in the salvation history of Israel. They appealed to a variety of symbols, metaphors, similes, and allusions, many of which drew from the sacrificial system

---

[76] McKnight, *Jesus and His Death*, 344, 350.
[77] 1 Cor. 15:45.
[78] 2 Cor. 5:17.
[79] Gal 4:4; 2 Cor. 4:4; 1 Cor. 11:7.
[80] Gal 1:4.
[81] Phil 2:15.
[82] Rom 8:2.
[83] Dunn, *Christology in the Making*, 105–6.
[84] Rom 8:29.
[85] Phil 3:21.
[86] 1 Cor. 15:45.
[87] Rudolf Bultmann, in H.W. Bartsch (ed.), *Kerygma and Myth: A Theological Debate* (trans. R. H. Fuller; New York: Harper & Row, 1961), 7.

and provided rich scriptural resources that effectively linked Jesus' death to the larger story of Israel. They searched the scriptures for exegetical parallels that could serve as proof-texts for their emerging theology.[88] They found the themes of the *rejected prophet*[89] and the psalms of the *suffering "righteous one"*[90] to be useful paradigms for prophetically foreshadowing Jesus' suffering and death.[91] Similar themes also seem to be present in 2 Maccabees, where the suffering of the martyrs seems to atone for the nation's sin. The martyrs are portrayed as having gone "gladly" to their deaths, believing that they would be raised to new life in the future.[92] In 4 Maccabees, martyrs are "dying for the law," a "ransom for the sin of our nation … an atoning sacrifice."[93] They also found the Suffering Servant of Isaiah 40–53, where the prophet portrays the Lord's Servant in four oracles or Songs.[94]

By the time of Paul, Jesus' death seems to have been associated with Isaiah 53.[95] The fate of the "Servant" ("Israel") was transferred to Jesus' death – now seen through the scriptural lens of Isaiah's Servant – as *salvific*:

> For I received from the Lord what I also *handed on* (παρέδωκα) to you, that the Lord Jesus on the night when he was *handed over* (παρεδίδετο) … (1 Cor   11:23)

> The Lord *handed him over* (παρέδωκεν) *for our sins* (LXX Isa 53:6)

> He bore the sins of *many* (πολλῶν) and was *handed over* (παρεδόθη) (LXX Isa 53:12)

[88] Joel Marcus, *The Way of the Lord*; "The Old Testament and the Death of Jesus: The Role of Scripture in the Gospel Passion Narratives," in John T. Carroll et al. (eds.), *The Death of Jesus in Early Christianity* (Peabody: Hendrickson, 1995), 205–33..

[89] 1 Thess. 2:15–16; Q 11:49–51; Q 6:22–23; Acts 7:51–53.

[90] Wis. 2:10–22; 5:1–7; Matt. 27:39–43; Dan. 3; 6; 11:33–35.

[91] Marcus, "The Old Testament and the Death of Jesus," 205–33. See esp. Ps. 22, 22:27, 10:7–8, 35:19, 42:5, 38:13–14, 109:3, 34:15, 17, 19; and from the LXX, 6:3–4, 140:8, 38:12, 4:6, 41:9, 27:12, 35:11, 69:21, 22:1, 6, 7, 8, 18, 31:5, 69:21, 34:20.

[92] 2 Macc. 6.30, 7.9, 11, 14, 16–17, 22–23, 29, 30–38.

[93] 4 Macc 6.27–29; 17.20–22. See Sam K. Williams, *Jesus' Death as Saving Event: The Background and Origin of a Concept* (HDR 2; Missoula: Scholars, 1975).

[94] Isa 42:1–7; 49:1–13; 50:4–11; 52:13–53:12..

[95] Crossan, *The Birth of Christianity*, 439.

Similarly, in Rom. 4:25, Paul claims that Jesus was

> given up (ὃς παρεδόθη) for (διὰ) our trespasses and raised for (διὰ) our justification.

These apparent allusions and references to Isaiah 53 are telling. There are few passages in the Hebrew Bible that have received as much attention as this "erratischer Block," a passage fraught with textual, historical, and theological ambiguities.[96] Who is the Servant? Is "he" an individual historical figure?[97] Or a typological archetype? Or a collective-group? Or a prophetic witness to Jesus' messianic suffering and death? Or a *symbol* of Israel during the messianic age? Many scholars and theologians hold the Servant Songs as the keystone in their Christological interpretations of Jesus' ministry and death.[98] Isa 52–53, in particular, plays a major role in Jewish/Christian relations to this day, just as it did for the authors of the Gospels. Matthew describes Jesus as healing the sick

> to fulfill what had been spoken through the prophet Isaiah, "He took our infirmities and bore our diseases."[99]

Similarly, the author of Luke-Acts's "Jesus" explicitly appeals to Isa 53:

> For I tell you, this scripture must be fulfilled in me:
> "And he was counted among the lawless."[100]

In the book of Acts, the apostle Philip identifies Jesus as the prophetic fulfillment of Isa 53:

> Like a sheep he was led to the slaughter,
> And like a lamb silent before its shearer,
> So he does not open his mouth.
> In his humiliation justice was denied him.[101]

---

[96] K. Koch, "Sühne und Sündenvergebung um die Wende von der exilischen zur nachexilischen Zeit," *EvT*, 26 (1966), 217–39, esp. 237.

[97] Antti Laato, *Who Is the Servant of the Lord? Jewish and Christian Interpretations on Isaiah 53 from Antiquity to the Middle Ages* (SRB 4; Winona Lake: Eisenbrauns, 2012), 10, 40, suggests that the individual features of the Servant *originally* referred to the death of Josiah in 609 BCE. The passage was then interpreted to refer to "the righteous and faithful Israelites" in exile (47).

[98] Wright, *Simply Jesus*, 154.

[99] Matt 8:17.

[100] Luke 22:37.

[101] Acts 8:26–39.

The Servant appears to die a vicarious, violent death for the sins of others.[102] His mission seems to be accomplished *through* this suffering and death, which he submits to in silence before his accusers. He is abused, "handed over," and "numbered with transgressors." His suffering and death are unjust, but redemptive.[103] He relies solely on God for vindication and God rescues him from death,[104] exalting him.[105] The Servant will be "a light to the nations."[106]

Our first interpretive hurdle is recognizing that the Servant Songs of Isa 40–53 represent different subjects and speakers: God, the Servant, and the collective ("we") voice of the Gentiles/nations. The first Song (42:1–7) refers to the Servant as an agent of divine justice. Here the Lord speaks in the first person:

> Here is *my servant* (עבדי; LXX: ὁ παῖς μου), whom I uphold, my chosen, in whom my soul delights; I have put my spirit upon him; he will bring forth justice to the nations. He will not cry or lift up his voice, or make it heard in the street (Isa 42:1–2)

In the second Song (49:1–6), the Servant describes how his mission will bring redemption to Israel and "a light to the nations":

> Listen to me, O coastlands, pay attention, you Gentiles/ nations (לאמים; LXX ἔθνη) ...
> The Lord called me before I was born, while I was in my mother's womb he named me ...

---

[102] See Anthony Gelston, "Knowledge, Humiliation, or Suffering: A Lexical, Textual, and Exegetical Problem in Isaiah 53," in R. N. Whybray, H. A. McKay, and D. J. A. Clines (eds.), *Of Prophets' Visions and the Wisdom of Sages: Essays in Honour of R. Norman Whybray on His Seventieth Birthday* (JSOT Sup 162; Sheffield: JSOT, 1993), 126–41. See also Christopher Richard North, *The Suffering Servant in Deutero-Isaiah: An Historical and Critical Study* (London: Oxford University Press, 1948).

[103] Isa 50:6; 53:9. On his redemptive work, see Isa 42:1–4; 49:5–8; 53:5, 6, 12. The Servant obeys God (Yahweh) (42:4; 49:7–8; 50:4–11; 52:13; 53:12) and fulfills his mission in the face of suffering (42:4; 49:4, 7–8; 50:6–9; 52:14–53:10) and ultimate exaltation (49:7; 52:13–15).

[104] Isa 49:8; 53:10–11. It is not necessarily clear whether the Servant actually dies. Isa 52:13–53:12 envisions the Servant *in danger* of a violent death. Isa 53:8 states that "He was cut off from the land of the living," which seems to depict death. Isa 53:9 states that "they prepared his grave," while Isa 53:12b notes that "He poured out his soul to death."

[105] Isa 52:13; 53:12, 15.

[106] Isa 42:1–4, 6–7; 49:5–6.

And he said to me, 'You are *my servant* (עבדי; LXX: δοῦλός),
Israel ...
I will give you as a light to the Gentiles/nations (לאור גוים;
LXX: εἰς φῶς ἐθνῶν).

It is the fourth Song (52:13–53:12), however, that fully describes
the nature of the Servant's suffering and role in God's plan of
redemption:[107]

Behold, *my servant* (עבדי) shall prosper: he shall he exalted
and lifted up, and shall be very high ... so he shall startle
many nations (ἔθνη πολλὰ);
kings shall shut their mouths because of him, for that
which had not been told them they shall see, and that which
they had not heard they shall contemplate.

Who would have believed our report? ...
He was despised and rejected by others; a man of suffering (איש מכאבות) and acquainted with infirmity ...
But he was wounded because of our transgressions,
crushed because of our iniquities; upon him was the punishment that made us whole, and by his bruises we were
healed ...[108]
For he was cut off from the land of the living, stricken
because of the transgression of my people (מפשע עמי נגע למו).[109]
And he gave his grave with the wicked and in his death(s)[110]
with the rich ... Yet it was the will of the Lord to crush him

---

[107] The third Song (50:4–11) describes the Servant's physical punishment he suffers.

[108] The MT reads Isa 53:5–8 as "*because of* our transgressions" (מפשעינו) and
"*because of* our iniquities" (מעונתינו) instead of "*for* our transgressions" and "*for* our
iniquities." The Hebrew Bible requires a reading that the Servant was hurt *because of*
the sinful acts of the Gentiles/nations, not (vicariously) "for them."

[109] In Isa 53:8 "my people" (עמי) refers to iniquities inflicted on Israel. When Isaiah
shifts back to the plural (למו: "them") in 53:8, it is a reference to Israel. The implication in the NRSV is that it is an individual who is afflicted ("*he* was stricken") whereas
in the MT, למו may be a synonym for להם meaning "them," "for/from them," or "to
them," suggesting that it is the nation (Israel) that is stricken. Indeed, The word is
translated usually as a plural form (see Isa 16:4; 23:1; 26:14; 30:5; 35:8; 43:8; 44:7;
44:15; 48:21; 53:8), except in Isa 44:15 and 53:8, where it is arguably mistranslated as
singular. If the correct translation is the third person plural ("*they* were stricken"), this
would confirm that the Servant is a nation, not a single individual.

[110] Isa 53:9 uses the plural form for "in his deaths" (במתיו) instead of "in his death."
This compound expression is a combination of a preposition and a noun; the noun

with pain. If his soul would acknowledge guilt, he shall see his
seed, he shall prolong his days (תשים אשם נפשו יראה זרע יאריך ימים
אם) ...[111] By his knowledge will my servant justify the righteous
before many,[112] and he shall bear their iniquities (ועונתם הוא יסבל
בדעתו יצדיק צדיק עבדי לרבים) ... because he poured out himself
to death, and was numbered with the transgressors; and he
bore the sin of many (καὶ αὐτὸς ἁμαρτίας πολλῶν ἀνήνεγκε),
and made intercession for the transgressors (LXX 53:12: "and
was handed over (παρεδόθη) because of their iniquities" (Isa
52:13–53:12).

The term "Servant" (עבד) is subject to a wide range of forms and
potential referents in the four Songs.[113] The Servant has been variously identified as (1) corporate national Israel; (2) the righteous
remnant of Israel; (3) the prophet Isaiah or Jeremiah; (4) the Israelite
king in exile; or (5) the ideal Davidic king/messiah.[114] While the
Servant's identity is, at times, ambiguous,[115] the Servant is also explicitly and repeatedly identified as Israel:[116]

מתו, is the inflection in the possessive third person singular, masculine gender of the
plural noun מותים, the plural of the root noun מות (death). The Hebrew term for "in
his death" would be במותו, not במתיו. If this is the case, then the Servant cannot be an
individual, but rather corportate Israel.

[111] Isa 53:10 is a conditional statement about Israel, not a reference to the vicarious
atonement by the Servant (NRSV: "When you make his life an offering for sin"). The
NRSV translates אשם as "an offering for sin" because it is used as a guilt offering, not
a sin offering (Lev 5:15; Num 6:12), but it is also used to refer to a sin or an iniquity
committed with intent (Jer 51:5; Prov 14:9). The conditional form of the verse suggests
that if Israel admits guilt and repents then there will be a "reward." The "seed" (זרע) of
reward refers to blood offspring, that is, physical descendants.

[112] In Isa 53:11, it is not the Servant who is called "righteous" (a covert messianic
reference); the Servant will justify the righteous. This is a reference to *Israel* being "a
light to the nations."

[113] It occurs thirty-nine times in singular and plural forms: "The Servant of
Yahweh," "His Servant," "My Servant," "the Servants of Yahweh," "His Servants,"
"Your Servants," and "My Servants."

[114] R. N. Whybray, *Thanksgiving for a Liberated Prophet* (JSOTS 4; Sheffield
University Press, 1978); David J. A. Clines, *I, He, We, and They: A Literary Approach
to Isaiah 53* (Sheffield: JSOT, 1976).

[115] Isa 42:1; 49:5, 6; 50:10; 52:13; 53:11.

[116] Isa 41:8, 9; 43:10; 44:1, 2, 21; 48:20; 49:3. The plural expression designates
corporate national Israel (54:17; 56:6; 63:17; 65:8, 9, 13, 14, 15; 66:14). Three singular expressions designate an individual: "My Servant David" (37:55), "My Servant
Eliakim" (22:20), and "My Servant Isaiah" (20:3). Eight singular expressions are

> But you, Israel, are my servant (עבדי), Jacob whom I have chosen, the seed of Abraham my friend (Isa 41:8)
>
> You are *my witnesses* (אתם עדי), says the Lord, *and my servant* (עבדי) (Isa 43:10)
>
> Yet hear now, O Jacob my servant (עבדי), and Israel, whom I have chosen (Isa 44:1)
>
> Remember these things, O Jacob, and Israel, for you are my servant (עבדי) (Isa 44:21)
>
> For the sake of my servant (עבדי) Jacob, and Israel my chosen one, I called to you by your name (Isa 45:4)
>
> And [God] said to me "you are my servant (עבדי), O Israel in whom I will be glorified" (Isa 49:3)

The Servant is clearly identified as Israel in numerous passages framing the fourth Servant Song. What this means is that it is the kings of the Gentiles/nations who are astonished at the Servant.[117] It is the Gentiles/nations who admit their guilt for mistreating Israel after they realize that Israel's role was to be "a light to the Gentiles/nations." This reading is made explicit in Isa 52:10 ("The Lord has revealed his holy arm *to* the eyes of all the Gentiles/nations"). The Gentiles/nations mistreated God's Servant, but now Israel will be exalted (53:2). It is Israel that has been despised, afflicted, and forsaken and now the Gentiles/nations realize that Israel has suffered for them (53:4). The Lord has used the Gentiles/nations to punish Israel (Isa 53:6) and it is Israel that has been massacred like sheep being slaughtered.[118] While Israel's suffering was in part a punishment for its sins, when Israel acknowledges her guilt and repents, Israel will be rewarded by growth, descendants, prolonged life, and success.

Isa 52–53 refers to the salvation of *Israel* and the eschatological redemption of the Gentiles/nations. The Song could thus be

---

collective for Israel: "Israel My Servant" (41:8, 9; 44:1, 2, 21; 48:20; 49:3). There are a number of cases where the singular title is not explicitly identified (42:1; 49:5, 6; 50:10; 52:13; 53:11). In two cases, "His Servant" (49:5) and "My Servant" (49:6) occur where the singular, "Israel My Servant" (49:3), appears immediately prior. Four other uses of "My Servant" (42:1; 52:13; 53:11) and "His Servant" (50:10) occur in oracles where the identity is not explicitly stated.

[117] Isa 52:14–15.

[118] Isa 53:7; cf. Zech 11:4–7; Ps 44:12, 23.

understood as "messianic" in a broad sense in so far as it refers to Israel's future vindication, but it does *not* refer to a future individual messianic *figure*. This reading is confirmed by Origen (c. 248 CE) who reported that contemporary Jews read the passage this way:

> Now I remember that, on one occasion, at a disputation held with certain Jews, who were reckoned wise men, I quoted these prophecies; to which my Jewish opponent replied, that these predictions bore reference to the whole [Jewish] people, regarded as one individual, and as being in a state of dispersion and suffering, in order that many proselytes might be gained, on account of the dispersion of the Jews among numerous heathen nations.[119]

The arguments *against* a Christological reading of Isa 53 are formidable. The arguments *for* the Christological reading are negligible. The Servant Songs were not recognized as "messianic" prophecies in the first century. Pre-Christian Jews did not expect their future ideal king to suffer and die in atonement for their sins. In the Gospel of Mark, the disciples are completely unfamiliar with the idea that the messiah "must" suffer and die as the fulfillment of Isaiah's Suffering Servant. The disciples simply do not understand what "Jesus" is saying:

> Then he began to teach them that the Son of Man must undergo great suffering, and be rejected by the elders, the chief priests, and the scribes, and be killed, and after three days rise again. He said all this quite openly, and Peter took him aside and began to rebuke him. (Mark 8:31–32)

> For he was teaching his disciples, saying to them, 'The Son of Man is to be betrayed into human hands, and they will kill him, and three days after being killed, he will rise again.' But they did not understand what he was saying and were afraid to ask him. (Mark 9:31–32)

Jesus' disciples had *no idea* that the messiah was to suffer and die. This is hardly surprising when we consider the fact that Isaiah's Servant is never described as "anointed" nor conforms to traditional Davidic conceptions of the royal role. Indeed, it is only if we were to posit

---

that Isaiah somehow (unwittingly?) slipped in two or three covert and ambiguous messianic references within a literary context where the Lord's Servant has already been identified as Israel (and the Lord's "Anointed" as Cyrus [45:1]) *and* ignore the numerous explicit references to the Servant-*as*-Israel that the Christological interpretation (Suffering Servant = Suffering and Dying Messiah = Jesus) works. Nonetheless, a further problem presents itself: while the Servant's suffering and death is allegedly described in *sacrificial* terms, the Torah clearly states that each person is responsible for their own sins.[120] We could conclude that it was *Jesus* who independently and innovatively combined these ambiguous Isaianic resonances by interpreting them as messianic and related them to his own imminent death.[121] But then we must reckon not only with the Torah's proscription of vicarious atonement, but the disturbing theological conclusion that Jesus believed that he was taking the wrath of God upon himself "for us," meaning that Jesus believed that God required his death in order to forgive humanity despite whatever Jesus may have said about God being a God of forgiveness, compassion, and mercy.[122]

One can hardly object to the conclusion that some of Jesus' early followers understood Jesus to be the prophetic fulfillment of Isaiah's Servant figure (and represented him accordingly), but this would have been a *post*-Easter development. Similarly, one cannot object to contemporary Christians seeing Jesus as the fulfillment of Isaiah's Servant, but this too is a theological interpretation that should not be projected back onto the *historical* Jesus. The idea that Jesus died as a sacrifice "for our sins" is simply not supported by the internal logic of the Torah's sacrificial system nor the enigmatic Servant Songs of Isaiah.

The identification of Jesus as the fulfillment of Isaiah 53 made good scriptural sense out of Jesus' suffering, death, and exaltation. Jesus' death was a historical fact demanding theological interpretation. We do not know who originally connected Jesus' death to the Isaianic motif of the Suffering Servant, but we can clearly see traces of this connection in Paul's letters and theology, a theology deeply embedded within a culture invested in sacrificial practice and ideology.

---

[120] Deut 24:16; cf. Exod 32:31–33; Num 35:33; Cf. 2 Kgs 14:6; Jer 31:29; Ezek 18:4, 20; Ps 49:7–8.

[121] Wright, *Simply Jesus*, 171.

[122] Wright, *Simply Jesus*, 184–5.

Jesus as Sacrifice

> The Christian language of sacrifice only makes sense within a context of the Fall and salvation.[123]
>
> Douglas Hedley, *Sacrifice Imagined*

The authors of the Gospels portray Jesus as knowing – well in advance – that he was going to die in Jerusalem. Yet the Gospels are not so much biographical reports on the sayings and deeds of Jesus as complex literary compositions combining historical narrative and theological reflection. The passion narratives echo multiple passages in Zechariah.[124] Jesus' entry into Jerusalem riding on a colt and being greeted by *Hosannas* echoes Zech. 9:9. Jesus' "cleansing" of the Temple echoes the purification of the Temple in Zech 14:21. Jesus' words at the Last Supper echo Zech 9:11. Jesus' crucifixion scene, where the inhabitants of Jerusalem "look on the one whom they have pierced," echoes Zech 12:10. Ps. 22 is repeated almost verbatim in the Markan narrative.[125] The speaker describes himself as "reviled by human beings and considered as nothing by people,"[126] and notes that "they divided up my clothes among themselves, and for my clothing they threw lots?"[127] In Mark, Jesus' final words on the cross are a quotation from the first verse of Ps. 22 ("My God, My God, why have you forsaken me?"), while in Luke, they are a quotation from Ps. 31.[128] Why are Jesus' last words in Mark different in Luke and John? Was Ps. 22 a prophecy fulfilled or a scriptural passage that made sense of Jesus' death "according to the scriptures?" Few scholars argue that Mark *invented* the story of Jesus' death; yet few also deny that Mark has literarily *crafted* a passion *narrative*.[129] What this means is that *post*-Easter understandings of Jesus and his death have been projected onto Jesus' ministry, with the result being that we tend to view the Jesus of history refracted through the lens of later theological convictions.

---

[123] Douglas Hedley, *Sacrifice Imagined: Violence, Atonement and the Sacred* (New York/London: Continuum, 2011), 7.

[124] Zech. 9–14; Zech. 13:7.

[125] Ps. 22:9; cf. Mark 27:43.

[126] Ps. 22:9; cf. Mark 15:29, 32; Matt. 27:39, 44.

[127] Ps. 22:19; cf. John 19:24.

[128] Ps. 31:5.

[129] Marcus, "The Old Testament and the Death of Jesus," 212.

Different Christians developed different views about Jesus' death, ranging from it being seen as accidental or unintended,[130] the fulfillment of the suffering son of man, the eschatological fulfillment of the Suffering Servant of Isaiah 53,[131] the fate of a prophet,[132] or a kind of Maccabean martyrdom.[133] The Maccabean martyrs are described as suffering a death that "atones."[134] 4 Macc 17:22 uses a number of terms associated with Lev. 16–17, that is, with the Day of

[130] Johannes Weiss, *Die Predigt Jesu vom Reiche Gottes* (1892; F. Hahn; 3rd edn.; Göttingen: Vandenhoeck & Ruprecht, 1964); Albert Schweitzer, *The Quest for the Historical Jesus: A Critical Study of its Progress from Reimarus to Wrede* (trans. W. Montgomery; London: Adam and Charles Black, 1910); Dale C. Allison, *Jesus of Nazareth: Millenarian Prophet* (Minneapolis: Fortress, 1999).

[131] Dodd, *The Parables of the Kingdom*, 57–60; *The Founder of Christianity* (London: Collins, 1971), 103–10; Vincent Taylor, *Jesus and His Sacrifice* (London: Macmillan, 1955); T. W. Manson, *Jesus the Messiah* (London: Hodder & Stoughton, 1943); *The Servant-Messiah* (Cambridge University Press, 1953); W. Wheeler Robinson, *Corporate Personality in Ancient Israel* (Philadelphia: Fortress, 1980); *The Cross in the Old Testament* (Philadelphia: Westminster, 1955); R. H. Fuller, *The Mission and Achievement of Jesus* (SBT 12; London: SCM, 1954); Meyer, *The Aims of Jesus*; Martin Hengel, "Der stellvertrentende Sühnetod Jesu. Ein Beitrag zur Entstehung des urchristlichen Kerygmas," *IKZ*, 9 (1980), 1–25, 135–47; Peter Stuhlmacher, *Reconciliation, Law, and Righteousness* (trans. E. Kalin; Philadelphia: Fortress, 1986), 16–29; "Jes 53 in den Evangelien und in der Apostelgeschichte," in B. Janowski and P. Stuhlmacher (eds.), *Der leidende Gottesknecht. Jesaja 53 und seine Wirkungsgeschichte* (Tübingen: Mohr Siebeck, 1996), 93–105; Otto Betz, "Jesus and Isaiah 53," in William H. Bellinger and William R. Farmer (eds.), *Jesus and the Suffering Servant: Isaiah 53 and Christian Origins* (Eugene: Wipf and Stock, 2009), 70–87; N. T. Wright, "The Servant and Jesus: The Relevance of the Colloquy for the Current Quest for Jesus," in W. H. Bellinger, Jr. and W. R. Farmer (eds.), *Jesus and the Suffering Servant: Isaiah 53 and Christian Origins* (Harrisburg: Trinity Press International, 1998), 281–97; G. B. Caird, *New Testament Theology* (Oxford: Clarendon, 1994); Moo, *The Old Testament in the Gospel*.

[132] Eduard Schweizer, *Lordship and Discipleship* (London: SCM, 1960), 22–41; Sanders, *Jesus and Judaism*; Jürgen Becker, *Jesus of Nazareth* (trans. J. E. Couch; New York: Walter de Gruyter, 1998), 327–42; Marinus de Jonge, *God's Final Envoy* (Grand Rapids: Eerdmans, 1998), 12–33; Luz, "Warum zog Jesus nach Jerusalem?" 409–27.

[133] 2 Macc. 7:37–38; 4 Macc. 6:27–29; 17:22; 18:4. See G. W. H. Lampe, "Martyrdom and Inspiration," in W. Horbury (ed.), *Suffering and Martyrdom in the New Testament* (Cambridge University Press, 1981), 118–35; D. Daube, "Death as Release in the Bible," *NovT*, 5 (1962), 82–104; D. W. Palmer, "To Die is Gain," *NovT*, 17 (1975), 203–18.

[134] Davies, "Did Jesus Die as a Martyr-Prophet?" 19–30. See esp. Marinus de Jonge, "Jesus' Death for Others and the Death of the Maccabean Martyrs," in T. Baarda, et al. (eds.), *Text and Testimony: Essays on the New Testament and Apocryphal Literature in Honour of A. F. J. Klijn* (Kampen: Kok, 1988), 146–7.

Atonement (ἱλαστήριον, αἷμα, and ἀντίψυχον). The martyr's death is associated with sacrifice, substitution, purification, atonement, and blood.[135] James Dunn has suggested that in the Diaspora the death of martyrs came to have an atoning significance in lieu of the Temple's sacrifices.[136] Yet the cultic terms employed in 4 Macc. are used in a *non*-cultic situation and context, that is, metaphorically.[137] There is no reference to sacrifice or the Temple in the text. The martyr's death assuages God's wrath against Israel,[138] so the martyr's endurance served as an ἱλαστήριον, an ideal example for other fellow Jews to follow. A further problem is that the Maccabean literature is itself dependent on Isaiah 53: the idea that a righteous person's suffering and death *atones* for the sins of others. Yet the Maccabean martyrs admit that they are dying for their *own* sins.[139] In Paul's thought, Jesus does not die for his own sins but "for" others. The Maccabean martyrs die "for the *law*,"[140] or "because of our [their] own sins,"[141] not as a redemptive act for others.

Most biblical scholars would agree that Jesus probably anticipated a premature death, saw himself as participating in the restoration of Israel, may have associated his own death with the fate of the prophets,[142] and expected a postmortem vindication, but this is where the general consensus breaks down. At first sight, it might seem incredible that anyone would have concluded that Jesus' brutal death was a *sacrifice*. Animal sacrifices were *unwilling* victims, but Jesus' death was voluntary. Sacrifices were conducted in the Temple, but Jesus' death took place on a cursed Roman cross. Sacrifices were offered by pilgrims, but Jesus was crucified by the Romans. Sacrifices were supposed to be pure and unblemished, but Jesus was scourged and badly beaten. Nonetheless, within the very first generation of Jesus' followers, the sacrificial metaphor became the dominant interpretive lens through which two millennia of Christians subsequently

---

[135] See Seeley, *The Noble Death*, 19–27, 83–112; Pobee, *Persecution and Martyrdom*, 61–3.

[136] See James D. G. Dunn, "Paul's Understanding of the Death of Jesus," in R. Banks (ed.), *Reconciliation and Hope: New Testament Essays on Atonement and Eschatology* (Exeter: Paternoster, 1974), 131–2.

[137] See Williams, *Jesus' Death*, 179–82.

[138] 2 Macc. 7:32–38. .

[139] 2 Macc. 7:32; 7:18.

[140] 2 Macc. 6:28; 7:9, 37.

[141] 2 Macc 7:18, 32.

[142] 1QS 5.6, 9.4–5; Pseudo-Philo, *Bib. Ant.* 18:5.

viewed Jesus' life *and* death. This view of Jesus' death in terms of sacrificial worship is now often assumed to be synonymous with "the Gospel."

Jesus' death in the New Testament is identified as a *willing* sacrifice: Jesus died because he believed it was the will of God and God required blood sacrifice in order to forgive sin or appease his own "wrath" (ὀργή).[143] In its most well-known form, the scriptural logic of penal substitution holds that the penalty or "wages" of sin is death.[144] Sinners deserve eternal punishment in hell and deserve God's wrath.[145] God, therefore, sent his Son Jesus to die on the cross to satisfy God's justice and bear the punishment of "our sins." Jesus offered himself up willingly, dying in our place,[146] and suffered the punishment "we" deserve(d). Jesus' purpose in this soteriological system is to "save" his followers from the suffering and death of the Torah's curses and the wrath of God. Jesus' death is a kind of Passover lamb; his spilled blood saves his people from the spirit of death, as in the biblical Exodus.[147] Ultimately, Jesus' efficacious act of atonement renders the Jewish sacrificial system superfluous, inefficacious, and irrelevant.[148] God accepted Jesus' sacrifice as the punishment meant "for us." Jesus' death thus put an end to the need for Temple sacrifices and/or replaced the sacrificial system.

Serious ethical and theological concerns have been registered with this model of atonement.[149] The portrayal of God as one who requires the violent death of His only Son for the sins of humankind is surely a disturbing image.[150] Whether or not we call this

---

[143] McKnight, *Jesus and His Death*, 142–3.

[144] Rom. 6:23.

[145] Rom. 1:18.

[146] 2 Cor. 5:21.

[147] Zachhuber, "Modern Discourse on Sacrifice," 20. Hedley, *Sacrifice Imagined*, 109–10, 128–30, argues that Christ represents "willing self-sacrifice" or self-renunciation.

[148] Pitre, *Jesus, the Tribulation*, 517. See also Dunn, *Jesus Remembered*, 824; Wright, *Jesus and the Victory of God*, 591–603; C. Marvin Pate and Douglas W. Kennard, *Deliverance Now and Not Yet: The New Testament and the Great Tribulation* (SBL 54; New York: Peter Lang, 2005).

[149] Green and Baker, *Recovering the Scandal*; Tom Stuckey, *The Wrath of God Satisfied?: Atonement in an Age of Violence* (Eugene: Wipf and Stock, 2012); Finlan, *Problems*, 112.

[150] See J. Sanders (ed.), *Atonement and Violence: A Theological Conversation* (Nashville: Abingdon, 2006); J. C. Brown and C. R. Bohn (eds.), *Christianity, Patriarchy, and Abuse: A Feminist Critique* (New York: Pilgrim, 1989).

substitutionary atonement, penal substitution, or satisfaction theory,
the idea that Jesus bore the wrath of God in our place has been a central tenet in Post-Reformation Protestantism and remains so among
many conservative Evangelical and Fundamentalist Christians. Put
simply, *substitutionary* atonement theology holds that humanity is
inherently sinful and deserves God's divine punishment: God wants
to forgive humanity, but requires a payment. This payment traditionally came through the sacrificial system. Our collective sin, however,
is so great that the sacrifice needed to be "perfect" and "unblemished," and since only a divine being could fulfill this function, God's
Son needed to take the punishment in our place, on our behalf, in
order to satisfy God: Jesus died "for us," paying the debt we owed
to God. While this model of atonement commands the allegiance of
many faithful Christians, it is actually based on a *medieval* notion of
debt-satisfaction in which Jesus' death is envisioned as a *payment* for
the sin-debt incurred by humanity.[151]

The idea that God requires blood sacrifice in order to forgive
human sin and that Jesus needed to *take our place* may not be the
earliest view of Jesus' death. Another view represented Jesus as victorious over the forces of evil.[152] Jesus defeated Satan by withstanding
the temptations to misuse his powers and healing diseases "by the
finger of God."[153] Finally, he defeated Satan on the cross, triumphing
over the powers of darkness. In Col. 2:13–15, "Paul" describe Jesus'
death as a *victory* over evil:

> erasing the record that stood against us with its legal
> demands. He set this aside, nailing it to the cross. He dis-
> armed the rulers and authorities and made a public example
> of them, triumphing over them in it.

This theory, often described as the Christus Victor model – where
Jesus overcomes the "powers" of the Devil, sin, and death that had
enslaved humanity since the fall of Adam – was held by Irenaeus,
Origen, and Augustine. Early Christians believed that Jesus' death
was orchestrated by Satanic powers, but this diabolical plan back-
fired when Jesus defeated those very "powers" by dying and rising

[151] Anselm, *Cur Deus Homo?* S. N. Deane, *St. Anselm: Basic Writings* (LaSalle: Open Court, 1962).
[152] Gustaf Aulén, *Christus Victor: An Historical Study of the Three Main Types of the Idea of Atonement* (trans. A. G. Herber; New York: Macmillan, 1969 [1931]), 4–5.
[153] Q 11:20.

from the grave. The theme of Jesus' cosmic victory over the "rulers" and "powers" of this world and age is ubiquitous throughout the New Testament from Q through the book of Revelation.

In Q, Jesus rejects the devil's offer of "all the kingdoms of this world."[154] For Paul, Jesus "set us free from the present evil age."[155] We "*were* enslaved to the elemental spirits of the world,"[156] but the creation will soon be set free from its "bondage of decay."[157] The "rulers of this age" are "doomed to perish."[158] Jesus has "put all his enemies under his feet."[159] According to the author of Luke-Acts, Jesus is "stronger" than the "strong man" and healed "all who were oppressed by the devil."[160] For the author of John, the "ruler of this world will now be driven out."[161] For the author of 1 John, Jesus' followers "have conquered the evil one" because Jesus came to "destroy the works of the devil."[162] Similarly, for the author of Hebrews, Jesus came to "destroy the one who has the power of death ... and free those who all their lives were held in slavery by the fear of death."[163] The author of Colossians asserts that Jesus "rescued us from the power of darkness."[164] He is "the head of every ruler and authority," "triumphing over them."[165] The author of Ephesians claims that Jesus "has put all things under his feet" although we struggle against "the rulers, against the authorities, against the cosmic powers of this present darkness, against the spiritual forces of evil in the heavenly places."[166] Nonetheless, Jesus is in heaven "with angels, authorities, and powers made subject to him," having freed us "from the snare of the devil, having been held captive by him."[167] This inventory of New Testament references illustrates that the theme of a cosmic battle between Jesus and the

---

[154] Q 4.
[155] Gal 1:4.
[156] Gal 4:3.
[157] Rom 8:19–22.
[158] 1 Cor 2:6.
[159] 1 Cor 5:25.
[160] Luke 11:21–22; Acts 10:38.
[161] John 12:31.
[162] 1 John 2:13–14; 3:8.
[163] Heb 2:14–15.
[164] Col 1:13.
[165] Col 2:10; 2:15.
[166] Eph 1:22; 6:12.
[167] 1 Pet 3:21–22; 2 Tim 2:26.

devil – a battle resulting in Jesus' victory over Satanic forces – is a dominant motif in the tradition.

According to the Christus Victor model, Jesus' death was also understood as a *ransom*-payment liberating humanity from sin and death. The Gospel of Mark explicitly uses the term "ransom" to refer to Jesus' death: he is the suffering son of man who "must" die at the hands of the religious authorities:

> For the son of man did not come (ἦλθεν) to be served, but to serve, and to give his life *a ransom for many*.[168]
> This is my blood of the covenant, which is poured out *for many* (ὑπὲρ πολλῶν).[169]

These two passages – the "words of institution" and the "ransom" saying – appear to be influenced by the Suffering Servant of Isaiah 53 who also surrenders his life "for many."[170] Mark 10:45 may have originated as an independent saying,[171] but it is frequently seen as betraying *Pauline* influence,[172] and having little to no claim to authenticity.[173] Here the Greek term for ransom (λύτρον) refers to the money used to release slaves,[174] a payment made to a hostage power,[175] the Greek equivalent of the Hebrew terms "ransom" (פדה) or "redeem" (גאל), referring to the release or deliverance from punishment, slavery, debt, guilt, sin, or death.[176] 1 Tim. 2:5–6 echoes the theme:

> Christ Jesus ... gave himself *a ransom for all* (ἀντίλυτρον ὑπὲρ πάντων).[177]

---

[168] Mark 10:45.

[169] Mark 14:24.

[170] Mark 14:24; 10:45. See Watts, "Jesus' Death, Isaiah 53, and Mark 10:45: A Crux Revisited," 125–51; Wright, *Jesus and the Victory of God*, 579–91, 605; H. E. Tödt, *The Son of Man in the Synoptic Tradition* (trans. D. M. Barton; Philadelphia: Westminster, 1965), 158–69, 202–211; De Jonge, *Jesus, the Servant Messiah*, 48–50.

[171] Dunn, *Jesus Remembered*, 812–15; Allison, *Jesus of Nazareth*, 54–5; Wright, *Jesus and the Victory of God*, 575, 602.

[172] See especially Nineham, *The Gospel of St. Mark*, 280–1.

[173] Sanders, *Jesus and Judaism*, 332.

[174] Josephus, *A.J.* 14.107, 371; *B.J.* 2.273.

[175] LXX Exod. 21:30; Sir. 29:15; 1 Macc. 2:50.

[176] From punishment, see Num 35:31, 32; Exod 30:12; Hos 7:13. From slavery, see Lev 19:20; 25:48, 49, 51, 52, 54; Exod 21:8. From debt, see Lev 25:25; 27:15, 19, 20, 27, 31. From guilt or sin, see Deut 21:8; Ps 25:22; 26:11; 32:7; 103:4; 130:8. From affliction, see 2 Sam 4:9; 1 Kgs 1:29; Ps 7:2; 31:5; 34:22; 55:18; 59:1; 69:18; 72:14; 118:34, 154; 144:10; Sir 48:20. From death, see Exod 21:30; Num 35:31, 32; Jer 15:21; Lam 3:58; Dan 6:28; Num 3:12, 46, 48, 49, 51; Exod 13:13–15; 34:20; Num 18:15, 17.

[177] See also Tit 2:11–14; Heb 9:11–15; 1 Pet 1:17–19; *Ep. Barn.* 14:5–6; *Diogn.* 9:2–3.

The Markan Jesus does *not* tell us what or who the "many" are ransomed from, but Paul tells us that Jesus "redeemed us from the curse of the law" and that this redemption was for the justification of sinners.[178] Several New Testament letters tell us that we have been ransomed from "all iniquity," from "the transgressions under the first covenant" and "the futile ways inherited from your fathers."[179] The problem with identifying Jesus' death as a "ransom," however, is that it is not clear who *receives* the "ransom." The ransom seems to have been made payable to *Satan*.[180] But the idea that Jesus and God needed to pay off Satan was theologically problematic, which is why Anselm introduced a new interpretation of the atonement in the eleventh-century: penal substitutionary atonement.[181]

The Christus Victor model may be an earlier view of Jesus' soteriological role, but it only captured certain *aspects* of the New Testament's many references to Jesus' death and atonement. It also left a set of troubling questions that continue to haunt its contemporary interpreters and advocates.[182] Why, for example, if Christ conquered sin, does sin persist? If Christ overcame the Devil, why does the Devil still have his way? How could Christ have defeated the "powers" when they are apparently still very much in "power?" And why does Jesus and/or God need to pay a "ransom" to the Devil in the first place? Why did Jesus have to die at all in order to achieve this so-called "victory?" Why did Jesus have to die *like that*? The Christus Victor model also seems to ignore, or misread, numerous references to Jesus in Paul's letters that describe his death in *substitutionary* terms. Paul repeatedly states that Christ died "for us" so that we could avoid receiving the wrath of God. Paul's many references to Jesus' atoning work do not all conform to the model of Christus Victor. The idea that Jesus died as a blood sacrifice of atonement *in our place* transfers the payment from Satan back to *God*, but raises a new set of disturbing questions. Did God really need Jesus' brutal death in order to forgive the sins of Israel and

---

[178] Gal 3:13; Rom 3:21–26.

[179] Tit 2:11–14; Heb 9:12–15; 1 Pet 1:17–19.

[180] Origen, *In Mattheum*, xvi 8, denies that it can be paid to God.

[181] For the authenticity of the ransom saying, see Bernd Janowski and Peter Stuhlmacher, *Biblische Theologie des Neuen Testaments* (vol. 1 of *Grundlegung von Jesus zu Paulus*; Göttingen: Vandenhoeck & Ruprecht, 1997), 128–9. For its inauthenticity, see Bultmann, *History*.

[182] Gregory A. Boyd, "Christus Victor View," in J. Beilby and P. R. Eddy (eds.), *The Nature of the Atonement* (Downers Grove: InterVarsity, 2006), 37, n. 23.

humanity? Did Jesus' death – as an efficacious blood sacrifice – render the Temple irrelevant? The idea that Jesus conquered death by dying still seems to be something of a scriptural riddle. These disturbing questions about Jesus' death require careful reexaminations of the fundamental historical and theological assumptions of early Christianity.

Conclusion

Did the Jesus of history think he would die "for our sins?" This does not seem very likely. Paul may have received this "tradition" from the Jerusalem leadership, but there is no way to confirm this, especially when Paul seems to have further developed the sacrificial interpretation of Jesus' death to such an extent that it rendered the sacrificial system in Jerusalem obsolete.[183]

Second, the idea of eating human flesh or drinking human blood is forbidden in both the Torah and the Jerusalem decree described in Acts 15.[184] This is antithetical to Jewish thought, law, and practice. It is not surprising that many scholars think that the idea of drinking Jesus' blood emerged in a pagan context.[185] Others hold that the Eucharist is modeled after Hellenistic customs of celebrating a memorial meal or drinking a cup in honor of a god.

Third, the Synoptics adopt the Pauline view of the Last Supper but the Gospel of John does not. In the Gospel of John, Jesus' "last supper" is not a Passover meal. Rather, it is a simple Jewish meal after which Jesus washes his disciples' feet as an example of how a Master must be a servant.

Fourth, the idea that Jesus sought to substitute his body and blood as efficacious sacrificial atonement offerings in order to replace the Temple sacrifices suggests that he thought the Temple sacrifices were no longer efficacious.[186] Did Jesus practice animal sacrifice in the Temple *and* simultaneously replace it with his death? The Christian theological tradition ultimately came to hold that Jesus *replaced* the Temple's sacrificial system – and thus abrogated a central part of the

---

[183] For Paul's critique, see 1 Cor. 15:35; Rom. 1:3–4; 3:25–26; 4:24–25; 10:8–9; 2 Cor. 5:21.

[184] Gen 9:4; Lev 3:17; 7:26–27; 17:10–16; *Jub* 21:17–20.

[185] See Funk and Seminar, *The Acts of Jesus*, 139–42.

[186] Chilton, *The Temple of Jesus; A Feast of Meanings*.

law or Torah – in and through his death. This supersessionistic tradition should not be traced back to Jesus.

Fifth, the Torah neither allows nor requires human sacrifice; in fact, God condemns human sacrifice. How could Jesus – whether as a human being or as the Son of God – be a divinely mandated or *halakhically* permitted sacrifice?

Sixth, the Torah does not require blood sacrifice for the forgiveness of sins.[187] The forgiveness of sins can also be mediated and attained by sincere prayer.

Seventh, the Torah does not allow one human being to die for another.[188]

Eighth, the identification of Jesus as a blood sacrifice portrays God as vengeful and punishing, a God virtually antithetical to Jesus' loving, forgiving, and compassionate God. There *are* Second Temple traditions that develop the theme of vicarious atonement (2 Macc.), but they are not in the Torah.

Ninth, the Suffering Servant of Isaiah is never identified as anointed, or a messianic figure, let alone a Davidic king, in the pre-Christian Jewish tradition. There is no suffering-and-dying messiah in pre-Christian Judaism. On the contrary, Isaiah's Servant *is* explicitly and repeatedly described as the collective nation of *Israel.*

Tenth, a number of Jewish and Jewish Christian texts and traditions do not attach any sacrificial significance to Jesus' death or last supper. The Essene texts from Qumran, for example, refer to a "messianic banquet" with the royal messiah blessing bread and wine, but the royal messiah does not die a salvific death nor identify his body and blood with the bread and wine. Q, our earliest source, is aware of Jesus' death, but does not attribute atoning significance to it.[189] Q calls for uncompromising conviction in the face of death, but Jesus' death does not save us from sin.[190] It is an inspiring example of courage and fortitude to be imitated.[191] Q does not contain a

---

[187] Lev 5:11–13; Num 16:47; Num 31:50; Hos 6:6; Isa 6:6–7; Mic 6:6; Ps 51:16–17; Ps. 40:6; Job 33:26; Jonah 3:10.

[188] Exod. 32:30–35; Deut. 24:16; Ezek. 18:20; Jer. 31:29–30). For the origin(s) of the idea of vicarious atonement, see Isa. 50–53, 2 Macc. 6.30, 7.9, 11, 14, 16–17, 22–23, 29, 30–38; 4 Macc. 6:27–29; 17:21–22; Pseudo-Philo, *Liber Ant. Bib.* 18:5, 35:3; *Test. of Moses* 9:7; Josephus, *A.J.* 11.169; 12.255–256.

[189] Q 14:27.

[190] Kloppenborg Verbin, *Excavating Q*, 370.

[191] Ibid., 242.

narrative of Jesus' crucifixion, prediction sayings of his death, or *any* passages in which Jesus announces his death as having saving significance. Jesus' death in Q is that of a rejected prophet; it is not an *atoning* death. Similarly, the *Didache* does not identify the bread and wine with Jesus' body and blood, nor with his salvific death. [192] The wine was associated with the "holy vine of David," with Jesus as the "Branch," and the bread symbolized a thanksgiving (εὐχαριστία) for the life and knowledge of Jesus. There is no reference to this being a Passover meal or any reference to the "sacrificial" death of Jesus. It has been suggested that the *Didache* represents an earlier, simpler nonsacrificial version of the Last Supper meal,[193] an early form of the Eucharist as a nonsacrificial commemorative thanksgiving meal held in honor of Jesus.[194] Did Paul (or his immediate predecessors) transform this meal by mixing metaphors and *innovating* a preexisting ritual practice? We don't know. The *Didache* meal may be a vestige of an early form of the Eucharist,[195] but it may also reflect a subsequent, derivative practice. Alternatively, it may have accidentally omitted the sacrificial elements described by Paul.

Jesus may have shared a "last supper" with his disciples, anticipated his imminent death, and referred to it during the meal; but it is unlikely that he directly identified his death as a blood sacrifice or identified the meal's bread and wine with his body and blood. The most likely explanation for the origin of the Eucharist is a post-Easter commemorative meal that rapidly developed into a ritual cultic-meal of mystical communion with Jesus.

[192] The *Didache* may represent an earlier, simpler nonsacrificial version of the Last Supper. See Johannes Betz, "Eucharist in the Didache," in J. A. Draper (ed.), *The Didache in Modern Research* (Leiden: Brill, 1996), 244–75. For the development of the tradition, see Willi Marxsen, *The Lord's Supper As a Christological Problem* (trans. L. Nieting; Philadelphia: Fortress, 1970); "The Meals of Jesus and the Lord's Supper of the Church," in *Jesus and the Church* (trans. P. I. Devenish; New York: Trinity, 1992), 137–46.

[193] Betz, "Eucharist in the Didache," 244–75; Mazza, "Didache 9–10: Elements of a Eucharistic Interpretation," 276–99; Crossan, *The Historical Jesus*, 360–7.

[194] See K. G. Kuhn, "The Last Supper and the Communal Meal of Qumran," in *The Scrolls and the New Testament* (London: SCM, 1958), 65–93; Theissen and Merz, *The Historical Jesus*, 412–13; Heinz-Wolfgang Kuhn, "The Qumran Meal and the Lord's Supper in Paul in the Context of the Graeco-Roman World," in A. Christophersen (ed.), *Paul, Luke and the Graeco-Roman World: Essays in Honour of Alexander J. M. Wedderburn* (JSNTSup 217; London: Sheffield Academic Press, 2002), 229.

[195] Marxsen, *The Lord's Supper*; "The Meals of Jesus and the Lord's Supper of the Church," 137–46; Riggs, "From Gracious Table," 83–101; "The Sacred Food of Didache 9–10," 256–83.

Our earliest evidence for the sacrificial identification of Jesus' death is Paul, but the concept of vicarious atonement is alien to and forbidden in the Torah and Isaiah 53 is not a messianic prophecy. Paul certainly appealed to and utilized the vocabulary of sacrifice, but his primary purpose was communicating the concept of Jesus' vicarious atonement to Gentiles, not Jews.[196] Paul drew on the symbolic system of sacrificial atonement in the Greco-Roman world (in the Diaspora) and attempted to graft the two systems together into a new soteriological synthesis, crossing the cultural boundaries of Greco-Roman religious ideology and Israelite sacrificial practice in order to construct an atonement theology based on biblical and sacrificial cultic metaphors.[197]

The sacrificial motif worked very well for Gentile communities, but Paul's theology and Christology also implied the replacement or substitution of the Torah and Temple with Christ and his sacrifice, and this radical solution did not appeal to his Jewish contemporaries. Paul's mission may have been an astounding success with Gentiles, but it resulted in failure, as he himself admits, among his own people.[198] The Gentile Christian response to Judaism, the Torah, and the Temple grew increasingly defensive, protective of Paul, apologetic in his defense, and, ultimately, hostile and aggressive in its rejection of Jewish Christianity.

Jesus' followers believed that he *reconciled* humanity and God. Jesus' death was an event of cosmic proportions to his followers who regarded it as the climax of his life, ministry, and teaching, the eschatological fulfillment of the "new creation" promised by the prophets. The life, example, and "faith of Jesus" (ἐκ πίστεως Ἰησοῦ) became the divine model to imitate.[199] We can hardly fault Paul for affirming these common conclusions with his Jewish Christian colleagues.[200] While many Christians today might feel threatened or disturbed by the potential loss of traditional penal substitutionary atonement theology,[201] Jesus' death can indeed be described as a "sacrifice" in so

---

[196] Hengel, *The Atonement*, 28–9.

[197] See Finlan, *Problems with Atonement*, 84–113; *Options on Atonement*.

[198] Rom. 9:32; 11:7, 11, 25.

[199] For the "faith *of* Christ" (πίστις Χριστοῦ) see Rom. 3:21–22; Gal. 2:16; 2:20; Phil. 3:9. On the subjective/objective genitive debate, see Richard B. Hays, *The Faith of Jesus Christ: The Narrative Substructure of Galatians 3:1–4:11* (BRS; Grand Rapids: Eerdmans, 2002); Matthew C. Easter, "The *Pistis Christou* Debate: Main Arguments and Responses in Summary," *CBR*, 9.1 (2010), 33–47.

[200] Rom. 3:26.

[201] Young, *Sacrifice and the Death of Christ*, 110.

far as he offered his life to God. In other words, we can retain the concept, language, and vocabulary of sacrifice – a vocabulary fundamental to the religious impulse, whether described and performed as prayer, thanksgiving, praise, purification, renunciation, or reconciliation – without concluding that Jesus' death was a *blood*-sacrifice *required* by God that *replaced* the Temple sacrifices or served as a *ransom*-payment to the Devil. If anything, the historical and theological problems of atonement theory might yet urge us now to reconsider the historical and theological significance of the *incarnation* of Jesus' *teachings* in a life lived and a faith forged in following an inspiring, divine vision even unto death.

SUMMARY AND CONCLUSION

This study began with the claim that Jesus' death might best be understood in light of his relationship to the two dominant cultural institutions of Early Judaism: the Torah and the Temple. The immediate problem with this claim is that our sources contain conflicting views of these relationships: Jesus is reported to have both affirmed and challenged these institutions. Building on recent Third Quest research into the Jewishness of Jesus, I have argued here that the Jesus movement can best be located within a spectrum of Early Jewish eschatological expectations that were variously enacted by different individuals, movements, and communities. The emergence of Jewish sectarianism in the Hasmonean period gave rise to a number of expressions of dissatisfaction with the Temple's administration. At the same time, the Enochic *Animal Apocalypse*, the book of *Jubilees*, the Qumran corpus, and Ben Sira all attest to a significant interest both in eschatological restoration and the law or Torah of creation, whether expressed in *Urzeit/Endzeit* paradigms or the idea of "heavenly tablets" supplementing, complementing, and sometimes correcting, Mosaic revelation.

The emergence of the early Jesus movement within this cultural milieu solves a number of pressing problems in the study of early Christian origins. Jesus' association with John the Baptist and his heightened sense of eschatological realization testify to this association. The most distinctive characteristic of Jesus' teaching career seems to have been his emphasis on the "kingdom of God." There is good reason to understand this expression as a metaphor representing the divinely realized will of God active in and through Jesus' ministry. There is also good reason to think that the distinctive hermeneutic Jesus applied to the Torah was one of eschatological restoration based on an appeal or argument to the law or Torah of creation, the best example being Jesus' saying on divorce.

The New Testament Gospels contain many conflict stories centered on Jesus' relationship(s) with his contemporaries. It seems reasonable to conclude that Jesus' teachings generated conflict, and that the force of Jesus' personal religious convictions and authority was sufficient both to attract followers and challenge opponents. While the New Testament Gospels are in virtual agreement that the Temple incident led to Jesus' death, they do not isolate the particular offense that led to Jesus' arrest, trial, and conviction, although they strongly suggest that Jesus criticized the Temple cult and predicted the Temple's destruction. After a careful survey of our sources, I have argued that Jesus' offense was challenging the soteriological efficacy, ethics, and violence of blood and animal sacrifice. Consequently, it is incorrect to charge Jesus with condemning the Torah, or the Temple in so far as these institutions could be purified and reformed to reflect *eschatological* ideals. Jesus' critique of the Temple cult was not a negative campaign against a central institution within Judaism, but a positive call for the restoration and transformation of that institution. The Mosaic Law was not upholding God's original law of creation; hence it was to be modified. The sacrificial rites were not originally intended by God, so they were no longer desirable or required. It is these kinds of ideological offenses that resulted in Jesus' politico-religious execution. Moreover, we find ancient support for our proposal in multiple "Jewish Christian" traditions consistent with an Early Jewish hermeneutic of creation.

The writings of the New Testament reflect the transformation of the early Jewish Jesus movement in its expansion throughout the Roman empire. The letters of Paul, in particular, had a significant influence on the composition of the Gospels, and Paul's identification of Jesus as a "sacrifice" – a tradition "received" from those who were "in Christ" before him – became the central symbol of Jesus' life and death. Sacrifice was a near-ubiquitous phenomenon in the ancient world and Paul's missionary efforts translated this cultural institution from Judaism into his new communities by utilizing a complex combination of sacrificial ideas and motifs. Sacrifice became the dominant symbol of Jesus' soteriological function and led to the innovative construction of the "Suffering Servant-Messiah" as a scripturally informed response to the scandal of the cross. The association of Jesus' blood – spilled during Passover – with the blood of the Passover lamb introduced further ideas into a rapidly developing tradition that would ultimately become traditional Christian replacement-theology.

The identification of Jesus as *savior*, once introduced to Gentile communities recognizable as voluntary associations centered on sacred meals and participatory identification with a deity, rapidly changed the constitution and ideological focus of the movement. Once Jesus' death was envisioned as an atoning sacrifice within the eschatological temple-community of the new covenant, it was ritually commemorated and inscribed in the passion narratives. The authors of the Gospels constructed biographical and historiographical accounts of Jesus' life culminating in the cross. As a result, the historical Jesus' criticism of blood/animal sacrifice was muted into ambivalent and ambiguous prioritizations of "mercy" over sacrifice alongside Jesus' alleged condemnation of the Temple and prediction of its destruction. The New Testament does not preserve Jesus' rejection of blood sacrifice because its authors identified Jesus *as* a blood sacrifice. The Gospels narrate the events that led to Jesus' death in order to proclaim and defend the sacrificial interpretation of Jesus' death. In this process, the historical circumstances, characters, and conflicts that led to Jesus' death were re-imagined as part of a cosmic drama, with Pilate re-described as the reluctant governor and Caiaphas and "the Jews" as bloodthirsty villians. The Gospels proclaimed the "good news" of Jesus' atoning death and resurrection, but they also subordinated Jesus' teachings and example as a faithful witness (martyr) to the kingdom of God – the original referent of "following Jesus" – to secondary status. After the destruction of the Temple in 70 CE, the Palestinian Jewish Jesus movement lost its authoritative center while Paul's Gentile communities came to see themselves as the new "spiritual Israel" replacing Israel "according to the flesh." A Jewish movement that once included Gentiles became a Gentile movement that excluded Jews. "Jesus" became known as one whose ministry abolished the Torah, destroyed the Temple, and transferred the covenantal promises from Jews to Christians, not the man who "sacrificed" his life by dedicating it to God, the man who lived and died for his vision of a redeemed Israel living according to the original Torah of creation.

BIBLIOGRAPHY

Abrahams, Israel 1917. *Studies in Pharisaism and the Gospels*. Cambridge University Press.

Adams, Rebecca 2000. "Loving Mimesis and Girard's "Scapegoat of the Text": A Creative Reassessment of Mimetic Desire," in Willar M. Swartley (ed.), *Violence Renounced: René Girard, Biblical Studies, and Peacemaking*. Studies in Peace and Scripture 4. Telford: Pandora Press, 277–307.

Ådna, Jostein 1999. "Jesus' Symbolic Act in the Temple (Mark 11:15–17): The Replacement of the Sacrificial Cult by his Atoning Death," in B. Ego, A. Lange, and P. Pilhofer (eds.), *Gemeinde ohne Tempel: Zur Substituierung und Transformation des Jerusalemer Tempels und seines Kults im Alten Testament, antiken Judentum und frühen Christentum*. Wissenschaftliche Untersuchungen zum Neuen Testament 118. Tübingen: Mohr Siebeck, 461–475.

Ådna, Jostein 2000. *Jesu Stellung zum Tempel: die Tempelaktion und das Tempelwort als Ausdruck seiner messianischen Sendung*. Wissenschaftliche Untersuchungen zum Neuen Testament II.119. Tübingen: Mohr Siebeck.

Ådna, Jostein 2011. "Jesus and the Temple," in Tom Holmén (ed.), *Handbook for the Study of the Historical Jesus*. 4 vols. Leiden: Brill, 3: 2635–2675.

Aitken, Ellen Bradshaw 2004. *Jesus' Death in Early Christian Memory: The Poetics of the Passion*. Novum Testamentum et orbis antiquus / Studien zur Umwelt des Neuen Testaments 53. Göttingen: Vandenhoeck and Ruprecht.

Akers, Keith 2000. *The Lost Religion of Jesus: Simple Living and Nonviolence in Early Christianity*. New York: Lantern Books.

Alexander, T. Desmond 2008. *From Eden to the New Jerusalem: An Introduction to Biblical Theology*. Grand Rapids: Kregel.

Alexander, T. Desmond and S. Gathercole (eds.) 2004. *Heaven on Earth: The Temple in Biblical Theology*. Carlisle: Paternoster.

Alexander, Philip S. 1988. "Jewish Law in the Time of Jesus: Towards a Clarification of the Problem," in B. Lindars (ed.), *Law and Religion: Essays on the Place of the Law in Israel and Early Christianity*. Cambridge: James Clarke & Co., 44–58.

Alexander, Philip S. 2007. "Jewish Believers in Early Rabbinic Literature (2nd to 5th Centuries)," in Oskar Skarsaune and Reidar Hvalvik (eds.), *Jewish Believers in Jesus: The Early Centuries*. Peabody: Hendrickson, 659–709.

Alexis-Baker, Andy 2012. "Violence, Nonviolence and the Temple Incident in John 2:13–15," *Biblical Interpretation* 20: 73–96.

Allison, Dale C. 1987. "Jesus and the Covenant: A Response to E.P. Sanders," *Journal for the Study of the New Testament* 29: 57–78.

Allison, Dale C. 1997. *The Jesus Tradition in Q*. Harrisburg: Trinity Press International.

Allison, Dale C. 1999. *Jesus of Nazareth: Millenarian Prophet*. Minneapolis: Fortress.

Allison, Dale C. 2000. *The Intertextual Jesus: Scripture in Q*. Harrisburg: InterVarsity.

Allison, Dale C. 2001. "Q's New Exodus and the Historical Jesus," in A. Lindemann (ed.), *The Sayings Source Q and the Historical Jesus*. Bibliotheca ephemeridum theologicarum lovaniensium 158. Leuven: Peeters, 395–428.

Allison, Dale C. 2002. "John and Jesus: Continuity and Discontinuity," *Journal for the Study of the Historical Jesus* 1.1, 6-27.

Allison, Dale C. 2005. *Resurrecting Jesus: The Earliest Christian Tradition and Its Interpreters*. New York: T & T Clark.

Allison, Dale C. 2010. *Constructing Jesus: Memory, Imagination, and History*. Grand Rapids: Baker Academic.

Alobaidi, Joseph (ed.) 1998. *The Messiah in Isaiah 53: The Commentaries of Saadia Gaon, Salmon ben Yeruham, and Yefer ben Eli on Isaiah 52:13–53:12*. New York: Peter Lang.

Amphoux, C-B. 1995. "L'Évangile selon les Hébreux: Source de L'Évangile de Luc," *Apocrypha* 6: 67–77.

Amsler, Frédéric 2003. "Les Reconnaissances du Pseudo-Clément comme catéchèse romaneque," in D. Marguerat (ed.), *La Bible en récits: L'exégese biblique à l'heure du lecteur*. Geneva: Labor et Fides, 141–167.

Anderson, B. W. (ed.) 1984. *Creation in the Old Testament*. Philadelphia: Fortress.

Anderson, Gary A. 1987. *Sacrifices and Offerings in Ancient Israel: Studies in their Social and Political Importance*. Harvard Semitic Monographs 41. Atlanta: Scholars.

Angel, Joseph L. 2010. *Otherworldly and Eschatological Priesthood in the Dead Sea Scrolls*. Studies on the Texts of the Desert of Judah 86. Leiden: Brill.

Antwi, Daniel J. 1991. "Did Jesus Consider His Death to be an Atoning Sacrifice?" *Interpretation* 45: 17–28.

Arai, S. 1988. "Zum 'Tempelwort' Jesu in Apostelgeschichte 6.14," *New Testament Studies* 34: 397–410.

Arens, E. 1976. *The ΗΛΘΟΝ-Sayings in the Synoptic Tradition*. Orbis Biblicus et orientalis 10. Göttingen: Vandenhoeck & Ruprecht.

Arnal, William E. 2005. *The Symbolic Jesus: Historical Scholarship, Judaism, and the Construction of Contemporary Identity*. London: Equinox.

Astell, Ann W. and Sandor Goodhart (eds.) 2011. "Substitutive Reading: An Introduction to Girardian Thinking, Its Reception in Biblical Studies, and This Volume," in A. W. Astell and S. Goodhart (eds.), *Sacrifice, Scripture, and Substitution: Readings in Ancient Judaism and Christianity*. Christianity and Judaism in Antiquity Series 18. Notre Dame University Press, 1–36.

Attridge, Harold W. 2014. "The Temple and Jesus the High Priest in the New Testament," in J. H. Charlesworth (ed.), *Jesus and the Temple: Textual and Archaeological Explorations*. Minneapolis: Fortress, 213–247.

Aulén, Gustaf 1969 (1931). *Christus Victor: An Historical Study of the Three Main Types of the Idea of Atonement*. Translated by A. G. Herber. New York: Macmillan.

Baarda, T. 1985. "*1 Thess. 2:14–16: Rodrigues in 'Nestle-Aland,'*" *Nederlands theologisch tijdschrift* 39: 186–93.

Badia, Leonard F. 1980. *The Qumran Baptism and John the Baptist's Baptism*. Lanham: University Press of America.

Bailie, Gil 1995. *Violence Unveiled: Humanity at the Crossroads*. New York: Crossroad.

Bammel, E. 1986. "A New Variant Form of the Testimonium Flavianum," in *Judaica*. Wissenschaftliche Untersuchungen zum Neuen Testament 37. Tübingen: Mohr Siebeck, 190–193.

Bandera, Pablo 2007. "Love vs. Resentment: The Absence of Positive Mimesis in Generative Anthropology," *Contagion: Journal of Violence, Mimesis, and Culture* 14: 13–26.

Banks, R. 1975. *Jesus and the Law in the Synoptic Tradition*. Society for New Testament Studies Monograph Series 28. Cambridge: Cambridge University Press.

Baras, Z. 1977. "Testimonium Flavianum: The State of Recent Scholarship," in M. Avi-Yonah and Z. Baras (eds.), *Society and Religion in the Second Temple Period*. The World History of the Jewish People VII. Jerusalem: Massada, 303–313, 378–385.

Barber, Michael Patrick 2013. "Jesus as the Davidic Temple Builder and Peter's Priestly Role in Matthew 16:16–19," *Journal of Biblical Literature* 132.4: 935–953.

Barclay, John and John Sweet (eds.) 1996. *Early Christian Thought in its Jewish Context*. Cambridge: Cambridge University Press.

Bareille, G. 1911. "Elcésaites," *Dictionnaire de théologie catholique* 4/2: 2233–2239.

Barnett, P. 1999. *Jesus and the Rise of Early Christianity: A History of New Testament Times*. Downers Grove: InterVarsity.

Barrett, C. K. 1955. *The Gospel According to St. John*. London: SPCK.

Barstad, Hans M. 1994. "The Future of the 'Servant Songs': Some Reflections on the Relationship of Biblical Scholarship to Its Own Tradition," in *Barr Festschrift*. Oxford: Clarendon, 261–270.

Barth, G. 1961. "Das Gesetzesverständnis des Evangelisten Mätthaus," in G. Bornkamm, G. Barth, and H. J. Held Neukirchern (eds.), *Überlieferung und Auslegung im Matthäusevangelium*. Wissenschaftliche Monographien zum Alten und Neuen Testament 1. Neukirchen-Vluyn: Neukirchener, 54–154.

Barth, G. 1992. *Der Tod Jesu Christi im Verständnis des Neuen Testaments*. Neukirchen-Vluyn: Neukirchener.

Bauckham, Richard 1986. "The Coin in the Fish's Mouth," in D. Wenham and C. Blomberg (eds.), *Gospel Perspectives VI: The Miracles of Jesus*. Sheffield: JSOT, 219–252.

Bauckham, Richard 1988. "Jesus' Demonstration in the Temple," in B. Lindars (ed.), *Law and Religion: Essays on the Place of the Law in Israel and Early Christianity*. Cambridge: James Clarke & Co., 72–89.

Bauckham, Richard 1990. *Jude and the Relatives of Jesus in the Early Church.* Edinburgh: T & T Clark.

Bauckham, Richard 2003. "The Origin of the Ebionites," in Peter J. Tomson and Doris Lambers-Petry (eds.), *The Image of the Judaeo-Christians in Ancient Jewish and Christian Literature.* Wissenschaftliche Untersuchungen zum Neuen Testament 158. Tübingen: Mohr Siebeck, 162–181.

Bauckham, Richard 2006. *Jesus and the Eyewitnesses: The Gospels as Eyewitness Testimony.* Grand Rapids: Eerdmans.

Bauckham, Richard 2011. *Living with Other Creatures: Green Exegesis and Theology.* Waco: Baylor University Press.

Bauer, Walter 1967. "Jesus der Galiläer," in G. Strecker (ed.), *Aufsätze und Kleine Schriften.* Tübingen: Mohr, 91–108.

Baumgarten, Albert I. 1994. "Josephus on Essene Sacrifice," *Journal of Jewish Studies* 45: 169–183.

Baumgarten, Albert I. 1997. *The Flourishing of Jewish Sects in the Maccabean Era: An Interpretation.* Supplements to the Journal for the Study of Judaism 55. Leiden: Brill.

Baumgarten, Albert I. (ed.) 2002. *Sacrifice in Religious Experience.* Studies in the History of Religions 93. Leiden: Brill.

Baumgarten, Joseph M. 1953. "Sacrifice and Worship among the Jewish Sectarians of the Dead (Qumran) Scrolls," *Harvard Theological Review* 46.3: 141–159.

Baumgarten, Joseph M. 1977. "The Essenes and the Temple: A Reappraisal," in *Studies in Qumran Law.* Leiden: Brill, 59–62.

Baumgarten, Joseph M. 1989. "4Q500 and the Ancient Conceptions of the Lord's Vineyard," *Journal of Jewish Studies* 40: 1–6.

Baumgarten, Joseph M. 1990. "The Qumran-Essene Restraints on Marriage," in L. H. Schiffman (ed.), *Archaeology and History in the Dead Sea Scrolls: The New York University Conference in Memory of Yigael Yadin.* Sheffield: Sheffield Academic Press, 13–24.

Baur, F. C. 1838. *Über den Ursprung des Episcopats in der christlichen Kirche.* Tübingen: Ludwig Friedrich Fues.

Baur, F. C. 1860. *Das Christentum und die christliche Kirche der drei ersten Jahrhunderte.* 2nd ed. Tübingen: Ludwig Friedrich Fues.

Beal, Todd S. 1988. *Josephus' Description of the Essenes Illustrated by the Dead Sea Scrolls.* Cambridge: Cambridge University Press.

Beasley-Murray, G. R. 1987. *John.* Word Biblical Commentary 36. Waco: Word Books.

Becker, Adam H. and Annette Yoshiko Reed (eds.) 2003. *The Ways that Never Parted: Jews and Christians in Late Antiquity and the Early Middle Ages.* Texte und Studien zum antiken Judentum 95. Tübingen: Mohr Siebeck.

Becker, Jürgen 1972. *Johannes der Täufer und Jesus von Nazareth.* Biblische Studien (Neukirchen) 63. Neukirchen-Vluyn: Neukirchener.

Becker, Jürgen. *Jesus of Nazareth* 1998. Translated by J. E. Couch. New York: Walter de Gruyter.

Beckwith, Roger T. 1988. "The Vegetarianism of the Therapeutae, and the Motives for Vegetarianism in Early Jewish and Christian Circles," *Revue de Qumran* 13: 407–410.

Beckwith, Roger T. and Martin Selman 1995. *Sacrifice in the Bible*. Grand Rapids: Baker Book House.

Beily, J. and P. R. Eddy (eds.) 2006. *The Nature of the Atonement*. Downers Grove: InterVarsity.

Bellinger, Jr., W. H. and W. R. Farmer 1998. *Jesus and the Suffering Servant*. Harrisburg: Trinity Press International.

Berger, K. 1972. *Die Gesetzesauslegung Jesu. Ihr historischer Hintergrund im Judentum und im Alten Testament. Teil I: Markus und Parallelen*. Wissenschaftliche Monographien zum Alten und Neuen Testament 40. Neukirchener-Vluyn: Neukirchener.

Berman, Saul J. 1975. "Lifnim Mishurat Hadin," *Journal of Jewish Studies* 26: 86–104.

Berman, Saul J. 1977. "Lifnim Mishurat Hadin," *Journal of Jewish Studies* 28: 181–193.

Bernard, John Henry 1928. *A Critical and Exegetical Commentary on the Gospel According to St. John*. 2 vols. Edinburgh: T & T Clark.

Bertrand, D. A. 1980. "L'Evangile des Ebionites: une harmonie évangélique antérieure au Diatessaron," *New Testament Studies* 26: 548–563.

Betz, Hans Dieter 1995. *The Sermon on the Mount*. Minneapolis: Fortress.

Betz, Hans Dieter 1997. "Jesus and the Purity of the Temple (Mark 11:15–18): A Comparative Religion Approach," *Journal of Biblical Literature* 116: 455–472.

Betz, Johannes 1996. "Eucharist in the Didache," in J. A. Draper (ed.), *The Didache in Modern Research*. Leiden: Brill, 244–275.

Betz, Otto 2009. "Jesus and Isaiah 53," in William H. Bellinger and William R. Farmer (eds.), *Jesus and the Suffering Servant: Isaiah 53 and Christian Origins*. Eugene: Wipf and Stock, 70–87.

Bickerman, Elias J. 1947. "The Warning Inscriptions of Herod's Temple," *The Jewish Quarterly Review* 37.4: 387–405.

Black, Matthew 1985. *The Book of Enoch or 1 Enoch: A New English Edition with Commentary and Textual Notes*. Studia in Veteris Testamenti pseudepigraphica 7. Leiden: Brill.

Blomberg, C. L. 1986. "The Law in Luke-Acts," *Journal for the Study of the New Testament* 22: 53–80.

Boccaccini, Gabriele 1998. *Beyond the Essene Hypothesis: The Parting of the Ways between Qumran and Enochic Judaism*. Grand Rapids: Eerdmans.

Boccaccini, Gabriele 1995. "The Preexistence of the Torah: A Commonplace in Second Temple Judaism, or a Later Rabbinic Development?" *Henoch* 17: 329–50.

Boccaccini, Gabriele 2009. "From a Movement of Dissent to a Distinct Form of Judaism: The Heavenly Tablets in Jubilees as the Foundation of a Competing Halakah," in G. Boccaccini and G. Ibba (eds.), *Enoch and the Mosaic Torah: The Evidence of Jubilees*. Grand Rapids: Eerdmans, 193–210.

Bock, Darrell L. 2012. "What Did Jesus Do that Got Him into Trouble? Jesus in the Continuum of Early Judaism-Early Christianity," in Tom Holmén (ed.), *Jesus in Continuum*. Wissenschaftliche Untersuchungen zum Neuen Testament 289. Tübingen: Mohr Siebeck, 171–210.

Bockmuehl, Markus 1989. "Matthew 5:32; 19:9 in the Light of Pre-Rabbinic Halakah," *New Testament Studies* 35: 291–95.

Bockmuehl, Markus 2000. *Jewish Law in Gentile Churches: Halakhah and the Beginnings of Christian Public Ethics.* Edinburgh: T & T Clark.

Bockmuehl, Markus 2001. "1 Thessalonians 2:14–16 and the Church in Jerusalem," *Tyndale Bulletin* 52.1: 1–31.

Bodewitz, Henk W. 1999. "Hindu *Ahimsā* and its Roots," in Jan E. M. Houben and Karel R. Van Kooij (eds.), *Violence Denied: Violence, Non-Violence and the Rationalization of Violence in South Asian Cultural History.* Brill's Indological Library 16. Leiden: Brill, 17–44.

Boismard, M.-E. 1966. "Evangile des Ebionites et problème synoptique (Mc 1, 2–6 and par.)," *Revue Biblique* 73: 321–352.

Bond, Helen K. 1998. *Pontius Pilate in History and Interpretation.* New York and Cambridge: Cambridge University Press.

Bond, Helen K. 2004. *Caiaphas: Friend of Rome and Judge of Jesus.* Louisville: Westminster John Knox.

Bond, Helen K. 2012. *The Historical Jesus: A Guide for The Perplexed.* London; New York: T & T Clark.

Bond, Helen K. 2013. "Dating the Death of Jesus: Memory and the Religious Imagination," *New Testament Studies* 59.4, 461–475.

Borg, Marcus J. 1984. *Conflict, Holiness, and Politics in the Teaching of Jesus.* New York: Edwin Mellen.

Böttrich, C. 1997 "Jesus und der Feigenbaum. Mk 11:12–14, 20–25 in der Diskussion," *Novum Testamentum* 39: 328–59.

Bourgel, Jonathan 2015. "*Reconnaissances* 1.27-71, ou la réponse d'un groupe judéo-chrétien de Judée au désastre du soulèvement de Bar-Kokhba," *New Testament Studies* 61.1, 30–49.

Boustan, Ra'anan 2005. *From Martyr to Mystic: Rabbinic Martyrology and the Making of Merkavah Mysticism.* Texts and Studies in Ancient Judaism 112. Tübingen: Mohr Siebeck.

Boustan, Ra'anan 2008. Review of Jonathan Klawans's *Purity, Sacrifice, and the Temple. AJS Review* 32:1: 169–219.

Boustan, Ra'anan and Annette Yoshiko Reed 2008. "Blood and Atonement in the Pseudo-Clementines and *The Story of the Ten Martyrs*: The Problem of Selectivity in the Study of 'Judaism' and 'Christianity,'" *Henoch* 30: 333–364.

Boyarin, Daniel 1999. *Dying for God: Martyrdom and the Making of Christianity and Judaism.* Stanford: Stanford University Press.

Boyarin, Daniel 2001. "Justin Martyr Invents Judaism," *Church History* 70: 427–461.

Boyarin, Daniel 2004. *Border Lines: The Partition of Judaeo-Christianity.* Divinations. Philadelphia: University of Pennsylvania Press.

Boyarin, Daniel 2009. "Rethinking Jewish Christianity: An Argument for Dismantling a Dubious Category (to which is Appended a Correction of my *Border Lines*)," *Jewish Quarterly Review* 99.1: 7–36.

Boyd, Gregory A. 2006. "Christus Victor View," in J. Beilby and P. R. Eddy (eds.), *The Nature of the Atonement.* Downers Grove: InterVarsity, 23–66.

Brandon, S. G. F. 1967. *Jesus and the Zealots: A Study of the Political Factor in Primitive Christianity.* New York: Scribners.

Brandt, W. 1912. *Elchasai, ein Religionsstifter und sein Werk. Beiträge zur jüdischen, christlichen und allgemeinen Religionsgeschichte.* Leipzig: J. C. Hinrichs.

Brandt, W. 1912. "Elkesaites," in *Encyclopedia of Religion and Ethics V.* 262–269.

Brawley, Robert L. 1987. *Luke-Acts and the Jews: Conflict, Apology, and Conciliation.* Society of Biblical Literature Monograph Series 23. Atlanta: Scholars.

Breytenbach, C. and J. Schröter (eds.) 2004. *Die Apostelgeschichte und die hellenistiche Geschichtsschreibung: Festschrift für Eckhard Plümacher zu seinem 65. Geburtstag.* Ancient Judaism and Early Christianity 57. Leiden: Brill.

Briggs, C. A. 1883. "The Argument *E Silentio*: With Special Relation to the Religion of Israel," *Journal of the Society of Biblical Literature and Exegesis* 3: 3–21.

Brin, G. 1997. "Divorce at Qumran," in M. Bernstein, F. García Martínez, and J. Kampen (eds.), *Legal Texts and Legal Issues: Proceedings of the Second Meeting of the International Organization for Qumran Studies Cambridge 1995.* Leiden: Brill, 231–249.

Broadhead, Edwin K. 1992. "Mark 1,44: The Witness of the Leper," *Zeitschrift für die neutestamentliche Wissenschaft* 83: 257–265.

Broadhead, Edwin K. 1992. "Christology as Polemic and Apologetic: The Priestly Portrait of Jesus in the Gospel of Mark," *Journal for the Study of the New Testament* 47: 21–34.

Broadhead, Edwin K. 2010. *Jewish Ways of Following Jesus: Redrawing the Religious Map of Antiquity.* Wissenschaftliche Untersuchungen zum Neuen Testament 266. Tübingen: Mohr Siebeck.

Broer, I. 1980. *Freiheit vom Gesetz und Radikalisierung des Gesetzes.* Stuttgarter Bibelstudien 98. Stuttgart: KBW.

Brooke, George J. 1985. *Exegesis at Qumran: 4QFlorilegium in its Jewish Context.* Supplements to the Journal for the Study of the Old Testament Sup 29. Sheffield: JSOT.

Brooke, George J. 1995. "4Q500 1 and the Use of Scripture in the Parable of the Vineyard," *Dead Sea Discoveries* 2: 268–294.

Brooke, George J. 1998. "Shared Intertextual Interpretations in the Dead Sea Scrolls and the New Testament," in M. E. Stone and E. G. Chazon (eds.), *Biblical Perspectives: Early Use and Interpretation of the Bible in Light of the Dead Sea Scrolls.* Studies on the Texts of the Desert of Judah 28. Leiden: Brill, 35–57.

Brooke, George J. 1999. "Miqdash Adam, Eden and the Qumran Community," in B. Ego, A. Lange, and P. Pilhofer (eds.), *Gemeinde ohne Tempel-Community without Temple: Zur Substituierung und Transformation des Jerusalemer Tempels und seines Kultes im Alten Testament, antiken Judentum und fruhen Christentum.* Wissenschaftliche Untersuchungen zum Neuen Testament 118. Tübingen: Mohr Siebeck, 285–330.

Brooke, George J. 2005. *The Dead Sea Scrolls and the New Testament.* Minneapolis: Fortress.

Brown, Raymond E. 1973. *The Virginal Conception and Bodily Resurrection of Jesus.* New York: Paulist.

Brown, Raymond E. 1983. "Not Jewish Christianity and Gentile Christianity but Types of Jewish/Gentile Christianity," *Catholic Biblical Quarterly* 45: 74–79.

Brown, Raymond E. 1994. *The Death of the Messiah: From Gethsemane to the Grave: A Commentary on the Passion Narratives in the Four Gospels.* 2 vols. New York: Doubleday.

Bruce, F. F. 1983. *The Gospel of John.* Grand Rapids: Eerdmans.

Bryan, Steven M. 2002. *Jesus and Israel's Traditions of Judgement and Restoration.* Society for New Testament Studies Monograph Series 117. Cambridge University Press.

Bultmann, Rudolf 1913. "Was läßt die Spruchquelle über die Urgemeinde erkennen," *Oldenburgisches Kirchenblatt* 19: 35–37, 41–44.

Bultmann, Rudolf 1961. "New Testament and Mythology: The Mythological Element in the Message of the New Testament and the Problem of its Re-Interpretation," in H.W. Bartsch (ed.), *Kerygma and Myth: A Theological Debate.* New York: Harper & Row.

Bultmann, Rudolf 1963. *The History of the Synoptic Tradition.* Translated by John Marsh. New York: Harper.

Bultmann, Rudolf 1967. "Das Verhältnis der urchristlichen Christusbotschaft zum historischen Jesus," in D. Dinkler (ed.), *Exegetica. Aufsätze zur Erforschung des Neuen Testaments.* Tübingen: Mohr Siebeck, 445–469.

Burkert, Walter 1983. *Homo Necans: The Anthropology of Ancient Greek Sacrificial Ritual and Myth.* Translated by Peter Bing. Berkeley: University of California Press.

Byrskog, Samuel 2000. *Story as History—History as Story: The Gospel Tradition in the Context of Ancient Oral History.* Wissenschaftliche Untersuchungen zum Neuen Testament 123. Tübingen: Mohr Siebeck.

Cadoux, A. T. 1931. *The Parables of Jesus: Their Art and Use.* New York: Macmillan.

Caird, G. B. 1995. *New Testament Theology.* L. D. Hurst (ed.). Oxford: Clarendon.

Cameron, Ron 1982. *The Other Gospels: Non-Canonical Gospel Texts.* Philadelphia: Westminster.

Campbell, K. M. 1978. "The New Jerusalem in Matthew 5:14," *Scottish Journal of Theology* 31: 335–363.

Carlson, Donald H. 2013. *Jewish-Christian Interpretation of the Pentateuch in the Pseudo-Clementine Homilies.* Minneapolis: Fortress.

Carroll, John T. and Joel B. Green 1995. "Paul's Theology of the Cross," in J. T. Carroll and J. B. Green (eds.), *The Death of Jesus in Early Christianity.* Peabody: Hendrickson, 113–132.

Carter, C. 2003. *Understanding Religious Sacrifice: A Reader.* London; New York: Continuum.

Casabona, Jean 1966. *Recherches sur le vocabulaire des sacrifices en grec, des origines à la fin de l'époque classique.* Paris: Editions Ophrys.

Casey, P. Maurice 1997. "Culture and Historicity: The Cleansing of the Temple," *Catholic Biblical Quarterly* 59: 306–332.

Casey, P. Maurice 1998. *Aramaic Sources of Mark's Gospel.* Society for New Testament Studies Monograph Series 102. Cambridge: Cambridge University Press.

Catchpole, David R. 1970. "The Problem of the Historicity of the Sanhedrin Trial," in E. Bammel (ed.), *The Trial of Jesus – Cambridge Studies in Honour of C. F. D. Moule.* Studies in Biblical Theology 2.13. London: SCM, 47–65.

Catchpole, David R. 1971. *The Trial of Jesus.* Studia Post-Biblica 18. Leiden: Brill.

Catchpole, David R. 1975. "The Synoptic Divorce Material as a Traditio-Historical Problem," *Bulletin of the John Rylands University Library of Manchester* 57: 92–127.

Catchpole, David R. 1987. "The Law and the Prophets in Q," in G. F. Hawthorne and O. Betz (eds.), *Tradition and Interpretation in the New Testament: Essays in Honor of E. Earle Ellis for his 60th Birthday.* Grand Rapids: Eerdmans, 95–109.

Catchpole, David R. 1993. *The Quest for Q.* Edinburgh: T & T Clark.

Cave, H. C. 1979. "The Leper: Mk 1:40–45," *New Testament Studies* 25: 245–250.

Chance, J. Bradley 1988. *Jerusalem, the Temple, and the New Age in Luke-Acts.* Macon: Mercer.

Chanikuzhy, Jacob 2012. *Jesus, The Eschatological Temple: An Exegetical Study of Jn 2,13–22 in the Light of the Pre-70 C.E. Eschatological Temple Hopes and the Synoptic Temple Action.* Contributions to Biblical Exegesis and Theology. Leuven: Peeters.

Chapman, David W. 2008. *Ancient Jewish and Christian Perceptions of Crucifixion.* Wissenschaftliche Untersuchungen zum Neuen Testament II.244. Tübingen: Mohr Siebeck.

Charlesworth, James H. (ed.) 2014. *Jesus and Temple: Textual and Archaeological Explorations.* Minneapolis: Fortress.

Chávez, Emilio G. 2002. *The Theological Significance of Jesus' Temple Action in Mark's Gospel.* Toronto Studies in Theology 87. Lewiston: Edwin Mellen.

Chilton, Bruce 1990. "A Coin of Three Realms (Matthew 17.24–27)," in D. J. A. Clines, S. E. Fowl, and S. E. Porter (eds.), *The Bible in Three Dimensions: Essays in Celebration of Forty Years of Biblical Studies in the University of Sheffield.* Supplements to the Journal for the Study of the Old Testament 87. Sheffield: Sheffield Academic Press, 269–282.

Chilton, Bruce 1992. *The Temple of Jesus: His Sacrificial Program Within a Cultural History of Sacrifice.* University Park: Pennsylvania State University Press.

Chilton, Bruce 1993. "René Girard, James Williams, and the Genesis of Violence," *Bulletin for Biblical Research* 3: 17–29.

Chilton, Bruce 1994. *Judaic Approaches to the Gospels.* Atlanta: Scholars.

Chilton, Bruce 1994. *A Feast of Meanings: Eucharistic Theologies from Jesus through Johannine Circles.* Leiden: Brill.

Chilton, Bruce 2008. *Abraham's Curse: The Roots of Violence in Judaism, Christianity, and Islam.* New York: Random House.

Chilton, Bruce 2011. "The Eucharist and the Mimesis of Sacrifice," in A. W. Astell and S. Goodhart (eds.), *Sacrifice, Scripture, & Substitution: Readings in Ancient Judaism and Christianity.* Christianity and Judaism in Antiquity 18. Notre Dame: University of Notre Damee Press, 140–154.

Chilton, Bruce and Craig A. Evans 1997. *Jesus in Context: Temple, Purity, and Restoration*. Leiden: Brill.

Clines, David J. A. 1976. *I, He, We, and They: A Literary Approach to Isaiah 53*. Sheffield: JSOT.

Cohn, Haim Hermann 1977. *The Trial and Death of Jesus*. New York: Ktav Publishing.

Cohn, Naftali S. 2013. *The Memory of the Temple and the Making of the Rabbis*. Divinations. Philadelphia: University of Pennsylvania Press.

Coloe, Mary L. 2001. *God Dwells with Us: Temple Symbolism in the Fourth Gospel*. Collegeville: Liturgical Press.

Collins, Adela Yarbro 2001. "Jesus' Action in Herod's Temple," in A. Yarbro Collins and M. Mitchell (eds.), *Antiquity and Humanity: Essays on Ancient Religion and Philosophy*. Tübingen: Mohr Siebeck, 45–61.

Collins, Adela Yarbro 2007. *Mark: A Commentary*. Hermeneia. Minneapolis: Fortress.

Collins, John J. 1978. "The Root of Immortality: Death in the Context of Jewish Wisdom," *Harvard Theological Review* 71: 17–92.

Collins, R. F. 1984. *Studies on the First Letter to the Thessalonians*. Bibliotheca ephemeridum theologicarum lovaniensium 66. Leuven: Peeters.

Collins, John J. 1997. "Creation and the Origin of Evil," in *Apocalypticism in the Dead Sea Scrolls*. London: Routledge, 30–51.

Conzelmann, H. 1960. *The Theology of Saint Luke*. London: Faber and Faber.

Conzelmann, H. 1965. "On the Analysis of the Confessional Formula in 1 Corinthians 15:3–5," *Interpretation* 20: 15–25.

Conzelmann, H. 1965. "Zur Analyse der Bekenntnisformel I. Kor 15,3–5," *Evangelische Theologie* 25: 1–11.

Cook, Michael J. 2011. "How Credible Is Jewish Scholarship on Jesus?" in Z. Garber (ed.), *The Jewish Jesus: Revelation, Reflection, Reclamation*. West Lafayette: Purdue University Press, 251–270.

Coté D. 2001. *Le thème de l'opposition entre Pierre et Simon dans les Pseudo-Clémentines*. Études Augustiniennes Série Antiquités 167. Paris: Institut d'Études Augustiniennes.

Cromhout, Markus 2007. *Jesus and Identity: Reconstructing Judean Ethnicity in Q*. Matrix: The Bible in Mediterranean Context. Eugene: Cascade.

Crook, Zeba A. 2013. "Collective Memory Distortion and the Quest for the Historical Jesus," *Journal for the Study of the Historical Jesus* 11, 53–76.

Cross, Frank Moore 1995. *The Ancient Library of Qumran*. 3rd edn. Minneapolis: Fortress.

Crossan, John Dominic 1971. "The Parable of the Wicked Husbandmen," *Journal of Biblical Literature* 90: 451–465.

Crossan, John Dominic 1973. *In Parables: The Challenge of the Historical Jesus*. New York: Harper San Francisco.

Crossan, John Dominic 1991. *The Historical Jesus: The Life of a Mediterranean Jewish Peasant*. San Francisco: HarperSanFrancisco.

Crossan, John Dominic 1995. *Who Killed Jesus? Exposing the Roots of Anti-Semitism in the Gospel Story of the Death of Jesus*. San Francisco: HarperSanFrancisco.

Crossan, John Dominic 1998. *The Birth of Christianity: Discovering What Happened in the Years Immediately After the Execution of Jesus*. San Francisco: HarperSanFrancisco.

Crossley, James G. 2004. *The Date of Mark's Gospel: Insights from the Law in Earliest Christianity*. London: T & T Clark.

Crossley, James G. 2006. *Why Christianity Happened: A Sociohistorical Account of Christian Origins* (26–50 CE). Louisville: Westminster John Knox.

Crossley, James G. 2010. "Mark's Christology and a Scholarly Creation of a Non-Jewish Christ of Faith," in J. G. Crossley (ed.), *Judaism, Jewish Identities and the Gospel Tradition: Essays in Honour of Maurice Casey*. London: Equinox, 118–151.

Crossley, James G. 2010. *The New Testament and Jewish Law: A Guide for the Perplexed*. London: T & T Clark International.

Crossley, James G. 2013. "A 'Very Jewish' Jesus: Perpetuating the Myth of Superiority." *Journal for the Study of the Historical Jesus* 11: 109–129.

Cullmann, Oscar 1963. *The Christology of the New Testament*. London: SCM.

Dahl, N.A. 1962. "The Problem of the Historical Jesus," in C.E. Braaten and R. A. Harrisville (eds.), *Kerygma and History: A Symposium on the Theology of Rudolf Bultmann*. Nashville: Abingdon, 138–171.

Dalman, Gustaf 1893. *Jesus Christ in the Talmud, Midrash, Zohar and the Liturgy of the Synagogue*. Cambridge: Deighton & Bell.

Daly, Robert J. 2005. "Eucharistic Origins: From the New Testament to the Liturgies of the Golden Age," *Theological Studies* 66: 3–22.

Daly, Robert 1978. *Christian Sacrifice: The Judaeo-Christian Background Before Origen*. Washington: Catholic University of America.

Danielou, Jean 1964. *The Theology of Jewish Christianity*. Translated by J. A. Baker. London: Darton, Longman, and Todd.

Das, A. Andrew 2001. *Paul, the Law, and the Covenant*. Peabody: Hendrickson.

Daube, David 1962. "Death as Release in the Bible," *Novum Testamentum* 5: 82–104.

Daube, David 1987. "Temple Tax," in E. P. Sanders (ed.), *Jesus, the Gospels and the Church*. Macon: Mercer University Press, 121–134.

Dautzenberg, Gerhard 1991. "Jesus und der Temple. Beobachtungen zur Exegese der Perikope von der Tempelsteuer (Mt 17,24–27)," in I. Oberlinner and P. Fiedler (eds.), *Salz der Erde – Licht der Welt: Exegetische Studien zum Matthäusevangelium. FS für Anton Vögtle zum 80. Geburtstag*. Stuttgart: KBW, 223–238.

Dautzenberg, Gerhard 1992. "Tora des Menschensohnes? Kritische?-erlegungen zu Daniel Kosch," *Biblische Zeitschrift* 36: 93–103.

Davies, M. 1993. *Matthew*. Readings: A New Biblical Commentary. Sheffield: JSOT.

Davies, P. R. 1987. *Behind the Essenes: History and Ideology in the Dead Sea Scrolls*. Atlanta: Scholars.

Davies, P. R. 1990. "Halakhah at Qumran," in P. R. Davies and R. T. White (eds.), *A Tribute to Geza Vermes: Essays on Jewish and Christian Literature and History*. Sheffield: JSOT: 37–50.

Davies, W. D. 1948. *Paul and Rabbinic Judaism: Some Rabbinic Elements in Pauline Theology*. London: SPCK.

Davis, Richard A. 1972. *"Lifnim Mishurat Hadin: The Rabbinic Concept."* Ph.D. dissertation. Hebrew Union College – Jewish Institute of Religion, New York.

De Heusch, Luc. 1982. "L'Evangile selon Saint-Girard." *Le Monde*: 19.

De Heusch, Luc 1985. *Sacrifice in Africa: A Structuralist Approach*. Translated by L. O'Brian and A. Morton. Bloomington: Indiana University Press.

De Jonge, Marinus 1988. "Jesus' Death for Others and the Death of the Maccabean Martyrs," in T. Baarda, A. Hilhorst, G.P. Luttikhuizen, and A.F.J. Klijn (eds.), *Text and Testimony: Essays on the New Testament and Apocryphal Literature in Honour of A. F. J. Klijn*. Kampen: Kok, 142–151.

De Jonge, Marinus 1991. *Jesus, The Servant-Messiah*. New Haven: Yale University Press.

De Jonge, Marinus 1998. *God's Final Envoy*. Grand Rapids: Eerdmans.

De Jonge, Henk Jan 2003. "The Cleansing of the Temple in Mark 11:15 and Zechariah 14:21," in C. Tuckett (ed.), *The Book of Zechariah and its Influence*. Burlington: Ashgate, 87–100.

De Smedt, Charles 1883. *Principes de la critique historique*. Paris: Librarie de la Societe Bibliographique.

De Waard, J. 1965. *A Comparative Study of the Old Testament Text in the Dead Sea Scrolls and in the New Testament*. Studies on the Texts of the Desert of Judah 4. Leiden: Brill.

Deane, S. N. 1962. *St. Anselm: Basic Writings*. LaSalle: Open Court.

Deines, R. 2004. *Die Gerechtigkeit der Tora im Reich des Messias: Mt 5,13–20 als Schlüsseltext der matthäischen Theologie*. Wissenschaftliche Untersuchungen zum Neuen Testament 177. Tübingen: Mohr Siebeck.

DeMaris, Richard E. 2013. "Sacrifice, an Ancient Mediterranean Ritual." *Biblical Theology Bulletin* 43: 60–73.

Denney, James 1903. *The Death of Christ: Its Place and Interpretation in the New Testament*. 3rd edn. New York: A. C. Armstrong and Sons.

Derrett, J. D. M. 1977. "The Zeal of thy House and the Cleansing of the Temple," *Downside Review* 95: 79–94.

Detienne, Marcel and Jean-Pierre Vernant 1989. *The Cuisine of Sacrifice among the Greeks*. Translated by Paula Wissing. Chicago: University of Chicago Press.

Dettwiler, Andreas 2008. "La source Q et la Torah," in A. Dettwiler and D. Marguerat (eds.), *La source des paroles de Jésus (Q): Aux origines du christianisme*. Le Monde de la Bible 62. Geneva: Labor et Fides, 221–254.

Dillmann, August 1853. *Das Buch Henoch übersetzt und erklärt*. Leipzig: Vogel.

Dillon, Richard J. 1987. "The Psalms of the Suffering Just in the Accounts of Jesus' Passion," *Worship* 61: 430–440.

Dimant, D. 1986. "4QFlorilegium and the Idea of Community as Temple," in A. Caquot, M. Hadas-Lebel, and J. Riaud (eds.), *Hellenica et Judaica: Hommage à Valentin Nikiprowetzky*. Leuven: Peeters, 165–189.

Doble, Peter 1996. *The Paradox of Salvation: Luke's Theology of the Cross*. Society for New Testament Studies Monograph Series 87. Cambridge University Press.

Dodd, C. H. 1961. *The Parables of the Kingdom*. New York: Charles Scribner's Sons.

Dodd, C. H. 1971. *The Founder of Christianity*. London: Collins.

Doering, Lutz 2009. "Marriage and Creation in Mark 10 and CD 4–5," in F. García Martínez (ed.), *Echoes from the Caves: Qumran and the New Testament*. Studies on the Texts of the Desert of Judah 85. Leiden: Brill, 131–163.

Doering, Lutz 2011. "*Urzeit-Endzeit* Correlation in the Dead Sea Scrolls and Pseudepigrapha," in J. Eckstein, C. Landmesser, and H. Lichtenberger (eds.), *Eschatologie: Eschatology*. Wissenschaftliche Untersuchungen zum Neuen Testament 272. Tübingen: Mohr Siebeck: 19–58.

Dombrowski, Daniel A. 1984. *The Philosophy of Vegetarianism*. Amherst: University of Massachusetts Press.

Donaldson, T. L. 1985. *Jesus on the Mountain: A Study in Matthean Typology*. Sheffield: JSOT.

Donfried, Karl Paul 2002. *Paul, Thessalonica, and Early Christianity*. Grand Rapids: Eerdmans.

Douglas, Mary 1982. *Natural Symbols: Explorations in Cosmology*. New York: Pantheon.

Droge, A. J. and J. D. Tabor 1992. *A Noble Death*. San Francisco: HarperSanFrancisco.

Dumbrell, W. J. 1981. "The Logic of the Law in Matthew V 1–20," *Novum Testamentum* 23.1: 1–21.

Dumouchel, P. (ed.) 1988. *Violence and Truth: On the Work of René Girard*. Stanford University Press.

Dunn, James D. G. 1980. *Christology in the Making: An Inquiry into the Origins of the Doctrine of the Incarnation*. London: SCM.

Dunn, James D. G. 1991. "Paul's Understanding of the Death of Jesus as Sacrifice," in S. Sykes (ed.), *Sacrifice and Redemption: Durham Essays in Theology*. New York and Cambridge: Cambridge University Press, 35–56.

Dunn, James D. G. 1998. *The Theology of Paul the Apostle*. Grand Rapids: Eerdmans.

Dunn, James D. G. 2008. *The New Perspective on Paul*. Rev. edn. Grand Rapids: Eerdmans.

Dunn, James D. G. 2003. *Jesus Remembered*. Grand Rapids: Eerdmans.

Dungan, D. 1971. *The Sayings of Jesus in the Churches of Paul: The Use of the Synoptic Tradition in the Regulation of Early Church Life*. Philadelphia: Fortress.

Easter, Matthew C. 2010. "The *Pistis Christou* Debate: Main Arguments and Responses in Summary," *Currents in Biblical Research* 9.1: 33–47.

Eberhart, Christian A. (ed.) 2011. *Ritual and Metaphor: Sacrifice in the Bible*. Resources for Biblical Study 68. Atlanta: Society of Biblical Literature.

Eckhardt, Benedikt 2014. "'Bloodless Sacrifice': A Note on Greek Cultic Language in the Imperial Era." *Greek, Roman, and Byzantine Studies* 54: 255–273.

Edwards, J. R. 1989. "Markan Sandwiches: The Significance of Interpolations in Markan Narratives," *Novum Testamentum* 31: 193–216.

Edwards, J. R. 2002. "The Gospel of the Ebionites and the Gospel of Luke," *New Testament Studies* 48: 568–586.

Ego, Beato 2005. "Vergangenheit im Horizont eschatologischer Hoffnung: Die Tiervision (1 Hen 85–90) als Beispiel apolkalypischer Geschichtskonzeption," in Eve-Marie Becker (ed.), *Die antike Historiographie und die Anfänge der christlichen Geschichtsschreibung.* Berlin: Walter de Gruyter, 171–195.

Ehrman, Bart D. 2012. *The New Testament: A Historical Introduction to the Early Christian Writings.* 5th edn. New York: Oxford University Press.

Eidevall, Göran 2011. "The Role of Sacrificial Language in Prophetic Rhetoric," in C. Eberhart (ed.), *Ritual and Metaphor: Sacrifice in the Bible.* Resources for Biblical Study 68. Atlanta: Society of Biblical Literature, 49–61.

Eisler, Robert 1931 (1929–1930). "The Baptist's Food and Clothing," in *The Messiah Jesus and John the Baptist according to Flavius Josephus' Recently Rediscovered 'Capture of Jerusalem' and Other Jewish and Christian Sources.* New York: L. MacVeagh [Dial], 235–240.

Elliott, John H. 2007. "Jesus the Israelite was neither a 'Jew' nor a 'Christian': On Correcting Misleading Nomenclature," *Journal for the Study of the Historical Jesus* 5/2: 119–154.

Eppstein, V. 1964. "The Historicity of the Gospel Account of the Cleansing of the Temple," *Zeitschrift für die neutestamentliche Wissenschaft* 55: 42–58.

Eschner, Christina 2010. *Gestorben und hingegeben "für" die Sünder. Die griechische Konzeption des Unheil abwendenden Sterbens und deren paulinische Aufnahme für die Deutung des Todes Jesu Christi.* Wissenschaftliche Monographien zum Alten und Neuen Testament 122. Neukirchen-Vluyn: Neukirchener.

Esler, P. 1987. *Community and Gospel in Luke-Acts: The Social and Political Motivations of Lucan Theology.* Society for New Testament Studies Monograph Series 57. Cambridge: Cambridge University Press.

Evans, Craig A. 1989. "Jesus' Action in the Temple: Cleansing or Portent of Destruction?" *Catholic Biblical Quarterly* 51: 237–270.

Evans, Craig A. 1989. "Jesus' Action in the Temple and Evidence of Corruption in the First-Century Temple," in D. J. Lull (ed.), *Society of Biblical Literature 1989 Seminar Papers.* Society of Biblical Literature Seminar Papers 28. Atlanta: Scholars, 522–539.

Evans, Craig A. 1992. "Predictions of the Destruction of the Herodian Temple in the Pseudepigrapha, Qumran Scrolls, and Related Texts," *Journal for the Study of the Pseudepigrapha* 10: 89–146.

Evans, Craig A. 1992. "Opposition to the Temple: Jesus and the Dead Sea Scrolls," in J. H. Charlesworth (ed.), *Jesus and the Dead Sea Scrolls.* New York: Doubleday, 235–253.

Evans, Craig A. 1993. "Jesus and the "Cave of Robbers": Toward a Jewish Context for the Temple Action," *Bulletin for Biblical Research* 2: 92–110.

Evans, Craig A. 1996. "Jesus' Parable of the Tenant Farmers in Light of Lease Agreements in Antiquity," *Journal for the Study of the Pseudepigrapha* 14: 25–83.

Evans, Craig A. 1997. "From 'House of Prayer' to 'Cave of Robbers': Jesus' Prophetic Criticism of the Temple Establishment," in C. A. Evans and

S. Talmon (eds.), *The Quest for Context and Meaning: Studies in Biblical Intertextuality in Honor of James A. Sanders*. Leiden: Brill, 417–442.

Evans, Craig A. 1997. "Jesus' Action in the Temple: Cleansing or Portent of Destruction?" in B. Chilton and C. A. Evans (eds.), *Jesus in Context: Temple, Purity and Restoration.* Arbeiten zur Geschichte des antiken Judtentums und des Urchristentums 39. Leiden: Brill, 395–439.

Evans, Craig A. 1999. "Jesus and James: Martyrs of the Temple," in B. D. Chilton and C. A. Evans (eds.), *James the Just and Christian Origins.* Novum Testamentum Supplements 98. Leiden: Brill, 233–249.

Evans, Craig A. 2001. *Mark 8:27–16:20.* Word Biblical Commentary 34B. Nashville: Thomas Nelson.

Evans, Craig A. 2003. "How Septuagintal is Isa 5:1–7 in Mark 12:1–9?" *Novum Testamentum* 45: 105–110.

Evans, Craig A. 2007. "The Jewish Christian Gospel Tradition," in O. Skarsaune and R. Hvalvik (eds.), *Jewish Believers in Jesus: The Early Centuries.* Peabody: Hendrickson, 241–277.

Evans, Craig A. 2014. *From Jesus to the Church: The First Christian Generation.* Grand Rapids: Westminster John Knox Press.

Fander, M. 1989. *Die Stellung der Frau im Markusevangelium. Unter besonderer Berücksichtigung kultur- und religionsgeschichtlicher Hintergründe.* Münsteraner Theologische Abhandlungen 8. Altenberge: Telos.

Faßbeck, Gabriele 2000. *Der Tempel der Christen. Traditionsgeschichtliche Untersuchungen zur Aufnahme des Tempelkonzepts im frühen Christentum.* Texte und Arbeiten zum neutestamentlichen Zeitalter 33. Tübingen: Francke.

Faraone, Christopher and F. S. Naiden (eds.) 2012. *Greek and Roman Animal Sacrifice: Ancient Victims, Modern Observers.* New York and Cambridge: Cambridge University Press.

Feldman, L. H. 1965. *Josephus: Jewish Antiquities, Books, XVIII-XIX.* Loeb Classical Library 433. Cambridge: Harvard University Press.

Fine, Steven 1997. *This Holy Place: On the Sanctity of the Synagogue during the Greco-Roman Period.* Notre Dame: University of Notre Dame Press.

Finlan, Stephen 2004. *The Background and Content of Paul's Cultic Atonement Metaphors.* Anchor Bible 19. Atlanta: Society of Biblical Literature.

Finlan, Stephen 2005. *Problems with Atonement: The Origins of, and Controversy about, the Atonement Doctrine.* Collegeville: Liturgical Press.

Finlan, Stephen 2007. *Options on Atonement in Christian Thought.* Wilmington.: Michael Glazier.

Finley, Gregory C. 2009. "The Ebionites and 'Jewish Christianity': Examining Heresy and the Attitudes of Church Fathers." Ph.D. dissertation. Catholic University of America.

Fiorenza, Elisabeth Schüssler 1976. "Cultic Language in Qumran and in the NT," *Catholic Biblical Quarterly* 38: 159–77.

Fitzmyer, Joseph A. 1955. "The Qumran Scrolls, the Ebionites and their Literature," *Theologicla Studies* 16: 335–372.

Fitzmyer, Joseph A. 1976. "The Matthean Divorce Texts and Some New Palestinian Evidence," *Theological Studies* 37: 197–226.

Fitzmyer, Joseph A. 1989. "The Jewish People and the Mosaic Law in Luke-Acts," in *Luke the Theologian: Aspects of his Teaching*. London: Chapman, 175–202.

Fleddermann, Harry T. 2005. *Q: A Reconstruction and Commentary*. Biblical Tools and Studies 1. Leuven: Peeters.

Flood, Gavin 2013. "Sacrifice as Refusal," in J. Zachhuber and J. T. Meszaros (eds.), *Sacrifice and Modern Thought*. Oxford: Oxford University Press, 115–131.

Flusser, David 1961. "Matthew XVII, 24–27 and the Dead Sea Sect," *Tarbiz* 31: 150–156.

Flusser, David 1969. *Jesus*. New York: Herder and Herder.

Fonrobert, Charlotte Elisheva 2001. "*The* Didascalia Apostolorum: *A Mishnah for the Disciples of Jesus*," *Journal of Early Christian Studies* 9: 483–509.

Foster, Paul 2004. *Community, Law and Mission in Matthew's Gospel*. Wissenschaftliche Untersuchungen zum Neuen Testament II.177. Tübingen: Mohr Siebeck.

Foster, Paul 2011. "Paul and Matthew: Two Strands in the Early Jesus Movement with Little Sign of Connection," in M. F. Bird and J. Willitts (eds.), *Paul and the Gospels: Christologies, Conflicts and Convergences*. Library of New Testament Studies 411. London: T & T Clark, 86–114.

Foster, Paul 2013. "Matthew's Use of 'Jewish' Traditions from Q," in M. Tiwald (ed.), *Kein Jota wird vergehen. Das Gesetzesverständnis der Logienquelle vor dem Hintergrund frühjüdischer Theologie*. Beiträge zur Wissenschaft vom Alten und Neuen Testament 200. Stuttgart: W. Kohlhammer, 179–201.

Foucault, Michel 1977. *Language, Counter-Memory, Practice: Selected Essays and Interviews*. Ithaca: Cornell University Press.

Fredriksen, Paula 1988 *From Jesus to Christ: The Origins of the New Testament Images of Jesus*. New Haven: Yale University Press.

Fredriksen, Paula 1990 "Jesus and the Temple, Mark and the War," in *SBL Seminar Papers, 1990*. Society of Biblical Literature Seminar Papers 29. Atlanta: Scholars, 293–310.

Fredriksen, Paula 1999. *Jesus of Nazareth, King of the Jews*. New York: Alfred A. Knopf.

Fredriksen, Paula 1999. "Did Jesus Oppose the Purity Laws?" *Biblical Research* 11.3: 20–25, 42–47.

Fredriksen, Paula 2008. "Gospel Chronologies, the Scene in the Temple, and the Crucifixion of Jesus," in F.E. Udoh (ed.) *Redefining First-Century Jewish and Christian Identities: Essays in Honor of Ed Parish Sanders*. Christianity and Judaism in Antiquity 16. Notre Dame: Universityof Notre Dame, 246–282.

Fredriksen, Paula 2015. "Arms and The Man: A Response to Dale Martin's 'Jesus in Jerusalem: Armed and Not Dangerous," *Journal for the Study of the New Testament* 37: 312–325.

Frey, Jörg 2012. "Die Fragmente des Ebionäerevangeliums," in C. Markschies and J. Schröter (eds.), *Antike christliche Apokryphen in deutscher Übersetzung 1: Evangelien und Verwandtes 1*. Tübingen: Mohr Siebeck, 607–620.

Fried, J. 2004. *Der Schleier der Erinnerung: Grundzüge einer historischen Memorik.* Munich: C.H. Beck.

Friedrich, G. 1982. *Die Verkündigung des Todes Jesu im Neuen Testaments.* Biblisch-theologische Studien 6. Neukirchen: Neukirchener.

Fuglseth, Kåre Sigvald 2005. *Johannine Sectarianism in Perspective: A Sociological, Historical, and Comparative Analysis of Temple and Social Relationships in the Gospel of John, Philo and Qumran.* Novum Testamentum Supplements 119. Leiden: Brill.

Fuller, Reginald H. 1954. *The Mission and Achievement of Jesus.* Studies in Biblical Theology 12. London: SCM.

Funk, Robert, Roy W. Hoover and the Jesus Seminar 1993. *The Five Gospels: The Search for the Authentic Words of Jesus: New Translation and Commentary.* New York: Macmillan.

García Martínez, Florentino 1997. "The Heavenly Tablets in the Book of Jubilees," in M. Albani, J. Frey, and A. Lange (eds.), *Studies in the Book of Jubilees.* Texte und Studien zum antiken Judentum 65. Tübingen: Mohr Siebeck, 243–259.

García Martínez, Florentino 1999. "Man and Woman: Halakhah Based upon Eden in the Dead Sea Scrolls," in G. P. Luttikuizen (ed.), *Paradise Interpreted: Representations of Biblical Paradise in Judaism and Christianity.* Themes in Biblical Narrative 2. Leiden: Brill, 95–115.

Gärtner, Bertil 1965. *The Temple and the Community in: Qumran and the New Testament: A Comparative Study in the Temple Symbolism of the Qumran Texts and the New Testament.* Cambridge: Cambridge University Press.

Gaston, Lloyd 1970. *No Stone on Another: Studies in the Significance of the Fall of Jerusalem in the Synoptic Gospels.* Novum Testamentum Supplements 23. Leiden: Brill.

Gelston, Anthony 1993. "Knowledge, Humiliation, or Suffering: A Lexical, Textual, and Exegetical Problem in Isaiah 53," in R. N. Whybray, H. A. McKay, and D. J. A. Clines (eds.), *Of Prophets' Visions and the Wisdom of Sages: Essays in Honour of R. Norman Whybray on His Seventieth Birthday.* Journal of the Study of the Old Testament: Supplement Series 162. Sheffield: JSOT, 126–141.

Gese, Hartmut 1981. *Essays on Biblical Theology.* Translated by Keith Crim. Minneapolis: Augsburg.

Gieseler, Johann Karl Ludwig 1820. "Über die Nazaräer und Ebioniten," *Archiv für alte und neue Kirchengeschichte* 4: 279–330.

Giesen, H. 1976. "Der verdorrte Feigenbaum – Eine symbolische Aussage? Zu Mk 11,12–14.20f," *Biblische Zeitschrift* 20: 95–111.

Gilders, William K. 2011. "Jewish Sacrifice: Its Nature and Function (According to Philo)," in Jennifer W. Knust and Zsuzsanna Várhelyi (eds.), *Ancient Meditteranean Sacrifice.* New York: Oxford University Press, 94–105.

Gilliard, Frank D. 1989. "The Problem of the Antisemitic Comma Between 1 Thessalonians 2.14 and 15," *New Testament Studies* 35: 481–502.

Girard, Réne 1977. *Violence and the Sacred.* Translated by Patrick Gregory. Baltimore: John Hopkins University Press.

Girard, Réne 1987. *Things Hidden since the Foundation of the World.* Stanford: Stanford University Press.

Girard, Réne 1986. *The Scapegoat*. Translated by Yvonne Frecerro. Baltimore: John Hopkins University Press.

Girard, Réne 2001. *Celui par qui le scandale arrive*. Paris: Desclée de Brouwer.

Girard, Réne 2003. *Sacrifice*. Translated by Matthew Pattilo and David Dawson. Breakthroughs in Mimetic Theory. East Lansing: Michigan State University Press.

Girard, Réne 2011. "Mimesis, Sacrifice, and the Bible: A Conversation with Sandor Goodhart," in A. W. Astell and S. Goodhart (eds.), *Sacrifice, Scripture, & Substitution: Readings in Ancient Judaism and Christianity*. Christianity and Judaism in Antiquity 18. Notre Dame: University of Notre Dame Press, 39–69.

Gnilka, G. 1979. *Das Evangelium nach Markus*. Evangelisch-katholischer Kommentar zum Neuen Testament 11/2. Zürich: Benzinger.

Goodacre, Mark 2006. "Scripturalization in Mark's Crucifixion Narrative," in G. van Oyen and T. Shepherd (eds.), *The Trial and Death of Jesus: Essays on the Passion Narrative in Mark*. Contributions to Biblical Exegesis and Theology 45. Leuven: Peeters, 33–47.

Goodblatt, David 1998. "From Judeans to Israel: Names of Jewish States in Antiquity," *Journal for the Study of Judaism* 29: 1–36.

Goodman, Martin 1996. "The Function of Minim in early Rabbinic Judaism," in P. Schäfer (ed.), *Tradition – Reflexion. Festschrift für Martin Hengel zum 70. Geburtstag, I*. Tübingen: Mohr Siebeck, 501–510.

Goodman, Martin 2007. "The Temple in First-Century CE Judaism," in J. Day (ed.), *Temple and Worship in Biblical Israel*. New York: T & T Clark, 459–468.

Goppelt, Leonhard 1981–1982. *Theology of the New Testament*. 2 vols. Translated by J. E. Alsup. Grand Rapids: Eerdmans.

Goulder, Michael 1995. *St. Paul versus St. Peter: A Tale of Two Missions*. Louisville: Westminster John Knox.

Grant, Michael 1977. *Jesus: An Historian's Review of the Gospels*. New York: Charles Scribner's Sons.

Grant, Robert M. and David N. Freedman 1960. *The Secret Sayings of Jesus*. Garden City: Doubleday.

Gray, Timothy C. 2010. *The Temple in the Gospel of Mark: A Study in Its Narrative Role*. Grand Rapids: Baker Academic.

Green, Joel B. 1988. *The Death of Jesus: Tradition and Interpretation in the Passion Narrative*. Wissenschaftliche Untersuchungen zum Neuen Testament II.33. Tübingen: Mohr Siebeck.

Green, Joel B. 1991. *The Way of the Cross: Following Jesus in the Gospel of Mark*. Nashville: Discipleship Resources.

Gregory, Andrew 2005. "Prior or Posterior? The Gospel of the Ebionites and the Gospel of Luke," *New Testament Studies* 51: 344–360.

Gregory, Andrew 2008. "Jewish-Christian Gospels," in P. Foster (ed.), *The Non-canonical Gospels*. London: T & T Clark, 54–67.

Greisch, Jean 1981. "Une anthropologie fondamentale du rite: René Girard," in *Le rite. Philosophie Institut catholique de Paris, présentation de Jean Greisch*. Paris: Beauchesne, 89–119.

Gubler, Marie-Louise 1977. *Die frühesten Deutungen des Todes Jesu*. Orbis biblicus et orientalis 15. Freiburg: Universitätsverlag.

Guelich, R. A. 1976. "The Antitheses of Matt 5:21–48: Traditional and/or Redactional?" *New Testament Studies* 22: 444–457.

Gupta, Nijay K. 2010. *Worship That Makes Sense to Paul: A New Approach to the Theology and Ethics of Paul's Cultic Metaphors.* New York and Berlin: de Gruyter.

Gurtner, Daniel M. 2007. *The Torn Veil: Matthew's Exposition of the Death of Jesus.* Society for New Testament Studies Monograph Series 139. Cambridge University Press.

Guthrie, W. K. C. 1966. *Orpheus and Greek Religion: A Study of the Orphic Movement.* New York: Norton.

Guttmann, Alexander 1969. "The End of the Jewish Sacrificial Cult," *Hebrew Union College Annual* 38: 137–148.

Gyanshruti, S. and S. Srividyananda 2006. *Yajna: A Comprehensive Survey.* Munger: Yoga Publications Trust.

Haas, N. 1970. "Anthropological Observations on the Skeletal Remains from Giv'at ha-Mivtar," *Israel Exploration Journal* 20: 38–59.

Haenchen, E. 1968. *Die Apostelgeschichte.* Kritisch-exegetischer Kommentar Uber das Neue Testament 111. Göttingen: Vandenhoeck und Ruprecht.

Haenchen, E. 1984. *John, 1, 2.* Hermeneia. Philadelphia: Fortress.

Hägerland, Tobias 2011. *Jesus and the Forgiveness of Sins: An Aspect of His Prophetic Mission.* Society for New Testament Studies Monograph Series 150. Cambridge: Cambridge University Press.

Hägglund, Fredrik 2008. *Isaiah 53 in the Light of Homecoming after Exile.* Tübingen: Mohr Siebeck.

Hagner, Donald A. 2003. "Matthew: Apostate, Reformer, Revolutionary?" *New Testament Studies* 49: 193–209.

Hagner, Donald A. 2009. "Jesus and the Synoptic Sabbath Controversies," in D. L. Bock and R. L. Webb (eds.), *Key Events in the Life of the Historical Jesus: A Collaborative Exploration of Context and Coherence.* Darrell L. Bock and Robert L. Webb (eds.). Grand Rapids: Eerdmans, 251–292.

Hahn, Ferdinand 1970. *Der urchristliche Gottesdienst.* Stuttgarter Bibelstudien 41. Stuttgart: KBW.

Hahn, Ferdinand 2002. *Die Einheit des Neuen Testaments: Thematische Darstellung.* Vol. 2, *Theologie des Neuen Testaments.* Tübingen: Mohr Siebeck.

Häkkinen, S. 2005. "Ebionites," in A. Marjanen and P. Luomanen (eds.), *A Companion to Second-Century Christian "Heretics."* Leiden: Brill, 247–278.

Hallo, William W. 1981. *The Torah: A Modern Commentary.* New York: Union of American Hebrew Congregations.

Hallo, William W. 1987. "The Origins of the Sacrificial Cult: New Evidence from Mesopotamia and Israel," in P. D. Miller Jr., P. D. Hanson, and S. Dean McBride (eds.), *Ancient Israelite Religion: Essays in Honor of Frank Moore Cross.* Philadelphia: Fortress, 3–13.

Hallo, William W. 1993. "Lugalbanda Excavated," *Journal of the American Oriental Society* 103: 165–180.

Hallo, William W. 2011. "The Origin of Israelite Sacrifice," *Biblical Archaeology Review* 37/6: 59–60, 71.

Hallo, William W. and W. K. Simpson 1971. *The Ancient Near East: A History.* New York: Harcourt Brace Jovanovich.

Ham, C. A. 2005. *The Coming King and the Rejected Shepherd: Matthew's Reading of Zechariah's Messianic Hope.* Sheffield: Sheffield Phoenix Press.

Hamerton-Kelly, Robert 1992. "Sacred Violence and the Messiah: The Markan Passion Narrative as a Redefinition of Messianology," in J. H. Charlesworth (ed.), *The Messiah: Developments in Earliest Judaism and Christianity.* Philadelphia: Fortress, 461–493.

Hamerton-Kelly, Robert 1992. *Sacred Violence: Paul's Hermeneutic of the Cross.* Minneapolis: Fortress.

Hamerton-Kelly, Robert 1994. *The Gospel and the Sacred: Poetics of Violence in Mark.* Minneapolis: Fortress.

Hamerton-Kelly, Robert (ed.) 1987. *Violent Origins: Walter Burkert, René Girard, and Jonathan Z. Smith on Ritual Killing and Cultural Formation.* Stanford: Stanford University Press.

Han, Kyu Sam 2002. *Jerusalem and the Early Jesus Movement: The Q Community's Attitude Toward the Temple.* Journal for the Study of the New Testament: Supplement Series 207. Sheffield: Sheffield Academic Press.

Hare, D. R. A. 2000. "How Jewish is the Gospel of Matthew?" *Catholic Biblical Quarterly* 62: 264–277.

Harrington, D, J. 1991. *The Gospel of Matthew.* Sacra Pagina 1. Collegevill e: Liturgical Press.

Harrington, D. J. 2008. "Matthew and Paul," in D. Sim and B. Repschinski (eds.), *Matthew and His Christian Contemporaries.* London: T & T Clark, 11–26.

Harvey, A. E. 1982. *Jesus and the Constraints of History.* London: Duckworth.

Harvey, Graham 1996. *The True Israel: Uses of the Name Jew, Hebrew and Israel in Ancient Jewish and Early Christian Literature.* Leiden: Brill.

Haussleiter, Johannes 1935. *Der Vegetarismus in der Antike.* Religionsgeschichtliche Versuche und Vorarbeiten 24. Berlin: Alfred Töpelmann.

Hays, Richard B. 1997. *First Corinthians.* Interpretation. Louisville: Westminster John Knox.

Hays, Richard B. 2002. *The Faith of Jesus Christ: The Narrative Substructure of Galatians 3:1–4:11.* Biblical Resource Series. Grand Rapids: Eerdmans.

Hays, Richard B. 1996. *The Jewish Temple: A Non-Biblical Sourcebook.* London: Routledge.

Head, P. M. 2004. "The Temple in Luke's Gospel," in T. D. Alexander and S. Gathercole (eds.), *Heaven on Earth: The Temple in Biblical Theology.* Carlisle: Paternoster, 102–119.

Hecht, Richard D. 1982. "Studies on Sacrifice," *Religious Studies Review* 8.3: 253–259.

Hedley, Douglas 2011. *Sacrifice Imagined: Violence, Atonement and the Sacred.* New York; London: Continuum.

Heil, Christoph 2013. "Nachfolge und Tora in Q 9 57–60," in M. Tiwald (ed.), *Kein Jota wird vergehen: das Gesetzesverständnis der Logienquelle vor dem Hintergrund frühjüdischer Theologie.* Beiträge zur Wissenschaft vom Alten und Neuen Testament 10. Stuttgart: Kohlhammer, 111–140.

Heil, John P. 1997. "The Narrative Strategy and Pragmatics of the Temple Theme in Mark," *Catholic Biblical Quarterly* 59.1: 76–100.

Hendel, Ronald S. 1989. "Sacrifice As a Cultural System: The Ritual Symbolism of Exodus 24, 3–8," *Zeitschrift für die alttestamentliche Wissenschaft* 101: 366–390.

Hengel, Martin 1961. *Die Zeloten: Untersuchungen zur Jüdischen Freiheitsbewegung in der Zeit von Herodes 1.bis 70 n. Chr.* Arbeiten zur Geschichte des antiken Judentums und des Urchristentums 1. Leiden: Brill.

Hengel, Martin 1971. *Was Jesus a Revolutionist?* Translated by William Klassen. Philadelphia: Fortress.

Hengel, Martin 1977. *Crucifixion in the Ancient World and the Folly of the Message of the Cross.* Translated by John Bowden. Philadelphia: Fortress.

Hengel, Martin 1980. "Der stellvertrentende Sühnetod Jesu. Ein Beitrag zur Entstehung des urchristlichen Kerygmas," *Internationale kirchliche Zeitschrift* 9: 1–25, 135–47.

Hengel, Martin 1981. *The Atonement: The Origins of the Doctrine in the New Testament.* Translated by John Bowden. Philadelphia: Fortress.

Hengel, Martin 1989. *The Zealots: Investigations into the Jewish Freedom Movement in the Period from Herod I Until 70 A. D.* Translated by D. Smith. Edinburgh: T & T Clark.

Hengel, Martin and Anna Maria Schwemer 2007. *Jesus und das Judentum. Vol. I: Geschichte des frühen Christentums.* Tübingen: Mohr Siebeck.

Henige, David P. 2005. *Historical Evidence and Argument.* Madison: University of Wisconsin Press.

Henne, P. 1994. "L'Evangile des Ebionites. Une fausse harmonie. Une vraie supercherie," in D. Van Damme, A. Kessler, T. Ricklin, and G. Wurst (eds.), *Peregrina curiositas. Eine Reise durch den Orbis antiquus. Zu Ehren von Dirk van Damme.* Novum Testamentum et orbis antiquus 27. Göttingen: Vandenhoeck & Ruprecht, 57–75.

Herr, Moshe David 1980. "Jerusalem, the Temple, and Its Cult – Reality and Concepts in Second Temple Times," in A. Oppenheimer, U. Rappaport, and M. Stern (eds.), *Jerusalem in the Second Temple Period: Abraham Schalit Memorial Volume.* Jerusalem: Yad Ben-Zvi, Ministry of Defense, 166–177.

Herzog II, William R. 2000. *Jesus, Justice, and the Reign of God.* Louisville: Westminster John Knox.

Heskett, Randall 2007. *Messianism within the Scriptural Scroll of Isaiah.* New York: T & T Clark.

Heyman, George 2007. *The Power of Sacrifice: Roman and Christian Discourses in Conflict.* Washington: Catholic University of America Press.

Himmelfarb, Martha 1991. "The Temple and the Garden of Eden in Ezekiel, the Book of Watchers, and the Wisdom of Ben Sira," in J. S. Scott and P. Simpson-Housely (eds.), *Sacred Places and Profane Spaces: Essays in the Geographies of Judaism, Christianity and Islam.* Westport: Greenwood, 63–78.

Himmelfarb, Martha 1993. *Ascent to Heaven in Jewish and Christian Apocalypses.* New York: Oxford University Press.

266   *Bibliography*

Himmelfarb, Martha 1999. "Torah, Testimony, and Heavenly Tablets: The Claim of Authority of the Book of Jubilees," in B. G. Wright (ed.), *A Multiform Heritage. Festschrift Robert A. Kraft.* Atlanta: Scholars, 19–29.

Hitch, Sarah and Ian Rutherford (eds.) 2015. *Animal Sacrifice in the Ancient World.* Cambridge University Press.

Hoffmann, Paul 1972. *Studien zur Theologie der Logienquelle.* Neutestamentliche Abhandlungen 8. Münster: Aschendorff.

Hogeterp, Albert L.A. 2006. *Paul and God's Temple: A Historical Interpretation of Cultic Imagery in the Corinthian Correspondence.* Biblical Tools and Studies 2. Leuven: Peeters.

Hogg, Michael A. and Dominic Abrams 2007. "Intergroup Behavior and Social Identity," in M. A. Hogg and J. Cooper (eds.), *The Sage Handbook of Social Psychology.* Concise Student Edition. Los Angeles: Sage, 335–360.

Holdrege, Barbara A. 1996. *Veda and Torah: Transcending the Textuality of Scripture.* Albany: State University of New York.

Holl, Karl (ed.) 1915, 1933. *Ancoratus und Panarion.* 3 vols. Leipzig: J. C. Hinrichs.

Holmås, Geir Otto 2005. "'My House Shall Be a House of Prayer,' Regarding the Temple as a Place of Prayer in Acts within the Context of Luke's Apologetic Objective," *Journal for the Study of the New Testament* 27: 394–416.

Holmén, Tom 2000. "The Temple Action of Jesus (Mark 11:15–17) in Historical Context," in K-J. Illman, T. Ahlbäck, S.-O. Back, and R. Nurmela (eds.), *A Bouquet of Wisdom: Essays in Honour of Karl-Gustav Sandelin.* Religionsvetenskapliga skrifter 48. Åbo: Åbo Akademi, 99–127.

Holmén, Tom 2001. *Jesus and Jewish Covenant Thinking.* Biblical Interpretation Series 55. Leiden: Brill.

Holmén, Tom 2004. "Jesus, Judaism and the Covenant," *Journal for the Study of the Historical Jesus* 2.1: 3–27.

Holmén, Tom 2007. "An Introduction to the Continuum Approach," in T. Holmén (ed.), *Jesus from Judaism to Christianity: Continuum Approaches to the Historical Jesus.* Library of New Testament Studies 352. London: T & T Clark, 1–16.

Hooker, Morna D. 1972. "On Using the Wrong Tool," *Theology* 75: 570–581.

Hooker, Morna D. 1988. "Traditions about the Temple in the Sayings of Jesus," *Bulletin of the John Rylands University Library of Manchester* 70: 7–19.

Hooker, Morna D. 1991. *A Commentary on the Gospel According to St. Mark.* Black's New Testament Commentaries 2. Peabody: Hendrickson.

Hooker, Morna D. 1994. *Not Ashamed of the Gospel.* Didsbury Lectures, 1988. Carlisle: Paternoster.

Hooker, Morna D. 1997. *The Signs of a Prophet: The Prophetic Actions of Jesus.* London: SCM.

Hopkins, Jamal-Dominique 2011. "The Dead Sea Scrolls and the Greco-Roman World: Examining the Essenes' View of Sacrifice in Relation to the Scrolls," in A. Lange, E. Tov, M. Weigold, and B. Reynolds III (eds.), *The Dead Sea Scrolls in Context: Integrating the Dead Sea*

Scrolls in the Study of Ancient Texts, Languages, and Cultures. 2 vols. Vetus Testamentum Supplements 140. Leiden: Brill: 367–383.

Horbury, William 1982. "The Benediction of the Minim and Early Jewish-Christian Controversy," *Journal of Theological Studies* 33: 19–61.

Horbury, William 1984. "The Temple Tax," in E. Bammel and C. F. D. Moule (eds.), *Jesus and the Politics of His Day.* New York and Cambridge: Cambridge University Press, 265–286.

Horsley, Richard 1984. "Popular Messianic Movements Around the Time of Jesus," *Catholic Biblical Quarterly* 46: 471–95.

Horsley, Richard 1987. *Jesus and the Spiral of Violence: Popular Jewish Resistance in Roman Palestine.* San Francisco: Harper & Row.

Horsley, Richard 1991. "Q and Jesus: Assumptions, Approaches, and Analyses," *Semeia* 55: 175–209.

Horsley, Richard 2007. *Scribes, Visionaries, and the Politics of Second Temple Judea.* Louisville: Westminster John Knox.

Horsley, Richard 2012. *The Prophet Jesus and the Renewal of Israel: Moving Beyond a Diversionary Debate.* Grand Rapids: Eerdmans.

Horsley, Richard and John S. Hanson 1985. *Bandits, Prophets, and Messiahs: Popular Movements in the Time of Jesus.* Minneapolis: Winston.

Hort, F. J. A. 1894. *Judaistic Christianity.* Cambridge: Cambridge University Press.

Horvath, Tibor 1979. *The Sacrificial Interpretation of Jesus' Achievement in the New Testament: Historical Development and its Reasons.* New York: Philosophical Library, Inc.

Hoskins, Paul M. 2006. *Jesus as the Fulfillment of the Temple in the Gospel of John.* Milton Keynes: Paternoster.

Hoskyns, E. C. 1947. *The Fourth Gospel.* London: Faber and Faber.

Hubert, Henri and Marcel Mauss 1964 (1898). *Sacrifice: Its Nature and Functions.* Translated by W. D. Halls. Chicago: University of Chicago Press.

Hübner, H. 1973. *Das Gesetz in der synoptischen Tradition.* Witten: Luther.

Huddleston, Jonathan 2012. *Eschatology in Genesis.* Forschungen zum Alten Testament 2/57. Tübingen: Mohr Siebeck.

Hulst, A. R. 1963. "Opmerkingen over de Ka'aser-Zinnen in Deuteronomium," *Nederlands Theologisch Tijdschrift* 18: 337–61.

Hultgren, Arland J. 2000. *The Parables of Jesus: A Commentary.* Grand Rapids: Eerdmans.

Humbert, J.-B. 1994. "L'espace sacré à Qumrân: Propositions pour l'archéologie," *Revue biblique* 101: 161–214.

Hummel, Reinhardt 1966. *Die Auseinandersetzung zwischen Kirche und Judentum im Matthäusevangelium.* München: Kaiser.

Hurtado, Larry H. 1983. *Mark.* The New International Biblical Commentary. Peabody: Hendrickson.

Hurtado, Larry H. 2003. *Lord Jesus Christ: Devotion to Jesus in Earliest Christianity.* Grand Rapids: Eerdmans.

Instone-Brewer, D. 1998. "Nomological Exegesis in Qumran 'Divorce' Texts," *Revue de Qumran* 18: 561–579.

Instone-Brewer, D. 2000. "Jesus' Old Testament Basis for Monogamy," in S. Moyise (ed.), *The Old Testament in the New Testament: Essays in Honour of J. L. North.* Sheffield Academic Press, 75–105.

Irmscher, J. 1992. "The Book of Elchasai," in W. Schneelmelcher (ed.), *New Testament Apocrypha II: Writings Relating to the Apostles, Apocalypses and Related Subjects*. Translated by R. McL. Wilson. Louisville: John Knox Press, 685–690.

Jackson, David R. 2004. *Enochic Judaism: Three Defining Paradigm Exemplars*. Library of Second Temple Studies 49. London: T & T Clark.

Jackson-McCabe, Matt (ed.) 2007. *Jewish Christianity Reconsidered: Rethinking Ancient Groups and Texts*. Minneapolis: Fortress.

Jacobson, Arland D. 1992. *The First Gospel: An Introduction to Q*. Sonoma: Polebridge.

Jaffee, M. S. 2001. *Torah in the Mouth: Writing and Oral Tradition in Palestinian Judaism, 200 BCE-400 CE*. New York: Oxford University Press.

Janowski, Brend, Peter Stuhlmacher, and Daniel P. Bailey (eds.) 2004. *The Suffering Servant: Isaiah 53 in Jewish and Christian Sources*. Grand Rapids: Eerdmans.

Janowski, Brend and Peter Stuhlmacher 1997. *Biblische Theologie des Neuen Testaments. Vol. 1: Grundlegung von Jesus zu Paulus*. Göttingen: Vandenhoeck and Ruprecht.

Jassen, Alex P. 2014. *Scripture and Law in the Dead Sea Scrolls*. New York and Cambridge: Cambridge University Press.

Jay, Nancy 1992. *Throughout Your Generations Forever: Sacrifice, Religion, and Paternity*. Chicago: University of Chicago Press.

Jeremias, J. 1955. *The Parables of Jesus*. London: SCM.

Jeremias, J. 1966. "Artikellos Χριστός. Zur Ursprache von 1. Kor 15.3b-5," *Zeitschrift für die neutestamentliche Wissenschaft* 57: 211–215.

Jeremias, J. 1971. *New Testament Theology*. New York: SCM.

Jeremias, J. 1972. *The Parables of Jesus*. New York: Charles Scribner's Sons.

Jervell, J. 1972. *Luke and the People of God: A New Look at Luke-Acts*. Minneapolis: Fortress.

Jewett, R. 1986. *The Thessalonian Correspondence*. Philadelphia: Fortress.

Johnson, Aaron P. 2013. *Religion and Identity in Porphyry of Tyre: The Limits of Hellenism in Late Antiquity*. New York and Cambridge: Cambridge University Press.

Jones, F. Stanley 1990. "An Ancient Jewish Christian Rejoinder to Luke's Acts of the Apostles: Pseudo-Clementine Recognitions 1.27–71," in R. Stoops (ed.), *Semeia 80: The Apocryphal Acts of the Apostles in Intertextual Perspectives*. Atlanta: Scholars, 223–245.

Jones, F. Stanley 1995. *An Ancient Jewish Christian Source On the History of Christianity: Pseudo-Clementine Recognitions I.27–71*. Atlanta: Scholars.

Jones, F. Stanley 2000. "Pseudo-Clementine Literature," in L. H. Schiffman and J. C. VanderKam (eds.), *Encyclopedia of the Dead Sea Scrolls*. 2 vols. New York: Oxford University Press, 2: 717–719.

Jones, F. Stanley 2001. "Jewish-Christian Chiliastic Restoration in Pseudo-Clementine Recognitions 1.27–71," in J. M. Scott (ed.), *Restoration: Old Testament, Jewish, and Christian Perspectives*. Journal for the Study of Judaism 72. Leiden: Brill, 529–547.

Jones, F. Stanley 2001. "Hegesippus as a Source for the History of Jewish Christianity," in S. Mimouni and F. S. Jones (eds.), *Le judéo-christianisme dans tous ses états*. Paris: Cerf, 201–212.

Jones, F. Stanley 2004. "The *Book of Elchasai* in its Relevance for Manichaean Institutions with a Supplement: The *Book of Elchasai* Reconstructed and Translated," *ARAM* 16: 179–215.

Jones, F. Stanley 2005. "Jewish Christianity of the Pseudo-Clementines," in A. Marjanen and P. Luomanen (eds.), *A Companion to Second Century Christian "Heretics."* Leiden: Brill, 315–334.

Jones, F. Stanley 2008. "Sonship in Some Early Jewish Christian Traditions." Occasional Papers of the Institute for Antiquity and Christianity 52. Claremont.

Jones, F. Stanley 2009. "The Genesis of Pseudo-Clementine Christianity." A paper presented for the Construction of Christian Identities Section at the 2009 Annual Meeting of the Society of Biblical Literature, New Orleans.

Jones, F. Stanley 2012. *Pseudoclementina Elchasaiticaque inter Judaeochristiana: Collected Studies.* Orientalia Lovaniensia analecta 203. Leuven: Peeters.

Joseph, Simon J. 2010. "The Ascetic Jesus," *Journal for the Study of the Historical Jesus* 8: 146–181.

Joseph, Simon J. 2011. "'Seek His Kingdom': Q 12,22b-31, God's Providence, and Adamic Wisdom," *Biblica* 92.3: 392–410.

Joseph, Simon J. 2012. *Jesus, Q, and the Dead Sea Scrolls: A Judaic Approach to Q.* Wissenschaftliche Untersuchungen zum Neuen Testament II.333. Tübingen: Mohr Siebeck.

Joseph, Simon J. 2014. *The Nonviolent Messiah: Jesus, Q, and the Enochic Tradition.* Minneapolis: Fortress.

Joseph, Simon J. 2014. "'For Heaven and Earth to Pass Away'? Reexamining Q 16,16–18, Eschatology, and the Law," *Zeitschrift für die neutestamentliche Wissenschaft* 105/2: 169–188.

Juel, D. 1977. *Messiah and Temple: The Trial of Jesus in the Gospel of Mark.* Society of Biblical Literature Dissertation Series 31. Missoula: Scholars.

Juel, D. 1983. *Luke-Acts: The Promise of History.* Atlanta: John Knox.

Juster, Jean 1914. *Les Juifs dans l'Empire Romain: leur Condition Juridique, Économique, Sociale.* Paris: Paul Geuthner.

Kähler, Martin 1964. *The So-Called Historical Jesus and the Historic Biblical Christ.* Philadelphia: Fortress.

Kalmin, R. 1994. "Christians and Heretics in Rabbinic Literature of Late Antiquity," *Harvard Theological Review* 87: 155–169.

Käsemann, Ernst 1964. "The Problem of the Historical Jesus," in *Essays on New Testament Themes.* Studies in Biblical Theology 41. London: SCM, 15–47.

Käsemann, Ernst 1970. "The Pauline Theology of the Cross," *Interpretation* 24: 151–177.

Kazen, Thomas 2008. "The Christology of Early Christian Practice." *Journal of Biblical Literature*, 127.3: 591–614.

Kazen, Thomas 2013. *Scripture, Interpretation, or Authority? Motives and Arguments in Jesus' Halakic Conflicts.* Wissenschaftliche Untersuchungen zum Neuen Testament 320. Tübingen: Mohr Siebeck.

Kazmierski, C. R. 1992. "Evangelist and Leper: A Socio-Cultural Study of Mk 1.40–45," *New Testament Studies* 38: 37–50.

Kee, Howard Clark 1975. "The Function of Scriptural Quotations and Allusions in Mark 11–16," in E. Earle Ellis and Erich Grässer (eds.), *Jesus und Paulus: Festschrift für Werner Georg Kümmel zum 70. Geburtstag.* Göttingen: Vandenhoeck-Ruprecht, 165–188.

Keener, Craig S. 2005. *1–2 Corinthians.* New Cambridge Bible Commentary. New York: Cambridge University Press.

Keith, Chris 2014. *Jesus Against the Scribal Elite: The Origins of the Conflict.* Grand Rapids: Baker Academic.

Kelber, W. H. 1979. *Mark's Story of Jesus.* Philadelphia: Fortress.

Kelhoffer, James A. 2005. *The Diet of John the Baptist: 'Locusts and Wild Honey' in Synoptic and Patristic Interpretation.* Wissenschaftliche Untersuchungen zum Neuen Testament 176. Tübingen: Mohr Siebeck.

Kelley, Nicole 2005. "Problems of Knowledge and Authority in the Pseudo-Clementine Romance of Recognitions," *Journal of Early Christian Studies* 13.3: 315–348.

Kelley, Nicole 2006. *Knowledge and Religious Authority in the Pseudo-Clementines: Situating the Recognition in Fourth-Century Syria.* Wissenschaftliche Untersuchungen zum Neuen Testament II.213. Tübingen: Mohr Siebeck.

Kerr, A. R. 2002. *The Temple of Jesus' Body: The Temple Theme in the Gospel of John.* Journal for the Study of the New Testament: Supplement Series 220. London: Sheffield Academic Press.

Kertelge, K. (ed.) 1976. *Der Tod Jesu.* Quaestiones disputatae 74. Freiburg: Herder.

Kieferndorf, Philipp 1921. "Seine Speise war Heuschrecken?" *Vegetarische Warte* 54: 188–189.

Kiilunen, Jarmo 1985. *Die Vollmacht im Widerstreit: Untersuchungen zum Werdegang von Mk 2,1–3,6.* Annales Academiae Scientiarum Fennicae. Diss. Humanarum litterarum 40. Helsinki: Suomalainen Tiedeakatemia.

Kilgallen, J. J. 1989. "The Function of Stephen's Speech (Acts 2–53)," *Biblica* 70: 177–181.

King, Karen L. 2003. *What is Gnosticism?* Cambridge: Harvard University Press.

Kinman, B. 1995. *Jesus' Entry into Jerusalem: In the Context of Lukan Theology and the Politics of His Day.* Arbeiten zur Geschichte des antiken Judentums und des Urchristentums 28. Leiden: Brill.

Kirk, Alan 1998. *The Composition of the Sayings Source: Genre, Synchrony, and Wisdom Redaction in Q.* Novum Testamentum Supplements 91. Leiden: Brill.

Kirk, Alan 2005. "The Memory of Violence and the Death of Jesus in Q," in A. Kirk and T. Thatcher (eds.), *Memory, Tradition, and Text: Uses of the Past in Early Christianity.* Semeia Studies 52. Atlanta: Society of Biblical Literature, 191–206.

Kister, M. 2009. "Divorce, Reproof, and Other Sayings in the Synoptic Gospels: Jesus Traditions in the Context of 'Qumranic' and Other Texts," in R. A. Clements and D. R. Schwartz (eds.), *Text, Thought, and Practice in Qumran and Early Christianity: Proceedings of the Ninth International Symposium of the Orion Center for the Study of the Dead Sea Scrolls and Associated Literature, Jointly Sponsored by the Hebrew University Center for the Study of Christianity, 11–12 January, 2004*. Studies on the Texts of the Desert of Judah 84. Leiden: Brill, 195–229.

Kister, Menahem 1999. "Studies in 4Miqsat Ma'aseh ha-Torah" and Related Texts: Law, Theology, Language and Calendar," *Tarbiz* 68.3: 317–372.

Kiuchi, N. 1987. *The Purification Offering in the Priestly Literature: Its Meaning and Function*. Sheffield: Sheffield Academic Press.

Klawans, Jonathan 2002. "Interpreting the Last Supper: Sacrifice, Spiritualization, and Anti-Sacrifice," *New Testament Studies* 48: 1–17.

Klawans, Jonathan 2005. *Purity, Sacrifice, and the Temple: Symbolism and Supersessionism in the Study of Ancient Judaism*. New York: Oxford University Press.

Klijn, A. F. J. 1974. "The Study of Jewish Christianity," *New Testament Studies* 20: 419–431.

Klijn, A. F. J. 1992. *Jewish-Christian Gospel Tradition. Vigiliae christianae*: Supplements Series 17. Leiden: Brill.

Klijn, A. F. J. and G. J. Reinink 1974. "Elchasai and Mani," *Vigiliae christianae* 28: 277–289.

Klinghardt, M. 1988. *Gesetz und Volk Gottes: Das lukanische Verständnis des Gesetzes nach Herkunft, Funktion und seinem Ort in der Geschichte des Urchristentums*. Wissenschaftliche Untersuchungen zum Neuen Testament II.32. Tübingen: Mohr Siebeck.

Klinzing, Georg 1971. *Die Umdeutung des Kultus in der Qumrangemeinde und im Neuen Testament*. Studien zur Umwelt des Neuen Testaments 7. Göttingen: Vandenhoeck and Ruprecht.

Kloppenborg, John S. 1978. "An Analysis of the Pre-Pauline Formula in 1 Cor 15:3b-5 in Light of Some Recent Literature," *Catholic Biblical Quarterly* 40.3: 351–357.

Kloppenborg, John S. 1986. "The Function of Apocalyptic Language in Q," in *Society of Biblical Literature Seminar Papers* 25. Atlanta: Scholars, 224–235.

Kloppenborg, John S. 1987. "Symbolic Eschatology and the Apocalypticism of Q," *Harvard Theological Review* 80.3: 287–306.

Kloppenborg, John S. 1987. *The Formation of Q: Trajectories in Ancient Christian Wisdom Collections*. Philadelphia: Fortress.

Kloppenborg, John S. 1990. "Nomos and Ethos in Q," in J. E. Goehring, J. T. Sanders, and C. W. Hedrick (eds.), *Gospel Origins and Christian Beginnings: In Honor of James M. Robinson*. Sonoma: Polebridge, 35–48.

Kloppenborg, John S. 1990. "Alms, Debt and Divorce: Jesus' Ethics in their Mediterranean Context," *Toronto Journal of Theology* 6: 182–200.

Kloppenborg, John S. 1991. "City and Wasteland: Narrative World and the Beginning of the Sayings Gospel (Q)," *Semeia* 52: 145–160.

Kloppenborg, John S. 1993. "The Sayings Gospel Q: Recent Opinion on the People behind the Document," *Currents in Research: Biblical Studies* 1: 9–34.

Kloppenborg, John S. 1996. "The Sayings Gospel Q and the Quest of the Historical Jesus," *Harvard Theological Review* 89: 307–44.

Kloppenborg, John S. 2001. "Discursive Practices in the Sayings Gospel Q and the Quest of the Historical Jesus," in A. Lindemann (ed.), *The Sayings*

Source Q and the Historical Jesus. Bibliotheca ephemeridum theologicarum lovaniensium 158. Leuven: Peeters, 149–190.

Kloppenborg, John S. 2002. "Preface," in Kyu Sam Han, *Jerusalem and the Early Jesus Movement: The Q Community's Attitude Toward the Temple*. Journal for the Study of the New Testament: Supplements Series 207. Sheffield Academic Press, 7–8.

Kloppenborg, John S. 2006. *The Tenants in the Vineyard: Ideology, Economics, and Agrarian Conflict in Jewish Palestine*. Wissenschaftliche Untersuchungen zum Neuen Testament 195. Tübingen: Mohr Siebeck.

Kloppenborg, John S. 2014. "A New Synoptic Problem: Mark Goodacre and Simon Gathercole on Thomas," *Journal for the Study of the New Testament* 36/3: 199–239.

Kloppenborg Verbin, John S. 2000. *Excavating Q: The History and Setting of the Sayings Gospel*. Edinburgh: T & T Clark.

Kloppenborg Verbin, John S. 2000. "Isaiah 5:1–7, the Parable of the Tenants, and Vineyard Leases on Papyrus," in S. G. Wilson and M. Desjardins (eds.), *Text and Artifact: Religions in Mediterranean Antiquity: Essays in Honor of Peter Richardson*. Studies in Christianity and Judaism 9. Waterloo: Wilfrid Laurier University Press, 111–134.

Kloppenborg Verbin, John S. 2002. "Egyptian Viticultural Practices and the Citation of Isa 5:1–7 in Mark 12.1–9," *Novum Testamentum* 44: 134–159.

Kloppenborg Verbin, John S. 2004. "Isa 5:1–7 LXX and Mark 12:1, 9, Again," *Novum Testamentum* 46: 12–19.

Knibb, Michael A. 1987. *The Qumran Community*. New York: Cambridge University Press.

Knust, Jennifer W. and Zsuzsanna Várhelyi (eds.) 2011. *Ancient Mediterranean Sacrifice*. New York: Oxford University Press.

Koch, G. A. 1976. "A Critical Investigation of Epiphanius' Knowledge of the Ebionites: A Translation and Critical Discussion of Panarion 30." Ph.D. dissertation, University of Pennsylvania Press.

Koch, K. 1966. "Sühne und Sündenvergebung um die Wende von der exilischen zur nachexilischen Zeit," *Evangelische Theologie* 26: 217–239.

Koester, Helmut 1983. "Three Thomas Parables," in A. H. B. Logan and A. J. M. Wedderburn (eds.), *The New Testament and Gnosis: Essays in Honor of Robert McL. Wilson*. Edinburgh: T & T Clark, 195–203.

Koester, Helmut 1990. *Ancient Christian Gospels: Their History and Development*. Philadelphia: Fortress.

Koester, Helmut 2000. *History and Literature of Early Christianity*. 2nd edn. New York: Walter de Gruyter.

Kosch, Daniel 1985. *Die Gottesherrschaft im Zeichen des Widerspruchs. Traditions- und redaktionsgeschichtliche Untersuchung von Lk 16,16/Mt 11,12 bei Jesus, Q und Lukas*. Europäische Hochschulschriften 23/257. Bern; New York: Peter Lang.

Kosch, Daniel 1989. *Die eschatologische Tora des Menschensohnes: Untersuchungen zur Rezeption der Stellung Jesu zur Tora in Q*. Novum Testamentum et Orbis Antiquus 12. Göttingen: Vandenhoeck and Ruprecht.

Kosch, Daniel 1992. "Q und Jesus," *Biblische Zeitschrift* 36: 30–58.

Kotila, M. 1988. *Umstrittene Zeuge. Studien zur Stellung des Gesetzes in der johanneischen Theologiegeschichte*. Helsinki: Suomalainen Tiedeakatemia.

Kraft, R. A. 1972. "In Search of 'Jewish Christianity' and its 'Theology': Problems of Definition and Methodology," *Recherches de Science Religieuse* 60: 81–92.

Kramer, W. 1966. *Christ, Lord, Son of God*. Studies in Biblical Theology 50. London: SCM.

Kuhn, Heinz-Wolfgang 1982. "Die Kreuzesstrafe während der frühen Kaiserzeit. Ihre Wirklichkeit und Wertung in der Umwelt des Urchristentums," *ANRW* II.25.1: 648–793.

Kuhn, Heinz-Wolfgang 2002. "The Qumran Meal and the Lord's Supper in Paul in the Context of the Graeco-Roman World," in A. Christophersen (ed.), *Paul, Luke and the Graeco-Roman World: Essays in Honour of Alexander J. M. Wedderburn*. Journal for the Study of the New Testament: Supplement Series 217. London: Sheffield Academic Press, 221–248.

Kuhn, K. G. 1958. "The Last Supper and the Communal Meal of Qumran," in *The Scrolls and the New Testament*. London: SCM, 65–93.

Laato, Antti 2012. *Who Is the Servant of the Lord? Jewish and Christian Interpretations on Isaiah 53 From Antiquity to the Middle Ages*. Studies in Rewritten Bible 4. Turku: Åbo Akademi University; Winona Lake: Eisenbrauns.

Lachs, Samuel Tobias 1987. *A Rabbinic Commentary on the New Testament: The Gospels of Matthew, Mark and Luke*. Hoboken: Ktav; New York: Anti-Defamation League of B'Nai Brith.

Lambrecht, Jan 1981. *Once More Astonished: The Parables of Jesus*. New York: Crossroad.

Lampe, G. W. H. 1981. "Martyrdom and Inspiration," in W. Horbury (ed.), *Suffering and Martyrdom in the New Testament*. Cambridge: Cambridge University Press, 118–135.

Lanci, John R. 1997. *A New Temple for Corinth: Rhetorical and Archaeological Approaches to Pauline Imagery*. New York: Peter Lang.

Lang, Bernhard 1997. *Sacred Games: A History of Christian Worship*. New Haven: Yale University Press.

Lange, John 1966. "The Argument from Silence," *History and Theology* 5: 288–301.

Langlois, Charles Victor and Charles Seignobos 1904. *Introduction to the Study of History*. Translated by G. G. Berry. New York: Henry Holt and Co..

Larsson, Edvin 1993. "Temple-Criticism and the Jewish Heritage: Some Reflections on Acts 6–7," *New Testament Studies* 39: 379–395.

Le Déaut, R. 1974. "Le Targumic Literature and New Testament Interpretation," *Biblical Theology Bulletin* 4: 243–289.

Le Donne, Anthony 2009. *The Historiographical Jesus: Memory, Typology, and the Son of David*. Waco: Baylor.

Lefebure, Leo D. 2000. *Revelation, the Religious, and Violence*. Maryknoll: Orbis.

Légasse, Simon 1997. *The Trial of Jesus*. Translated by John Bowden. London: SCM.

Lémonon, J.-P. 1981. *Pilate et le gouvernement de la Judée*. Paris: Gabalda.

Leonhardt, Jutta 2001. *Jewish Worship in Philo of Alexandria*. Texts and Studies in Ancient Judaism 84. Tübingen: Mohr Siebeck.

Levenson, Jon D. 1984. "The Temple and the World," *Journal of Religion* 64: 275–298.

Levenson, Jon D. 1993. *The Death and Resurrection of the Beloved Son: The Transformation of Child Sacrifice in Judaism and Christianity*. New Haven: Yale University Press.

Levine, Amy-Jill 1988. *The Social and Ethnic Dimensions of Matthean Salvation History: "Go nowhere among the Gentiles ..." (Matt. 10:5b)*. Studies in the Bible and Early Christianity 14. Lewiston: Edwin Mellen.

Levine, Amy-Jill 2000. "Jesus, Divorce, and Sexuality: A Jewish Critique," in B. F. le Beau, L. Greenspoon, and D. Hamm (eds.), *The Historical Jesus through Catholic and Jewish Eyes*. Harrisburg: Trinity, 113–129.

Levine, Amy-Jill 2014. *Review of Patrick Oliver, Torah Praxis after 70 CE*. Reviews of the Enoch Seminar. Retrieved from www.enochseminar.org.

Levine, Baruch A. 1968. "On the Presence of God in Biblical Religion," in Jacob Neusner (ed.), *Religions in Antiquity: Essays in Memory of Erwin Ramsdell Goodenough*. Leiden: Brill, 71–87.

Levine, Baruch A. 1974. *In the Presence of the LORD: A Study of the Cult and Some Cultic Terms in Ancient Israel*. Studies in Judaism in Late Antiquity. Leiden: Brill.

Levinson, Bernard M. 2008. *Legal Revision and Religious Renewal in Ancient Israel*. New York and Cambridge: Cambridge University Press.

Lindsey, E. Duane 1985. *The Servant Songs: A Study in Isaiah*. Chicago: Moody Press.

Lietzmann, H. 1953–1979 (1926). *Mass and Lord's Supper: A Study in the History of the Liturgy*. Leiden: Brill.

Lindars, B. 1972. *The Gospel of John*. New Century Bible Commentary 25. London: Oliphants.

Linzey, Andrew 2003. "The Bible and Killing for Food," in S. J. Armstrong and R. G. Botzler (eds.), *The Animal Ethics Reader*. London: Routledge, 227–234.

Loader, William R. G. 2002. *Jesus' Attitude towards the Law: A Study of the Gospels*. Grand Rapids: Eerdmans.

Loader, William R. G. 2004. *The Septuagint, Sexuality, and the New Testament: Case Studies on the Impact of the LXX in Philo and the New Testament*. Grand Rapids: Eerdmans.

Loader, William R. G. 2011. "Attitudes to Judaism and the Law and Synoptic Relations," in P. Foster, A. Gregory, and J. S. Kloppenborg (eds.), *New Studies in the Synoptic Problem Oxford Conference, April 2008*. Bibliotheca ephemeridum theologicarum lovaniensium 239. Leuven: Peeters, 347–369.

Lohse, E. 2008. "Christus, des Gesetzes Ende? Die Theologie des Apostels Paulus in kritischer Perspektive," *Zeitschrift für die neutestamentliche Wissenschaft* 99: 18–32.

Longenecker, R. N. 1970. *The Christology of Early Jewish Christianity*. Studies in Biblical Theology 2/17. London: SCM.

Longenecker, R. N. 1983. "Jews, Hebrews and Christians: Some Needed Distinctions," *Novum Testamentum* 24: 194–208.

Lüdemann, Gerd 1989. *Opposition to Paul in Jewish Christianity*. Translated by M. Eugene Boring. Minneapolis: Fortress.

Lüdemann, Gerd 1989. *Early Christianity according to the Traditions in Acts: A Commentary*. Minneapolis: Fortress.

Lüdemann, Gerd 1996. *Heretics: The Other Side of Early Christianity*. Translated by John Bowden. Louisville: Westminster John Knox.

Lüdemann, Gerd 2001. *Jesus After 2000 Years: What He Really Said and Did*. Amherst: Prometheus.

Lührmann, Dieter 1969. *Die Redaktion der Logienquelle*. Wissenschaftliche Monographien zum Alten und Neuen Testament 33. Neukirchener-Vluyn: Neukirchener.

Lührmann, Dieter 1981. "Markus 14, 55–64: Christologie und Zerstörung des Tempels im Markusevangelium," *New Testament Studies* 27: 457–474.

Lundquist, John M. 1984. "The Common Temple Ideology of the Ancient Near East," in T. G. Madsen (ed.), *The Temple in Antiquity: Ancient Records and Modern Perspectives*. Provo: Religious Studies Center, Brigham Young University, 53–76.

Luomanen, Petri 2012. *Recovering Jewish Christian Sects and Gospels*. Vigiliae christianae Supplements 110. Leiden: Brill.

Luttikhuizen, Gerard P. 1985. *The Revelation of Elchasai: Investigations into the Evidence for a Mesopotamian Jewish Apocalypse of the Second Century and its Reception by Judeo-Christian Propagandists*. Texte und Studien zum antiken Judentum 8. Tübingen: Mohr Siebeck.

Luz, Ulrich 2002. "Warum zog Jesus nach Jerusalem?" in J. Schröter and R. Brucker (eds.), *Der historische Jesus*. Edited by. Beihefte zur Zeitschrift für die neutestamentliche Wissenschaft 114. Berlin: Walter de Gruyter, 409–427.

Maccoby, Hyam 1987. *The Mythmaker: Paul and the Invention of Christianity*. New York: Harper and Row.

MacGregor, G. H. C. 1961. "The Concept of the Wrath of God in the New Testament," *New Testament Studies* 7: 101–109.

Mack, Burton L. 1987. "Introduction: Religion and Ritual," in R. Hamerton-Kelly (ed.), *Violent Origins: Ritual Killing and Cultural Formation*. Stanford: Stanford University Press, 1–70.

Mack, Burton L. 1988. *A Myth of Innocence: Mark and Christian Origins*. Philadelphia: Fortress.

Magness, Jodi 2003. *The Archaeology of Qumran and the Dead Sea Scrolls*. Studies in the Dead Sea Scrolls and Related Literature. Grand Rapids: Eerdmans.

Maier, Johann 1982. *Jüdische Auseinandersetzung mit dem Christentum in der Antike*. Erträge der Forschung 177. Darmstadt: Wissenschaftliche Buchgesellschaft.

Maimonides 1956. *Guide to the Perplexed*. Translated by M. Friedlander. New York: Dover Publications.

Majumdar, Ramesh Chandra (ed.) 1951. *The History and Culture of the Indian People. Vol. 1: The Vedic Age*. Bombay [Mumbai]: Bharatiya Vidya Bhavan.

Malina, B. J. 1976. "Jewish Christianity or Christian Judaism: Toward a Hypothetical Definition," *Journal for the Study of Judaism* 7: 46–57.

Mann, C. S. 1986. *Mark*. Anchor Bible. Garden City: Doubleday.

Manson, T. W. 1943. *Jesus the Messiah*. London: Hodder and Stoughton.

Manson, T. W. 1953. *The Servant-Messiah*. Cambridge: Cambridge University Press.

Marcus, Joel 1992. *The Way of the Lord: Christological Exegesis of the Old Testament in the Gospel of Mark*. Louisville: John Knox Westminster.

Marcus, Joel 1995. "The Old Testament and the Death of Jesus: The Role of Scripture in the Gospel Passion Narratives," in John T. Carroll and Joel B. Green (eds.), *The Death of Jesus in Early Christianity*. Peabody: Hendrickson, 205–233.

Marcus, Joel 2000. *Mark 1–8: A New Translation with Introduction and Commentary*. Anchor Bible 27. New York: Doubleday.

Marcus, Joel 2000. "Mark – Interpreter of Paul," *New Testament Studies* 46: 473–487.

Martin, Dale B. 2014. "Jesus in Jerusalem: Armed and Not Dangerous," *Journal for the Study of the New Testament* 37/1: 3–24.

Martin, Dale B. 2015. "Response to Downing and Fredriksen," *Journal for the Study of the New Testament* 37.3: 334–345.

Martin, Ralph 1967. *Carmen Christi: Philippians ii.5–11 in Recent Interpretation and in the Setting of Early Christian Worship*. Society for New Testament Studies Monograph Series 4. Cambridge: Cambridge University Press.

Martyn, J. L. 1977. "Clementine Recognitions 1,33–71, Jewish Christianity, and the Fourth Gospel," in J. Jervell and W. A. Meeks (eds.), *God's Christ and His People: Studies in Honour of Nils Alstrup Dahl*. Oslo: Universitetsforlaget, 265–295.

Marx, Alfred 2005. *Les systèmes sacrificiels de l'Ancien Testament: Formes et fonctions du culte sacrificiel à Yhwh*. Vetus Testamentum Supplements 105. Leiden: Brill.

Marxsen, Willi 1970. *The Lord's Supper As a Christological Problem*. Translated by Lorenz Nieting. Philadelphia: Fortress.

Marxsen, Willi 1992. "The Meals of Jesus and the Lord's Supper of the Church," in *Jesus and the Church*. Translated by P. I. Devenish. New York: Trinity, 137–146.

Mason, Steve 1992. *Josephus and the New Testament*. Peabody: Hendrickson.

Mason, Steve 2009. *Josephus, Judea and Christian Origins: Methods and Categories*. Peabody: Hendrickson.

Massaux, Édouard 1950. *Influence de l'Évangile de saint Matthieu sur la littérature chrétienne avant saint Irénée*. Universitas Catholica Lovaniensis 2.42. Leuven: Leuven University Press.

Matson, Mark A. 1992. "The Contribution to the Temple Cleansing by the Fourth Gospel," in E. H. Lovering (ed.), *Society of Biblical Literature 1992 Seminar Papers*. Society of Biblical Literature Seminar Papers 31. Atlanta: Scholars, 489–506.

Matthews, Kenneth A. 1988. "John, Jesus and the Essenes: Trouble at the Temple," *Criswell Theological Review* 3.1: 101–126.

McClymond, Kathryn 2008. *Beyond Sacred Violence: A Comparative Study of Sacrifice*. Baltimore: John Hopkins University Press.

McGowan, Andrew 2012. "Eucharist and Sacrifice: Cultic Tradition and Transformation in Early Christian Ritual Meals," in M. Klinghardt and H. Taussig (eds.), *Mahl und religiöse Identität im frühen Christentum. Meals and Religious Identity in Early Christianity*. Tübingen: Francke, 191–206.

McGrew, Timothy J. 2013. "The Argument from Silence," *Acta Analytica* 29.2: 215–228.

McGuckin, J. A. 1989. "Sacrifice and Atonement: An Investigation into the Attitude of Jesus of Nazareth towards Cultic Sacrifice," in Y. Bauer, A. Eckardt, F. H. Littell, D. Patterson, E. Maxwell, and R. Maxwell (eds.), *Remembering for the Future: Working Papers and Addenda; Volume 1: Jews and Christians During and After the Holocaust*. 3 vols. Oxford: Pergamon, 1: 548–661.

McHugh, John 2009. *A Critical and Exegetical Commentary on John 1–4*. International Critical Commentary on the Holy Scriptures of the Old and New Testaments. London: Continuum.

McKelvey, R. J. 1969. *New Temple: The Church in the New Testament*. Old Testament Message. Oxford: Oxford University Press.

McKenna, Andrew J. 1991. *Violence and Difference: Girard, Derrida, and Deconstruction*. Urbana: University of Illionis Press.

McKnight, Scot 2005. *Jesus and His Death: Historiography, the Historical Jesus, and Atonement Theory*. Waco: Baylor University Press.

McLean, Bradley H. 1992. "The Absence of an Atoning Sacrifice in Paul's Soteriology," *New Testament Studies* 38: 531–553.

McLean, Bradley H. 1996. *The Cursed Christ: Mediterranean Expulsion Rituals and Pauline Soteriology*. Journal for the Study of the New Testament: Supplements Series 126. Sheffield: Sheffield Academic Press.

Mealand, David L. 1978. "The Dissimilarity Test," *Scottish Journal of Theology* 31: 41–50.

Meier, John P. 1990. "Jesus in Josephus, a Modest Proposal," *Catholic Biblical Quarterly* 52: 76–103.

Meier, John P. 1991. *A Marginal Jew: Rethinking the Historical Jesus. Vol. 1: The Roots of the Problem of the Person*. New York: Doubleday.

Meier, John P. 1994. *A Marginal Jew: Rethinking the Historical Jesus. Vol. 2: Mentor, Message, and Miracles*. ABRL. New York: Doubleday.

Meier, John P. 2001. *A Marginal Jew: Rethinking the Historical Jesus. Vol. 3: Companions and Competitors*. New York: Doubleday.

Meier, John P. 2003. "The Historical Jesus and the Historical Law: Some Problems within the Problem," *Catholic Biblical Quarterly* 65: 52–79.

Meier, John P. 2009. *A Marginal Jew: Rethinking the Historical Jesus. Vol. 4: Law and Love*. Anchor Bible Reference Library. New Haven: Yale University Press.

Mendenhall, G. E. and G. A. Herion 1992. "Covenant," *Anchor Bible Dictionary* 1: 1179–1202.

Merklein, H. 1978. *Die Gottesherrschaft als Handlungsprinzip. Untersuchung zur Ethik Jesu*. Forschung zur Bibel 34. Würzburg: Echter.

Merklein, H. 1989. *Jesu Botschaft von de Gottesherrschaft. Eine Skizze*. 3rd edn. Stuttgart: Katholisches Bibelwerk.

Mermelstein, Ari 2014. *Creation, Covenant, and the Beginnings of Judaism: Reconceiving Historical Time in the Second Temple Period.* Journal for the Study of Judaism: Supplements Series 168. Leiden: Brill.

Meshorer, Yaakov 1984. "One Hundred Ninety Years of Tyrian Shekels," in A. Houghton, L. Mildenberg, and A. A. Houghton (eds.), *Festschrift für/Studies in Honor of Leo Mildenberg.* Wetteren: Editions NR, 171–191.

Mettinger, Tryggve N. D. 1983. *A Farewell to the Servant Songs: A Critical Examination of the Exegetical Axiom.* Lund: C. W. K. Gleerup.

Metzner, Rainer 2010. *Kaiphas. Der Hohepriester jenes Jahres. Geschichte und Deutung.* Ancient Judaism and Early Christianity 75. Leiden: Brill.

Meyer, Ben F. 1979. *The Aims of Jesus.* London: SCM.

Meyer, P. D. 1967. "The Community of Q." Ph.D. dissertation, University of Iowa.

Milgrom, Jacob 1971. "A Prolegomenon to Leviticus 17:11," *Journal of Biblical Literature* 90: 149–56.

Milgrom, Jacob 1971. "Sin Offering or Purification Offering?" *Vetus Testamentum* 21: 237–239.

Milgrom, Jacob 1976. "Profane Slaughter and the Composition of Deuteronomy," *Hebrew Union College Annual* 47: 1–17.

Milgrom, Jacob 1976. *Cult and Conscience: The Asham and the Priestly Doctrine of Repentance.* Leiden. Brill.

Milgrom, Jacob 1983. *Studies in Cultic Theology and Terminology.* Leiden: Brill.

Milgrom, Jacob 1992. *Leviticus 1–16: A New Translation with Introduction and Commentary.* Anchor Bible 3. New York: Doubleday.

Milgrom, Jacob 2002. *Pesharim, Other Commentaries, and Related Documents.* J. H. Charlesworth (ed.), Princeton Theological Seminary Dead Sea Scrolls Project 6B. Louisville: Westminster John Knox.

Mimouni, Simon Claude 1997. "La 'Birkat ha-minim': Une prière juive contre les judéo-chrétiens," *Recherches de science religieuse* 71: 275–298.

Mimouni, Simon Claude 1998. *Le Judéo-christianisme ancien: Essais historiques.* Série Patrimoines. Paris: Cerf.

Mimouni, Simon Claude 2006. *Les fragments évangéliques Judéo-chrétiens "apocryphisés": Recherches et perspectives.* Cahiers de la Revue biblique 66. Paris: Gabalda.

Mimouni, Simon Claude 2012. *Early Judaeo-Christianity: Historical Essays.* Interdisciplinary Studies in Ancient Culture and Religion 13. Translated by R. Fréchet. Leuven: Peeters.

Mimouni, Simon Claude and F. S. Jones (eds.) 2001. *Le Judéo-Christianisme dans tous ses états: acts du colloque de Jérusalem 6–10 Juillet 1998.* Paris: Les Éditions du Cerf.

Montefiore, Hugh 1962. "A Comparison of the Parables of the Gospel according to Thomas and the Synoptic Gospels," in H. E. W. Turner and H. Montefiore (eds.), *Thomas and the Evangelists.* Studies in Biblical Theology 35. Naperville: Alec R. Allenson, 455–465.

Montefiore, Hugh 1965. "Jesus and the Temple Tax," *New Testament Studies* 10: 60–71.

Moo, Douglas J. 1983. *The Old Testament in the Gospel Passion Narratives.* Sheffield: Almond.

Morris, Leon 1962. *The Cross in the New Testament*. Grand Rapids: Eerdmans.

Muddiman, John 2009. "The Triumphal Entry and Cleansing of the Temple (Mark 11.1–17 and Parallels): a Jewish Festival Setting?" in C. M. Tuckett (ed.), *Feast and Festivals*. Contributions to Biblical Exegesis and Theology 53. Leuven: Peeters, 77–86.

Mueller, J. R. 1980. "The Temple Scroll and the Gospel Divorce Texts," *Revue de Qumran* 10: 247–256.

Müller, K. 1986. "Gesetz und Gesetzeserfüllung im Frühjudentum," in K. Kertelge (ed.), *Das Gesetz im Neuen Testament*. Freiburg: Herder, 11–27.

Müller, K. 2000. "Forschungsgeschichtliche Anmerkungen zum Thema 'Jesus von Nazareth und das Gesetz': Versuch einer Zwischenbilanz," *Kirche und Volk Gottes. FS. Jürgen Roloff*. Neukirchen-Vluyn: Neukirchener, 58–77.

Munck, Johannes 1960. "Jewish Christianity in Post-Apostolic Times," *New Testament Studies* 6, 103–116.

Munck, Johannes 1965. "Primitive Jewish Christianity and Later Jewish Christianity: Continuation or Rupture?" in *Aspects du Judéo-Christianisme: Colloque de Strasbourg 23–25 avril 1964*. Université de Strasbourg, Centre de recherches d'histoire des religions. Paris: Presses Universitaires de France, 77–93.

Münderlein, Gerhard 1963. "Die Verfluchung Des Feigenbaumes (Mk. XI.12–14)," *New Testament Studies* 10/1: 89–104.

Murphy O'Connor, Jerome 1970. "An Essene Missionary Document? CD II, 4–VI, 1," *Revue Biblique* 77: 201–229.

Murphy O'Connor, Jerome 1981. "Tradition and Redaction in 1 Cor 15:3–7," *Catholic Biblical Quarterly* 43.4: 582–589.

Murphy O'Connor, Jerome 2000. "Jesus and the Money Changers (Mark 11:15–17; John 2:13–17)," *Revue Biblique* 107: 42–55.

Murry, R. 1974. "Defining Judaeo-Christianity," *Heythrop* 15: 303–310.

Murry, R. 1982. "Jews, Hebrews and Christians: Some Needed Distinctions," *Novum Testamentum* 24: 194–208.

Myers, C. 1988. *Binding the Strong Man: A Political Reading of Mark's Story of Jesus*. Maryknoll: Orbis.

Myllykoski, Matti 2007. "James the Just in History and Tradition: Perspectives of Past and Present Scholarship (Part II)," *Currents in Biblical Research* 6: 11–98.

Naiden, F.S. 2013. *Smoke Signals for the Gods: Ancient Greek Sacrifice from the Archaic through Roman Periods*. New York and Oxford: Oxford University Press.

Najman, Hindy 1999. "Interpretation as Primordial Writing: Jubilees and Its Authority Conferring Strategies," *Journal for the Study of Judaism* 30: 379–410.

Najman, Hindy 2009. "Reconsidering Jubilees: Prophecy and Exemplarity," in G. Boccaccini and G. Ibba (eds.), *Enoch and the Mosaic Torah: The Evidence of Jubilees*. Grand Rapids: Eerdmans, 229–243.

Nanos, Mark D. 1996. *The Mystery of Romans*. Minneapolis: Fortress.

Nanos, Mark D. 2002. *The Irony of Galatians: Paul's Letter in First-Century Context*. Minneapolis: Fortress.

Nasrallah, Laura 2011. "The Embarrassment of Blood: Early Christians and Others on Sacrifice, War, and Rational Worship," in Jennifer W. Knust and Zsuzsanna Várhelyi (eds.), *Ancient Meditteranean Sacrifice*. New York: Oxford University Press, 142–166.

Neufeld, Thomas R. Yoder 2011. *Killing Enmity: Violence and the New Testament*. Grand Rapids: Baker Academic.

Neusner, Jacob 1976. "First Cleanse the Inside," *New Testament Studies* 22.4: 486–495.

Neusner, Jacob 1989. "Money-Changers in the Temple: The Mishnah's Explanation," *New Testament Studies* 35: 287–290.

Newman, Louis E. 1989. "Law, Virtue and Supererogation in the Halakha: The Problem of '*Lifnim Mishurat Hadin*' Reconsidered," *Journal of Jewish Studies* 40/1: 61–88.

Nickelsburg, George W. E. 1999. "The Nature and Function of Revelation in 1 Enoch, Jubilees, and Some Qumranic Documents," in E. G. Chazon and M. Stone (eds.), *Pseudepigraphic Perspectives: The Apocrypha and Pseudeipgrapha in Light of the Dead Sea Scrolls*. Studies on the Texts of the Desert of Judah 31. Leiden: Brill, 92–120.

Nickelsburg, George W. E. 2001. *1 Enoch: A Commentary on the Book of 1 Enoch*. Hermeneia. Philadelphia: Fortress.

Nickelsburg, George W. E. 2003. *Ancient Judaism and Christian Origins: Diversity, Continuity, and Transformation*. Minneapolis: Fortress.

Nineham, D. E. 1963. *The Gospel of St. Mark*. Pelican New Testament Commentaries. Harmondsworth: Penguin.

Nolland, John 2005. *The Gospel of Matthew*. The New International Greek Testament Commentary. Grand Rapids: Eerdmans.

Nolland, John 2008. "The King as Shepherd: The Role of Deutero-Zechariah in Matthew," in T. R. Hatina (ed.), *Biblical Interpretation in Early Christian Gospels. Volume 2: The Gospel of Matthew*. London: T & T Clark International, 133–146.

Noland, John 1718. *Nazarenus: Or, Jewish, Gentile, and Mahometan Christianity*. 2nd edn. London: J. Brotherton, J. Roberts, and A. Dodd.

North, Christopher Richard 1948. *The Suffering Servant in Deutero-Isaiah: An Historical and Critical Study*. Oxford: Oxford University Press.

O'Leary, A. M. 2006. *Matthew's Judaization of Mark: Examined in the Context of the Use of Sources in Graeco-Roman Antiquity*. Journal for the Study of the New Testament: Supplements Series 323. London: T & T Clark.

Och, Bernard 2014. "Creation and Redemption: Toward a Theology of Creation," in L. Michael Morales (ed.), *Cult and Cosmos: Tilting toward a Temple-Centered Theology*. Biblical Tools and Studies 18. Leuven: Peeters, 331–350.

Oliver, Isaac W. 2013. *Torah Praxis after 70 CE: Reading Matthew and Luke-Acts as Jewish Texts*. Wissenschaftliche Untersuchungen zum Neuen Testament II.355. Tübingen: Mohr Siebeck.

Olson, Daniel C. 2013. *A New Reading of the Animal Apocalypse of 1 Enoch: "All Nations Shall Be Blessed": With A New Translation and Commentary*. Studia in Veteris Testamenti Pseudepigrapha 24. Leiden: Brill.

Origen 1965. *Contra Celsum*. Translated by Henry Chadwick. Cambridge: Cambridge University Press.

Ottenheijm, Eric 2014. "'So the Sons are Free': The Temple Tax in the Matthean Community," in A. Houtman, M. Poorthuis, J. Schwartz, and Y. Turner (eds.), *The Actuality of Sacrifice: Past and Present*. Jewish and Christian Perspectives 28. Leiden: Brill, 71–88.

Overman, J. A. 1990. *Matthew's Gospel and Formative Judaism: The Social World of the Matthean Community*. Minneapolis: Fortress.

Paesler, Kurt 1999. *Das Tempelwort Jesu. Die Traditionen von Tempelzerstörung und Tempelerneuerung im Neuen Testament*. Forschungen zur Religion und Literatur des Alten und Neuen Testaments 184. Göttingen: Vandenhoeck and Ruprecht.

Paget, James Carleton 2001. "Some Observations on Josephus and Christianity," *Journal of Theological Studies* 52.2: 539–624.

Paget, James Carleton 2010. *Jews, Christians, and Jewish Christians in Antiquity*. Wissenschaftliche Untersuchungen zum Neuen Testament 251. Tübingen: Mohr Siebeck.

Painter, John 1997. *Mark's Gospel: Worlds in Conflict*. New Testament Readings. London: Routledge.

Painter, John 1997. *Just James: The Brother of Jesus in History and Tradition*. Columbia: University of South Carolina Press.

Pallis, Alexander 1903. *A Few Notes on the Gospels according to St. Mark and St. Matthew: Based Chiefly on Modern Greek*. Liverpool: Liverpool Booksellers.

Palmer, D. W. 1975. "To Die is Gain," *Novum Testamentum* 17: 203–218.

Pancaro, S. 1975. *The Law in the Fourth Gospel: The Torah and the Gospel, Moses and Jesus, Judaism and Chrsitianity according to John*. Novum Testamentum Supplements 42. Leiden: Brill.

Patai, Raphael 1947. *Man and Temple in Ancient Jewish Myth and Ritual*. London: Thomas Nelson.

Pate, C. Marvin and Douglas W. Kennard 2005. *Deliverance Now and Not Yet: The New Testament and the Great Tribulation*. Studies in Biblical Literature 54. New York: Peter Lang.

Patte, D. 1987. *The Gospel According to Matthew: A Structural Commentary on Matthew's Faith*. Philadelphia: Fortress.

Patterson, Stephen J. 1993. *The Gospel of Thomas and Jesus*. Sonoma: Polebridge.

Penella, Robert J. (ed.) 1979. *The Letters of Apollonius of Tyana: A Critical Text with Prolegomena, Translation and Commentary*. Leiden: Brill.

Perkins, Pheme 1981. *Hearing the Parables of Jesus*. New York: Paulist Press.

Perrin, Nicholas 2010. *Jesus the Temple*. Grand Rapids: Baker Academic.

Perrin, Norman 1967. *Rediscovering the Teaching of Jesus*. New York: Harper and Row.

Perrin, Norman 1974. *The New Testament: An Introduction: Proclamation and Parenesis, Myth and History*. New York: Harcourt Brace Jovanovich.

Pervo, Richard I. 1987. *Profit With Delight: The Literary Genre of the Acts of the Apostles*. Philadelphia: Fortress.

Pesch, Rudolf 1986. *Die Apostelgeschichte I*. Evangelisch-katholischer Kommentar zum Neuen Testament 5. Zürich: Benziger.

Pesch, Rudolf 1977. *Das Markusevangelium.* 2 vols. Herders theologischer Kommentar zum Neuen Testament 2. Freiburg im Breisgau: Herder.

Petersen, William L. 1997. "From Justin to Pepys: The History of the Harminonised Gospel Tradition," *Studia Patristica* 30: 71–96.

Petersen, William L. 2001. "Constructing the Matrix of Judaic Christianity from Texts,"in F. S. Jones and S. C. Mimouni (eds.), *Le Judéo-Christianisme dans tous ses états: acts du colloque de Jérusalem 6–10 Juillet 1998.* Paris: Cerf, 126–145.

Peterson, David 2004. "The New Temple: Christology and Ecclesiology in Ephesians and 1 Peter," in T. D. Alexander and S. Gathercole (eds.), *Heaven on Earth: The Temple in Biblical Theology.* Carlisle: Paternoster, 161–176.

Petropolou, Maria-Zoe 2008. *Animal Sacrifice in Ancient Greek Religion, Judaism, and Christianity, 100 BC-AD 200.* New York and Oxford: Oxford University Press.

Pobee, John 1985. *Persecution and Martyrdom in the Theology of Paul.* Journal for the Study of the New Testament: Supplements Series 6. Sheffield: JSOT.

Porphyry 2000. *On Abstinence from Killing Animals.* Translated by Gillian Clark. Ithaca: Cornell University Press.

Pounds, Brian 2015. "The Crucifiable Jesus." Ph.D. dissertation, University of Cambridge.

Porter, Anne and Glenn M. Schwartz (eds.) 2012. *Sacred Killing: The Archaeology of Sacrifice in the Ancient Near East.* Winona Lake: Eisenbrauns.

Powery, E. B. 2003. *Jesus Reads Scripture: The Function of Jesus' Use of Scripture in the Synoptic Gospels.* Leiden: Brill.

Pratscher, W. 1987. *Der Herrenbruder Jakobus und die Jakobustradition.* Forschungen zur Religion und Literatur des Alten und Neuen Testaments 139. Göttingen: Vandenhoeck & Ruprecht.

Prescendi, Francesca 2007. *Décrire et comprendre le sacrifice. Les réflexions des Romains sur leur propre religion à partir de la littérature antiquaire.* Stuttgart: Franz Steiner.

Quispel, Gilles 1957. "The Gospel of Thomas and the New Testament," *Vigiliae christianae* 11: 205–206.

Rahner, J. 1998. *Er aber sprach vom Tempel seines Leibes. Jesus von Nazaret als Ort der Offenbarung Gottes im vierten Evangelium.* Bonner biblische Beiträge 117. Bodenheim: Philo.

Räisänen, Heikki 1987. *Paul and the Law.* 2nd edn. Wissenschaftliche Untersuchungen zum Neuen Testament. Tübingen: Mohr Siebeck.

Räisänen, Heikki 1992. *Jesus, Paul and Torah: Collected Essays.* Journal for the Study of the New Testament Supplements 43. Sheffield: JSOT.

Reasoner, Mark 1999. *The Strong and the Weak: Romans 14.1–15.13 in Context.* Society for New Testament Studies Monograph Series 103. Cambridge: Cambridge University Press.

Redekop, Vern Neufeld and Thomas Ryba (eds.) 2014. *René Girard and Creative Mimesis.* Lanham: Lexington Books.

Redman, Judith C. S. 2010. "How Accurate are Eyewitnesses? Bauckham and the Eyewitnesses in the Light of Psychological Research," *Journal of Biblical Literature,* 129, 177–197.

Reed, Annette Yoshiko 2003. "'Jewish Christianity' after the 'Parting of the Ways,'" in A. Y. Reed and A. Becker (eds.), *The Ways that Never Parted: Jews and Christians in Late Antiquity and the Early Middle Ages.* Texte und Studien zum antiken Judentum 95. Tübingen: Mohr Siebeck, 189–231.

Reed, Annette Yoshiko 2005. *Fallen Angels and the History of Judaism and Christianity: The Reception of Enochic Literature.* New York and Cambridge: Cambridge University Press.

Reed, Annette Yoshiko 2008. "'Jewish Christianity' as Counter-history?: The Apostolic Past in Eusebius' Ecclesiastical History and the Pseudo-Clementine Homilies," in G. Gardner and K. Osterloh (eds.), *Antiquity in Antiquity: Jewish and Christian Pasts in the Greco-Roman World.* Texte und Studien zum antiken Judentum 123. Tübingen: Mohr Siebeck, 173–216.

Reed, Annette Yoshiko 2008. "Heresiology and the (Jewish-) Christian Novel: Narrativized Polemics in the Pseudo-Clementines," in E. Iricinschi and H. Zelletin (eds.), *Heresy and Self-Definition in Late Antiquity.* Tübingen: Mohr Siebeck, 273–298.

Regev, Eyal 2003. "Abominated Temple and a Holy Community: The Formation of the Notions of Purity and Impurity in Qumran," *Dead Sea Discoveries* 10/2: 243–278.

Regev, Eyal 2004. "Moral Impurity and the Temple in Early Christianity in Light of Qumranic Ideology and Ancient Greek Practice," *Harvard Theological Review* 79: 383–411.

Regev, Eyal 2010. "Temple Concerns and High-Priestly Prosecutions from Peter to James: Between Narrative and History," *New Testament Studies* 56: 64–89.

Rehm, Bernhard 1994. *Die Pseudoklementinen II: Rekognitionen in Rufins Übersetzung.* Die griechische christliche Schriftsteller der ersten Jahrhunderte 51. 2nd edn. Berlin: Akademie.

Rehm, Bernhard 2010. *The Pseudo-Clementines.* Studies on Early Christian Apocrypha 10. Edited by J. N. Bremmer. Leuven: Peeters.

Rehm, Bernhard and Georg Strecker 1992. *Die Pseudoklementinen I: Homilien.* Die griechische christliche Schriftsteller der ersten Jahrhunderte 42. 3rd edn. Berlin: Akademie-Verlag.

Reinhartz, Adele 2013. "The Temple Cleansing and the Death of Jesus," in C. S. Ehrlich, A. Runesson, and E. Schuller (eds.), *Purity, Holiness, and Identity in Judaism and Christianity: Essays in Memory of Susan Haber.* Wissenschaftliche Untersuchungen zum Neuen Testament 305. Tübingen: Mohr Siebeck, 100–111.

Rembaum, Joel E. 1982. "The Development of a Jewish Exegetical Tradition regarding Isaiah 53," *Harvard Theological Review* 75.3: 289–311.

Repschinski, B. 2009. *Nicht aufzulösen, sondern zu erfüllen: Das jüdische Gesetz in den synoptischen Jesuserzählungen.* Forschung zur Bibel 120. Würzburg: Echter.

Reumann, John 1966. "The Gospel of the Righteousness of God: Pauline Interpretation in Romans 3:21–32," *Interpretation* 20: 434–439, 450–451.

Reventlow, Henning Graf 1998. "Basic Issues in the Interpretation of Isaiah 53," in *Jesus and the Suffering Servant.* Harrisburg: Trinity Press International, 23–38.

Richard, Earl 1995. *First and Second Thessalonians*. Collegeville: Liturgical Press.

Richardson, Peter 1992. "Why Turn the Tables? Jesus' Protest in the Temple Precincts," in E. H. Lovering (ed.), *SBL 1992 Seminar Papers*. Society of Biblical Literature Seminar Papers 31. Atlanta: Scholars, 507–523.

Richardson, Peter 2004. *Building Jewish in the Roman East*. Journal for the Study of Judaism: Supplements Series 92. Waco: Baylor.

Richardson, Peter and S. Westerholm 1991. *Law in Religious Communities in the Roman Period: The Debate over Torah and Nomos in Post-Biblical Judaism and Early Christianity*. Studies in Christianity and Judaism 4. Waterloo: Wilfred Laurier University Press.

Ridderbos, H. N. 1974. "The Earliest Confession of the Atonement in Paul," in R. Banks (ed.), *Reconciliation and Hope*. Grand Rapids: Eerdmans, 76–89.

Riegel, S. K. 1978. "Jewish Christianity: Definitions and Terminology," *New Testament Studies* 24: 46–57.

Riggs, John W. 1984. "From Gracious Table to Sacramental Elements: The Tradition-History of *Didache* 9 and 10," *Second Century* 4: 83–101.

Riggs, John W. 1995. "The Sacred Food of Didache 9–10 and Second-Century Ecclesiologies," in C. N. Jefford (ed.), *The Didache in Context: Essays on Its Text, History, and Transmission*. Novum Testamentum Supplements 77. Leiden: Brill, 256–283.

Rives, James 2011. "The Theology of Animal Sacrifice in the Ancient Greek World: Origins and Developments," in Jennifer W. Knust and Zsuzsanna Várhelyi (eds.), *Ancient Mediterranean Sacrifice*. New York: Oxford University Press, 187–202.

Rivkin, Ellis 1984. *What Crucified Jesus? The Political Execution of a Charismatic*. Nashville: Abingdon Press.

Robins, William 2000. "Romance and Renunciation at the Turn of the Fifth Century," *Journal of Early Christian Studies* 8: 531–537.

Robinson, James M. 1992. "The Sayings Gospel Q," in F. Van Segbroek (ed.), *The Four Gospels 1992: Festschrift Frans Neirynck*. Bibliotheca ephemeridum theologicarum lovaniensium 100. Leuven: Peeters, 361–388.

Robinson, James M. 1993. "The Jesus of the Sayings Gospel Q." Institute for Antiquity and Christianity Occasional Papers 28. Claremont: Claremont Graduate School.

Robinson, James M. 2001. "The Critical Edition of Q and the Study of Jesus," in A. Lindemann (ed.), *The Sayings Source Q and the Historical Jesus*. Leuven: Peeters, 27–52.

Robinson, James M. 2005. *The Sayings Gospel Q: Collected Essays*. Bibliotheca ephemeridum theologicarum lovaniensium 189. C. Heil and J. Verheyden (eds.), Leuven: Peeters.

Robinson, James M., Paul Hoffmann, and John S. Kloppenborg (eds.) 2000. *The Critical Edition of Q*. Minneapolis: Fortress.

Robinson, W. Wheeler 1955. *The Cross in the Old Testament*. Philadelphia: Westminster.

Robinson, W. Wheeler 1980. *Corporate Personality in Ancient Israel*. Rev. ed. Philadelphia: Fortress.

Rogerson, J. W. 1980. "Sacrifice in the Old Testament: Problems of Method and Approach," in M. F. C. Bourdillon and Meyer Fortes (eds.), *Sacrifice in the Old Testament*. London: Academic Press, 45–59.

Roloff, J. 1970. *Das Kerygma und der irdische Jesus. Historische Motive in den Jesus-Erzählungen der Evangelien.* Göttingen: Vandenhoeck and Ruprecht.

Rosner, Brian S. 2013. *Paul and the Law: Keeping the Commandments of God.* New Studies in Biblical Theology 31. Downers Grove: Apollos/ InterVarsity.

Roth, Cecil 1960. "The Cleansing of the Temple and Zecharia xiv.21," *Novum Testamentum* 4: 174–181.

Rowland, Christopher 2007. "The Temple in the New Testament," in J. Day (ed.), *Temple Worship in Biblical Israel.* London: T&T Clark, 469–483.

Runnalls, D. 1983. "The King as Temple Builder: A Messianic Typology," in E. J. Furcha (ed.), *Spirit within Structure: Essays in Honor of George Johnston.* Allison Park: Pickwick Publications, 15–37.

Sacchi, Paolo 1997. *Jewish Apocalyptic and Its History.* Translated by W. J. Short. Journal for the Study of the Pseudepigrapha: Supplements Series 20. Sheffield: Sheffield Academic Press.

Safrai, Shmuel 1985. *Pilgrimage at the Time of the Second Temple.* Jerusalem: Akademon.

Saldarini, Anthony J. 1994. *Matthew's Christian-Jewish Community.* Chicago: University of Chicago Press.

Salo, K. 1991. *Luke's Treatment of the Law: A Redactional-Critical Investigation.* Helsinki: Suomalainen Tiedeakatemia.

Samuelsson, Gunnar 2011. *Crucifixion in Antiquity: An Inquiry into the Background and Significance of the New Testament Terminology of Crucifixion.* Wissenschaftliche Untersuchungen zum Neuen Testament II.310. Tübingen: Mohr Siebeck.

Sanders, E. P. 1985. *Jesus and Judaism.* Philadelphia: Fortress.

Sanders, E. P. 1990. "Jewish Association with Gentiles and Galatians 2:11–14," in R. T. Forna and B. R. Gaventa (eds.), *The Conversation Continues: Studies in Paul and John in Honor of J. Louis Martyn.* Nashville: Abingdon, 170–188.

Sanders, E. P. 1992. *Judaism: Practice and Belief, 63 BCE – 66 CE.* London: SCM.

Sanders, E. P. 1993. *The Historical Figure of Jesus.* London: Penguin.

Sanders J. (ed.) 2006. *Atonement and Violence: A Theological Conversation.* Nashville: Abingdon.

Sanders, J. T. 1987. *The Jews in Luke-Acts.* London: SCM.

Sariola, H. 1990. *Markus und das Gesetz: Eine redaktionskritische Untersuchung.* Annales Academiae scientiarum fennicae 56. Helsinki: Suomalainen Tiedeakatemia.

Schäfer, Peter 1974. "Die Torah der Messianischen Zeit," *Zeitschrift für die Neutestamentliche Wissenschaft* 65: 27–42.

Schäfer, Peter 2007. *Jesus in the Talmud.* Princeton: Princeton University Press.

Scharlemann, Martin Henry 1968. *Stephen: A Singular Saint.* Anchor Bible 34. Rome: Pontifical Biblical Institute.

Schelkle, K. H. 1983. "Israel und Kirche im Anfang," *Theologische Quartalschrift* 163: 86–95.

Schiffman, Lawrence H. 1975. *The Halakhah at Qumran.* Studies in Judaism in Late Antiquity 16. Leiden: Brill.

Schiffman, Lawrence H. 1992. "Laws Pertaining to Women in The Temple Scroll," in D. Dimant and U. Rappaport (eds.), *The Dead Sea Scrolls: Forty*

Years of Research. Studies on the Texts of the Desert of Judah 10. Leiden: Brill, 210–228.

Schiffman, Lawrence H. 1994. *Reclaiming the Dead Sea Scrolls: The History of Judaism, the Background of Christianity, the Lost Library of Qumran.* Philadelphia: Jewish Publication Society.

Schiffman, Lawrence H. 1996. "The Place of 4QMMT in the Corpus of Qumran Manuscripts," in J. Kampen and M. J. Bernstein (eds.), *Reading 4QMMT, New Perspectives on Qumran Law and History.* Society of Biblical Literature Symposium Series 2. Atlanta: Scholars, 81–98.

Schiffman, Lawrence H. 1998. *Texts and Traditions.* Hoboken: Ktav.

Schiffman, Lawrence H. 1999. "Community without Temple: The Qumran Community's Withdrawal from the Jerusalem Temple," in B. Ego, A. Lange, and P. Pilhofer (eds.), *Gemeinde ohne Tempel/Community without Temple: Zur substituierung und Transformation des Jerusalemer Tempels und seines Kultes im Alten Testament, antiken Judentum und frühen Christentum.* Wissenschaftliche Untersuchungen zum Neuen Testament 118. Tübingen: Mohr Siebeck, 267–284.

Schiffman, Lawrence H. 2001. "Halakhah and Sectarianism in the Dead Sea Scrolls," in T. H. Lim, et al (eds.), *The Dead Sea Scrolls in their Historical Context.* Edinburgh: T & T Clark, 123–142.

Schlarb, E. and D. Lührmann 2000. *Fragmente apokryph gewordener Evangelien in griechischer und lateinischer Sprache.* Marburg: N. G. Elwert.

Schmidt, Francis 2001 (1994). *How the Temple Thinks: Identity and Social Cohesion in Ancient Judaism.* Translated by J. Edward Crowley. Sheffield Academic Press.

Schnackenburg, R. 1987. *The Gospel According to John.* 2 vols. New York: Crossroad.

Schneider, Gerhard 1980. *Die Apostelgeschichte: I. Teil: Einleitung, Kommentar zu Kap. 1,1–8, 40.* Herders theologischer Kommentar zum Neuen Testament 5.1. Freiburg: Herder.

Schnellbächer, Ernst L. 1983. "The Temple as Focus of Mark's Theology," *Horizons in Biblical Theology* 5: 95–113.

Schoeps, Hans Joachim 1949. *Theologie und Geschichte des Judenchristentums.* Tübingen: Mohr Siebeck.

Schoeps, Hans Joachim 1969. *Jewish Christianity: Factional Disputes in the Early Church.* Translated by Douglas R. A. Hare. Philadelphia: Fortress.

Schremer, A. 2000. "Qumran Polemic on Marital Law: CD 4:20–5:11 and Its Social Background," in J. M. Baumgarten, E. G. Chazon, and A. Pinnick (eds.), *The Damascus Document: A Centennial of Discovery. Proceedings of the Third International Symposium of the Orion Center for the Study of the Dead Sea Scrolls and Associated Literature, 4–8 February 1998.* Studies on the Texts of the Desert of Judah. Leiden: Brill, 147–160.

Schröter, Jens 1997. "Erwägungen zum Gesetzverständnis in Q anhand von Q 16, 17–18," in C. M. Tuckett (ed.), *The Scriptures in the Gospels.* Bibliotheca ephemeridum theologicarum lovaniensium 131. Leuven: Peeters, 441–458.

Schröter, Jens 1998. "Markus, Q und der historische Jesus: Methodologische und exegetische Erwägungen zu den Anfängen der Rezeption der Verkündigung Jesu," *Zeitschrift für die neutestamentliche Wissenschaft* 89: 173–200.

Schröter, Jens 2006. *Das Abendmahl: Frühchristliche Deutungen und Impulse für die Gegenwart.* Stuttgarter Bibelstudien 210. Stuttgart: Katholisches Bibelwerk.

Schröter, Jens 2013. *From Jesus to the New Testament: Early Christian Theology and the Origin of the New Testament Canon.* Translated by W. Coppins. Baylor-Mohr Siebeck Studies in Early Christianity. Waco: Baylor University Press.

Schulz, Siegfried 1964. "Die Bedeutung des Markus für die Theologiegeschichte des Urchristentums," *Studia Evangelica* 2.1: 135–145.

Schulz, Siegfried 1972. *Q: Spruchquelle der Evangelisten.* Zurich: Theologischer.

Schürer, Emil 1973–1979. *The History of the Jewish People in the Age of Jesus Christ (175 B. C. – A. D. 135).* Revised and edited by Geza Vermes, Fergus Millar, and Matthew Black with Pamela Vermes. Edinburgh: Clark.

Schwager, Raymund 1985. "Christ's Death and the Prophetic Critique of Sacrifice," *Semeia* 33: 109–123.

Schwager, Raymund 1987. *Must There Be Scapegoats? Violence and Redemption in the Bible.* San Francisco: Harper and Row.

Schwartz, Daniel R. 2007. "'Judean' or 'Jew'? How Should We Translate *Ioudaios* in Josephus?" in J. Frey, D. R. Schwartz and S. Gripentrog (eds.), *Jewish Identity in the Greco-Roman World: Jüdische Identität in der griechisch-römischen Welt.* Ancient Judaism and Early Christianity 71. Leiden: Brill, 3–27.

Schwegler, Albert 1846. *Das nachapostolische Zeitalter in den Hauptmomenten seiner Entwicklung.* 2 vols. Tübingen: Ludwig Friedrich Fues.

Schweitzer, Albert 1910. *The Quest for the Historical Jesus: A Critical Study of its Progress from Reimarus to Wrede.* Translated by W. Montgomery. London: Adam and Charles Black.

Schweitzer, Albert 1914. *The Mystery of the Kingdom of God.* Translated by W. Lowrie. New York: Dodd, Mead.

Schweizer, Eduard 1960. *Lordship and Discipleship.* London: SCM.

Schweizer, Eduard 1970. *The Good News According to Mark.* Translated by D. H. Madvig. Atlanta: John Knox.

Scott, James M. 2002. *Geography in Early Judaism and Christianity: The Book of Jubilees.* Society for New Testament Studies Monograph Series 113. Cambridge: Cambridge University Press.

Scroggs, Robin 1966. *The Last Adam: A Study in Pauline Anthropology.* Philadelphia: Fortress.

Seeberg, A. 1906. *Der Katechismus der Urchristenheit.* Leipzig: Deichert.

Seeley, David 1990. *The Noble Death: Graeco-Roman Martyrology and Paul's Concept of Salvation.* Journal for the Study of the New Testament: Supplement Series 28. Sheffield: JSOT.

Seeley, David 1993. "Jesus' Temple Act," *Catholic Biblical Quarterly* 55: 263–283.

Segal, Alan F. 1992. "Jewish Christianity," in H. W. Attridge and G. Hata (eds.), *Eusebius, Christianity, and Judaism.* Studia post-Biblica 42. Leiden: Brill, 326–351.

Segal, Alan F. 2004. *Life After Death: A History of the Afterlife in Western Religion.* New York: Doubleday.

Segal, Peretz 1989. "The Penalty of the Warning Inscription from the Temple in Jerusalem," *Israel Exploration Journal* 39.1/2: 79–84.

Selong, G. 1971. "The Cleansing of the Temple in Jn 2,13–22 with a Reconsideration of the Dependence of the Fourth Gospel upon the Synoptics." Ph.D. dissertation, University of Leuven. Faculty of Theology, Leuven.

Senior, Donald 1995. "The Death of Jesus and the Meaning of Discipleship," in J. T. Caroll and J. B. Green (eds.), *The Death of Jesus in Early Christianity.* Peabody: Hendrickson, 234–255.

Sevrin, J-M. 2001. "Mark's Use of Isaiah 56:7 and the Announcement of the Temple Destruction," in A. Niccacci (ed.), *Jerusalem: House of Prayer for All Peoples in the Three Monotheistic Religions: Proceedings of a Symposium Held in Jerusalem, February 17–18, 1997.* Studium Biblicum Franciscanum Analecta 52. Jerusalem: Franciscan Printing Press, 45–57.

Shemesh, Aharon 1998. "4Q271.3: A Key to Sectarian Matrimonial Law," *Journal of Jewish Studies* 49: 244–263.

Shemesh, Aharon 2009. *Halakhah in the Making: The Development of Jewish Law from Qumran to the Rabbis.* Taubman Lectures in Jewish Studies 6. Berkeley; Los Angeles: University of California Press.

Shimoff, Sandra R. 1995. "Gardens: From Eden to Jerusalem," *Journal for the Study of Judaism* 26: 145–155.

Siegert, F 2002. "Zerstört diesen Tempel ...!" Jesus als 'Tempel' in den Passionsüberlieferungen," in J. Hahn (ed.) *Zerstörungen des Jerusalemer Tempels: Geschehen-Wahrnehmung-Bewältigung.* Wissenschaftliche Untersuchungen zum Neuen Testament 147. Mohr Siebeck: Tübingen, 108–139.

Sim, David C. 1998. *The Gospel of Matthew and Christian Judaism: The History and Social Setting of the Matthean Community.* Edinburgh: T & T Clark.

Sim, David C. 2002. "Matthew's Anti-Paulinism: A Neglected Feature of Matthean Studies," *Harvard Theological Studies* 58: 767–783.

Sim, David C. 2007. "Matthew 7.21–23: Further Evidence of Its Anti-Pauline Perspective," *New Testament Studies* 53: 325–343.

Sim, David C. 2008. "Matthew, Paul and the Origin and Nature of the Gentile Mission: The Great Commission in Matthew 28:16–20 as an Anti-Pauline Tradition," *Harvard Theological Studies* 64: 377–392.

Sim, David C. 2009. "Paul and Matthew on the Torah: Theory and Practice," in P. Middleton, A. Paddison, and K. Wenelll (eds.), *Paul, Grace and Freedom: Essays in Honour of John K. Riches.* London: T & T Clark, 50–64.

Sim, David C. 2011. "Matthew's Use of Mark: Did Matthew Intend to Supplement or to Replace His Primary Source?" *New Testament Studies* 57: 176–192.

Simon, Marcel 1948. *Verus Israel: Étude sur les relations entre Chrétiens et Juifs dans l'Empire Romain (135–425).* Bibliothèques des écoles francaises d'Athènes et de Rome. Paris: Editions de Boccard.

Simon, Marcel 1958. *St. Stephen and the Hellenists in the Primitive Church: The Haskell Lectures Delivered at the Graduate School of Theology Oberlin College, 1956.* London: Longmans, Green, and Co.

Skarsaune, Oskar 1987. *The Proof from Prophecy: A Study in Justin Martyr's Proof-Text Tradition: Text-Type, Provenance, Theological Profile*. Novum Testamentum Supplements 56. Leiden: Brill.

Skarsaune, Oskar 2002. *In the Shadow of the Temple: Jewish Influences on Early Christianity*. Downer's Grove: InterVarsity Press.

Skarsaune, Oskar 2007. "The Ebionites," in O. Skarsaune and R. Hvalvik (eds.), *Jewish Believers in Jesus: The Early Centuries*. Peabody: Hendrickson, 419–462.

Skarsaune, Oskar 2007. "Cerinthus, Elxai, and Other Alleged Jewish Christian Teachers or Groups," in O. Skarsaune and R. Hvalvik (eds.), *Jewish Believers in Jesus: The Early Centuries*. Peabody: Hendrickson, 488–502.

Smallwood, E. Mary. 1981. *The Jews Under Roman Rule: From Pompey to Diocletian: A Study in Political Relations*. 2nd edn. Leiden: Brill.

Smart, Ninian 1980. Review of Girard, *Violence and the Sacred, Religious Studies Review* 6.3: 173–77.

Smith, Brian K. 1989. *Reflections on Resemblance, Ritual and Religion*. Oxford: Oxford University Press.

Smith, D. Moody. 2011. "Jesus Traditions in the Gospel of John," in S. E. Porter and T. Holmén (eds.), *Handbook for the Study of the Historical Jesus*. 4 vols. Leiden: Brill, 3: 1997–2039.

Smith, Dennis E. 2003. *From Symposium to Eucharist: The Banquet in the Early Christian World*. Minneapolis: Fortress.

Smith, F. M. 2000. "Indra Goes West: Report on a Vedic Soma Sacrifice in London," *History of Religions* 36/3: 247–267.

Smith, Jonathan Z. 1982. *Imagining Religion: From Babylon to Jonestown*. Chicago: Chicago University Press.

Smith, Jonathan Z. 1987. "The Domestication of Sacrifice," in R. G. Hamerton-Kelly (ed.), *Violent Origins: Walter Burkert, Rene Girard, and Jonathan Z. Smith on Ritual Killing and Cultural Formation*. Stanford: Stanford University Press, 191–205.

Smith, William Robertson 1894. *Lectures on the Religion of the Semites*. London: Adam and Charles.

Smith, William Robertson 1927. *Lectures on the Religion of the Semites: The Fundamental Institutions*. 3rd edn. New York: Macmillan.

Snodgrass, Klyne R. 1975. "The Parable of the Wicked Husbandmen: Is the Gospel of Thomas Version the Original?" *New Testament Studies* 21: 142–144.

Snodgrass, Klyne R. 1983. *The Parable of the Wicked Tenants: An Inquiry into Parable Interpretation*. Wissenschaftliche Untersuchungen zum Neuen Testament 27. Tubingen: Mohr Siebeck.

Snodgrass, Klyne R. 2009. "The Temple Incident," in R. L. Webb and D. L. Bock (eds.), *Key Events in the Life of the Historical Jesus*. Tübingen: Mohr Siebeck, 429–480.

Söding, T. 1992. "Die Tempelaktion Jesu," *Trierer theologische Zeitschrift* 101: 36–64.

Soler, Jean 1997. "The Semiotics of Food in the Bible," in C. Counihan and P. Van Esterik (eds.), *Food and Culture: A Reader*. London: Routledge, 55–66.

Stager, Lawrence E. 1999. "Jerusalem and the Garden of Eden," *Eretz-Israel* 26: 183–194.

Stanton, Graham 1992. *A Gospel for a New People: Studies in Matthew.* Louisville: Westminster John Knox.

Stanton, Graham 2007. "Jewish Christian Elements in the Pseudo-Clementine Writings," in O. Skarsaune and R. Hvalvik (eds.), *Jewish Believers in Jesus: The Early Centuries.* Peabody: Hendrickson, 305–324.

Steck, Odil Hannes 1967. *Israel und das gewaltsame Geschick der Propheten: Untersuchungen zur Überliererung des deuteronomistischen Geschichtsbildes im Alten Testament, Spätjudentum und Urchristentum.* Wissenschaftliche Monographien zum Alten und Neuen Testament 23. Neukirchen-Vluyn: Neukirchener.

Stegemann, Hartmut 1982. "Der lehrende Jesus: Der sogenannte biblische Christus und die geschichtliche Botschaft Jesu von der Gottesherrschaft," *Neue Zeitschrift für Systematische Theologie und Religionsphilosophie Berlin* 24: 3–20.

Stegemann, Hartmut 1985. "Some Aspects of Eschatology in Texts from the Qumran community and in the Teachings of Jesus," in *Biblical Archaeology Today: Proceedings of the International Congress on Biblical Archaeology, Jerusalem, April 1984.* Jerusalem: Israel Exploration Society, Israel Academy of Sciences and Humanities, American Schools of Oriental Research, 408–426.

Steinmair-Pösel, Petra 2007. "Original Sin, Grace, and Positive Mimesis," *Contagion: Journal of Violence, Mimesis, and Culture* 14: 1–12.

Steudel, A. 1993. "The Houses of Prostration: CD XI 21-XII 1 – Duplicates of the Temple," *Revue de Qumran* 16, 49–68.

Still, Todd D. 1999. *Conflict at Thessalonica: A Pauline Church and its Neighbours.* Journal for the Study of the New Testament: Supplement Series 183. Sheffield Academic Press.

Stone, Michael E. 2011. *Ancient Judaism: New Visions and Views.* Grand Rapids: Eerdmans.

Stötzel, Arnold 1982. "Die Darstellung der ältesten Kirchengeschichte nach den Pseudo-Clementinen," *Vigiliae christianae* 36: 24–37.

Stowers, Stanley K. 1994. *A Rereading of Romans: Justice, Jews and Gentiles.* New Haven: Yale University Press.

Stowers, Stanley K. 1995. "Greeks Who Sacrifice and Those Who Do Not: Toward and Anthropology of Greek Religion," in L. Michael White and O. L. Yarbrough (eds.), *The Social World of the First Christians: Essays in Honor of Wayne A. Meeks.* Minneapolis: Fortress, 293–333.

Stowers, Stanley K. 2011. "The Religion of Plant and Animal Offerings versus the Religion of Meanings, Essences, and Textual Mysteries," in Jennifer W. Knust and Zsuzsanna Várhelyi (eds.), *Ancient Mediterranean Sacrifice.* Oxford: Oxford University Press: 35–56

Strecker, Georg 1958. *Das Judenchristentum in den Pseudoclementinen.* Berlin: Akademie.

Strecker, Georg 1959. "Elkesaï," *Reallexikon für Antike und Christentum* 4: 1171–1186.

Strecker, Georg 1971. "On the Problem of Jewish Christianity," in R. A. Kraft and G. Krodel (eds.), *Orthodoxy and Heresy in Earliest Christianity* by Walter Bauer. 2d edn. Translated by the Philadelphia Seminar on Christian Origins. Philadelphia: Fortress, 241–285.

Strecker, Georg 1981 (1958). *Das Judenchristentum in den Pseudoklementinen*. Texte und Untersuchungen zur Geschichte der altchristlichen Literatur 70. 2nd rev. edn. Berlin: Akademie.

Strenski, Ivan 1993. *Religion in Relation: Method, Application, and Moral Location*. Columbia: University of South Carolina Press.

Stroumsa, Guy G. 2009. *The End of Sacrifice: Religious Transformations in Late Antiquity*. Translated by Susan Emanuel. Chicago: University of Chicago Press.

Stuckenbruck, Loren T. 2005. "'Reading the Present' in the Animal Apocalypse (1 Enoch 85–90)," in K. de Troyer and A. Lange (eds.), *Reading the Present in the Qumran Library: The Perception of the Contemporary by Means of Scriptural Interpretations*. Society of Biblical Literature Symposium Series 30. Atlanta: Society of Biblical Literature, 91–102.

Stuckenbruck, Loren T. 2010. "The Dead Sea Scrolls and the New Testament," in Pages 131–170 in N. Dávid and Armin Lange (eds.), *Qumran and the Bible: Studying the Jewish and Christian Scriptures in Light of the Dead Sea Scrolls*. Leuven: Peeters.

Stuckenbruck, Loren T. 2014. *The Myth of Rebellious Angels: Studies in Second Temple Judaism and New Testament Texts*. Wissenschaftliche Untersuchungen zum Neuen Testament 335. Tübingen: Mohr Siebeck, 240–256.

Stuckey, Tom 2012. *The Wrath of God Satisfied?: Atonement in an Age of Violence*. Eugene: Wipf and Stock.

Strugnell, J. and E. Qimron (eds.) 1994. *Qumran Cave 4, V, Miqsat Ma'aśe Ha-Torah*. Discoveries in the Judaean Desert 10. Oxford: Clarendon.

Stuhlmacher, Peter 1986. *Reconciliation, Law, and Righteousness*. Translated by E. Kalin. Philadelphia: Fortress.

Stuhlmacher, Peter 1996. "Jes 53 in den Evangelien und in der Apostelgeschichte," in B. Janowski and P. Stuhlmacher (eds.), *Der leidende Gottesknecht. Jesaja 53 und seine Wirkungsgeschichte*. Tübingen: Mohr Siebeck, 93–105.

Suggs, M. J. 1970. *Wisdom, Christology and Law in Matthew's Gospel*. Cambridge: Harvard University Press.

Svartvik, J. 2000. *Mark and Mission: Mk 7:1–23 in its Narrative and Historical Contexts*. Coniectanea biblica, New Testament 32. Stockholm: Almqvist and Wiksell International.

Svartvik, J. 2008. "Matthew and Mark," in D. C. Sim and B. Repschinski (eds.), *Matthew and His Christian Contemporaries*. Library of New Testament Studies 333. London: T & T Clark, 27–49.

Swartley, Willard M. (ed.) 2000. *Violence Renounced: René Girard, Biblical Studies, and Peacemaking*. Telford: Pandora Press; Scottdale: Herald Press.

Sylva, Dennis 1987. "The Meaning and Function of Acts 7.46–50," *Journal of Biblical Literature* 106: 261–275.

Tait, Michael 2009. "The End of the Law: The Messianic Torah in the Pseudepigrapha," in M. Tait and P. Oakes (eds.), *The Torah in the New Testament: Papers Delivered at the Manchester-Lausanne Seminar of June*

2008. Library of New Testament Studies 401. London: T & T Clark, 196–207.

Tajfel, Henri and John C. Turner 1986. "The Social Identity Theory of Intergroup Behavior," in S. Worchel and W. G. Austin (eds.), *Psychology of Intergroup Relations.* 2nd edn. Chicago: Nelson-Hall, 7–24.

Tan, K. H. 1997. *The Zion Traditions and the Aims of Jesus.* Society for New Testament Studies Monograph Series 91. Cambridge University Press.

Taylor, Joan E. 1990. "The Phenomenon of Early Jewish Christianity: Reality or Scholarly Invention?" *Vigiliae Christianae* 44: 313–334.

Taylor, Joan E. 2003. *Jewish Women Philosophers of First-Century Alexandria: Philo's "Therapeutae" Reconsidered.* New York: Oxford University Press.

Taylor, Joan E. 2012. *The Essenes, the Scrolls, and the Dead Sea.* New York: Oxford University Press.

Taylor, N. H. 1999. "Jerusalem and the Temple in Early Christian Life and Teaching," *Neotestamentica* 33: 445–461.

Taylor, Vincent 1955 (1937). *Jesus and His Sacrifice.* Repr. edn. London: Macmillan.

Taylor, Vincent 1966. *The Gospel According to St. Mark.* London: Macmillan.

Telford, William R. 1980. *The Barren Temple and the Withered Tree.* Journal for the Study of the New Testament: Supplement Series 1. Sheffield: JSOT

Telford, William R 1999. *The Theology of the Gospel of Mark.* New Testament Theology. Cambridge: Cambridge University Press.

Teppler, Yaakov Y. 2007. *Birkat haMinim: Jews and Christians in Conflict in the Ancient World.* Translated by S. Weingarten. Texte und Studien zum antiken Judentum 120. Tübingen: Mohr Siebeck.

Theissen, Gerd 1976. "Die Tempelweissagung Jesu: Prophetie im Spannungsfeld von Stadt und Land," *Theologische Zeitschrift* 32: 144–158.

Theissen, Gerd 1997. "Jesus und die symbolpolitischen Konflikte seiner Zeit. Sozialgeschichtliche Aspekte der Jesusforschung," *Evangelische Theologie* 57: 378–400.

Theissen, Gerd 2009. "Die Bedeutung der Tempelprophetie Jesu für die ersten Christen: Die Wirkungsgeschichte der Tempelprophetie im 1. Jh. n. Chr," in G. Theissen, H. U. Steymans, S. Ostermann, M. Schmidt, and A. Moresino-Zipper (eds.), *Jerusalem und die Länder: Ikonographie – Topographie – Theologie. Festschrift für Max Küchler zum 65. Geburtstag.* Göttingen: Vandenhoeck & Ruprecht, 149–202.

Theissen, G. and Annette Merz 1998. *The Historical Jesus: A Comprehensive Guide.* Translated by J. Bowden. Minneapolis: Fortress.

Theissen, G. and Dagmar Winter 2002. *The Quest for the Plausible Jesus: The Question of Criteria.* Translated by M. Eugene Boring. Louisville: Wesminster John Knox.

Thomas, J. 1935. *Le mouvement baptiste en Palestine et Syrie (150 v.J.C. – 300 apr. J.C.).* Gembloux: Duculot.

Thompson, James W. 1979. "Hebrews 9 and Hellenistic Concepts of Sacrifice," *Journal of Biblical Literature* 98: 574.

Thornton, T. C. G. 1987. "Christian understandings of the Birkat ha-Minim in the Eastern Roman Empire," *Journal of Theological Studies* 38: 419–431.

Tigchelaar, Eibert 2010. "Manna-Eaters and Man-Eaters: Food of Giants and Men in the Pseudo-Clementine Homilies 8," in J. N. Bremmer (ed.), *The Pseudo-Clementines*. Studies on Early Christian Apocrypha 10. Leuven: Peeters, 92–114.

Tiwald, Markus 2012. "Jewish-Christian Trajectories in Torah and Temple Theology," in T. Holmén (ed.), *Jesus in Continuum*. Wissenschaftliche Untersuchungen zum Neuen Testament 289. Tübingen: Mohr Siebeck, 385–409.

Tiwald, Markus 2013. "Hat Gott sein Haus verlassen (vgl. Q 13,35)? Das Verhältnis der Logienquelle zum Frühjüdentum," in M. Tiwald (ed.), *Kein Jota wird vergehen: das Gesetzesverständnis der Logienquelle vor dem Hintergrund frühjüdischer Theologie*. Beiträge zur Wissenschaft vom Alten und Neuen Testament 10. Stuttgart: Kohlhammer, 63–89.

Tödt, Heinz E. 1965. *The Son of Man in the Synoptic Tradition*. Translated by Dorothea M. Barton. Philadelphia: Westminster.

Tomson, Peter J. 1990. *Paul and the Jewish Law: Halakha in the Letters of the Apostle to the Gentiles*. Assen: van Gorcum.

Tomson, Peter J. 2010. "Halakhah in the New Testament: A Research Overview," in R. Bieringer, F. García Martínez, D. Pollefeyt, and P. J. Tomson (eds.), *The New Testament and Rabbinic Literature*. Journal for the Study of Judaism Supplements 136. Leiden: Brill: 135–206.

Townsend, John T. 1984. "The Date of Luke-Acts," in C. H. Talbert (ed.), *Luke-Acts: New Perspectives from the Society of Biblical Literature*. New York: Crossroad, 47–62.

Trautmann, M. 1980. *Zeichenhafte Handlungen Jesu. Ein Beitrag zur Frage nach dem geschichtlichen Jesu*. Forschung zur Bibel 37. Würzburg: Echter.

Tuckett, Christopher M. 1983. *The Contemporary Revival of the Griesbach Hypothesis*. Society for New Testament Studies Monograph Series 44. Cambridge: Cambridge University Press.

Tuckett, Christopher M. 1988. "Q, the Law and Judaism," in B. Lindars (ed.), *Law and Religion: Essays on the Place of the Law in Israel and early Christianity*. Cambridge: James Clarke, 90–101.

Tuckett, Christopher M. 1996. *Q and the History of Early Christianity: Studies on Q*. Peabody: Hendrickson.

Tuckett, Christopher M. 1997. "Scripture in Q," in C. M. Tuckett (ed.), *The Scriptures in the Gospels*. Bibliotheca ephemeridum theologicarum lovaniensium 131. Leuven: Peeters, 3–26.

Tuckett, Christopher M. 2014. "What is 'New Testament Study'? The New Testament and Early Christianity," *New Testament Studies* 60/2: 157–184.

Turner, M. M. B. 1982. "The Sabbath, Sunday, and the Law in Luke/Acts," in D. Carson (ed.), *From Sabbath to Lord's Day: A Biblical, Historical and Theological Investigation*. Grand Rapids: Zondervan, 99–157.

Tylor, Edward Burnett 1871. *Primitive Culture: Researches into the Development of Mythology, Philosophy, Religion, Language, Art, and Custom*. 2 vols. London: John Murray.

Ullucci, Daniel C. 2008. "Before Animal Sacrifice: A Myth of Innocence," *Religion & Theology* 15: 357–374.

Ullucci, Daniel C. 2011. *The Christian Rejection of Animal Sacrifice*. Oxford: Oxford University Press.

Van Henten, Jan Willem 1997. *The Maccabean Martyrs as Saviours of the Jewish People: A Study of 2 and 4 Maccabees*. Journal for the Study of Judaism Supplements 57. Leiden: Brill.

Van Kooij, Karel R. 1999. "Iconography of the Battlefield: The Case of Chinnamastā," in J. E. M. Houben and K. R. Van Kooij (eds.), *Violence Denied: Violence, Non-Violence and the Rationalization of Violence in South Asian Cultural History*. Brill's Indological Library 16. Leiden: Brill, 249–274.

Van Voorst, Robert E. 1989. *The Ascents of James: History and Theology of a Jewish-Christian Community*. Society of Biblical Literature Dissertation Series 112. Atlanta: Scholars.

VanderKam, James C. 1994. "Genesis 1 in Jubilees 2," *Dead Sea Discoveries* 1: 300–321.

VanderKam, James C. 1995. *Enoch: A Man For All Generations*. Columbia: University of South Carolina Press.

VanderKam, James C. and J. T. Milik (eds.) 1994. *DJD XIII*. Oxford: Clarendon.

Vermes, Geza 1956. *Discovery in the Judean Desert*. New York: Desclee Co..

Vermes, Geza 1974. "Sectarian Matrimonial Halakhah in the Damascus Rule," *Journal of Jewish Studies* 25: 197–202.

Vermes, Geza 1981 (1973). *Jesus the Jew: A Historian's Reading of the Gospels* Philadelphia: Fortress.

Vermes, Geza 1997. *The Complete Dead Sea Scrolls in English*. New York: Penguin.

Vermes, Geza 2003. *The Authentic Gospel of Jesus*. London: Allen Lane.

Vermes, Geza and Martin Goodman 1989. *The Essenes According to the Classical Sources*. Oxford Classical Texts 1. Sheffield: JSOT.

Vielhauer, P. and G. Strecker 1991. "The Gospel of the Ebionites," in W. Schneelmelcher (ed.), *New Testament Apocrypha*. Vol. 1. Cambridge: James Clarke & Co., 167–168.

Visotzky, Burton L. 1989. "Prolegomenon to the Study of Jewish-Christianities," *Association for Jewish Studies Review* 14: 47–70.

Von Rad, Gerhard 1966. "The Theological Problem of the Old Testament Doctrines of Creation," in *The Problem of the Hexateuch and Other Essays*. Edinburgh: Oliver and Boyd, 131–143.

Vouga, F. 1988. *Jésus et la Loi selon la Tradition synoptique*. Geneve: Labor et Fides.

Wardle, Timothy 2010. *The Jerusalem Temple and Early Christian Identity*. Wissenschaftliche Untersuchungen zum Neuen Testament II.291. Tübingen: Mohr Siebeck.

Watson, Francis 2013. *Gospel Writing: A Canonical Perspective*. Grand Rapids: Eerdmans.

Watty, W. W. 1982. "Jesus and the Temple – Cleansing or Cursing?" *Expository Times* 93: 235–239.

Webb, B. G. 1990. "Zion in Transformation: A Literary Approach to Isaiah," in D. J. A. Clines, S. E. Fowl, and S. E. Porter (eds.), *The Bible in Three Dimensions*. Journal for the Study of the Old Testament: Supplement Series 87. Sheffield: JSOT, 65–84.

Webb, Robert L. 1991. *John the Baptizer and Prophet: A Socio-Historical Study*. Journal for the Study of the New Testament: Supplement Series 62. Sheffield: JSOT.

Webb, Robert L. 1994. "John the Baptist and His Relationship to Jesus," in B. D. Chilton and C. A. Evans (eds.), *Studying the Historical Jesus: Evaluations of the State of Current Research*. New Testament Tools and Studies 19. Leiden: Brill, 179–229.

Webb, Robert L. 2006. "Jesus Heals a Leper: Mark 1.40–45 and *Egerton Gospel* 35–47," *Journal for the Study of the Historical Jesus* 4.2: 177–202.

Webb, Robert L. 2009. "Jesus' Baptism by John: Its Historicity and Significance," in D. L. Bock and R. L. Webb (eds.), *Key Events in the Life of the Historical Jesus: A Collaborative Exploration of Context and Coherence*. Wissenschaftliche Untersuchungen zum Neuen Testament 247. Tübingen: Mohr Siebeck, 95–150.

Webb, Robert L. 2009. "The Historical Enterprise and Historical Jesus Research," in D. L. Bock and R. L. Webb (eds.), *Key Events in the Life of the Historical Jesus: A Collaborative Exploration of Context and Coherence*, Tübingen: Mohr Siebeck, 60–75.

Wedderburn, Alexander J. M. 1999. *Beyond Resurrection*. Peabody: Hendrickson.

Wedderburn, Alexander J. M.. 2006. "Jesus' Action in the Temple: A Key or a Puzzle?" *Zeitschrift für die Neutestamentliche Wissenschaft* 97: 1–22.

Weeden, T. J. 1971. *Mark – Traditions in Conflict*. Philadelphia: Fortress.

Wehnert, Jürgen 1983. "Literarkritik und Sprachanalyse: kritische Anmerkungen zum gegen wärtigen Stand der Pseudoklementinen – Forschung," *Zeitschrift für die neutestamentliche Wissenschaft* 74: 268–300.

Weiss, Johannes 1964 (1892). *Die Predigt Jesu vom Reiche Gottes*. 3rd edn. Göttingen: Vandenhoeck & Ruprecht.

Wenham, Gordon J. 1979. *The Book of Leviticus*. New International Commentary on the Old Testament. Grand Rapids: Eerdmans.

Wenham, Gordon J. 1986. "Sanctuary Symbolism in the Garden of Eden Story," *Proceedings of the World Congress of Jewish Studies* 9: 19–25.

Wenschkewitz, Hans 1932. *Die Spiritualisierung der Kultusbegriffe: Tempel, Priester und Opfer im Neuen Testament*. Angelos-Beiheift 4. Leipzig: E. Pfeiffer.

Wenthe, Dean O. 1974. "An Exegetical Study of 1 Corinthians 5:7b," *Springfielder* 38: 134–140.

Weren, W. J. C. 1997. "Jesus' Entry into Jeruasalem: Mt 21, 1–17 in the Light of the Hebrew Bible and the Septuagint," in C. M. Tuckett (ed.), *The Scriptures in the Gospels*. Bibliotheca ephemeridum theologicarum lovaniensium 131. Leuven University Press, 117–141.

Weren, W. J. C. 1998. "The Use of Isaiah 5,1–7 in the Parable of the Tenants (Mark 12, 1–12; Matthew 21,33–46)," *Biblica* 79: 1–26.

White, Hayden 1978. "Ethnological 'Lie' and Mystical 'Truth,'" *Diacritics* 8: 2–9.

Whybray, R. N. 1978. *Thanksgiving for a Liberated Prophet*. Journal for the Study of the Old Testament: Supplements Series 4. Sheffield: Sheffield Univesity Press.

Wilckens, Ulrich 1982. *Der Brief an die Römer*. Evangelisch-katholischer Kommentar zum Neuen Testament 6. 3 vols. Neukirchen-Vluyn: Neukirchener.

Wilckens, Ulrich 2003. *Theologie des Neuen Testaments*. Vol. I.2 Neukirchen-Vluyn: Neukirchener.

Williams, James G. 1991. *The Bible, Violence, and the Sacred: Liberation from the Myth of Sanctioned Violence*. San Francisco: HarperSanFrancisco.

Williams, James G. 1994. "Steadfast Love and Not Sacrifice," in M. I. Wallace and T. H. Smith (eds.), *Curing Violence*. Forum Facsimiles 3. Sonoma: Polebridge, 71–99.

Williams, James G._ (ed.) 1996. *The Girard Reader*. Translated by Yvonne Freccero. New York: Crossroad.

Williams, Michael Allen 1996. *Rethinking "Gnosticism": An Argument for Dismantling a Dubious Category*. Princeton: Princeton University Press.

Williams, Rowan 1982. *Eucharistic Sacrifice: The Roots of a Metaphor*. Bramcote: Grove.

Williams, Sam K. 1975. *Jesus' Death as Saving Event: The Background and Origin of a Concept*. Harvard Dissertations in Religion 2. Missoula: Scholars.

Williamson, Lamar 1983. *Mark: Interpretation: A Biblical Commentary for Teaching and Preaching*. Louisville: Westminster John Knox.

Wilson, J. V. Kinnier 1961. "The Story of the Flood," in D. Winton Thomas (ed.), *Documents from Old Testament Times*. New York: Harper and Row, 17–26.

Wilson, S. G. 1983. *Luke and the Law*. Society for New Testament Studies Monograph Series 50. Cambridge: Cambridge University Press.

Winter, P. 1958. "1 Corinthians XV, 3b-7," *Novum Testamentum* 2: 142–150.

Wise, Michael O. 1991. "4QFlorilegium and the Temple of Adam," *RevQ* 15: 103–132.

Witherington III, Ben 1994. *Paul's Narrative Thought World: The Tapestry of Tragedy and Triumph*. Louisville: Westminster John Knox.

Witherington III, Ben 1995. *John's Wisdom*. Cambridge: Lutterworth Press.

Witherington III, Ben 2001. *The Gospel of Mark: A Socio-rhetorical Commentary*. Grand Rapids: Eerdmans.

Wolter, Michael 2011. *Paulus: ein Grundriss seiner Theologie*. Neukirchen-Vluyn: Neukirchener Verlagsgesellschaft.

Wright, David P. 1987. *The Disposal of Impurity: Elimination Rites in the Bible and in Hittite and Mesopotamian Literature*. Society of Biblical Literature Dissertation Series 101. Atlanta: Scholars.

Wright, N. T. 1996. *Jesus and the Victory of God. Vol. 2: Christian Origins and the Question of God*. Minneapolis: Fortress.

Wright, N. T. 2009. "The Servant and Jesus: The Relevance of the Colloquy for the Current Quest for Jesus," in W. B. Bellinger and W. R. Farmer (eds.), *Jesus and the Suffering Servant: Isaiah 53 and Christian Origins*. Eugene: Wipf and Stock, 281–297.

Wright, N. T. 2011. *Simply Jesus: A New Vision of Who He Was, What He Did, and Why He Matters*. New York: HarperOne.

Wright, N. T. 2013. *Paul and the Faithfulness of God, Vol. 4 of Christian Origins and the Question of God*. 2 vols. Minneapolis: Fortress Press.

Yee, G. A. 1989. *Jewish Feasts and the Gospel of John*. Wilmington: Glazier.

Yerkes, R. K. 1953. *Sacrifice in Greek and Roman Religions and Early Judaism*. London: Adam & Charles Black.

Young, Frances M. 1972. "Temple Cult and Law in Early Christianity: A Study in the Relationship between Jews and Christians in the Early Centuries," *New Testament Studies* 19: 325–338.

Young, Frances M. 1975. *Sacrifice and the Death of Christ*. Cambridge: Cambridge University Press.

Young, Frances M. 1979. *The Use of Sacrificial Ideas in Greek and Christian Writers from the New Testament to John Chrysostom*. Cambridge: Philadelphia Patristic Foundation.

Zachhuber, Johannes 2013. "Modern Discourse on Sacrifice and its Theological Background," in J. Zachhuber and J. T. Meszaros (eds.), *Sacrifice and Modern Thought*. Oxford: Oxford University Press, 12–28.

Zager, W. 1996. "Wie kam es im Urchristentum zur Deutung des Todes Jesu als Sühnegeschehen?" *Zeitschrift für die neutestamentliche Wissenschaft* 87: 165–186.

Zager, W. 1999. *Jesus und die frühchristliche Verkündigung*. Neukirchen-Vluyn: Neukirchener.

Zahn, Theodor 1922. *Das Evangelium des Matthäus*. Leipzig: A. Deichert.

Zeitlin, Solomon 1942. *Who Crucified Jesus?* New York: Harper & Brothers.

Zenos, Andrew Constantinides 1895. *The Elements of the Higher Criticism*. New York: Funk & Wagnalls.

Zerbe, Gordon Mark 1993. *Non-Retaliation in Early Jewish and New Testament Texts: Ethical Themes in Social Contexts*. Supplements to the Journal for the Study of the Pseudepigrapha 13. Sheffield: JSOT.

Zias, J. and E. Sekeles 1985. "The Crucified Man from Giv'at ha-Mivtar: A Reappraisal," *Israel Exploration Journal* 35: 22–27.

Zohar, Noam 1988. "Repentance and Purification: The Significance and Semantics of חטאת in the Pentateuch," *Journal of Biblical Literature* 107: 609–618.

INDEX OF ANCIENT SOURCES

Greek and Latin Literary Sources

INDEX OF AUTHORS

Elliott, John H., 169
Eppstein, V., 144n57, 144n58, 147n82
Eschner, Christina, 210
Esler, P., 64n222, 65n228
Evans, Craig A., 7, 69, 69n18, 108,
    109n25, 110, 111, 117n65, 141n47,
    144, 144n57, 145, 153, 175
Fander, M., 53
Faraone, C., 72
Feldman, L.H., 21
Fine, Steven, 82n89
Finlan, Stephen, 81, 82n89, 84n106,
    89n137, 91n143, 211, 232n149,
    240n198
Finley, Gregory C., 176n44, 180n71
Fiorenza, Elisabeth Schüssler, 104
Fitzmyer, Joseph A., 49, 52n131,
    52n134, 53n138, 64n222, 178,
    192n139
Fleddermann, Harry T., 47n97,
    56n166
Flood, Gavin, 71n23
Flusser, David, 145, 147n82
Fonrobert, Charlotte Elisheva, 189
Foster, Paul, 47n93, 60, 61
Fredriksen, Paula, 3, 9, 67, 108, 142n48,
    145n61, 157n133
Freedman, David N., 114
Frey, Jörg, 189
Fried, J., 4n8
Fuglseth, Kåre Sigvald, 129
Fuller, R.H., 230
Funk, Robert W., 212n17, 214n33,
    237n186

Gärtner, B., 51n127, 99, 112n40
Gaston, L., 68
Gathercole, S., 162
Gelston, Anthony, 223
Gese, Hartmut, 34, 154
Gieseler, Johann Karl Ludwig, 176
Giesen, H., 108
Gilders, William K., 102n190
Gilliard, Frank D., 22
Girard, René, 9, 73, 73n37, 74, 75, 76,
    77n63, 132n150
Gnilka, G., 108, 114n51
Goodblatt, David, 169
Goodhart, Sandor, 74
Goodman, Martin, 6, 102, 170
Goppelt, Leonhard, 103
Goulder, Michael, 174
Grant, Robert M., 114

Gray, Timothy C., 106, 108n17, 117n63,
    165n178
Green, Joel B., 210, 216n45, 217
Gregory, Andrew, 180, 182n81, 189n124
Greisch, Jean, 75
Guelich, R.A., 55
Gupta, Nijay K., 211n11
Guthrie, W.K.C., 82
Guttmann, Alexander, 171n11
Gyanshruti, S., 77

Haas, N., 27n145
Haenchen, E., 64, 130n140, 131n143,
    144n58
Hägerland, Tobias, 163
Hagner, Donald A., 60, 208n221
Hahn, F., 114
Häkkinen, S., 177, 192n139
Hallo, William W., 78, 79, 79n72, 80,
    80n76, 190
Ham, C.A., 115
Hamerton-Kelly, Robert, 74, 75, 109
Han, Kyu Sam, 41, 44n79, 134n6
Hanson, John S., 104
Hare, D.R.A., 60
Harrington, D.J., 61, 108
Harvey, A.E., 144
Harvey, Graham, 169
Hays, Richard B., 240
Hayward, C.T.R., 85n111
Head, P.M., 124
Hecht, Richard D., 75
Hedley, Douglas, 229
Heil, Christoph, 49n111, 55n157
Heil, John P., 108
Hendel, Ronald S., 87
Hengel, Martin, 7, 14, 15n77, 21, 26, 68,
    144, 161, 176n41, 210, 210n9, 230,
    240n197
Henige, David P., 201
Henne, P., 179
Herion, G.A., 38n42
Herr, Moshe David, 6
Herzog, Williarm R., 165
Heyman, George, 10
Himmelfarb, Martha, 32,
    94n155, 100
Hitch, Sarah, 72
Hoffmann, Paul, 42, 46n90, 47n98,
    48n105
Hogeterp, Albert L.A., 211n11
Hogg, Michael A., 43
Holdrege, Barbara A., 77
Holmås, Geir Otto, 125

Levinson, Bernard M., 30
Lietzmann, H., 215
Lindars, B., 130
Loader, William R.G., 45, 45n85, 46n89,
    53, 54, 57n170, 57n175, 58n181, 60,
    63n213, 64n218, 109n25, 117n66,
    118n68, 119n76, 120n79, 147n88,
    165n179, 181n80, 185n101
Lohse, E., 35
Longenecker, R.N., 173
Lüdemann, Gerd, 13, 136, 174, 184n92
Lührmann, Dieter, 42, 48n105, 107,
    134n6, 179
Lundquist, John M., 79
Luomanen, Petri, 168, 173, 176n40
Luttikhuizen, Gerard P., 179
Luz, Ulrich, 230n132

Maccoby, Hyam, 174
MacGreggor, G.H.C., 215
Mack, Burton L., 73n35, 108
Magness, Jodi, 99n173, 147n81
Magnin, J.M., 192
Maier, J., 21n113
Malina, B.J., 173
Mann, C.S., 144
Manson, T.W., 230
Marcus, Joel, 61, 117, 217n55, 221n88,
    229n129
Martin, Dale B., 3, 157n133
Martin, Ralph, 215
Martínez, F. García, 32, 52
Martyn, J.L., 191, 192n139
Marx, Alfred, 78
Marxsen, Willi, 239, 239n196
Mason, Steve, 21
Massaux, Édouard, 179
Matson, M., 130, 131n143, 138n28
Matthews, Kenneth A., 129
Mauss, Marcel, 71
Mazza, Enrico, 239n194
McClymond, Kathryn, 73, 77, 78,
    86n112
McGowan, Andrew, 216
McGrew, Timothy, 201
McGuckin, J., 160, 160n155
McGuckin, J.A., 120
McHugh, John, 130
McKelvey, R.J., 217
McKenna, Andrew J., 74
McKnight, Scot, 7, 8n26, 139n33,
    215n34, 219n71, 220n76, 232n143
McL. Wilson, R., 136n20
McLean, B.H., 73, 87, 89n134, 211n14

Mealand, David L., 206
Meier, John P., 21, 48, 49, 55n161, 67,
    108n19, 206n213, 212n19, 213
Mendenhall, G.E., 38n42
Merklein, H., 48, 159
Mermelstein, Ari, 31, 33n12,
    34n20
Merz, Annette, 108n19, 135, 138n28,
    157n133, 165n180, 181n75, 185n99,
    212n16, 213n24, 239n195
Meshorer, Yaakov, 146
Meszaros, J.T., 71
Metzner, Rainer, 16
Meyer, B.F., 230
Meyer, Paul, 41
Milgrom, Jacob, 72, 78, 79, 88, 88n130,
    98n171
Milik, J.T., 96
Millar, Fergus, 15
Mimouni, Simon C., 168, 170, 170n8,
    176n44, 178n56, 179n65, 179n67,
    180n71
Montefiore, Hugh, 113, 146
Moo, Douglas J., 230n131
Morris, Leon, 215
Muddiman, John, 128
Mueller, J.R., 52
Müller, K., 30, 61
Munck, J., 173, 174
Münderlein, Gerhard, 108
Murphy-O'Connor, Jerome, 52, 144, 214
Murry, R., 173
Myers, C., 109, 109n24
Myllykoski, Matti, 124n104, 184

Naiden, Fred S., 72
Najman, Hindy, 32, 33n11
Nanos, Mark D., 57
Neufeld, Thomas R. Yoder, 131
Neusner, Jacob, 45n86, 129, 146n67,
    146n76, 151n106, 157n132, 158,
    165n180
Newman, Louis E., 164
Nickelsburg, George W.E., 14, 32,
    55n158, 94n155, 195
Nineham, D.E., 60, 235n172
Noland, John, 176
Nolland, J., 61, 115
North, Christopher Richard, 223

O'Leary, A.M., 62
Och, Bernard, 35
Oliver, Isaac W., 63
Olson, Daniel C., 95

322   *Index of Authors*

INDEX OF SUBJECTS

Galilee, 20
Gerousia, 20
The *Gospel of the Ebionites*, 179
  literary dependence, 181
  rejection of sacrifice, 180
  vegetarianism, 182
Gospel of John, 65
  chronology of Temple Incident, 128
  relationship to Mark, 128
  supersessionism, 65
Gospel of Luke, 63
  as apologetic, 65
  and the law, 64
Gospel of Mark, 57
  date, 58
  Jesus as sacrifice, 153
  kosher laws, 58
  messianic secret, 118
  and Pauline theology, 57
  Sabbath, 58
  suffering son of man, 152
  Temple Incident, 116
Gospel of Matthew, 60
  antitheses, 63
  and Gentiles, 62
  and the Gospel of Mark, 61
  as "Jewish-Christian", 60
  "Jewishness", 60
  and the law, 61, 63
  and Pauline thought, 61
  redaction of Mark, 119
  Temple tax, 120
Gospel of Thomas, 109, 136
  Parable of Wicked Tenants, 113
  Temple saying, 136
the Gospels, 8
grain offering, 89
the Greatest Commandment, 119
guilt offering, 88

Hasmonean, 16
heavenly tablets, 31, 32, 33, 34
Hebrews, 131
Hegesippus, 127
Herod Antipas, 104
Herod the Great, 16, 20
high priest
  corruption, 69
high priests
  as collaborators, 17
  as illegitimate, 18
  involvement in Jesus' death, 23n118
  responsibility for Jesus' death, 19
Hillel, 45n86, 153n113
Holy of Holies, 107, 111, 211

Holy Spirit, 126

Idumaea, 16
imperial cult, 16

Jainism, 78
James
  death, 25
  murder, 69
Jesus, 1
  and animal sacrifice, 14, 204, 208, 243
  and animals, 198
  as apocalyptic prophet, 2
  and "apostasy", 25
  arrest, 1
  arrival in Jerusalem, 20
  as ascetic, 84
  attitude towards the Temple, 12
  and "blasphemy", 25, 29
  as charismatic prophet, 190
  and "common Judaism", 3
  in conflict with Temple leaders, 10
  and the "covenant", 37
  and creation-Torah, 54, 57
  criticism of the Temple's
    adminstration, 6
  crucifixion, 26, 28
  death, 1, 2, 15, 18, 230
  death as atoning, 215
  death as sacrifice, 6, 7, 8, 210, 216,
    219, 231, 237
  disrespect for the Temple, 19
  disturbing commerce in the Temple,
    26
  and divorce, 49, 53, 205
  as eschatological Adam, 219
  and eschatological restoration, 163
  and eschatology, 156
  execution for sedition, 3
  as failed messiah, 2
  final meal with disciples, 218
  and forgiveness of sins, 162
  halakhah, 36, 38, 39
  as healer, teacher, and prophet, 205
  and the kingdom of God, 38, 161,
    205, 242
  and "kingship", 26
  Jewishness, 36
  and the Last Supper, 11
  and the law, 35, 37, 56
  and nonviolence, 161, 205
  as "observant Jew", 14, 58,
    70, 207
  as "offering" his life to God, 84
  and Passover, 11

JESUS AND THE TEMPLE

Most Jesus specialists agree that the Temple incident led directly to Jesus' arrest, but the precise relationship between Jesus and the Temple's administration remains unclear. *Jesus and the Temple* examines this relationship, exploring the reinterpretation of Torah observance and traditional Temple practices that are widely considered central components of the early Jesus movement. Challenging a growing tendency in contemporary scholarship to assume that the earliest Christians had an almost uniformly positive view of the Temple's sacrificial system, Simon J. Joseph addresses the ambiguous, inconsistent, and contradictory views on sacrifice and the Temple in the New Testament. This volume fills a significant gap in the literature on sacrifice in Jewish Christianity. It introduces a new hypothesis positing Jesus' enactment of a program of radically nonviolent eschatological restoration, an orientation that produced Jesus' conflicts with his contemporaries and inspired the first attributions of sacrificial language to his death.

SIMON J. JOSEPH is Adjunct Professor of Religion at California Lutheran University. He is the author of *Jesus, Q, and the Dead Sea Scrolls* and *The Nonviolent Messiah*.

SOCIETY FOR NEW TESTAMENT STUDIES

MONOGRAPH SERIES

General Editor: Paul Trebilco

165

JESUS AND THE TEMPLE

SOCIETY FOR NEW TESTAMENT STUDIES

MONOGRAPH SERIES

Recent titles in the series: